# LAW RELATING TO THEFT

# LAW RELATING TO THEFT

**Edward Phillips, LLB, BCL,**
Principal Lecturer in Law, University of Greenwich

**Charlotte Walsh, MA (Oxon), PGCE, LLB,**
Associate Dean of Law, University of Buckingham

**Paul Dobson, LLB, Barrister,**
Visiting Professor at Anglia Polytechnic
University and Greenwich University

First published in Great Britain 2001 by Cavendish Publishing Limited,
The Glass House, Wharton Street, London WC1X 9PX, United Kingdom
Telephone: +44 (0)20 7278 8000     Facsimile: +44 (0)20 7278 8080
Email: info@cavendishpublishing.com
Website: www.cavendishpublishing.com

British Library Cataloguing in Publication Data

Phillips, E
Law relating to theft
1 Larceny – England  2 Larceny – Wales
I Title  II Walsh, C  III Dobson, AP
345.4'2'0262

ISBN 1 85941 200 9

Printed and bound in Great Britain

# PREFACE

Anyone writing in this field of law owes a great debt to the two eminent professors who have already written extensively in it – to the late Professor Griew and, especially, to Professor Sir John Smith. We gratefully acknowledge that debt and where on occasion we have expressed views at variance with theirs we have done so with feelings of some awe and diffidence.

In organising the book, we sought to follow as far as was sensible the order in which the sections appear in the 1968 Act (with the obvious addition of a chapter on the 1978 Act). We opted for an arrangement whereby a section of the Act is set out verbatim in the body of the text immediately before the commentary on it. We hope that this makes it possible for the reader's eye to move easily between the commentary and the statutory words as the need arises.

Although the focus of the book is the substantive law of theft, we have throughout included some information on mode of trial and sentencing as well as covering, in the first chapter, some procedural matters including jurisdiction and, in the final chapter, the law of attempts – the latter because the attempts cases presenting difficulties have often been ones involving a charge of attempting to commit an offence under the Theft Act 1968.

Finally we would like to record our thanks: to Cavendish for their patience, to Janis Dear of the Law School at Greenwich University for reading through, and commenting upon, much of the manuscript; to our respective families for putting up with our irritabilities whilst completing this book. Charlotte extends a special thanks to Rachel, Guy and Barney for their patience and endurance.

We have endeavoured to state the law as it is on the second of April 2001.

*Edward Phillips, Charlotte Walsh and Paul Dobson*

## Postscript

More years ago than I care to remember I agreed to write a book on the Theft Acts. I am very grateful to my two co-authors who came along and took the bulk of the work off me and I applaud them for their commitment and dedication. Of course, we have each written different parts of the book and each takes responsibility for the whole. I just know that without my co-authors the book would never have seen the light of day.

*Paul Dobson*

# CONTENTS

# Contents

# TABLE OF CASES

# TABLE OF STATUTES

# TABLE OF ABBREVIATIONS

The following abbreviations are used in this book. References are to the editions mentioned in this list, except where an earlier edition is expressly identified.

| | |
|---|---|
| Archbold | *Archbold Criminal Pleading, Evidence & Practice*, 2001, London: Sweet & Maxwell |
| Arlidge & Parry | *Arlidge & Parry on Fraud*, 2nd edn, 1996, London: Sweet & Maxwell, by Anthony Arlidge, Jacques Parry and Ian Gatt |
| Ashworth | *Principles of Criminal Law*, 3rd edn, 1999, Oxford: OUP, by Andrew Ashworth |
| Eighth Report, Cmnd 2977 | Criminal Law Revision Committee, *Eighth Report Theft and Related Offences*, 1966, Cmnd 2977 |
| Griew | *The Theft Acts 1968 and 1978*, 7th edn, 1995, London: Sweet & Maxwell, by Edward Griew |
| Law Comm No 155 (1999) | *Legislating the Criminal Code: Fraud and Deception*, Law Commission Consultation Paper No 155 (1999) |
| Smith, ATH | *Property Offences*, 1994, Sweet & Maxwell, by ATH Smith |
| Smith, JC | *Theft*, 8th edn, 1997, London: Butterworths, by Professor Sir John Smith |
| Thirteenth Report, Cmnd 6733 | *Criminal Law Revision Committee, Thirteenth Report Section 16 of the Theft Act 1968*, 1977, Cmnd 6733 |

# CHAPTER 1

# HISTORY AND PRELIMINARY MATTERS

## 1 THEFT OF PROPERTY

1-01     It is crucial to locate the law on theft within the wider context of the law's protection of private property (including criminal damage). However, the concept of 'property' is extremely complex and encompasses fundamental issues of ownership and title and is expressed in terms of varying degrees of exclusive and shared 'rights'. These rights to ownership and title receive protection under civil, as well as, criminal law. This creates its own set of problems (unfortunately, not unique) for the law of theft. One long enduring controversy is the extent to which definitions and concepts employed by the civil law can be appropriated for the purposes of the criminal law. This is especially important as English law has traditionally sought to draw a distinction between the protection of property rights (either through an action for damages, or through those equitable remedies developed as a means for dealing with those situations where a remedy in damages would be inappropriate or unsuitable)[1] and the assignment of criminal culpability and blameworthiness. It is submitted that the inability of the common law and, in some cases, the refusal of the common law judges, to acknowledge these incompatibilities, were responsible for the chaotic nature of the early law relating to theft. This takes on an added significance in the light of the harsh sentencing practices, including transportation and capital punishment, applicable to property offences in the centuries leading up to the passing of the Theft Act (TA) in 1968.[2]

1-02     By the beginning of the 19th century, it was recognised that the law was in an impossibly complicated state, as a consequence of judicial and parliamentary attempts to utilise and extend larceny and the doctrine of constructive possession, as the fundamental mechanisms for protecting property. The Criminal Law Commissioners of 1834 expressed it as follows:

> The numerous subtle distinctions upon the subject of constructive possession especially as to the cases where the owner has a constructive possession against

---

1     A prime example would be the use of injunctions to deal with breaches of property (ie, land) rights.

2     The historical background to the English criminal law relating to property is adequately dealt with elsewhere. Reference may usefully be made to: Smith, ATH, Chapter 1; Lacey, N and Wells, C, *Reconstructing Criminal Law*, 2nd edn, 1998, Butterworths, Chapter 3. See, also, the introductory chapters in Smith, JC and Griew.

one person and not against another, and where the person in actual possession may or may not be guilty of stealing another's goods, are much too technical for convenient use or the general comprehension of the community.[3]

1-03    An attempt was made in the Larceny Acts (LA) 1861 and 1916 to deal with the mass of unnecessarily complicated, and often contradictory, rules that had developed. With the benefit of hindsight, however, it can be seen that this was doomed to failure, primarily because of the unfortunate categorisation of offences as larceny, embezzlement, obtaining by false pretences and fraudulent conversion and the continued use of language that was divorced from the ordinary understanding of what was to be regarded as stealing.[4] Moreover, the single most important explanation for some of the strange pathways down which the courts chose to go was the refusal to release their adherence to the previous case law. Consequently, there continued to be perpetuated:

> ... an immensely and unnecessarily complicated structure, full of difficult distinctions of a purely technical character and bristling with traps for the judges, magistrates, prosecutors and police who had to administer the law.[5]

## 2 THE THEFT ACT 1968

1-04    The TA 1968 was an attempt to sweep away the whole crumbling edifice of the previous law, and the piecemeal statutory tinkering, to create what was intended to be a code dealing with theft and a number of associated offences. As ATH Smith puts it:

> The Act sought to shift the whole conceptual basis of the law of theft, so that ownership could be protected directly rather than through the series of clumsy stratagems devised by judges over the centuries. It was intended to make an entirely fresh start, unlike the LAs of 1916 and before, which had been consolidating measures.[6]

The 1968 Act itself was based on the Eighth Report of the Criminal Law Revision Committee (CLRC), 'Theft and related offences'.[7]

> As Lacey and Wells put it:

> ... this project of codification was informed by rule of law values such as clarity, comprehensiveness, coherence and consistency and, in particular, by the idea that the criminal law should be accessible to the citizen and that its technicality should hence be reduced.[8]

---

3    Criminal Law Commissioners, First Report, 1834, *Parliamentary Papers xxvi*, p 117.
4    There is a brief account of these in Smith, JC, para 1-13.
5    Smith, JC, para 1-02.
6    Smith, ATH, para 1-15.
7    CLRC, Eighth Report, Cmnd 2977, 1966, London: HMSO.
8    *Op cit*, Lacey and Wells, fn 2, p 263.

It was the view of the Committee that it was the dishonest appropriation of another's property that was the concern of the criminal law and that this was to be reflected in a 'new' offence of theft:

> The committee generally are strongly of opinion that larceny, embezzlement and fraudulent conversion should be replaced by a single new offence of theft. The important element of them all is undoubtedly the dishonest appropriation of another's property ... and we think it not only logical, but right in principle, to make this the central element of the offence. In doing so, the law would concentrate on what the accused dishonestly achieved or attempted to achieve and not on the means – taking or otherwise – which he used in order to do so.[9]

1-05   It was the express intention of the CLRC that the Act should be both simple and understandable. Moreover, the language that was used was to be given its ordinary meaning. This can be seen in the fact that crucial terms, such as 'dishonesty', were not provided with an interpretation (apart from the explanation in s 2 as to what was *not* to be regarded as dishonest). This was welcomed by the courts (although, sometimes, in word and not in deed). In *Treacy v DPP*, Lord Diplock opined that the Act:

> ... is expressed in simple language as used and understood by ordinary literate men and women. It avoids, so far as possible, those terms of art which have acquired a special meaning understood only by lawyers in which many of the penal enactments which it supersedes were couched.[10]

1-06   This is not to say, however, that the Committee's work is beyond criticism. There were a number of areas where insufficient thought had gone into the recommendations put forward. These have become the subject of much subsequent difficulty. One instance of this may be mentioned here. The Committee had concluded that it was not practicable for any definition of theft to encompass the offence of obtaining by false pretences. This was finally settled by the House of Lords in *Gomez*, to the effect that obtaining property (with the exception of land) by deception, under s 15, would also constitute theft.[11]

1-07   Simplification, moreover, has frequently created its own problems. The price of simplification has meant that too many issues have been left to be resolved by the courts. In some areas, this simplification has meant that matters which should, in reality, be questions of law are left as merely questions of fact to be determined by individual juries. In the intervening period since the introduction of the 1968 Act, some judges, too, have voiced dissatisfaction. The modernising process of 1968 may have been radical for the time but, judged by present day standards, it did not go far enough. As Beldam LJ, in *Hallam*, remarked, the present law is:

---

9   *Op cit*, Lacey and Wells, fn 2, para 33. See, below, para 2-07 for a discussion of the Committee's preference for 'dishonesty' rather than 'fraudulently'.
10   [1971] AC 537, p 565.
11   [1993] AC 442; see, below, paras 2-31ff.

... in urgent need of simplification and modernisation, so that a jury of 12 ordinary citizens do not have to grapple with the antiquated 'franglais' of choses in action and scarce public resources are not devoted to hours of semantic argument divorced from the true merits of the case.[12]

As Smith points out, however, this is hardly a fair criticism.[13] In a number of situations, covered at various points in the text below, it is the judges who must bear responsibility for endless and unnecessary semantic quibbling. It is true, however, that there are too many issues which remain unresolved. The Law Commission, among other commentators, has pointed out that '... the time may be approaching when a thorough review of the TAs is required'.[14]

# 3 THE THEFT ACT 1978

1-08    When the original Theft Bill was making its way through Parliament, there was, on occasion, a certain amount of meddling with the proposals put forward by the CLRC. An example of this occurred in relation to s 16 (the obtaining of pecuniary advantage by deception). Here, a provision not scrutinised by the CLRC was enacted as s 16(2)(a). This proved to be so unsatisfactory and unworkable that the Home Secretary referred it back to the Committee.[15]

Upon their recommendation (the *Thirteenth Report*), this was repealed and replaced by new offences in the TA 1978.[16]

# 4 ISSUES OF INTERPRETATION

1-09    Any evaluation of the TAs will inevitably raise a number of issues that may conveniently be covered under this general heading.

## The use of pre-1968 law

1-10    The LA of 1916 had been little more than an attempt at consolidating the common law position. Accordingly, the pre-1916 cases had continued to be applied, with all of the consequent deleterious results. The 1968 Act was,

---

12  (1994) Court of Appeal, No 92/4388, cited in Smith, ATH, para 1-04.
13  *Ibid*, Smith, ATH.
14  *Conspiracy to Defraud*, 1987, Law Commission Working Paper No 104, para 1.10.
15  Smith, ATH, para 1-04.
16  There has been a need for subsequent statutory changes, primarily caused by technological developments not foreseen by the CLRC. An example of this is the Theft (Amendment) Act 1996, dealing with new methods of transferring funds.

however, intended to be much more in the nature of codifying legislation, enacting a radically different approach to the law on theft. So much was this the prevalent view, that an attempt was made to prohibit completely any reference to the previous cases. Lord Wilberforce proposed an amendment to the 1968 Bill in the House of Lords that would have prohibited any reference '... to any decisions of any courts prior to the passing of this Act, other than decisions in general terms dealing with the interpretation of statutes'. While there may be some measure of understanding for the spirit with which the amendment was proposed, it is fortunate that this amendment was eventually withdrawn. In most areas, of course, the changes introduced by the 1968 Act have meant that the old cases are now irrelevant and no longer to be considered good law.[17] Continued references to these cases, while interesting from an academic perspective, would serve only to confuse. On the other hand, there are also a number of limited situations where the old cases may serve to illuminate the current provisions. These have been adequately discussed elsewhere and may be summarised as follows:[18]

(a) in situations where the Act incorporates the provisions of earlier statutes, it is unnecessary to reconsider points of interpretation that had been previously well settled. An instance of this would be s 12, which replaced s 217 of the Road Traffic Act 1960. Cases such as *Roberts*,[19] decided under the 1960 Act, would continue to be decided the same way today;[20]

(b) the old law may be relevant when considering the mischief which the Act was intended to deal with. This would be particularly useful in persuading the courts that Parliament could not have intended to legalise conduct which was previously criminal under the old law. The decision of the House of Lords in *Treacy v DPP* is a case in point.[21]

Here, Lord Diplock, expressing the majority view, had no hesitation in referring to the old s 29 of the LA 1916 and the cases thereunder in disposing of the defence argument that a blackmailing letter sent from the UK to an address in Germany was no longer within the jurisdiction of the English courts;[22]

(c) there are situations where a term used in the TAs is intended to bear a technical, rather than its ordinary, meaning. In these situations, it may be useful to refer to the interpretation accorded to such a term by the previous law.

---

17  See, below, para 8-21.
18  Smith, JC, paras 1-08–1-12.
19  [1965] QB 448.
20  See, below, para 6-15. For another specific example, see, below, para 8-08.
21  [1971] AC 537.
22  See, below, para 11-05.

## The use of the CLRC's *Eighth Report*

1-11 One of the general principles for the construction of statutes is that, where the words of the statute are vague or ambiguous, reference may be made to the preparatory material that culminated in the enactment of that statute. Instances of the use of this principle include the landmark decisions in *Ghosh* and *Preddy*.[23]

In the latter case, Lord Goff also utilised the *Thirteenth Report* (on s 16). The use of this principle of construction in the cases decided under the TAs is noted at various points in this text. On the other hand, there are notable instances of the judicial reluctance to adopt this approach to construction. In *Gomez*,[24] for instance, the majority of the House of Lords declined to consider the *Eighth Report* on the grounds, first, that it would not serve any useful purpose and, secondly, that there was already a decision of the House of Lords on that very point. Lord Lowery in a strong dissenting judgment, however, made the point that the majority were, in effect, defeating Parliament's intention in enacting provisions which were virtually identical to the proposals of the CLRC. There have now been significant comments on this issue in the recent decision in *Hinks*.[25] Lord Steyn, in providing a summary of the evolution of the law relating to s 1(1), referred to the use of the Eighth Report as being 'relevant as part of the background against which Parliament enacted the Bill which became the 1968 Act'.[26] Nonetheless, there was no doubt in his Lordship's mind that logical limits must be placed on such a technique of construction and he could see no reason to disagree with the views on this matter expressed in *Gomez*: 'The starting point must be the words of the statute as interpreted by the House in its previous decisions'.[27]

## Questions of civil law

1-12 The TAs utilise many technical legal terms that are undefined within the Acts. Examples of these include 'trespasser',[28] 'proprietary rights',[29] 'trust',[30] 'real or personal' property[31] and 'restitution',[32] among others. These are terms that have long been utilised by the civil law and it was clearly the intention of the CLRC

---

23 [1982] QB 1053; [1996] AC 815.
24 [1993] AC 442.
25 [2000] 4 All ER 833.
26 *Ibid*, p 839.
27 *Ibid*.
28 Section 9.
29 Section 5(1).
30 Section 5(2).
31 Section 4(1).
32 Section 28.

that the use of these terms implied a civil law interpretation. Indeed, the provisions of the Acts would be unworkable without this approach:

> Section 5 qualifies and defines the expression 'belonging to another' and specifically makes use of a number of civil law concepts. Under sub-s (1) the jury may have to decide who had the possession of the article, or whether someone other than the defendant had a 'proprietary right or interest', including an equitable interest (subject to the stated exception) and receive the requisite direction as to the civil law. Sub-sections (2) and (3) necessitate the consideration of the law of trusts and the rights of beneficiaries and the law of bailment and agency. Sub-section (4) makes provision for the situation 'where a person gets property by another's mistake'. The criterion which the sub-section then applies is whether or not the recipient came under an obligation to make restoration of the property (or its value, or proceeds). This is a sophisticated criterion wholly dependent upon distinctions to be drawn from the civil law ... Section 5 and, particularly, s 5(4), demonstrates that the 1968 Act has been drafted so as to take account of and require reference to the civil law of property, contract and restitution.[33]

1-13    However, leaving aside the whole philosophy of assigning an ordinary meaning to these terms, the question remains as to whether civil law concepts can be shoehorned into fulfilling criminal law functions. The principle of justifying punishment on the basis of criminal culpability and blameworthiness (as required by the *mens rea* requirement criteria) sits rather uneasily with those concepts devised and utilised for civil obligations which, after all, apply horizontally (individual versus individual) as opposed to the criminal law's verticality (the state versus the individual). On occasion, the courts, too, have expressed their unease at this approach, for instance, in relation to 'appropriation', under s 3, and 'trespass', under s 9. In *Baxter*, Sachs LJ stated the, not uncommon, judicial view that 'this court deprecates attempts to bring into too close consideration the finer distinctions in civil law as to the precise moment when contractual communications take effect, or when property passes.[34]

1-14    Nonetheless, the recent judgment of the House of Lords, in *Hinks*,[35] indicates that this is not a matter that causes undue concern. Lord Steyn acknowledged that there might exist some 'tension between the civil and the criminal law', especially in those situations, such as the instant appeal, where conduct which is not wrongful in a civil law sense may constitute the crime of theft. Nonetheless, the purposes of the civil and the criminal law are different and the 'tension' was not sufficiently serious to sway the views of the Law Lords.[36]

---

33  *Hinks* [2000] 4 All ER 833, p 855, *per* Lord Hobhouse.
34  This issue is further discussed at various points below; see, eg, paras 2-44 and 4-17.
35  [2000] 4 All ER 833, p 843, *per* Lord Steyn.
36  See the further discussion of this issue, below, para 2-44.

## Questions of law and questions of fact

1-15    It is trite law to state that ordinary words used in a statute do not need judicial explanation: they are questions of fact upon which the jury, or the magistrates, as the tribunal of fact, are perfectly capable of answering. However, it has often proved impossible, in the common law tradition of distinguishing questions of law from questions of fact.[37] The cynical approach to resolving the matter has been offered by Lord Denning in *Griffiths v JP Harrison Ltd*: 'Here is question of law, if your Lordships please to treat it a such.'[38] In an earlier decision, however, he had stated that something was a question of law, if it was a question that only a trained lawyer could answer:

> ... the correct conclusion to be drawn from the primary facts requires, for its correctness, determination by a trained lawyer because it involves the interpretation of documents, or because the law and the facts cannot be separated, or because the law on the point cannot properly be understood or applied except by a trained lawyer.[39]

Such views, of course, cannot be consistent with the stated aim of the CLRC to make the law on theft accessible to the general public.

1-16    It is submitted that the distinction is important for at least the following reasons:

(a) judges answer questions of law; juries answer questions of fact;

(b) appellate courts act only if there is an error of law;

(c) appellate courts rarely interfere with an exercise of discretion based on a finding of fact;

(d) as far as the doctrine of precedent is concerned, a decision of a higher court on a question of law (but not a question of fact) binds lower courts.

1-17    The CLRC had chosen to utilise concepts, such as 'dishonesty', without definition on the basis that these were ordinary words to be given an ordinary meaning. This does not necessarily, and automatically, mean that these words *have* to be treated as questions of fact: the courts could, instead, have developed their own legal definitions (much as 'recklessly' in the Criminal Damage Act 1971 was defined by the House of Lords in *Caldwell*).[40] Instead, generally speaking, the courts have chosen to treat these words as questions of fact and to leave the meaning of such words to the jury. While this may be consistent with the ideal of ensuring that the law remains undivorced from the norms of reasonable men and women, such an approach presents its own dangers. In particular, it contradicts another set of ideals that any legal system should hold

---

37   See, for instance, Endicott, T, 'Questions of law' (1988) 114 LQR 292.
38   [1963] AC 1.
39   *British Launders Research Association v Hendon Rating Authority* [1949] 1 KB 462.
40   [1982] AC 341.

dear: the lack of fixed standards, inconsistency and unpredictability may be too high a price to pay for making the law accessible.[41]

1-18     This, in turn, focuses attention on the proper function of judge and jury (not, it must be said, unique to the law on theft). The principle is easy enough to state: the judge decides questions of law and directs the jury accordingly; the jury decides questions of fact and applies the law to those facts. The reality, however, is not so clear cut. Where a statute uses an 'ordinary word', is it acceptable for the judge to simply leave this to the jury? Or, should he go further and explain what this 'ordinary word' means? Two opposing views may be put forward. First, the failure of the trial judge adequately to direct the jury may amount to an abdication of his responsibility to conduct a trial that is fair to the defendant, especially where the defendant's liberty is at stake. The lack of jury direction can only lead to inconsistency of jury decisions. As Griew puts it: '... it is the business of the judiciary, gradually by a course of decisions, to help the lay tribunal to as consistent an application of the criminal law as can reasonably be achieved.'[42]

1-19     On the other hand, there are many situations where treating the issue as one of fact and leaving it to the jury may provide the only pragmatic solution. In *Feely*, Lawton LJ was of the view that juries are perfectly capable of deciding whether a defendant's conduct was dishonest:

> In their own lives, they have to decide what is and what is not dishonest. We can see no reason why, when in a jury box, they should require the help of a judge to tell them what amounts to dishonesty.[43]

Moreover, leaving these matters to the jury has the advantage of avoiding unnecessary and futile legal niceties, something that had led to the reform of the law in the first place.[44] The debate, as to which of these views is the better one, is not likely to be resolved; perhaps, after all, the search for certainty in the criminal law is a futile one. As Lord Macmillan put it, in *Read v Lyons*: 'Your Lordships are not called upon to rationalise the law of England.'[45] If the second of the views put forward above is accepted, however, it must be on the clear understanding that one particular consequence will follow. If these matters are to be treated as questions of fact and left to the jury, then substantial obstacles will face the defendant who wishes to mount an appeal against a conviction. The appellate courts have traditionally refused to overturn jury determinations on the facts. This is illustrated by the case of *Brutus v Cozens*.[46] The House of Lords

---

41   This is not a problem unique to the law of theft. A similar problem underlies, for instance, the law on negligent manslaughter, where a conviction is ultimately dependent on whether the conduct of the defendant was so grossly negligent that the jury considers a conviction for manslaughter is justified: *Adomako* [1995] 1 AC 171.

42   Griew, para 1-22.

43   [1973] 1 QB 530; see, below, para 2-17.

44   See para 4-27, below, in relation to a burglar who enters a part of a building.

45   [1947] AC 156.

46   [1973] AC 854.

refused to interfere with a finding of the magistrates that the defendant's conduct did not constitute insulting behaviour likely to occasion a breach of the peace, under the Public Order Act 1936, on the basis that the magistrates had made a finding of fact which was beyond the scope of appellate review.[47]

## Tribunals of fact

1-20    The approach adopted in this text has been to avoid the cumbersome phraseology of referring to 'juries and/or magistrates' in those situations where a discussion of questions of fact has been called for. Instead, the authors have opted to refer to the jury alone, with the understanding that the same issue will arise equally with magistrates when they, too, are dealing with questions of fact. As Griew succinctly puts it, 'for "jury" read also "magistrate(s)" whenever the context permits'.[48]

# 5 JURISDICTION

1-21    The general principle in relation to criminal jurisdiction is that it is territorial: the courts of England and Wales do not accept jurisdiction over criminal activities committed outside the territory. Apart from piracy, the main exceptions to this rule are now all contained in statute. However, there are numerous statutes where there is an absence of either a geographical limitation, or extension. This issue was dealt with by the House of Lords in *Treacy v DPP*.[49] Lord Diplock, for the majority, was of the opinion that, where a provision relating to extra-territorial jurisdiction was not expressed, it was to be implied by applying some presumption as to the intention of Parliament. Lord Reid dissented from this approach, being of the opinion that, if it was intended that a statute should have extra-territorial jurisdiction, this had to be stated in express terms. The view of Lord Diplock has been subsequently approved by the Privy Council[50] and applied in the Court of Appeal.[51] There is nothing in precedent, the principles of international comity, or good sense to inhibit the common law from regarding as justiciable in England, inchoate crimes committed abroad which are intended to result in the commission of criminal offences in England.

1-22    In any case, these decisions have now been superseded by ss 1–6 of the Criminal Justice Act (CJA) 1993, which was brought into force with effect from

---

47  On this issue, Scrutton LJ remarked in *Currie v Comrs of Inland Revenue* [1921] 2 KB 332: 'There has been a very strong tendency ... in a judge to say, if he agrees with the decision of the Commissioners, that the question is one of fact, and if he disagrees with them that it is one of law, in order that he may express his own opinion the opposite way.'

48  Griew, para 1-04.

49  [1971] AC 537.

50  *Somchai Liangsiripraesert v Government of the USA* [1991] 1 AC 225.

51  *Sansom* [1991] 2 QB 130.

1 June 1999.[52] Where it has been necessary to do so, the issues of territorial jurisdiction have been dealt with in the main body of the text.[53] As many of the problems arising out of territorial jurisdiction in relation to the TA offences relate to charges for attempts, the main discussion of this issue is to be found in that chapter.[54]

# 6 SENTENCE

1-23     The average person in the UK is more likely to be the victim of a property offence than of any other kind of crime. The Criminal Statistics for 1996 indicate that over 90% of crime is property related, while theft offences account for 50% of all reported crime in England and Wales.[55] These figures must be viewed in the light of the underreporting of theft offences. This would be especially true in relation to shoplifting offences, for instance, indicating the immense scale of theft offences.[56]

1-24     It is difficult to make any wide ranging generalisation in relation to the sentences awarded for the offences under the TAs. The alternative sentences available range from a maximum sentence of life imprisonment down to various non-custodial sentences and fines. This reflects the fact that the theft offences themselves range from the professional robbery and burglary, involving the possible infliction of grievous bodily injury, down to conduct that may be said to lie at the fringes of criminality. There is no typical 'thief' and the sentencing for offences under the TAs must reflect this. Moreover, there have been numerous statutes introduced over the last 20 years or so with the aim of dealing with the rising crime rates and the even higher rates of recidivism. These have also to be seen in the context of even further legislative innovations in relation to the particular problems posed by youth offending. It is beyond the scope of this text to deal with all of these here. Nonetheless, the authors have attempted, in individual chapters, to provide some indications of sentencing practice.

1-25     One particular issue of concern has been the disparity of sentences awarded for those offences dealt with by magistrates.[57] An attempt has been made by the

---

52   The 1993 Act is not intended to have retrospective effect. Moreover, as this part of the Act deals only with offences of dishonesty and blackmail, it may be possible to argue that the approach put forward by Lord Diplock, in *Treacy* [1971] AC 537, continues to be applicable for the other offences under the TAs. See the discussion on this point in relation to thefts from mails, para 7-12.

53   In relation to blackmail, see below, para 11-05.

54   See, below, para 13-06.

55   *Criminal Statistics, England and Wales, 1996,* Cm 3764, London: HMSO.

56   See, for instance, Mirrlees-Black, C and Ross, P, *Crime Against Retail Premises in 1993,* 1995, HORF No 26, where it is suggested that only about 20% of customer thefts are reported (p 44) and that this type of theft costs retail premises about £200 m (p 11).

57   See the discussion of this issue in Ashworth, A, 'Disentangling disparity', in Pennington, D and Lloyd-Bostock, S (eds), *The Psychology of Sentencing,* 1987, Oxford: OUP, pp 24–27.

Magistrates' Association to publish 'Sentencing guidelines' for use by its members. These come in the form of folders for individual offences. Originally, these were confined to motoring offences, but now cover practically all the offences which regularly come before the magistrates' courts. The guidelines indicate a 'starting point' for sentence and then list the various features of a case that might be considered as aggravating, or mitigating. The 'Sentencing guidelines' for the offence of taking vehicles without consent under s 12 of the TA 1968 may be used as an example. Magistrates are, first, required to consider the seriousness of the offence (including the impact on the victim). Secondly, in terms of the base guideline, three questions are posed: is compensation, discharge, or fine appropriate?; is it serious enough for a community penalty?; is it so serious that only custody is appropriate? Thirdly, a list of aggravating and mitigating factors in relation to the offence, which are not intended to be exhaustive, are suggested. The aggravating factors include: group action, premeditation, related damage, professional hallmarks, vulnerable victims, offence committed on bail, previous convictions and failure to respond to previous sentences. The mitigating factors include: misunderstanding with owner, vehicle soon returned, or vehicle belonging to family, or friend. Fourthly, the factors of offender mitigation are listed. These include: age, health, co-operation with the police, voluntary compensation and remorse. The magistrates are then asked to consider their sentence in relation to the suggested guideline and to consider a discount for a guilty plea. These guidelines offer a form of structured decision making and are not intended to suggest an 'answer'.

1-26     As far as the Crown Court is concerned, there are a plethora of sentencing guidelines issued by the Court of Appeal,[58] as well as those contained in the various statutes themselves. An example of such a statutory provision is s 1 of the CJA 1991, which seeks to restrict the powers of the Crown Court to impose a custodial sentence. Such a sentence should be imposed, under s 1(2)(a), only if the court is of the opinion that the offence is so serious that a custodial sentence is justified or, under s 1(2)(b), if such a sentence is necessary in order to protect the public. Judicial guidance, in relation to the imposition of any maximum sentence provided by law, has been offered in cases such as *Byrne*, where it was laid down that these should be reserved only for the most serious examples of the offence.[59]

# 7 MISCELLANEOUS MATTERS

1-27     There a number of matters covered by the TAs which are beyond a book of this nature. These relate to the provisions on evidence and procedure (including the

---

58   For an example of this in relation to burglary, see below, para 4-08.
59   (1976) 62 Cr App R 159.

search for stolen goods), orders for restitution and the various commencement and transitional provisions. Where it has been necessary to do so, these have been incorporated in the main body of the text. So, for instance, some of the provisions relating to evidence, in s 27, have been referred to in Chapter 2 on theft and Chapter 12 on handling stolen goods. One remaining issue is dealt with briefly.

## Husband and wife

1-28 The TA 1968 contains two provisions, ss 30 and 31, which are specifically applicable to spouses. Two main factors account for these sections. The first relates to the commonality of property as it exists between spouses. The second relates to the nature of the marital relationship where an offence is alleged in the following situations where a spouse is (a) the defendant, (b) the victim, or (c) a witness. These provisions were intended to clarify the legal position, rather than to lay down new provisions. In relation to one spouse as a witness, in criminal proceedings against the other, the law is now effectively contained in s 80 of the Police and Criminal Evidence Act 1984, as amended by the Youth Justice and Criminal Evidence Act 1999.

Only one remaining point needs to be made. The general principle in the law of evidence is to the effect that, when a witness in criminal proceedings is required to answer any question, he cannot refuse to do so on the grounds that the answer may incriminate either himself, or anyone else. Section 31(1) applies this general principle in relation to the spouse of the witness. However, the general principle also states that any such incriminating answer may be admissible in any subsequent criminal proceedings. Section 31(1) provides an exception to this general principle in that no such incriminating statement or admission shall be admissible in evidence in relation to any offence under the Act, against either that person, or the spouse of that person.

## 8 EVALUATION

1-29 While it might not seem so today, the TAs of 1968 and 1978 represented a radical attempt at dealing with the problems posed in an area of the law noted for confusion and complexity. The basic definition of theft, in s 1, as the dishonest appropriation of another's property, whether for gain or otherwise, with an intention permanently to deprive, was and remains, shocking in its simplicity. It applies through the whole spectrum of 'stealing', from shoplifting and pickpocketing to professional and organised thievery and deception. Consequently, it does not detract from the achievements of the CLRC to observe that changes are needed 30-odd years later. The law on theft has had to deal with issues that could not have been anticipated at that time: for instance, the use of credit and charge cards, together with electronic methods of money transfer. Moreover, the provisions in the Act often sit uneasily with more recent changes in other areas of the law. This requires that the student and the practitioner, no less than the commentator, should consider much broader contexts:

> In considering criminal law's construction of property offences, we should not, however, confine our view to the TAs. We need to bear in mind the laws relating to criminal damage, computer misuse, conspiracy to defraud, offences relating to forgery and counterfeiting, criminal nuisances or trespasses and, indeed, offences relating to terrorism and hijacking which may have considerable implications for property holdings. Many 'regulatory offences', such as those relating to pollution and safety precautions, are also relevant, as are laws relating to 'intellectual property' and the protection of copyrights, computer software and data and performing rights.[60]

Unfortunately, while successive governments are ready to enact piecemeal reforms for short term effect, they appear to lack the political will for the root and branch reforms suggested by the various commentators and the Law Commission.[61] It also remains to be seen if the law on theft will be immune to any challenge raised by the incorporation of the European Convention for the Protection of Human Rights and Fundamental Freedoms in the Human Rights Act 1998. Concern has already been raised by the Law Commission, in its Consultation Paper on *Fraud and Deception*,[62] on possible incompatibility.[63]

---

60  *Op cit*, Lacey and Wells, fn 2, p 254.
61  *A Criminal Code for England and Wales*, 1989, Law Commission No 177, 1989, HMSO: London; see Bingham, 'A criminal code; must we wait forever?' [1998] Crim LR 694.
62  1999, Law Commission, No 155, HMSO, London, para 5.52.
63  For a discussion of this point in relation to the decisions in *Gomez* [1993] AC 442 and *Hinks* [2000] 4 All ER 833, see, below, para 2-47.

# CHAPTER 2

# THEFT

## 1 BASIC DEFINITION AND INTRODUCTION

2-01 **Section 1 of the Theft Act (TA) 1968**

(1) A person is guilty of theft if he dishonestly appropriates property belonging to another with the intention of permanently depriving the other of it; and 'thief' and 'steal' shall be construed accordingly.

(2) It is immaterial whether the appropriation is made with a view to gain, or is made for the thief's own benefit.

(3) The five following sections of this Act shall have effect as regards the interpretation and operation of this section (and except as otherwise provided by this Act, shall apply only for the purposes of this section).

**Section 7 of the TA 1968**

A person guilty of theft shall on conviction on indictment be liable to imprisonment for a term not exceeding seven years.

## Mode of sentence and trial

2-02 The offence is triable either way.[1] If tried on indictment, theft is a class 4 offence, with a maximum penalty of imprisonment for seven years.[2] Following summary trial, the magistrates can sentence to imprisonment for up to six months, a fine up to the statutory maximum, or both.[3] According to the *Practice Note (Mode of Trial: Guidelines)* (1990),[4] theft should be tried summarily, unless the court considers that one or more of the following features is present and that its sentencing powers are insufficient:

(a) breach of trust by a person in a position of substantial authority, or in whom a high degree of trust is placed;

(b) theft which has been committed or disguised in a sophisticated manner;

(c) theft committed by an organised gang;

---

1 Magistrates' Courts Act 1980, s 17(1) and Sched 1, para 28.

2 The TA 1968, s 7 (as amended by the Criminal Justice Act (CJA) 1991, s 26(1)). The maximum was originally 10 years.

3 Magistrates' Courts Act 1980, s 32(1) and Sched 1, para 28. The statutory maximum is currently £5,000.

4 The guidelines are unreported, but broadly follow the guidelines published in *Practice Note (Mode of Trial: Guidelines)* [1990] 1 WLR 1439. The guidelines also apply to offences involving fraud.

(d) the victim is particularly vulnerable to theft (for example, the elderly or infirm);

(e) the unrecovered property is of high value (at least £10,000).

An offence of theft, or attempted theft, of a motor vehicle carries discretionary disqualification.[5] However, it has been held that disqualification should be restricted to cases involving bad driving or where there have been persistent motoring offences, or where the vehicle has been used for the purpose of crime.[6]

## Elements of theft

2-03    It has been stated that the basic definition of theft 'involves four elements: (a) a dishonest (b) appropriation (c) of property belonging to another (d) with the intention of permanently depriving the owner of it'.[7] However, this chapter will consider theft as containing five elements, since it is sometimes important to give separate consideration to the meaning of 'property' from that of 'belonging to another'. Although the basic offence is contained in s 1 of the TA 1968, ss 2–6 provide explanations (in part and to varying degrees) of how each of these elements operate. The *mens rea* is dealt with in s 2, which gives examples of when a defendant will not be regarded as dishonest, and in s 6 which extends the general meaning of 'an intention permanently to deprive'. The *actus reus* is contained in s 3 which deals with the meaning of 'appropriation', and in ss 4 and 5, which elaborate on the meaning of 'property' and 'belonging to another' respectively. Note that ss 2–6 are purely explanatory and have no other function but to interpret the content of the basic definition.

Each element of theft will be examined in the order in which it appears in the basic definition. However, it may be helpful to note throughout that theft is essentially a crime against rights of ownership in property and need not necessarily involve a taking into possession. Note, too, that the wording of s 1(2) of the Act means that it is not necessary to show that the thief has appropriated property for his own benefit – throwing a person's handbag down a deep well is as much theft of the handbag as if the thief had taken the handbag home and used it as a replacement for an old one of his own. Furthermore, due to the wide definition of property in s 4, almost anything can, in principle, be the subject of theft. In addition, the House of Lords has given an extraordinarily wide meaning to the concept of 'appropriation', which means that the offence of theft is drawn very broadly. However, no act which is done in relation to property belonging to another with the intention of permanently depriving another's rights in that property will amount to theft, unless it is done dishonestly.

---

5    Road Traffic Offenders Act 1988, ss 34 and 97 and Sched 2, Pt II.

6    *Callister* [1993] RTR 70.

7    In *Lawrence* (1970) 55 Cr App R 73, p 78, Court of Appeal, *per* Megaw LJ, and specifically approved by the House of Lords [1972] AC 626, p 632, *per* Viscount Dilhorne.

## 2 DISHONESTY

2-04    **Section 2 of the TA 1968**

2(1) A person's appropriation of property belonging to another is not to be regarded as dishonest –

(a) if he appropriates the property in the belief that he has in law the right to deprive the other of it, on behalf of himself or of a third person;

(b) if he appropriates the property in the belief that he would have the other's consent if the other knew of the appropriation and the circumstances of it; or

(c) (except where the property came to him as trustee or personal representative) if he appropriates the property in the belief that the person to whom the property belongs cannot be discovered by taking reasonable steps.

(2) A person's appropriation of property belonging to another may be dishonest notwithstanding that he is willing to pay for the property.

## Background

2-05    Dishonesty is a concept which unites most of the offences in the TAs and which distinguishes them from other offences against property, such as criminal damage. In addition to theft itself, eight other offences under the TA 1968, and all three under the TA 1978, require dishonesty as an essential ingredient. Under the 1968 Act, these offences are: s 13, abstracting electricity; s 15, obtaining property by deception; s 15A,[8] obtaining a money transfer by deception; s 16, obtaining a pecuniary advantage by deception; s 17, false accounting; s 20(1) suppression of documents; s 20(2), procuring the execution of a valuable security by deception; s 22 handling stolen goods; and s 24A,[9] dishonestly retaining a wrongful credit. Under the 1978 Act, the offences are: s 1, obtaining services by deception; s 2, evasion of liability by deception; and s 3, making off without payment. In addition to these offences, s 8, robbery, presupposes an offence of theft having taken place and thus requires dishonesty; ss 9 and 10, burglary and aggravated burglary may also include a theft; finally, s 25, going equipped for stealing, will invariably involve an intent to commit an offence requiring dishonesty as an essential ingredient.

### *'Dishonesty' not defined*

2-06    It will be noted immediately that there is no actual definition of the word dishonest in the Act. Other key words in the Act are defined as a matter of law,

---

8    Created by the Theft (Amendment) Act 1996, s 1(1).

9    *Ibid*, s 2.

such as 'appropriation' and 'property', but not the word dishonest. There is only a partial definition in terms of three situations where dishonesty is negated, in s 2(1), and merely one positive example of potential dishonesty, in s 2(2). This lack of assistance is particularly strange, as the concept of dishonesty is so central to the notion of criminality throughout the TAs. Now that the concept of appropriation has been interpreted so widely that it has been almost neutralised by the decision of the House of Lords in *Gomez*,[10] the concept of dishonesty is crucial in deciding what type of interference with another's property will attract criminal sanction. That is not to say that dishonesty on its own is criminalised: there will be instances where dishonest behaviour involving, for example, temporary deprivation of property, however dishonestly undertaken, will not amount to theft. Nevertheless, it is also the concept that justifies prosecution for what we might consider 'minor offences', such as stealing 50 p rather than £50, or in situations where it would seem more appropriate to pursue a remedy through the civil courts or the regulatory bodies. It is society's condemnation of dishonest behaviour that enables such prosecutions to go ahead because the concept of dishonesty strikes at the very heart of criminal culpability. It is where the overlap between morality and criminal culpability is most clearly seen and why crimes of theft (and deception, etc) are regarded as so morally reprehensible. It is not simply the interference with another's property that is morally repugnant but, the essential ingredient of dishonesty points to a personal choice having been made. Dishonesty is that crucial factor which enables us to decide whether wrongs that are committed against another's property are serious enough to justify criminalisation.[11]

The problem for the law is thus twofold: first, what standards of morality should be upheld – if, indeed, there is such a norm of moral behaviour – and secondly, whether this should be left to the jury to decide as a matter of fact, or for the judge to decide as a matter of law.

### The word 'dishonestly' preferred to 'fraudulently'

2-07    When the Criminal Law Revision Committee (CLRC) published its *Eighth Report*, on which the TA 1968 was based,[12] they deliberately chose the word 'dishonestly' to replace the expression 'fraudulently and without a claim of right made in good faith' used in the old Larceny Act (LA) 1916, the meaning of which had led to 'a mass of difficult and conflicting case law'.[13] The precise meaning of the word 'fraudulently' and, indeed, whether it added anything to

---

10   [1993] AC 442; see para 2-31, below.
11   Griew believes dishonesty merely has a negative function in the Act, similar to the word 'unlawful': para 2-122.
12   CLRC, *Eighth Report*, Cmnd 2977, 1966, London: HMSO.
13   See *Samuels*, below.

'claim of right', had been uncertain and so the word 'dishonestly' was thought to be more modern and easier for a jury to understand:

> 'Dishonestly' seems to us to be a better word than 'fraudulently'. The question 'was this dishonest?' is easier for a jury to answer than the question 'was this fraudulent?'. Dishonesty is something which laymen can easily recognise when they see it, whereas 'fraudulently' may seem to involve technicalities which have to be explained by a lawyer.[14]

There seems little doubt that the CLRC thought of 'dishonestly' (in the same way as 'fraudulently') in terms of it being descriptive of the defendant's state of mind, a word 'chosen to mark out the moral reprehensibility' of the action; s 2(1) was included merely to preserve certain aspects of the law of larceny, rather than to provide a new 'defence' of honest behaviour. But, by leaving the word undefined in law, the CLRC left open the possibility of expansion and, it is submitted, inconsistency.[15] Leaving it to the jury gives them the unenviable, and deceptively straightforward, task of assessing the defendant's state of mind in terms of the morality of his action. Other *mens rea* words, such as 'intention' and 'recklessness', are not necessarily linked to a moral norm in quite the same way.

## Where D will not be dishonest: the meaning of s 2(1)

2-08    Section 2(1) provides for three situations where a defendant might claim as a matter of law that his appropriation of property is not dishonest because he holds a particular belief. What counts is the defendant's own state of mind in relation to the act done. The emphasis in s 2(1) is on what the defendant believes at the time that he appropriates property belonging to another. As it relates to the belief of the defendant, it is arguable that it covers situations where the defendant may have made a mistake, as long as that belief is honestly held and relates to his appreciation that he was doing something which is regarded as dishonest. The decision whether a defendant had such a belief is one for the jury to decide.

### Section 2(1)(a) belief in a right to deprive – a claim of right

2-09    If the defendant holds the belief 'that he has in law the right to deprive the other' of property, then he is entitled to an acquittal, the jury having been directed in accordance with s 2(1)(a). This is so, even if the belief is in relation to another person; or if that belief is unreasonably held;[16] or, arguably, mistakenly held as

---

14   *Op cit*, CLRC, fn 12 , para 39.
15   See Law Commission No 155, 1999, para 3.7.
16   *Small* (1987) 86 Cr App R 170 and para 2-10, below.

the result of intoxication.[17] This is the same as the approach previously taken by the law of larceny, where the court, in *Bernhard*,[18] approved the passage in Stephen's *History of the Criminal Law of England*: 'Fraud is inconsistent with a claim of right made in good faith to do the act complained of. A man who takes possession of property which he really believes to be his own does not take it fraudulently, however unfounded his claim might be. This, if not the only, is nearly the only case in which ignorance of the law affects the legal character of acts done under its influence.'[19]

The belief is as to a legal right to appropriate the property; even the old law of larceny gave no protection to a belief in a moral right.[20] For example, where a customer in a shop legitimately buys a loaf of bread but, believing it to be overpriced, then helps himself to another loaf while the shopkeeper is not looking, the customer cannot claim the protection of s 2(1)(a), however much he feels morally entitled to do so.[21] By the same token, if a defendant were to remove money from the pocket of his more highly paid work colleague in the belief that he has a moral right to be paid the same, he is not entitled to a s 2(1)(a) direction. He will be, however, if he removes the same amount of money from the same pocket in the belief that his colleague owed him an equivalent sum, provided he also thinks that the debt entitles him in law to help himself to that money. This is because s 2(1)(a) requires only that the accused believed he was entitled to take the property. It is not necessary for him to believe he is entitled to take it in the way in which he does: it seems that he may take the property by fair means or foul. This is because his mistake is as to the civil rather than the criminal law – even though he may be aware that the criminal law prohibits him from doing so.[22] According to *Robinson*,[23] this would be so even if the money were taken by force. In that case, it was held to be a misdirection for a judge to direct a jury that an honest belief by the defendant that he was entitled in law to get his money in a particular way was necessary before he could avail himself of s 2(1)(a). If Robinson believed that he had the right in law to deprive his victim

---

17   Cf *Jaggard v Dickinson* [1981] 1 QB 527.

18   [1938] 2 KB 264.

19   1883 (republished 1996, Routledge), Vol III, p 124.

20   *Harris v Harrison* [1963] Crim LR 497.

21   Note that he may still be acquitted of theft, if a sympathetic jury interprets the *Ghosh* test in his favour. In *Woolven* (1983) 77 Cr App R 231, it was stated that where a defendant asserted a belief in a claim of right then a *Ghosh* direction should be given, since it would cover all such circumstances relevant to s 2(1)(a). However, since *Woolven* was a case concerned with a s 15 offence to which s 2 does not apply, it seems preferable that a s 2(1)(a) direction should always be given as a matter of law, where the defendant is asserting his belief as of right on a charge of theft.

22   Provided, of course, that this knowledge of the criminal prohibition does not make it impossible for him to claim he believed he was 'entitled' to take the property. Cf *Forrester* [1992] Crim LR 793.

23   [1977] Crim LR 173; see also *Skivington* [1968] 1 QB 166 (decided before the TA 1968).

of the money, he could not be guilty of theft, even if he knew that he was not entitled to use force to recover the money.[24]

## Where D 'finds' the property

2-10 Where a defendant mistakenly believes himself to be entitled to hold onto property that he has 'found', he may still assert that he is not dishonest according to s 2(1)(a), despite the fact he knows the whereabouts of the true owner. This is because he may believe himself to have acquired ownership under the principle of 'finders keepers'.[25] Of course, a defendant who makes a mistake as to the true ownership of property need not be forced to rely solely on s 2(1)(a) for protection when defending a theft charge. For example, if a defendant takes another's criminal law book in the belief that it is his own, it is difficult to see how he intends permanently to deprive property belonging to another person.[26] A charge of theft may then fail, on this basis, rather than the need to rely on s 2(1)(a).

## Section 2(1)(b) belief that the victim would consent

2-11 This section provides a defence where a defendant believes that the victim would have consented to the taking of the property, if he had known of the appropriation *and the circumstances of it*. Since the decision in *Gomez*,[27] an appropriation can take place even where the victim consents to it, but he may not have genuinely agreed to the passing of property so that the defendant may be guilty of theft, unless he can claim successfully that he believed his victim would still have consented had he had both knowledge of the actual appropriation and of the relevant circumstances. The victim's knowledge (or assumed knowledge) of the true circumstances of the appropriation is, therefore, relevant before the defendant can claim that he is not dishonest. In simplest terms, this section covers situations such as helping yourself to food from a neighbour's fridge, or petrol from his garage. An intention permanently to deprive another of property belonging to him is present but the defendant thinks his neighbour 'wouldn't mind' and, therefore, there is no dishonesty.[28] Thus, where a defendant takes a bottle of milk from a stack of crates outside business hours, and leaves the appropriate money for it, he is entitled to claim the protection of s 2(1)(b) if he believed that the milkman would have consented

---

24 He may, however, be guilty of blackmail. For discussion of the offences of blackmail and robbery, see Chapters 11 and 3, respectively.

25 See *Small* (1987) 86 Cr App R 170; and 'Commentary' [1987] Crim LR 777.

26 For, further comment on abandoned property, see para 2-95, below.

27 [1993] AC 422 (HL).

28 Of course, if he asserted that he was going to replace it later, particularly if he knew his neighbour might object, then the *Ghosh* test would apply. See para 2-18.

to him doing this – even if it is established that he was wrong in his surmise, as all the milk was already accounted for. It is a matter of what the defendant believes the owner of the property's attitude would have been, not what would have been the property owner's attitude in reality.[29] However, it would not be sufficient for the defendant to believe that the milkman would have sold him the milk had he been present. The defendant's belief must be that the milkman – if he had known of the circumstances in which the milk was taken – would have consented to what the defendant did, namely taking the milk in the milkman's absence.

### Application of s 2(1)(b) to company controllers

2-12    Where one or more persons are in control of a limited liability company, by reason of their shareholdings and directorship, he or they can still be convicted of stealing property from that company, notwithstanding s 2(1)(b). It was so held in *AG Ref (No 2 of 1982)*[30] where Kerr LJ rejected a submission that there was no issue in relation to dishonesty when it was claimed that, as the respondents were the sole will and directing mind of the company, the company was bound to consent to all to which they themselves consented. It was held that, in such circumstances, a defendant cannot impute consent to the company, as it is a separate entity. The defendant's belief must be 'an honest belief in a true consent, honestly obtained'.[31] Whether or not such persons could establish a defence under s 2(1)(a) (above) would depend on whether the prosecution could prove (to the satisfaction of the jury) that they did not honestly believe that they were entitled to do what they did.

### Section 2(1)(c) belief that owner cannot be discovered

2-13    Property that has been truly abandoned by its owner cannot normally be stolen, since it has ceased to be property belonging to the person who abandoned it.[32] Even where property has been inadvertently lost, if the defendant believes that he cannot, by taking reasonable steps, discover the owner, he will not be guilty of theft because he is not dishonest according to s 2(1)(c). This is so even if his belief was unreasonable, provided the jury accept he genuinely had such a belief. That he had taken such steps as he, the defendant, thought reasonable in order to discover the true owner would be evidence that he held such a belief. However, there may be some circumstances where he deems it unnecessary to take any steps at all. For example, where he finds a £50 note on top of

---

29   See 'Commentary' on *Pryor* (1969) 119 NLJ 561; *Fynn* [1970] Crim LR 118.
30   [1984] QB 624.
31   *Ibid*, p 641; see, also, *Pearlberg* [1982] Crim LR 829.
32   However, there may be circumstances in which the property 'belongs' to the person on whose land it is: the landowner may then have a better title than the 'finder'. For further discussion of abandoned property, see para 2-95, below.

Snowdonia, or a diamond ring in a car park and, unreasonably, though genuinely, believes that the only way to trace the owner is to advertise on national television which he decides is too expensive. The same will be true where he obtains the property by mistake, or has been asked to look after the property and later cannot discover the whereabouts of the owner.[33]

This sub-section preserves the common law idea of 'finders keepers' without fear of prosecution. However, it does make one important change to the old offence of larceny in that a defendant will now be guilty of theft if, having believed it impossible to discover the owner, he later discovers his true identity but dishonestly retains the property. This will now be an appropriation under s 3(1).[34]

### Application of s 2(1)(c) to trustees

2-14   Section 2(1)(c) does not give protection to a trustee or personal representative because such a person may not personally retain property, but holds it on behalf of the beneficiaries; if the beneficiaries cannot be traced, then the property should revert to the Crown as *bona vacantia*.[35] Presumably, if a trustee or personal representative were to hold onto property in the mistaken belief that they were legally entitled to it, it is at least arguable that s 2(1)(a) would apply.

## A willingness to pay may still be dishonest: the meaning of s 2(2)

2-15   This is the only positive definition of dishonesty in the TAs 1968 and 1978, and it is only a partial one at that. The section makes a thief out of the determined buyer who, even though he is prepared to pay a reasonable price for the property (perhaps, a long coveted painting or sports car), does so knowing that the owner is unwilling to sell; similarly, he may take another's pint of beer from the table in a bar, leaving the full price for it. He has appropriated property belonging to another with the intention of permanently depriving the owner of it; the only ingredient left to establish is dishonesty. In these circumstances, s 2(2) leaves the issue of dishonesty to the jury to decide on the basis of the *Ghosh* test (see, below). However, it is a question of fact whether an appropriation in such circumstances is dishonest,[36] and it is arguable (in some circumstances) that leaving the money is evidence of belief in consent under s 2(1)(b).

---

33   *Holden* [1991] Crim LR 478; cf *Small* (1987) 86 Cr App R 170.
34   See, further, para 2-52, below.
35   Administration of Estates Act 1925, s 46(1)(iv).
36   *Boggeln v Williams* [1978] 1 WLR 873, and 'Commentary' [1978] Crim LR 242.

## Where s 2(1) does not apply

2-16    Section 2(1) provides only limited assistance and where the facts of a situation fall outside those described in s 2(1), then guidance must be sought elsewhere. For example, if a student takes books from the library without permission, knowing that such conduct is forbidden but intending to return them the next day, nothing in s 2(1) offers a solution as to whether he is dishonest. The section leaves fundamental questions unanswered in particular, whether dishonesty is to be decided as a matter of law by the judge, in which case it seems logical to expect a legal definition, or whether it is to be decided as a matter of fact by the jury, in which case, should it be determined subjectively, or objectively?

The first issue has been resolutely settled by the decision in *Feely*.[37] Whether the defendant is dishonest is a matter of fact for the jury; after all, the whole reason why the CLRC chose the word 'dishonestly' in preference to 'fraudulently' was because they thought that it was a word more easily understood by a jury.[38] The second issue is more difficult to resolve as it relates to how a society decides to criminalise behaviour. If it is to be determined in terms of the harm done, then it will be irrelevant how the defendant actually viewed his own behaviour; his state of mind must be tested objectively, with reference to reasonable norms of behaviour. On the other hand, if we punish behaviour only where the defendant himself is considered blameworthy or evil, then his state of mind must be tested subjectively.[39] The emphasis of s 2(1) is subjective, reflecting the approach taken by the CLRC that it is the defendant's own state of mind which is paramount. Where s 2(1) does not apply, the law has sought a compromise between these two approaches and the leading case is now *Ghosh*, which will be discussed below.

## Dishonesty is a matter for the jury

2-17    The Court of Appeal in *Feely* believed that, since a jury was comprised of 'ordinary decent people', they were best able to judge whether the defendant was dishonest. Feely was the manager of a betting shop who 'borrowed' money from his employer's safe, claiming in his defence that he had intended to repay the money at a later date. Feely was well aware that his employer disapproved of any such practice and so he could not claim the protection of s 2(1)(b). He was convicted of theft, after the judge had directed the jury that a willingness to repay was no defence and they could convict him if they, the jury, found that he did not believe that his employers would have consented to him taking the

---

37    [1973] QB 530.
38    See para 2-07, above.
39    There is always the possibility of a third approach, that it be regarded purely in terms of strict liability.

money. However, this was held to be a misdirection and his conviction was quashed: dishonesty was a matter for the jury to decide and they did not need a judge to tell them what it was. Dishonesty was 'an ordinary word';[40] it was 'in common use'. As Lawton LJ explained: 'Jurors, when deciding whether an appropriation was dishonest can be reasonably expected to, and should, apply the current standards of ordinary decent people. In their own lives they have to decide what is and what is not dishonest. We can see no reason why, when in a jury box, they should require the help of a judge to tell them what amounts to dishonesty.'

Of course the jury needed to consider what was in the defendant's mind, but it was to be judged by the standards of 'ordinary decent people'. But what if the defendant did not know that such people would regard his behaviour as dishonest? While it was clear from *Feely* that it is for the jury, and not for the judge, to determine whether the defendant acted dishonestly, confusion remained as to whether these ordinary decent people would decide the matter subjectively or objectively. In *Boggeln v Williams*,[41] it was held that a defendant's own state of mind was crucial in deciding whether he was dishonest: the relevant question for the jury to consider was whether the defendant, himself, believed that what he had done was dishonest. Something similar was said in *Landy*,[42] referring to the earlier decision in *Gilks*,[43] where it was held correct to consider the defendant's own standards of honesty, even while recognising they might not be those of the ordinary decent person.

The dangers implicit in such a situation were recognised in *Greenstein*, as potentially allowing as many acquittals as there were defendant states of mind. In that case, the Court of Appeal believed that a more objective approach was required and approved the judge's direction that the jury should apply only its own standards: 'It is no good, you see, applying the standards of anyone accused of dishonesty otherwise everybody accused of dishonesty, if he were to be tested by his own standards, would be acquitted automatically, you may think. The question is essentially one for a jury to decide and it is essentially one which the jury must decide by applying its own standards.'[44]

There was an opportunity to resolve these two lines of authority in *McIvor*,[45] where the defendant was convicted of theft after the trial judge had directed the jury to disregard what McIvor had said about his own state of mind and, instead, ask themselves whether his conduct could be regarded as honest by 'ordinary people'. Unfortunately, the Court of Appeal only confused matters

---

40   *Brutus v Cozens* [1973] AC 854 (HL).
41   [1978] 1 WLR 873.
42   [1981] 1 WLR 355.
43   [1972] 1 WLR 1341.
44   [1975] 1 WLR 1353, p 1358 (but, note that a subjective approach can still lead to a conviction as the jury are not bound to believe the defendant).
45   [1981] 1 WLR 409.

further by sidestepping the issue and simply distinguishing *Landy*, stating that while the subjective approach was appropriate to a charge of conspiracy to defraud, it did not apply to theft. In considering a charge of theft, the jury must apply its own standards of dishonesty, although where a defendant gives evidence as to his own belief, the jury should give that evidence such weight as they think fit.

The matter was finally, if not entirely satisfactorily, resolved in *Ghosh*,[46] where a similarly constituted Court of Appeal rejected this distinction between conspiracy and theft and proposed 'some other solution'.[47]

## Meaning of dishonesty: the *Ghosh* direction

2-18    In giving the judgment of the court, the Lord Chief Justice stated that while dishonesty is a matter for the jury to decide 'the knowledge and belief of the accused are at the root of the problem', and later, 'if the mind of the accused is honest, it cannot be deemed dishonest merely because members of the jury would have regarded it as dishonest to embark on that course of conduct'.[48] The test is neither fully objective, nor fully subjective, but the jury must be directed to consider the issue in two stages: (1) was the defendant's conduct dishonest according to the standards of reasonable and honest people? If the answer is no, then the matter ends and the prosecution fails. If the answer is yes, then a second question must be considered; (2) did the defendant realise that reasonable and honest people would regard what he did as dishonest? If the jury finds the answer to this question also to be yes, then dishonesty is established.

The first question is derived from *Feely* and is objective, but when combined with the second question, the *Ghosh* test maintains the principle of subjectivity, while at the same time not altogether abandoning all states of mind but that of the accused himself. In this way, Lord Lane believes the approach takes care of (that is, negates) the so called 'Robin Hood defence'. He gives the example of 'ardent anti-vivisectionists' who remove animals from vivisection laboratories, who, he says, will not be able to rely on their belief of moral justification because they know that ordinary people would consider their actions to be dishonest. The jury must decide on the facts presented to them, so in *Ghosh* itself, Lord Lane CJ states: 'If the judge had asked the jury to determine whether the defendant might have believed that what he did was in accordance with the ordinary man's ideas of honesty, there could have only been one answer – and that is no, once the jury had rejected the defendant's explanation of what had happened.'

---

46    [1982] QB 1053.
47    *Ibid*, p 1061, *per* Lane LCJ.
48    *Ibid*, p 1064.

On the other hand, to use another of Lord Lane's examples, a man who comes from a country where public transport is free, travels on a bus and gets off without paying will not be regarded as dishonest because it is 'conduct to which no moral obloquy could possibly attach'. As a stranger to the land, he could not know that ordinary decent people would regard that conduct as dishonest.

## *Academic criticism of the Ghosh test*

2-19    The *Ghosh* view has many critics.[49] Spencer criticises it for being far too complicated and oversophisticated ('clearly intelligence tests for juries will soon be needed'), but also because, by letting the defendant say, 'I'm sorry, I thought society tolerated till-dipping, or cheating bookmakers, or fiddling the NHS', it allows something like a mistake of law as a defence.[50]

One of its most vehement critics was Professor Griew who regarded the decision in *Ghosh* as flawed from the start, as it is based on *Feely* and perpetuates the circular argument of defining dishonesty in terms of honest men. He points out that there is no ordinary standard of honesty, no community norm and, therefore, leaving dishonesty as a matter of fact for the jury to decide, without the benefit of legal guidance from the judge, will inevitably lead to inconsistent verdicts, uncertainty, and long and expensive trials.[51] Furthermore, neither Griew nor Elliott believes that the second part of the test takes care of the so called 'Robin Hood defence', as Lord Lane CJ thought that it did. After all, if the defendant passionately believes in the moral right of his action, then he may well believe that right-minded members of society will agree with him; this will inevitably lead to an acquittal. Professor Griew thinks such a result is remarkable.[52]

However, it is submitted that it need not be regarded so. Surely there would be no 'moral obloquy' in such circumstances, neither must we lose sight of the fact that it is always open to a jury to disbelieve the defendant's claim. If Robin Hood genuinely thought that the plain man would not consider what he had done as dishonest, then it is at least arguable to a jury that he lacks a state of mind traditionally recognised as sufficiently blameworthy in order to turn a civil wrong into a criminal one.

---

49   Griew, E, 'Dishonesty: the objections to *Feely* and *Ghosh*' [1985] Crim LR 341; Elliot, DW, 'Dishonesty in theft: a dispensable concept' [1982] Crim LR 395; Spencer, JR, 'Dishonesty: what the jury thinks the defendant thought the jury would have thought' (1982) CLJ 222; Glazebrook, PR, 'Revising the Theft Acts' [1993] CLJ 191; Campbell, K, 'Test of dishonesty in *R v Ghosh*' [1984] CLJ 349.

50   See, also, Smith, JC [1982] Crim LR 609; Glanville-Williams, *Textbook of Criminal Law*, 2nd edn, 1983, Stevens, p 728 on this point.

51   The Law Commission share similar anxieties: see, Law Commission Consultation Paper No 155, 1999. It may even be that a judge is abdicating his constitutional responsibility by handing over such an important matter to the jury alone to decide.

52   See also Smith, JC, para 2-124.

2-20    Professor Griew believes most of these pitfalls could be avoided if dishonesty became a matter of law, but he does not attempt a definition. Glazebrook does do so, based on the premise that it surely cannot be considered dishonest to do what one is entitled (at civil law) to do. His proposal is to rewrite s 2:

> A person's appropriation of property belonging to another *is to be regarded as dishonest unless* –
>
> (a) done in the belief that he has in law the right to deprive the other of it, on behalf of himself or of a third person; or
>
> (b) done in the belief that he would have the other's consent if the other knew of the appropriation and the circumstances of it; or
>
> (c) done (otherwise than by a trustee or personal representative) in the belief that the person to whom the property belongs is unlikely to be discovered by taking reasonable steps; or
>
> (d) *he received it in good faith and for value; or*
>
> (e) *the property is money, some other fungible, a thing in action or intangible property, and it is appropriated with the intention of replacing it, and in the belief that it will be possible for him to do so without loss to the person to whom it belongs; or*
>
> (f) *it consists in picking (otherwise than for reward, or for sale or other commercial purpose) mushrooms, flowers, fruit or foliage growing wild.*

It is arguable that this definition would create as many problems as it would solve. Judicial creativity on interpretation of statutes has often led to conflicting case law and may not necessarily produce any more certainty or generate any more public confidence in justice than the verdict of the good sense of 12 ordinary men and women based on their everyday experience of 'moral obloquy'.[53] Thus, Elliott proposes going further by dispensing with the word 'dishonestly' altogether and adding a new sub-s (3) to s 2:

> No appropriation of property belonging to another which is not detrimental to the interests of the other in a significant way shall amount to theft of the property.[54]

Finally, Professor Smith believes that interpreting dishonest to be '*knowing* [emphasis added] that the appropriation will or may be detrimental to the interests of the owner in a significant practical way' would achieve a satisfactory result – but it would require legislation or a revisitation of the matter by the House of Lords.[55]

---

53  *Samuels* [1974] Crim LR 493.
54  *Op cit*, Elliot, fn 49, p 410.
55  Smith, JC, para 2-124.

## The status of the Ghosh test

2-21    Early optimism by critics[56] that the *Ghosh* test would soon be re-examined by the House of Lords has proved unfounded and, despite all the criticism, the test has remained unchallenged in the English courts for almost 20 years.[57] It is now clear that the *Ghosh* test applies to all offences where dishonesty is an issue and where s 2(1) of the TA 1968 does not apply.

## How and when a Ghosh direction should be given

2-22    The Court of Appeal has made it clear that the second question should be used only in circumstances where there is doubt as to whether the defendant himself believed that ordinary people would regard his actions as dishonest.[58] When the jury is directed in terms of both questions, it has been held by the Court of Appeal in *Hyam*[59] that it is not compulsory to use Lord Lane's exact words as long as the two essential ingredients of the test are explained to the jury. However, it will always be desirable to do so in order to avoid the risk of appeal – after all the judge has the easy bit, the difficult part is for the jury.[60]

# 3 APPROPRIATION

2-23    **Section 3 of the TA 1968**

3(1) Any assumption by a person of the rights of an owner amounts to an appropriation, and this includes, where he has come by the property (innocently or not) without stealing it, any later assumption of a right to it by keeping or dealing with it as owner.

(2) Where property or a right or interest in property is or purports to be transferred for value to a person acting in good faith, no later assumption by him of rights which he believed himself to be acquiring shall, by reason of any defect in the transferor's title amount to theft of the property.

---

56    *Op cit*, Spencer, fn 49.

57    Although, even before *Ghosh*, in *Salvo* [1980] VR 401, the Supreme Court of Victoria refused to follow *Feely*, preferring the meaning of dishonest to be a matter of law, as it was the duty of a judge to explain to the jury that it meant, 'with disposition to defraud, ie, with disposition to withhold from a person what is his right'. See 'Commentary' [1982] Crim LR 410.

58    *Roberts* (1987) 84 Cr App R 117; *Price* (1990) 90 Cr App R 409; *Clowes (No 2)* [1994] 2 All ER 316.

59    [1997] Crim LR 440.

60    *Green* [1992] Crim LR 292 and 'Commentary'; *Ravenshead* [1990] Crim LR 398.

## Introduction

2-24   Before the enactment of the TA 1968, English law required that the defendant 'takes and carries away' property 'without the consent of the owner' before stealing was complete. The requirement that there had to be a mere 'appropriation' of property is thus a new concept created by the TA 1968 and is much broader in scope than the old law of larceny.

Despite the fact that the CLRC expressed the belief that the concept of 'dishonest appropriation' would 'easily be understood even without the aid of further definition',[61] an interpretation of appropriation was offered in s 3(1). However, the definition was not exhaustive and two major issues remained unexplained by s 3 alone. First, just exactly how many of the rights of an owner must be assumed before an appropriation has occurred; and, secondly, whether it is possible for an appropriation to take place with the consent of the owner. Both these issues have been addressed by the House of Lords, who have had to consider the meaning of the word 'appropriates' on four occasions since the enactment of the TA 1968; s 3 must now be read in the light of these decisions.

In *Morris*,[62] it was held that the assumption of any of the rights of the owner in property amounts to an appropriation; and in *Gomez*[63] (confirming the earlier decision in *Lawrence v Metropolitan Police Commissioner*),[64] it was held that there may be an assumption of a right to property belonging to another, even where the owner *consents or authorises* the property being taken. These decisions have their critics,[65] but undoubtedly represent the law. Indeed, as recently as July 2000, the House of Lords, in *Hinks*,[66] felt it unnecessary to depart from either decision when they held that an indefeasible gift of property is capable of amounting to an 'appropriation' of property belonging to another for the purposes of s 1(1) of the TA 1968. The meaning of appropriation is thus very wide indeed, although, of course, the actual offence of theft will not be complete until a dishonest intention permanently to deprive is proven. The implications of each of these decisions are examined below.

---

61   *Op cit*, CLRC, fn 12, para 38.
62   [1984] AC 320, see paras 2-25 and 2-29, below.
63   [1993] AC 442, see para 2-31, below.
64   [1972] AC 626, see para 2-27 below.
65   See Smith, JC [1993] Crim LR 304 and [1998] Crim LR 904; Griew, para 2-84; Smith, ATH, 'Gifts and the law of theft' [1999] CLJ 10. But cf *op cit*, Glazebrook, fn 49; Gardner, S, 'Property and theft' [1998] Crim LR 35.
66   [2000] 3 WLR 1590; see para 2-42, below.

## Appropriation is an interference with any of the rights of an owner

2-25   Because the old larceny laws stated that property was to be 'taken away', it implied that it must be taken out of the control, or possession, of the victim and into the possession of the thief. But the owner of property has a variety of rights in relation to his property, not merely a right of possession, and it was held in *Morris* that it was not necessary for D to assume all of the owner's rights, an assumption of any of these rights will amount to an appropriation. *Morris* was a consolidated appeal involving two cases of price label switching in supermarkets. In both cases, the defendant had removed the proper price label and replaced it with a lower price before taking the goods to the checkout, where he intended to pay the lower price. In the first case, the defendant was detected at the checkout point before he had paid for the goods and, in the second, he paid the lower price at the checkout so that property passed into his ownership. The issue was simply whether and when, an appropriation had taken place. Lord Roskill, with whose speech their Lordships all concurred, concluded that the defendant had been rightly convicted of theft in both cases. It was not necessary for the accused to have assumed all the rights of the owner: 'it is enough for the prosecution if they have proved ... the assumption by the defendants of *any* of the rights of the owner of the goods' (emphasis added). The appropriation had taken place when the defendants removed the goods from the shelves and switched over the labels, as it was at this point that one of the owner's rights, namely to price goods as he pleased, was 'assumed' within the meaning of s 3. For an appropriation to take place, there is no need for the defendant actually to deprive the owner of his property (whether permanently or temporarily). If, but only if, at the time of appropriating the property, the defendant intends permanently to deprive the owner of the property, the appropriation is capable of amounting to theft. A layman might suppose that, by offering to pay for the goods, D is acknowledging that he is not the true owner, but it seems from *Morris* that an appropriation can take place irrespective of whether D has taken the goods into his possession.

The decision in *Morris* fixes the point of 'appropriation' early on and means that the offence of theft criminalises a defendant at a much earlier stage than some commentators felt acceptable,[67] but it is consistent with earlier decisions.[68] For example, in *Pitham and Hehl*,[69] it was held that a person who went to the house of a man whom he knew to be in prison and offered to sell his furniture to the two defendants, had appropriated the furniture. The Court of Appeal was

---

67   Notably Leigh, 'Remarks on appropriation in the law of theft after *Morris*' [1985] 48 MLR 167: 'If X kicks my camel, he surely does not appropriate it. The notion of assumption must surely involve a taking unto oneself or a denial of the owner's right or title to a thing for the benefit of another.' Note, since *Gomez* [1993] AC 422 (HL), the appropriation occurs even earlier (see below).

68   Although, *ibid*, Leigh argues to the contrary.

69   (1976) 65 Cr App R 45.

clear that when he 'showed them the furniture and invited them to buy what they wanted', he had 'assumed the rights of the owner'. This was despite the fact that the defendants knew that the offeror had no title to pass on; neither was it necessary to show even a touching of the goods, let alone a taking into possession.[70] In *Corcoran v Anderton*,[71] mere forcible tugging at a handbag in an effort to release it from its owner's grasp was regarded as an act of appropriation, even though the defendant later dropped the handbag and ran away. His conduct in tugging at the bag had been an assumption of the owner's rights.

## Appropriation and the owner's consent

2-26    Section 3 does not contain the words 'without the consent of the owner', as the old Larceny Acts did. Whether this was an oversight, or deliberate, or simply irrelevant, and whether there could be an 'appropriation' if the victim had given his consent to the passing of his property, unfortunately remained a matter of debate for some 24 years after the TA 1968 was enacted. Nevertheless, it is now clear that the decision in *Lawrence*, that the words were not to be read into the section, and which was decided a mere four years after the Act was passed, is correct.

### The decision in Lawrence

2-27    Lawrence was a taxi driver who picked up an Italian student, Mr Occhi, who spoke very little English. He produced £1 from his wallet to pay for his fare but was told by Lawrence that it would be more expensive. Lawrence then helped himself to a further £6 from the wallet that Mr Occhi was still holding open. In fact, the correct fare was only 50p. Had the prosecution proceeded under s 15, we might have heard no more of this case, but Lawrence was charged and convicted of theft and he appealed, ultimately to the House of Lords. They had to consider the extent to which the question of consent was relevant to the issue of whether or not there had been an appropriation within the meaning of s 1, and by implication whether ss 1 and 15 could be alternative charges on the same facts. Lawrence's principal submission was that Mr Occhi had consented to the taking of the £6 and that the wording of the new offence of theft only made sense if the words 'without the consent of the owner' were inserted after 'appropriates'. It followed, he argued, that if Mr Occhi had consented, then ownership in the £6 would have passed to him and it would have meant that he had appropriated his own property and, therefore, could not be guilty of theft

---

70    For a critical discussion of this case, see Glanville Williams, *Textbook of Criminal Law*, 2nd edn, 1983, Stevens, p 724.

71    (1980) 71 Cr App R 104.

However, on the facts of the case, it was possible to say that the appropriation took place the moment Lawrence took hold of the notes and before he removed the £6 – and, therefore, before ownership had passed from Mr Occhi.

Their Lordships also held that the facts of the case fell short of establishing that Mr Occhi ever did truly consent to giving away his £6. Even if he had consented, Lawrence's conduct would still have amounted to an appropriation as the words 'without the consent of the owner' were not to be read into the wording of s 3(1). Viscount Dilhorne, delivering an opinion with which all their Lordships concurred, said (p 632):

> I see no ground for concluding that the omission of the words 'without the consent of the owner' was inadvertent and not deliberate, and to read the sub-section as if they were included is, in my opinion, wholly unwarranted. Parliament by the omission of these words has relieved the prosecution of the burden of establishing that the taking was without the owner's consent. That is no longer an ingredient of the offence ... Belief or the absence of belief that the owner had with such knowledge consented to the appropriation is relevant to the issue of dishonesty, not to the question whether or not there had been an appropriation. That may occur even though the owner has permitted or consented to the property being taken.

Thus, there can be no objection to charging either s 1 or s 15 of the TA 1968 on the same facts. Indeed, Viscount Dilhorne expressly refers to the overlap between the two offences.[72]

2-28    Despite these clear words,[73] the Court of Appeal and the Divisional Court, in a series of subsequent decisions, refused to accept that an act done with the owner's consent could amount to an appropriation. In *Skipp*,[74] a lorry driver, posing as a haulage contractor and intending all along to deprive the owner permanently of his goods, had collected consignments of oranges from three different locations in London, with instructions to deliver them to Leicester. He set off according to those instructions but, somewhere outside London, he deviated from the route to Leicester. The Court of Appeal held that he did not commit theft prior to deviating from the route to Leicester because, until then, he had not committed any unauthorised act. Until that point, he had done nothing to exceed his authority. In *Eddy v Niman*,[75] the defendant entered a supermarket intent on theft. He selected goods from the shelf and put them into a basket belonging to the supermarket, before having second thoughts about the whole enterprise and abandoning the basket within the supermarket and leaving the premises without the goods. It was held that he was not guilty of theft because

---

72   Page 633. As to lack of dishonesty due to a belief that D would have had the owner's consent, TA 1968, s 2(1)(b), see para 2-11 above.

73   Although, for further discussion of the controversy surrounding the decision in *Lawrence*, see Williams, G, 'Theft, consent and illegality' [1977] Crim LR 127.

74   [1975] Crim LR 114.

75   (1981) 73 Cr App R 237.

he had not done anything with the goods which had not been authorised by the owner.

These, and other decisions of the Court of Appeal,[76] inconsistent though they were with *Lawrence*, were nevertheless given the stamp of approval by the House of Lords in *Morris*.

## The decision in Morris

2-29    In *Morris*,[77] Lord Roskill (with whom the rest of their Lordships concurred) said: 'In the context of s 3(1), the concept of appropriation in my view involves not an act expressly or impliedly authorised by the owner but an act by way of adverse interference with or usurpation of [the owner's] rights.' He specifically disagreed with a submission made by counsel for the Crown (and apparently approved by Lord Lane CJ in the Court of Appeal) that any removal from the shelves of the supermarket, even if unaccompanied by label switching, was without more an appropriation.[78] The customer was merely doing what they had been invited or permitted to do by the owner of the supermarket. Although the statutory wording was not to be read as if it included the words 'without the consent of the owner', nevertheless, there could be no appropriation unless there was an unauthorised act, that is, an act done which is against the wishes of the owner.

Strictly speaking, this part of the decision in *Morris* was *obiter*, since, as we have seen earlier, on the facts of the case,[79] the defendants had carried out what were clearly unauthorised acts and 'it is enough for the prosecution if they have proved ... the assumption by the defendants of *any* of the rights of the owner of the goods'. Oddly, Lord Roskill took the view that nothing he said in *Morris* was in conflict with the decision in *Lawrence*, on the basis that in *Lawrence*, there had been, without question, a dishonest appropriation and, therefore, it had not been necessary for the House to consider the precise meaning of 'appropriation' in s 3(1). Nevertheless, in consequence of his decision in *Morris*, there was, for several years, confusion as to the status of *Lawrence*, and also confusion over when to charge s 1 and when to charge s 15 of the Act in cases where the (apparent) consent had been gained by fraud. Thus, in an otherwise sound decision, the House of Lords in *Morris* confirmed that an appropriation had to be an unauthorised act and, thus, gave approval to the approach taken by the Court of Appeal since *Lawrence*.

Fortified by the approval of the House of Lords, the Court of Appeal, in *Fritschy*,[80] continued in the same fashion as before. The accused in that case had,

---

76   Including *Hircock* (1978) 67 Cr App R 278; *Meech* [1974] QB 549; *Kaur v Chief Constable of Hampshire* [1981] 1 WLR 578.
77   See para 2-25 above for facts and issues other than consent.
78   As, undoubtedly, it would have been under *Lawrence*.
79   See para 2-25 above.
80   [1985] Crim LR 744.

on instructions from the owner, collected some krugerrands from bullion dealers in England and taken them to Switzerland. In Switzerland, he had deviated from the owner's instructions and, as he had intended all along, disposed of them for his own benefit. The Court of Appeal held that he had not committed any theft within the jurisdiction of the English courts, since all his acts in England had been authorised and, therefore, no appropriation had taken place.

### An attempt at reconciliation between Lawrence and Morris

2-30 A valiant attempt to reconcile the two House of Lords decisions was made in the civil case of *Dobson v General Accident Fire and Life Assurance Corp plc*.[81] Dobson advertised his Rolex watch and a diamond ring for sale that he had previously insured against theft. A rogue, using a stolen cheque that turned out to be worthless, purchased the goods. The Civil Division of the Court of Appeal had to decide if there had been a 'theft' within the meaning of the Act of 1968 in order to determine whether he had a valid claim on his insurance policy. Parker LJ highlighted the conflict between *Lawrence* and *Morris* and, after 'anxious consideration', ultimately chose to follow *Lawrence.* He reached the conclusion that: 'Whatever *R v Morris* did decide, it cannot be regarded as having overruled the very plain decision in *R v Lawrence* that appropriation can occur even if the owner consents and that *R v Morris* itself makes it plain that it is no defence to say that the property passed under a voidable contract.'[82] It was held that the fact that Dobson had voluntarily parted with the items did not prevent him from being a victim of theft: appropriation did not necessarily involve an absence of consent. Even if, as the insurers claimed (and the court doubted), the ownership in the goods had passed when a contract was made over the telephone, with the result that when the rogue collected the goods, he was taking delivery of his own property, Parker LJ's response was '... the result would merely be that the making of the contract constituted the appropriation. It was by that act that the rogue assumed the rights of an owner and at that time the property did belong to the plaintiff'.[83]

In trying to reconcile the two lines of authority, Bingham LJ attempted to draw a distinction between express authorisation (where property would pass) and 'mere permission or consent' (where it would not). The victim in Lawrence 'had permitted or allowed his money to be taken, he had not in truth consented to the taxi driver taking anything in excess of the exact fare'.[84] Thus, an uneasy compromise seemed to have been reached: property might be appropriated although the overt act appears to have the consent of the owner – but it was mere permission rather than express authorisation.

---

81   [1990] 1 QB 274.
82   *Ibid*, p 285.
83   *Ibid*, p 280.
84   *Ibid*, p 289.

*The decision in Gomez*

2-31    After 20 years, it was inevitable that the conflict would have to be revisited and resolved by the House of Lords, and so to *Gomez*.[85] The defendant was employed as an assistant manager of an electrical goods shop. He agreed with two accomplices that goods would be supplied by the shop in return for two building society cheques that he knew to be worthless. He asked the shop manager to authorise supply of the goods, pretending that he had checked with the bank and telling the shop manager that they were 'as good as cash'. The Court of Appeal quashed his conviction for theft, holding that there was a voidable contract between the owner of the shop and the dishonest receivers of the goods and that, since the transfer of goods had been with the consent of the owner, there had been no appropriation. The following question was certified to the House of Lords:

> When theft is alleged and that which is alleged to be stolen passes to the defendant with the consent of the owner, but that has been obtained by a false representation, has (a) an appropriation within the meaning of s 1(1) of the Theft Act 1968 taken place, or (b) must such a passing of property necessarily involve an element of adverse [interference] with or usurpation of some right of the owner?

Their Lordships were, thus, asked to decide between the correctness of the decision in *Lawrence* and the correctness of the various Court of Appeal decisions that had preceded and followed *Morris*.

By a majority of 4:1 (Lord Lowry dissenting), their Lordships reversed the decision of the Court of Appeal, answering yes to branch (a) and no to branch (b). The actual decision in *Morris* was correct, but the House disapproved Lord Roskill's *dictum* and preferred the *ratio* in *Lawrence*. Lord Keith could not have been clearer: the observations of Lord Roskill in *Morris* were unnecessary for the decision in that case, they were in clear conflict with the *ratio* of *Lawrence* and they were wrong: 'The actual decision in *R v Morris* was correct, but it was erroneous, in addition to being unnecessary for the decision, to indicate that an act expressly or impliedly authorised by the owner could never amount to an appropriation.'[86] *Lawrence* must be accepted as authoritative and correct and 'there was no question of it now being right to depart from it'. At the same time Lord Keith endorsed the judgment of Parker LJ in *Dobson*, although he declared unsound Bingham LJ's attempt at reconciliation. The plain fact of the matter is that, on this point, *Lawrence* is to be preferred to *Morris*.

After *Gomez*, there is no doubt now that an act may be an appropriation, notwithstanding that it is done with the consent of the owner. No distinction is to be made between consent obtained by fraud and consent obtained in other circumstances. *Skipp* and *Fritschy* are expressly overruled and, by implication, so

---

85    [1993] AC 442.
86    *Ibid*, p 464, *per* Lord Keith.

too must be all of those cases which were decided on the basis that appropriation required an act not authorised by the owner. For example, *Eddy v Niman*, *Meech* and *Hircock*.[87]

## Emergent principles on the meaning of appropriation

2-32    From the above history and, in particular, the decision in *Gomez*, a number of principles are now clearly established. First, an authorised act (or an act done with the owner's consent) can be an appropriation, as well as an unauthorised one. Secondly, an appropriation can be entirely innocent (although it will not amount to theft unless all the other ingredients of theft are present). Thirdly, an appropriation can be effected by the assumption of any one (or more) of the rights of the owner and, fourthly, the offence of theft, defined in s 1, and the offence of obtaining property by deception, contrary to s 15, are not mutually exclusive and there is a substantial overlap between the two.

### Examples of the first three principles

2-33    The first three principles can be illustrated by reference to examples set in a self-service supermarket. The honest and lawful shopper is expected to remove articles from the shelves and put then into the supermarket's trolley or basket. This activity is authorised by the supermarket and is done with the owner's consent. It is, nevertheless, an appropriation. Provided that the shopper intends to pay the supermarket's price, it is an honest appropriation and, so, does not amount to theft. Equally, a shopper who swaps price labels on goods in the supermarket, thereby commits an appropriation of those goods. If this is done with the requisite *mens rea* for theft, then the act of theft is complete as soon as the goods are removed from the shelves: or, when the labels are swapped, if that is earlier. Lord Keith, in *Gomez*, was of the opinion that there would be an appropriation at this point, even where the labels were removed as a practical joke, although of course such a person would lack the intention permanently to deprive necessary for a theft conviction. The same principle applies to a motorist visiting a self-service station. At the moment that motorist takes the petrol, that is by squeezing the petrol pump handle and causing petrol to come out into the petrol filler pipe of his car, the motorist 'appropriates' that petrol. If when he does so, he intends to drive off without paying, he commits theft of the petrol. It is no defence to say that the act of taking it was an authorised one.[88]

---

87    See para 2-28.
88    As to whether he is appropriating petrol 'belonging to another', see para 2-84 below.

*The overlap between ss 1 and 15 of the TA 1968*

2-34   This was confirmed by their Lordships in both *Lawrence* and *Gomez*. In *Gomez*, it was suggested that virtually every offence of obtaining by deception contrary to s 15 would also amount to theft. Lord Browne-Wilkinson observed[89] that this did not render s 15 otiose, because whereas (as a general rule) land cannot be stolen,[90] it can be obtained by deception. This seems to acknowledge that, apart from the peculiar case of land, every other example of obtaining by deception contrary to s 15 will also amount to theft: it would seem that every 'obtaining' amounts to an appropriation.

It is unsatisfactory to lump together thieves and swindlers in this way.[91] There is a common sense moral distinction between theft and obtaining property by deception. In simple terms, theft is normally regarded as a crime when an owner is deprived of his property against his wishes and often without his knowledge,[92] whereas deception somehow implies tricking a victim into 'consenting' to part with his property. This view can no longer be supported after *Gomez*. This was surely not the intention of the CLRC, '... obtaining by false pretences is ordinarily thought of as different from theft ... To create a new offence of theft to include conduct which ordinary people would find difficult to regard as theft would be a mistake'.[93] In his dissenting judgment in Gomez, Lord Lowry went to some length to explain that the ruling in *Lawrence* and the decision of the majority in *Gomez* were inconsistent with the intention of the Report of the CLRC[94] upon which the TA 1968 had been based. But, in reference to this Report, Lord Keith, speaking for the majority, ruled in crystalline terms that '... it serves no useful purpose at the present time to seek to construe the relevant provisions of the Theft Act by reference to the report which preceded it'. It is submitted that it is valid to ask, why not?

## Interpretations of *Gomez*

*The accepted interpretation*

2-35   As the above examples show, the confirmation in *Gomez* that an act done with the consent of the owner can be an appropriation means that the scope of appropriation is now so wide that almost anything can amount to an appropriation, with the result that behaviour which is not inherently theftuous is

---

89   [1993] AC 442, p 496.

90   TA 1968, s 4(2).

91   See Shute, S and Horder, J, 'Thieving and deceiving: what is the difference?' (1993) 56 MLR 548; Clarkson, CMV, 'Theft and fair labelling' (1993) 56 MLR 554.

92   Although, of course, the modern concept of appropriation need not involve a 'taking'.

93   CLRC, *Theft (General)*, 1965, HMSO, para 38; see, Ashworth, A [2000] Crim LR 185, pp 382–85, for analysis of *Gomez*.

94   *Op cit*, CLRC, fn 12.

potentially a criminal offence, provided that the required *mens rea* is present. Professor Smith concludes that an appropriation is now committed by: 'Anyone doing anything whatever to property belonging to another, with or without the authority or consent of the owner.'[95] While Professor Griew suggests that 'almost any act done in relation to property belonging to another, the doing or authorisation of which is one of "the rights of an owner", may be an appropriation'.[96] In effect, it seems that 'the ordinary meaning of appropriation has gone out of the window'.[97]

It is submitted that this wide interpretation is the correct reading of the decision in *Gomez*.

### A narrower interpretation

2-36    Given the fact that the certified question in *Gomez* was framed in terms of where the consent was gained by fraud or deception, it may be possible to interpret its ambit less widely. Lord Keith said that, while it was correct to say that appropriation within the meaning of s 3(1) included an act by way of adverse interference with, or usurpation of, the owner's rights, 'it does not ... follow that no other act can amount to an appropriation and in particular that no act expressly or impliedly authorised by the owner can in any circumstances do so'.[98] It is possible, therefore, to understand Lord Keith to be saying that there are two categories of appropriation: category (a) acts of adverse interference with, or usurpation of, one or more of the owner's rights; and category (b) other acts which assume one or more of the owner's rights. He expressed himself as in full agreement with the extensive extracts he quoted from the judgment of Parker LJ in *Dobson*.[99] Parker LJ referred to 'label swapping', clearly identifying that as an 'interference with or usurpation of an owner's rights' and pointing out that it would be a trespass to goods and only the owner would have the right to do such an act. It could, thus, be argued that 'label swapping' is properly categorised as category (a) appropriation, and this would include the practical joker. It is equally clear that the shopper in the self-service shop who removes an article from the shelf and takes it to the checkout commits as appropriation in category (b). Parker LJ also instanced the situation where goods on display were to be taken from the shelves only by an attendant and said that 'in such a case, a customer who took from the shelves would clearly be usurping the right of the

---

95   Smith, JC, para 2-05.
96   Griew, para 2-64.
97   *Op cit*, Smith, JC, 1993, fn 65, p 309.
98   [1993] AC 442, p 461.
99   [1990] 1 QB 274 (and see above).

owner. Indeed, he would be doing so if he did no more than move an item from one place on a shelf to another'.[100] Both these instances would then be examples of category (a) appropriation.[101]

Nowhere in his speech does Lord Keith state that all acts done in relation to the property will amount to appropriations. Indeed, there are suggestions in passages of his speech that, before an act which is not a category (a) appropriation can be described as an appropriation, some justification is required, other than that it is an act done in relation to the property. When discussing *Morris*, he referred to whether '... the mere taking of an article from the shelf and putting it in a trolley, or other receptacle provided, amounted to an assumption of one of the rights of the owner and hence an appropriation'. He said: '... there was much to be said in favour of the view that it did, in respect that doing so gave the shopper control of the article and capacity to exclude any other shopper from taking it.' Indeed, it could be said that each of the examples in his speech of an appropriation within category (b) is a situation where the defendant had exerted, or obtained, effective control of the property. This is certainly true of the facts in *Skipp* and in *Fritschy*. If this is the correct reading of *Gomez*, then it would seem that an act in relation to the goods will be an appropriation within category (b), if either the defendant already has, or that act gives him, effective control of the property. If it does not give him effective control, then it will not amount to an appropriation in the absence of some other reason justifying the conclusion that it was an assumption of one or more rights of the owner.

Thus, it may be, that a customer who pushes aside some goods on the shelf of a self service supermarket in order to be able more easily to reach the item he wants, does not thereby appropriate the goods moved. The same might be said of someone who taps on the window of a car in order to attract the attention of someone sitting inside. According to Lord Browne-Wilkinson, in determining whether an act amounts to an appropriation, one leaves aside entirely the mental state of the defendant and of the owner.[102] Even ignoring the actor's motive or intention, it does seem difficult to accept that tapping on the window of a car can amount to an appropriation of the car and, thus, if accompanied by *mens rea*, also to its theft. If the above analysis of *Gomez* is correct, one has to ignore the accused's mental state and ask first, is tapping on the car's window an adverse interference with the car? And, secondly, if not, what factor justifies describing it as an assumption of one of the rights of an owner? It is submitted that there is none.

---

100 [1990] 1 QB 274, p 284.

101 Although, it must be admitted that the logic of Parker LJ's judgment quoted by Lord Keith is to make no distinction between the situation where the act is done with, and where it is done without, the consent of the owner.

102 [1993] AC 442, p 495.

*Some difficult cases to reconcile with Gomez*

2-37 There are three cases which may be difficult to reconcile with the law as it now appears to be after *Gomez* and which illustrate the wide ranging effect of that decision. They are *Kaur*,[103] *Monaghan*[104] and *Gallasso*.[105]

*Kaur* was a case tried by magistrates where the defendant, a customer in a self-service shop, had spotted a pair of shoes with different price labels attached to the two shoes, £4.99 and £6.99. She realised that £6.99 was the correct price but, nevertheless, picked up the pair and took them to the checkout in the hope that the cashier would charge her only the lower price. The cashier did indeed only notice the lower price, took the shoes from the defendant, bagged them and accepted the £4.99 from the defendant who then picked up the shoes and left. The defendant was convicted of theft and, in a case stated, the magistrates indicated that the basis of the conviction was that the cashier was not authorised to make the contract at an undervalue and that the contract was therefore void. When Mrs Kaur had picked up the bagged shoes she had appropriated property belonging to the shop. The Divisional Court quashed the conviction holding that the cashier had authority to make the contract, which was, therefore, not void. That being so, property passed to Mrs Kaur when she paid for the goods, with the result that when she picked up the bagged shoes she was not picking up property 'belonging to another'.

There is absolutely nothing wrong with the reasoning in this decision and it perfectly accords with the law on the passing of property (ownership) under a contract made in a supermarket, where, unless the parties agreed otherwise, the law assumes that the property passes when the buyer pays the price.[106] The Divisional Court did not, however, consider the possibility that Mrs Kaur might have committed theft at an earlier stage. However, it can now be said, after *Gomez*, that she appropriated the shoes in the shop when she took them off the shelf. If, at that moment, she intended to buy them and if she was dishonest, as the magistrates must have considered she was, in intending to buy them at a lower price, then we can now say she committed theft in the shop.

The facts of *Monaghan* were that the defendant, a shop cashier working at the checkout, took £3.99 payment from a customer and put it into the till without ringing it up. It was established that she intended subsequently to remove £3.99 from the till, but she was apprehended before she had done this. Her conviction for theft of £3.99 was upheld on appeal. It may be that putting money into the till was an act in relation to the goods and thus was correctly, in the light of *Gomez*, regarded as appropriation, it being no defence that the act was an authorised one which she was supposed to do. If so, it seems that hundreds of shop cashiers

---

103 [1981] 1 WLR 578.
104 [1979] Crim LR 673.
105 (1992) 98 Cr App R 284.
106 *Lacis v Cashmarts* [1969] 2 QB 400.

up and down the country commit the *actus reus* of theft every time they accept and put in the till the money they receive from their customers. Alternatively, her act was an appropriation only because of the presence of the circumstance that she omitted to ring up the £3.99. Maybe her act is correctly to be regarded as an appropriation, as assuming one or other of the rights of an owner and the justification for designating it so was her omission to ring up the money.[107]

2-38    *Gallasso* is the most difficult case to reconcile with *Gomez*. Yet, it was decided by the Court of Appeal with express reference to the House of Lords' decision in *Gomez*. The defendant was a nurse in charge of a home for severely mentally handicapped people and was also in charge of their finances. She received cheques payable to one of the patients, J. Although J had a trust account at a building society, the defendant paid one of J's cheques (for £18,000) into a new account (a cash card account) which she opened at the building society in J's name. On the basis of that act being the appropriation, she was convicted of theft of the cheque, the prosecution case being that she had no need to open the new account and had done so to enable her later to make unauthorised withdrawals. The Court of Appeal, acknowledging that, after *Gomez*, taking property with the owner's consent could be an appropriation, nevertheless quashed the conviction, holding that paying the cheque into J's account was not an appropriation since it was an act affirming J's rights, rather than an assumption of them. The facts of the case are close to those of *Monaghan*, since the act in each case was authorised and was done to facilitate a later unauthorised withdrawal. However, there is a distinction because, in *Gallasso*, the act was not accompanied by any feature such as Monaghan's failure to ring up the amount. It might be that the Court of Appeal reached the correct decision – but for the wrong reasons. Part of the appellant's successful argument was that there must be a 'taking' and it seems to have been accepted by the Court of Appeal that 'the paying in was not a taking at all'. This cannot be correct, even in pre-*Gomez* days,[108] and certainly not in 'post'. It does appear that Gallasso did nothing against the consent of the owner, but, as the law stands, that is now enough to amount to an appropriation. It is submitted that it is difficult to reconcile the decision in *Gallasso* with the House of Lords' decision in *Gomez*, although Lloyd LJ saw no contradiction. He observed:

> In *Gomez*, Lord Keith said that there was much to be said in favour of the view that the mere taking of an article from a shelf in a supermarket and putting it in a trolley or other receptacle amounted to an appropriation in so far as it gave the shopper control over the article and the capacity to exclude any other shopper from taking it. But Lord Keith did not mean to say that every handling is an appropriation. Suppose, for example, the shopper carelessly knocks an article off

---

107 It is, in any case, difficult to see that she intended to deprive the owner permanently of the money which she put into the till, since it was not proved that she intended later to take out of the till the very same notes and coins as she put into the till – but this point seems not to have been taken in the case.

108 See Smith, JC, 'Commentary' [1993] Crim LR 459.

the shelf; if he bends down and replaces it on the shelf nobody could regard that as an act of appropriation. Or suppose a lady drops her purse in the street, if a passer-by picks it up and hands it back, there is no appropriation even though the passer-by is in temporary control. It would be otherwise if he were to make off with the purse.[109]

With the greatest of respect, this is exactly what Lord Keith does seem to say.

## *Appropriation after Gomez*

2-39    It is impossible to escape the wider interpretation of *Gomez*. In fact, the full horror of following the decision to its logical conclusion is now revealed by the House of Lords in *Hinks*,[110] which will be explored below. It must be accepted that any touching of any article belonging to someone else, with or without the consent of the owner is capable of being an appropriation. This puts great emphasis on the concept of dishonesty, with all its inherent difficulties, that has been explored above. It also offends against the need for 'manifest criminality', by creating such a wide conduct element that may only be distinguished from honest dealings by the whim of a jury and the intent of the defendant.[111] The House of Lords does not seem to find this a problem. Indeed, Lord Browne-Wilkinson observes unashamedly in *Gomez*: 'I regard the word "appropriation" in isolation as being an objective description of the act done irrespective of the mental state of either the owner or the accused. It is impossible to reconcile the decision in *Lawrence* ... with the views expressed in *Morris*, which latter views in my judgment are incorrect.'[112]

## Appropriation and gifts

2-40    The very wide ambit of *Gomez* is confirmed by the way in which it has been applied to the transfer of *inter vivos* gifts. It is one thing to say that lack of consent is unnecessary for an appropriation to take place and quite another to say that where consent has been freely given to the passing of property in the form of a gift, that too amounts to an appropriation by the recipient. Can the recipient of a validly made gift, obtained with no element of deception, really be a potential thief? If a donor has made such an indefeasible gift of property to another and retains no proprietary interest, or any right to resume or recover any proprietary interest in the property, then it is hard to see that his property has been stolen in the accepted sense of the word. Nevertheless, this is what the

---

109 (1994) 98 Cr App R 284, p 288.
110 See para 2-42 below.
111 Giles, M and Uglow, S, 'Appropriation and manifest criminality in theft' (1992) 56 J Crim Law 179.
112 [1993] AC 442, p 495.

House of Lords has decided in *Hinks*,[113] settling conflicting decisions of the Court of Appeal and affirming the *Gomez* approach to appropriation.

Of course, if the alleged victim-donor lacked the mental capacity to make a gift, there will have been no valid transfer of ownership and a potential theft conviction becomes acceptable. But if the donor is mentally sound and the gift is neither void nor voidable for fraud, duress, undue influence or any other reason, there will have been a valid transfer of ownership at civil law.[114] But as a result of the decision in *Hinks*, there may nevertheless be an appropriation with potential for a criminal conviction for theft. This means that it is possible to conceive of a transaction that is valid at civil law and yet constitutes a serious crime at the same time. Therefore, the issue of appropriation and gifts goes to the heart of the relationship between civil and criminal law and needs to be examined in detail.

### The Court of Appeal cases

2-41 In *Mazo*,[115] D had received a series of cheques and some valuables from her employer who was an elderly woman and whose mental state was failing fast. The defendant said that they were gifts from a grateful employer, but she was convicted of theft. The Court of Appeal quashed her conviction deciding that it was 'common ground' that the receiver of a valid gift, *inter vivos*, could not be guilty of theft. If the gift was valid at civil law, the donee acquired an absolute, indefeasible title to the property.

However, *Mazo* was distinguished and not followed in *Kendrick and Hopkins*,[116] where the Court of Appeal cast doubt on the approach taken in that case. The appellants ran a residential home for the elderly and were given power of attorney on behalf of a 99 year old resident who was virtually blind and incapable of managing her own affairs. After cashing in all her investments and helping themselves to the proceeds, they got her to sign a new will naming them both as beneficiaries. Rather implausibly, their defence to a charge of conspiracy to steal was that they acted at all times with her consent and for her benefit. The Court of Appeal, in dismissing their appeals against conviction, held that, whatever the circumstances of the making of the 'gift', an appropriation had taken place. Other factors, such as the capacity of the donor and the issue of fraud, were only of importance in relation to dishonesty. This was an issue for the jury to decide, where a simple *Ghosh* direction would suffice. The court criticised the judgment in *Mazo* as not adequately reflecting what was said in

---

113 [2000] 3 WLR 1590.

114 For criteria required for the making of a valid *inter vivos* gift, see *Re Beaney* [1978] 1 WLR 770.

115 [1997] Cr App R 518.

116 [1997] 2 Cr App R 524, although, see Lord Hobhouse's dissenting judgment in *Hinks* [2000] 3 WLR 1590, p 1622, where he believed 'there was probably no conflict between the actual decisions in the two cases'.

*Gomez*, particularly Lord Browne-Wilkinson's emphasis on appropriation being a neutral concept to be treated quite distinctly from dishonesty.

## The decision in Hinks

2-42   It was inevitable that the matter of a validly given gift would eventually arrive at the House of Lords, and it did so with the case of *Hinks*. Miss Hinks was a 38 year old woman with a young son who was friendly with a 53 year old man, John Dolphin, a man described as of limited intelligence. Over a period of six months, Mr Dolphin, accompanied by Miss Hinks, withdrew sums totalling about £60,000 from his building society account which were then deposited in Miss Hinks' account. He also gave her son a television set. She was charged with various counts of theft: the prosecution case being, in a nutshell, that she had taken Mr Dolphin for as much as she could get. She submitted that there was no case to answer, arguing that the money was a gift from Mr Dolphin and that, since the title in the money had validly passed to her with the consent of the owner, there could be no theft. The judge rejected the submission and, following *Gomez*, held that a gift was capable of amounting to an appropriation, so the issue was simply one of whether she had been dishonest in accepting it. The relevant question in relation to any gift would be: 'Was Mr Dolphin so mentally incapable that the defendant herself realised that ordinary and decent people would regard it as dishonest to accept that gift from him?' The jury decided that she did and Miss Hinks was convicted of theft and appealed ultimately to the House of Lords with the following certified question: 'Whether the acquisition of an indefeasible title to property is capable of amounting to an appropriation of property belonging to another for the purposes of s 1(1) of the TA 1968.' In other words, according to Lord Steyn, could a person '"appropriate" property belonging to another where that other person makes him an indefeasible gift of property, *retaining no proprietary interest or any right to resume or recover any proprietary interest in the property'* (emphasis added) .

In a majority decision (Lord Hutton and Lord Hobhouse dissenting), the House of Lords said yes to the certified question and dismissed the appeal, settling the matter on a straightforward interpretation of *Gomez* that appropriation could be looked at in isolation and consent was immaterial. It is worth noting that the majority of their Lordships found it unnecessary to review the trial judge's directions on dishonesty.[117] The convictions were entirely safe. Speaking for the majority, Lord Steyn cited with approval Rose LJ in the Court of Appeal:

> In our judgment, in relation to theft, one of the ingredients for a jury to consider is not whether there has been a gift, valid or otherwise, but whether there has been an appropriation. A gift may be clear evidence of appropriation. But a jury

---

117 But note Lord Hutton dissenting on this issue [2000] 3 WLR 1590, p 1607 and below.

should not, in our view, be asked to consider whether a gift has been validly made because, first, that is not what s 1 of the TA 1968 requires; secondly, such an approach is inconsistent with *Lawrence* and *Gomez*; and thirdly, the state of mind of the donor is irrelevant to appropriation.[118]

This is a telling statement. It shows a willingness to accept that *Gomez* is capable of very wide interpretation indeed and is not limited to situations that may be void or voidable for deception. It is significant that Lord Steyn dismisses so assertively the appellant's submission in *Hinks* that the conviction of a donee for receiving a perfectly valid gift is a completely new departure. Counsel for the appellant had relied on academic criticism of the earlier decisions of *Lawrence* and *Gomez* and, in particular, on a passage from a note by Professor Smith on the decision of the Court of Appeal in *Hinks*,[119] where he cited as evidence a memorandum from the draftsman of the TA 1968, writing to members of the Larceny Sub-Committee of the CLRC in 1964:

> I trust the Sub-Committee will not agree with Dr [Glanville] Williams when he says ... that a person appropriates for himself property of which another person is the owner every time he gratefully accepts a gift or buys an apple. If this is what the words mean, then the whole language of the clause ought to be changed, because one really cannot have a definition of stealing which relies on the word 'dishonestly' to prevent it covering every acquisition of property.

It appears that Lord Steyn saw no such contradiction and showed no compunction in stating that reliance on such evidence goes beyond the limits of statutory interpretation and 'cannot conceivably be relevant [to interpretation of the TA 1968] ... The starting point must be the words of the statute as interpreted by the House in its previous decisions'.

## Hinks as a logical extension of Gomez?

2-43    Arguably, it is these previous decisions which are the problem and *Hinks* is just the logical result of the saga that began with *Lawrence* and was made explicit in *Gomez*. It follows that any criticism of the decision in *Hinks*, is a criticism of the decision in *Gomez* as well. In that case, the House of Lords were expressly invited to hold that 'there is no appropriation where the entire proprietary interest passes', but that submission was rejected. The rejection is affirmed in *Hinks*, when Lord Steyn, speaking for the majority, stated: 'The *ratio* [in *Gomez*] involves a proposition of general application. *Gomez* therefore gives effect to s 3(1) of the Act by treating "appropriation" as a neutral word comprehending "any assumption by a person of the rights of an owner." If the law is as held in *Gomez*, it destroys the argument advanced in the present appeal, namely that an indefeasible gift of property cannot amount to an appropriation.'[120]

118 [2000] 3 WLR 1590, p 1595.
119 [1998] Crim LR 904, pp 904–05.
120 [2000] 3 WLR 1590, p 1599.

But at least in *Lawrence* and in *Gomez*, there was an element of deception based on the facts. This meant that both transactions were voidable so that the owner of the property still retained a right to recover the goods (even though that was not part of the *ratio decidendi* in *Gomez*). That was not the case in *Hinks*: there was no deception, only a perfectly valid gift and, therefore, no such right was retained. It is for that reason that the decision has been greeted with little enthusiasm from academics, who have largely condemned it as an unnecessary and unwise extension of *Gomez*.[121] The property had passed to Miss Hinks as an indefeasible gift and, as Professor Smith argues, it was preposterous that the money belonged to Miss Hinks in civil law and yet she stole it!

The problem is that the majority judgments in *Gomez* do not differentiate between cases of consent induced by fraud and consent given in any other circumstances. However, it was to be hoped that having been given the opportunity to reconsider *Gomez*, the House of Lords might have accepted this distinction. Instead, they seem to have followed the logic of that omission to the very brink of folly. And they have done this simply on the basis that any narrower interpretation of *Lawrence* and *Gomez* would be 'likely to put beyond the reaches of the criminal law dishonest persons who should be found guilty of theft'.

## *Civil v Criminal Law*

2-44    The decision also creates a strain between the civil and the criminal law. It means that conduct which is perfectly valid at civil law (that is, obtaining good title to property by way of a validly made gift) may nevertheless constitute the crime of theft.[122] However, Simon Gardner[123] has argued that, while recognising interaction between criminal law and civil law can cause problems, this is not necessarily cause for concern. Whereas the civil law is concerned to respect established property rights, even if unsatisfactorily acquired, the criminal law concentrates on penalising the unsatisfactory way in which those rights were acquired. His views were cited with approval by Lord Steyn in *Hinks*:[124]

> The purposes of the civil law and the criminal law are somewhat different. In theory, the two systems should be in perfect harmony. In a practical world, there will sometimes be some disharmony between the two systems. In any event, it would be wrong to assume on *a priori* grounds that the criminal law rather than

---

121   Eg, Smith, JC, 'Commentary' [2001] Crim LR 162; Beatson, J and Simester, AP, 'Stealing one's own property'[1999] LQR 372. But the decision does have its supporters: *op cit*, Gardner, fn 65, a response to *Hinks* in the Court of Appeal.

122   *Op cit*, Williams, fn 73. See, also, Smith, ATH, para 5-49: '... if the civil law sees no reason to permit the owner to complain of an interference with his property why should the criminal law do so?' Also, *op cit*, Beaston and Simester, fn 121.

123   *Op cit*, Gardner, fn 65.

124   [2000] 3 WLR 1590, p 1601.

the civil law is defective ... While in some contexts of the law of theft the judge cannot avoid explaining the civil law concepts to a jury (for example, in respect of s 2(1)(a)), the decisions of the House of Lords eliminate the need for such explanations in respect of appropriation.

This is certainly a bold approach. It might even be a pragmatic one. It certainly has the advantage that it will be unnecessary to explain to a jury the niceties of such civil law terms as void and voidable contracts, since the distinction will be irrelevant in the context of whether an appropriation has taken place. It seems that as long as the *Gomez* interpretation of the meaning of appropriation prevails this conflict between civil and criminal law will have to be accepted.

## The relevance of dishonesty in Hinks

2-45      There is some comfort in recognising that establishing an appropriation has taken place is not the same as establishing there has been a theft. Even if there has been an appropriation with an intention permanently to deprive, it still remains for a jury to find that the recipient has been dishonest in accepting it, for example, because he set out to gain the gift by fraud or took advantage of the donor's mental frailty. *Hinks* is merely a further illustration of how the concept of 'appropriation' has been neutralised and relegated to an almost insignificant issue in the law of theft. In affirming the *Gomez* interpretation of appropriation, the House of Lords has once again emphasised the importance of the element of dishonesty. This is now the all important decisive element. It may even mean that we have to redefine the offence of theft as a crime that primarily criminalises dishonesty, in direct contradiction to the arguably accepted view that the civil law of property is the essential foundation for the criminal law of theft.[125] This is why Lord Hutton's dissenting judgment in *Hinks* places such importance on the way in which the judge explains the meaning of dishonesty to the jury. He said:

> But in my opinion in a case where the defendant contends that he or she received a gift, a direction based only on *Ghosh* is inadequate because it fails to make clear to the jury that if there is a valid gift, there cannot be dishonesty and, in the present case, there is the danger that, if the gift was not void for want of mental capacity, the jury might nevertheless convict on the basis that ordinary and decent people would think it dishonest for a younger woman to accept very large sums of money which constituted his entire savings from a naïve man of low intelligence, and that the woman would have realised this.[126]

---

125 See Smith, JC [1997] 359; [1998] Crim LR 80, who believes that retrospective adjustments of property rights turning simply on a jury's perception of dishonest behaviour is inconceivable; also, Smith, ATH, 'Commentary' on *Hinks* Court of Appeal [1999] CLJ 11. But note that *inter vivos* gifts of land will be unaffected by the decision as land is not regarded as 'property' for the purposes of theft: TA 1968, s 4.

126 [2000] 3 WLR 1590, p 1607.

While he agreed with the majority view on the issue of appropriation, he would have allowed the appeal on the basis of a misdirection on dishonesty.

## *Lawrence, Morris, Gomez and Hinks*

2-46    In his dissenting judgment in *Hinks*, Lord Hobhouse believed that the 'damaging legacy' of *Lawrence* has been that the courts have adopted a 'fragmented approach' to interpreting the components of theft, enabling Lord Browne-Wilkinson in *Gomez* to adopt a 'sanitised concept of appropriation' isolated from any concept of interdependence with the other sections. He states:

> The relevant law is contained in ss 1–6 of the Act. They should be construed as a whole and applied in a manner that presents a consistent scheme both internally and with the remainder of the Act. The phrase 'dishonestly appropriates' should be construed as a composite phrase. It does not include acts done in relation to the relevant property which are done in accordance with the actual wishes or actual authority of the person to whom the property belongs. This is because such acts do not involve any assumption of the rights of that person within s 3(1) or because, by necessary implication from s 2(1), they are not to be regarded as dishonest appropriations of property belonging to another.[127]

But, it is too late to turn the clock back now. While in theory it may still be possible to argue, as Lord Hobhouse does, that Lord Keith in *Gomez* was not saying that consent and authorisation are irrelevant to appropriation but, rather that they do not necessarily exclude the possibility of appropriation, it seems too late to continue to argue that Lord Roskill's statements in *Morris* are misunderstood. We now have two further House of Lords' decisions based on a wide interpretation of *Lawrence*, rather than *Morris*. Lord Browne-Wilkinson's view of appropriation in *Gomez* must prevail. Once Lord Roskill's views in *Morris* had been rejected, then *Hinks* is the natural progression. Appropriation can be so wide ranging as to include an indefeasible gift and the only aspect which will stop it being theft is the dishonest intention of the receiver. That much seems clear. What is less clear is whether a simple *Ghosh* direction on dishonesty will suffice as it is surely open to the defendant to seek the protection of s 2(1)(a): if the defendant has been given a gift, then surely the jury should have the opportunity of deciding whether to believe a defendant's assertion that he, the defendant, was entitled to it in law.

## *Gomez, Hinks and the Human Rights Act 1998*

2-47    The majority judgments in *Hinks* put a rather touching faith in the mental requirement of theft being 'an adequate protection against injustice'. But this may not be enough. It may be that the wide meaning of appropriation, with its consequent implications will meet its Waterloo from another quarter, namely

---

127 [2000] 3 WLR 1590, p 1623.

the Human Rights Act 1998, s 3 of which requires UK legislation as far as possible to 'be read and given effect in a way which is compatible with Convention rights'. Fair warning has already been given by the Law Commission in their Consultation Paper on *Fraud and Deception*,[128] where they express concern that a general dishonesty defence would be incompatible with certain Convention rights. In their view, the element of dishonesty should provide only additional – not sole – protection for rights and interests already protected by the civil law of property and obligations: 'To apply it to conduct giving rise to no civil liability is to extend it beyond its proper function.'[129] The problem is that there is too much inherent uncertainty in the *Ghosh*[130] test for dishonesty as it leaves everything to be decided on the opinion of the jury, so making it impossible to state the limits of the prohibited conduct with any precision. In the opinion of the Commissioners this would make it impossible for the Home Secretary to make a declaration of compatibility on legislation giving effect to a general dishonesty defence. It would not meet the requirements of legality and certainty which underpin, for example, Arts 5 and 7 of the European Convention on Human Rights (ECHR).

Fuel for the pyre may now have been added by the decision in *Hashman and Harrup v UK*.[131] A violation of Art 10 was found where the appellants had been convicted on the basis of an expression that was imprecise because it gave no guidance as to how the defendant was to behave in the future; any law relied on had to satisfy the 'quality of law' tests developed by the European Court of Human Rights. It is essential that there should be certainty in the law and, although rigidity in the law could be an unwelcome by-product of establishing certainty, this has to be balanced against the need for an individual to be clear about the type of conduct which he must avoid in order to avoid criminal sanction. The principle is not limited to Art 10 and it is likely that this test for certainty will have an impact on the law of theft as it now stands. There is little in the present law of theft, with its present reliance on dishonesty, to give rise to this requirement for certainty. This is because a person's criminal liability depends on behaviour which is described by current moral standards rather than describing 'behaviour by reference to its effects', which is required by community law. In his commentary on the case, Andrew Ashworth warns: 'In view of the breadth of [the law of theft] following *Gomez*, it seems that the need to prove an intention permanently to deprive the other of his property rights is all that saves [the law of theft] from incompatibility.'[132] It seems that the House of Lords may yet be forced to reconsider not only their approach to appropriation but to the law on dishonesty as well. One thing is certain – it will

---

128 *Op cit*, Law Commission, fn 15, para 5.52.
129 *Op cit*, Law Commission, fn 15, para 5.28.
130 See para 2-18, above.
131 [2000] Crim LR 185 and 'Commentary'.
132 *Ibid*, p 186.

no longer be open to them to regard dishonesty alone as sufficient bulwark against injustice. The conduct element in theft will have to be restored to its proper place.

## Appropriation and bank accounts

2-48 Increasingly, the victim of theft might be a bank, or a person who has money wrongfully transferred from his bank account to that of the defendant. Monies held in bank accounts are things in action and therefore property capable of being stolen. In *Kohn*,[133] a company director was convicted of theft when he used company cheques to pay for his own expenses. It was held that he had appropriated the cheque and stolen a thing in action, namely the money held in the company account.[134] With modern methods of automated transfer, the problem extends beyond mere appropriation by means of a cheque.[135] It is then necessary to ascertain not only what conduct amounts to an appropriation, but also the exact point at which the appropriation takes place.

Two different situations might arise. First, where a person, knowing he has insufficient funds in the bank and no overdraft arrangements, uses his bank card to support a cheque which must then be honoured by the bank. Secondly, where a person causes his own bank account to be credited and that of his victim to be debited. The decision in *Navvabi*[136] covers the first scenario. The defendant wrote cheques, supported by a cheque guarantee card, in excess of his permitted limit on his account. It was held that there was no theft from the bank, either when the cheque was handed to the payee or when it was presented for payment and the funds ultimately transferred, since the bank was obliged to honour the cheque and so there had been no assumption of the right of an owner over any part of the bank's funds (even though, of course, D had caused the bank itself to lose money). The use of the cheque card and presentation of the cheque did no more than give the payee a contractual right against the bank to be paid a specified sum from the bank's funds on presentation of the guaranteed cheque. Furthermore, there was no property to steal because, as there were no funds in the defendant's bank account, there was no debt (a thing in action) to steal.

---

133 *Kohn* (1979) 69 Cr App R 395; for things in action generally under the Act, see para 2-62 below.

134 *Ibid*, where Lane LJ's observation that 'the completion of the theft does not take place until the transaction has gone through to completion' was held to be *obiter* in *R v Gov of Pentonville Prison ex p Osman* [1990] 1 WLR 277.

135 It is thought inappropriate to charge a person with theft of the actual cheque itself – that is the piece of paper, because there will be no intention permanently to deprive the owner of it, since it will eventually find its way back to the drawer via his bank: *Preddy* [1996] AC 815.

136 [1986] 1 WLR 1311.

In the second scenario, the outcome is different, as there has been an assumption of the rights of the owner-victim to deal with his own bank account. In *Chan Man-Sin v AG of Hong Kong*,[137] the appellant was a company accountant who was convicted of theft when he wrote unauthorised cheques in order to withdraw funds from two companies' bank accounts. Since no bank has the authority to honour a forged cheque, he claimed, on appeal, that there had been no appropriation because the bank was obliged to re-instate the account when it was discovered that the cheques were forgeries. Consequently, he claimed, the companies were no worse off and so he could not have assumed the rights of the account owner.[138] However, the Privy Council dismissed his appeal. Following *Morris*, they held it was not necessary that the appropriation should assume all the rights of the owner, it is enough that 'one who draws, presents and negotiates a cheque on a particular bank account is assuming the rights of the owner of the credit in the account or (as the case may be) of the pre-negotiated right to draw on the account up to the agreed figure'.[139] It seems from the decision that there is no requirement for the assumption of rights to be 'legally efficacious' in order to amount to an appropriation. In other words, it is immaterial that the end result of the transaction may be a legal nullity.[140] Professor Smith has argued that this means that it is now possible to have a conviction for theft where there is no loss to the victim – a situation quite at variance with the old common law and under the Larceny Acts which supported the popular conception of stealing being where the thief makes a gain and his victim suffers a corresponding loss.[141] It is at least arguable that, in this respect, the decision is less satisfactory than that in *Kohn*, where the facts meant the defendant had the authority to draw the cheques (and, therefore, they were not forgeries), even though that authority was abused for personal gain.

## Where the appropriation takes place

2-49    Another feature of the decision in *Chan Man-Sin v AG of Hong Kong*, is that the Privy Council did not deem it necessary (on the facts of the case) to decide the exact point at which the appropriation took place. It may, however, be necessary in situations which involve cross-jurisdictional boundaries. Where does the appropriation (and theft) take place if the request for transferring funds was made in a different country from the one in which the funds were held? This

---

137 [1988] 1 WLR 196.

138 He also argued that, since the company whose property was alleged to have been stolen had not, in fact, been deprived of anything, there could not have been an intention permanently to deprive the company of its property.

139 *Ibid*, *per* Lord Oliver.

140 See criticism by Smith, ATH, para 5-52; cf civil case of *Tai Hing Cotton Mill Ltd v Liu Chong Hing Bank Ltd* [1986] AC 80.

141 Smith, JC, para 2-54; see, also, *op cit*, Ashworth, fn 93, p 381: 'The decision penalises dishonesty, but reduces appropriation to a will o' the wisp.'

matter was considered in *R v Governor of Pentonville Prison ex p Osman*,[142] in connection with extradition proceedings. The defendant, without authority, sent instructions by telex from Hong Kong to a bank in New York instructing the bank to transfer funds from one account to another. For jurisdictional purposes, it was necessary to establish whether the theft had taken place in Hong Kong or the USA. Counsel for Osman claimed that the moment of appropriation must be when the account in the USA was debited, but the Divisional Court accepted the Crown's argument that the appropriation took place as soon as the request was sent by telex from Hong Kong. Lloyd LJ concluded that, if the act of sending the telex was the act of appropriation, then the place where the act was performed is the place where the appropriation took place, namely Hong Kong.[143] The very act of sending a telex instructing the bank to debit an account had assumed the account holder's rights to have his own instructions met and was an act of theft, even though the theft may not be complete in fact until the account is actually debited. Despite this decision, the Court of Appeal appears to have taken a different view in *Hilton*,[144] where it was held that the appropriation occurred when the defendant instructed the bank to make a transfer of funds and the transfer was actually completed.

Hopefully, the matter may be resolved by the decision in *Ngan*,[145] where the defendant, with full knowledge that her bank account had been mistakenly credited with a large sum on money, signed a number of blank cheques and sent them to her sister in Scotland so that her sister could complete them and present the cheques to her own bank in Scotland. It was held that the appellant's acts of signing and sending blank cheques (in England) to her sister in Scotland were preparatory acts and not an appropriation. Consequently, there had been no theft within the jurisdiction. The appropriation only occurred when the cheque was presented to the bank (in Scotland). The Court of Appeal seemed to take the view that they were following *Osman* in equating *presentation* of the cheque with the *issuing* of a telex instruction, as the court in *Osman* had said an appropriation takes place when a defendant 'dishonestly issues a cheque'. But is the act of presentation and issuing really the same? If D presents a cheque at the bank himself then presentation may equate with issuing. But if he sends that cheque to someone else (as happened in *Ngan*) and that other person presents it at the bank then it is hard to see that the issuing and the presenting are the same. On a strict interpretation of *Osman*, it is surely arguable that the issuing of the cheque in England could be equated with the sending of the telex from Hong Kong,

---

142 [1990] 1 WLR 277 (DC).

143 *Ibid*, p 295, although he did not rule out the possibility that there may be a simultaneous appropriation in the place where the telex was received. The court declined to follow *Tomsett* [1985] Crim LR 369 where it was said that *prima facie* theft takes places where the property stolen is appropriated and *prima facie* appropriation takes place where the property is situated.

144 [1997] 2 Cr App R 445.

145 [1998] 1 Cr App R 331.

especially as it would not have made any difference in *Osman* if the account at the paying bank had never, in fact, been debited. Nevertheless, it is probably right to deal with Ngan's situation as an attempt since, until the cheque was presented in Scotland, no right as against the bank had been exercised.

2-50     Can it be different where use of a computer is involved? *Osman* was distinguished in *Governor of Brixton Prison ex p Levin*,[146] in which the defendant operated a computer in Russia to gain access to the computer of a bank in the USA and thence to divert funds from that bank to accounts held at other banks. The court held that the appropriation of the account holder's right to give instructions to their own bank had taken place in the USA. This was because, although he had to begin by accessing the computer in Russia, it was impossible to give instructions to the bank in the USA until he had gained access to the computer in the USA whereas, in *Osman*, the instructions were sent straight to the bank without more ado. Just as in *Osman*, however, the court intimated that it would be more realistic to regard the appropriation as taking place simultaneously, if the English courts were ever to adopt the view that a crime may have a dual location. Until that time, it made more sense to attach significance to the operation of the magnetic disks of the computer in the USA rather than the defendant's physical presence in Russia – the appropriation of the client's rights had taken place inside the computer in the USA. It is submitted that this is the better view, in that it makes sense that the theft should occur where it has an effect on the property.[147]

## Appropriation of company assets by company controllers

2-51     It was established in *Bonner*[148] that it is possible for one partner to appropriate partnership property from another partner and be liable for theft of that property (provided that the other elements are present), even though the property was co-owned. There has been more controversy when it comes to the abstraction of money from companies by those who are wholly in control of them, because the property which is owned by the company may be identified with those very persons who are in complete control it. This means that, if there are one or more persons who are, between them, the sole shareholders in a company and, if they were to transfer the entire funds of that company into their personal accounts, it might be difficult to say that they had appropriated property 'belonging to another'.[149] However, this difficulty has been overcome

---

146 [1997] QB 65 (the case went to the House of Lords on a different point: [1997] AC 741).
147 Since the coming into force in 1999 of the CJA 1993, Pt I, the rules on jurisdiction have been considerably widened and it is now irrelevant where any act occurred, proof of which is required for conviction of theft. See, further, para 14-06 below.
148 [1970] 1 WLR 838.
149 For property belonging to another, see para 2-83, below.

by the decision in *AG Ref (No 2 of 1982)*,[150] which established that such activity may, in principle, amount to theft. This is because, since the company is a separate legal entity from those who control it[151] – in effect a separate person in law (with the directors being the directing mind and will of the company) – it may therefore own property and that property is capable of being stolen. However, although this decision may have settled one aspect of the problem, there was still the issue of appropriation, since those pillaging the company assets are the very people who are in a position to give the consent to their own wrongdoing.

The pre-*Gomez* case of *Phillipou*[152] illustrates both the dilemma and the solution. The appellant and his colleague were sole directors of Budget Holiday group in London which was made up of three principal companies, one of which was Sunny Tours. They withdrew money from the Sunny Tours account in London and used it to buy property in Spain, which they then put into a separate Spanish company, of which they were also the sole director and shareholders. The result was that Sunny Tours was forced into liquidation with substantial debts. The appellant and his colleague were charged, *inter alia*, with theft. The Court of Appeal upheld their convictions despite argument that the appellant and his colleague were the mind of the Sunny Tours company, and that their instruction to the London bank to transfer money to Spain were the instructions of the Sunny Tours company which consequently had, in effect, consented to the transfer. A similar argument had earlier found favour with the Court of Appeal in *McHugh and Tringham*,[153] but the Court of Appeal in *Phillipou* took the view that the acquisition of the property in Spain was really for the appellants' own personal benefit and demonstrated their dishonest intention permanently to deprive Sunny Tours of its money; this was clearly adverse to the rights of Sunny Tours and, therefore, was an act without its consent and so an appropriation had taken place. The decision appears to follow *Morris* and yet it is difficult to reconcile entirely with that case, in that the 'consent' of the appellants in transferring Sunny Tours' assets was clearly regarded as irrelevant. In that sense, the decision favours *Lawrence* and it seems that the Court of Appeal believed the two decisions to be reconcilable. In any event, the court made no reference to *McHugh and Tringham* (decided only four months before *Phillipou* by a differently constituted Court of Appeal), or to the Australian case of *Roffel*,[154] both of which clearly followed the decision in *Morris*.

---

150 [1984] QB 624.
151 *Salomon v Salomon* [1897] AC 22.
152 (1989) 89 Cr App R 290.
153 (1988) 88 Cr App R 385.
154 [1985] VR 511 where the Supreme Court took the view that, however dishonest the conduct of the directors in such a situation, there was no appropriation.

The present position is best summed up by Lord Browne-Wilkinson in *Gomez*. Approving *AG Ref (No 2 of 1982)* and the decision in *Phillipou*, and specifically disapproving *Roffel* and *McHugh and Tringham*, he stated:

> Where a company is accused of a crime the acts and intentions of those who are the directing minds and will of the company are to be attributed to the company. That is not the law where the charge is that those who are the directing minds and will themselves have committed a crime against the company ... Whether or not those controlling the company consented or purported to consent to the abstraction of the company's property by the accused, he will have appropriated the property of the company. The question will be whether the other necessary elements are present, viz was such appropriation dishonest and was it done with the intention of permanently depriving the company of such property?[155]

There is a hint of policy here. One of the reasons that Lord Browne-Wilkinson welcomed the decision in *Gomez* is because it would prevent the 'pillaging of companies by those who control them': it is no longer possible for those in control of a company to say there has been no appropriation if they have consented to the transfer of company assets – the question of their consent is now irrelevant.

## Appropriation of property acquired innocently (or by those already in possession)

2-52    The second part of s 3(1) provides that an appropriation may take place even where the defendant comes by the property innocently, if he later decides to keep it, or deal with it as owner. It is further indication that an appropriation is an act interfering with ownership and not just simply possession. This part of the section is meant to deal with cases such as when a person borrows or hires property intending to return it; or finds property and takes it into his possession, having at that time the intention of returning it to its owner; or is handed property through the mistake of another, for example, when too much money is mistakenly included in his pay packet,[156] or too much of a commodity is mistakenly weighed out for him as purchaser of a stated lesser quantity. The effect of the closing words of s 3(1) is that if, after coming by the property without stealing it, the possessor keeps it or deals with it 'as owner', he will commit theft provided that when he does so he is dishonest and intends permanently to deprive the owner of his property.[157]

---

155 [1993] AC 442, p 496; Lord Keith (with whom Lord Slynn and Lord Jauncey agree) refers to Lord Browne-Wilkinson's speech with approval.

156 Cf *Ngan* [1998] 1 Cr App R 331, above, where Leggatt LJ thought: '"Keeping" as owner in relation to a [overcredited] bank account may be difficult to prove in a case where a defendant does no more than refrain from bringing the mistake to the attention of the Bank.'

157 Provided that, at the time, the property can be said to belong to another: if it no longer belongs to another, then the later keeping or dealing with it cannot be theft. See *Greenberg* [1972] Crim LR 33.

### 'Keeping' or 'dealing'

2-53    The words 'keeping or dealing' with the property 'as owner' are important and it would seem that D must do something with the property to demonstrate the proprietorial nature of his intentions if he is to be said to be 'dealing' with it; for example, he might paint it.[158] It is sometimes more difficult to demonstrate a 'keeping', as this may be denoted by a mental act on behalf of the defendant. For example, if D borrows a book from a friend and then makes a decision not to give it back, it may be that some overt act is required in order to provide evidence that he has indeed intended to appropriate the book by 'keeping' it 'as owner'. Merely continuing to read the book (at least before the period of the loan expires) would probably not be sufficient for an appropriation, some evidence of behaving 'as owner' is required.[159] So, if he wrote his name in the book, or placed it on his own library shelf, D would be both 'dealing' with the book as owner and demonstrating his intention of 'keeping' it. In *Broom v Crowther*,[160] it was held that there was no 'keeping ... as owner' while D simply held on to property while he was making up his mind what to do with it. A clear demonstration of doing something which only an owner could do would be to sell the book to someone else, or even offer it for sale.[161] The point at which he does either of these things is the point at which the appropriation takes place by 'keeping' or 'dealing' with the book as an owner.

2-54    Can this mean that there are two appropriations? That is, an 'innocent' one followed by a 'guilty' one. After all, since *Gomez*, the meaning of appropriation is so wide that even when the book is lent with the consent of the owner an appropriation takes place when the borrower picks up the book. Furthermore, by speaking of a 'later assumption', the section surely envisages that there can be more than one. It may be that the second part of s 3(1) is superfluous (or at least amounts to overkill) and these later acts described are better left to be examined within the context of dishonesty. As it stands, however, the concluding words of s 3(1) usefully make it clear that someone who is already in possession of property can steal that property provided he has not already done so.

### *Bailees*

2-55    As was indicated earlier, a common example of someone who might already be in 'innocent' possession of property is a bailee. A bailee is a person who is entrusted with possession of property for some temporary purpose, on the

---

158 *Russell* [1977] 2 NZLR 20.

159 See Smith, ATH, para 5-64.

160 (1984) 148 JP 592 (DC).

161 Cf *Pilgrim v Rice-Smith* [1977] 1 WLR 671 (DC) where goods were dishonestly underpriced by an assistant in a supermarket acting in collusion with a customer. It is now clear that the underpricing would be an appropriation within the meaning of s 3(1).

understanding that he is to return it to the owner, or some other person; it is possible to be either a 'voluntary' or an 'involuntary' bailee. Examples of bailees are borrowers, hirers, hire purchasers, repairers, persons who receive things for safe custody and people like auctioneers who receive property for sale on behalf of the owner. If a baillee dishonestly decides to keep the property bailed, and puts that decision into effect by appropriating within the meaning of the latter part of s 3(1), then the bailee has committed theft.

However, it has been suggested[162] that someone who has hired property cannot be guilty of theft by virtue of any act which his contract of bailment entitles him to carry out. That is, his act of keeping (or indeed using) the property during the period of contractual hire, cannot be an appropriation. This would seem to have the effect of distinguishing between the gratuitous bailee and the bailee for reward. According to the closing words of s 3(1), the former would be guilty as soon as he decided not to return the goods. The latter could be guilty only if he did some act outside the terms of his contract. Thus, if, for example, D hires a car under a contract that did not prohibit the export of the property, he would not be guilty of theft if he took the car to France; if the contract did prohibit it, then presumably taking the property abroad would amount to an appropriation. The argument is that the hire contract is a contract of bailment and, thus, gives the bailee proprietary rights which it cannot be an appropriation to exercise because he is not assuming any right belonging to anyone other than himself.

On the other hand, this approach does not accord well with the very wide interpretation given to the word 'appropriation' in *Gomez*,[163] which says that authorisation or consent is irrelevant to appropriation. Indeed, it does not sit very well with any interpretation of *Gomez*. The approach is also thoroughly inconsistent with *Hinks*. The hirer, like the donee, may well have civil law rights over the property. Exercising those rights can still be an appropriation. If the borrower (that is a gratuitous bailee) commits an appropriation by keeping or using the property, it is difficult to see why the hirer (a bailee for reward) should not also. Assuming that, in each case, the possessor has dishonestly decided not to return the property, why treat them any differently? The answer seems to be 'because, otherwise, exercising a contractual right can amount to a crime'. Initially, there seems some merit in this reply, but the effect of *Gomez* is that a lot of actions that are perfectly normal and lawful may still amount to an appropriation. However, an appropriation can only become theft if it is accompanied by the necessary *mens rea*. The potential for ultimate conflict between the law of theft and the law of contract is not as great as might at first appear. In a situation where the hirer is proved to have retained the property under the terms of the hire agreement and to have done so dishonestly and with no intention to return the property at the end of the hire, he is likely, in most

162 Smith, JC, para 2–29.
163 See para 2–31, above.

cases, to have done an act which amounts to a repudiation of the contract of hire – that is, the action or statement which provides the evidence of his intention not to return the property at the end of the hire period, is likely to amount to such a repudiation. It is only where there is no such repudiation that it can be said that the law of theft ensnares something that is the exercise of a contractual right. In any case, if it were to be a defence that the defendant was exercising a contractual right, then it ought to be a defence that he was performing a contractual duty. Assuredly, however, there is no such defence. Otherwise, the House of Lords could not sensibly have overruled *Skipp*,[164] where the defendant, in collecting the consignments, was performing a contractual duty.[165]

A variation of the argument that a bailee cannot commit an appropriation by carrying out an act which is within his proprietary rights as bailee, is that, if the entire proprietary interest is transferred to the defendant, the defendant cannot commit an appropriation because he cannot 'assume' any of the rights of an owner, since in these circumstances, he is the entire owner. According to Professor Glanville Williams, theft cannot be committed 'by a person who has or obtains an indefeasible right to the property when he commits the act charged as appropriation'.[166] We have already seen, however, that despite protestations from Professor JC Smith *et al*, the House of Lords has decided otherwise in *Hinks*.[167]

## Appropriation and the *bona fide* purchaser

2-56    Section 3(2) protects the *bona fide* purchaser from the ambit of s 3(1). Such a person will not have appropriated property if he acquires that property for value[168] and, at the moment he acquires the goods, he is acting in good faith. No later assumption of the rights he believed himself to have acquired can amount to an appropriation – even if, later, he realises that the property was stolen, or he has not acquired good title.[169] So, if student D buys a book from student B, believing that student B is the lawful owner, but later finds out that he had stolen it from student C, any refusal by student D to return the book to student C would not amount to theft, as there would be no appropriation. This is so, even if D later decides to give the property away; but if he should sell it and represent expressly, or impliedly, that he has the title to do so, he will probably commit the offence of obtaining the purchase price by deception.[170]

---

164 See para 2-28, above.

165 In any case, see *Atakpu* [1994] QB 69 (para 2-58 below), where the appropriation was said to take place at the point at which the defendant hired the cars.

166 [1977] Crim LR 127.

167 See para 2-42 above.

168 But not as a gift.

169 *Adams* [1993] Crim LR 72.

170 Smith, JC, para 2-45.

## Appropriation as a continuing act?

2-57    Theft can be an instantaneous matter. For example, a £10 note can be taken from the victim's pocket and the whole incident completed in a few seconds. However, it is possible for the process of theft to last a little longer. The issue of when a particular instance of theft is finished can be important in relation to offences such as handling or robbery. For example, the offence of handling stolen property[171] can be committed only 'otherwise than in the course of stealing'. Thus, an act which is part of the theft in question cannot amount to handling. The offence of robbery[172] is committed if theft is accompanied, or immediately preceded, by the use or threat of force. If, however, the theft is finished before force is used or threatened, there is no robbery. The matter can also be important in other contexts, for example, with regard to accomplices: once the commission of the offence by D has finished, others who become involved only afterwards cannot be guilty as accomplices. There may also be jurisdictional reasons for deciding when the theft has 'finished'. If the thief has first stolen the property abroad (outside the jurisdiction), he cannot then be guilty of later stealing that same property inside the jurisdiction: 'If goods have once been stolen ... they cannot be stolen again by the same thief exercising the same or other rights of ownership over the property.'[173]

It is clear that as soon as an appropriation, within the very wide meaning now attached to that concept, is committed with the necessary *mens rea*, the offence of theft is complete. Thus, for example, someone who takes goods from a supermarket shelf and puts them into the supermarket's trolley with the intention of leaving the store with the goods and without paying for them, commits the offence of theft as soon as he removes the goods from the shelf. For one of the above reasons, the question may arise as to whether the offence, though complete, has actually finished. How long does it continue?

Before *Gomez*, there is authority to indicate that an act of appropriation did not suddenly cease and it may be a continuous act. We have already seen in *Pitham and Hehl* that the two defendants appealed against their conviction of handling stolen property on the basis that their handling of the goods was 'in the course of stealing'.[174] Dismissing the appeal, the Court of Appeal held that theft was complete when M offered to sell them the goods and that their subsequent receipt of the goods was, therefore, not in the course of the stealing. Discussing this case, in *Atakpu and Abrahams*,[175] Ward J said: 'On the facts of that case the appropriation was instantaneous for the thief had clearly done all he was going to in relation to the property.' But he went on to say that the wording

---

171 Contrary to the TA 1968, s 22; see Chapter 12.
172 Contrary to the TA 1968, s 8; see Chapter 3.
173 In *Atakpu* [1994] QB 69, *per* Ward LJ (see below).
174 See para 2-25 above.
175 [1994] QB 69.

of s 22(1) of the TA 1968, 'otherwise than in the course of stealing', means that, in other cases, 'the act of stealing may run a longer course than an instant'. In *Hale*,[176] the defendant and another had rushed into the victim's house wearing stocking masks, rushed upstairs, taken her jewellery and then gagged and tied her up before threatening her and leaving with the jewellery. They appealed against their conviction for robbery, claiming that the violence and threats were not used until after the theft was complete. The Court of Appeal dismissed their appeal and held that the act of appropriation was a continuing one and it was for the jury to decide whether or not the act of appropriation had finished. In *Gregory*,[177] the defendant was convicted of burglary upon the basis that someone else had originally burgled the premises and he had gone there as a receiver. It was suggested that a single theft might comprise more than one appropriation: 'In the case of burglary of a dwelling house and before any property is removed from it, it may consist of a continuing process and involve either a single appropriation by one or more persons or a number of appropriations of the property in the house by several persons at different times during the same incident.'[178]

### Property stolen once cannot be stolen again by the same thief

2-58    In *Atakpu and Abrahams*,[179] the Court of Appeal had their first opportunity, in the light of the decision of the House of Lords in *Gomez*, to consider both the duration of theft and the question of whether property could be appropriated more than once. The case concerned 'a pair of thoroughly dishonest rascals' who were involved in a conspiracy to hire expensive motor cars in Germany and Belgium and then drive them to England with the intention of selling them on to unsuspecting customers. In considering their appeal against conviction for conspiracy to steal, the Court of Appeal had to decide where the appropriation had taken place – in England or on the continent, or, indeed, whether it could have taken place in both places. Having reviewed the above authorities, Ward J summarised the law as follows:

> (1) Theft can occur in an instant by a single appropriation but it can also involve a course of dealing with property lasting longer and involving several appropriations before the transaction is complete; (2) theft is a finite act – it has a beginning and it has an end; (3) at what point the transaction is complete is a matter for the jury to decide upon the facts of each case; (4) though there may be several appropriations in the course of a single theft or several appropriations of different goods each constituting a separate theft as in *R v Skipp*, no case suggests that there can be successive thefts of the same property ...[180]

---

176 (1978) 68 Cr App R 415.
177 (1983) 77 Cr App R 41.
178 *Ibid*, p 46, *per* Watkins LJ.
179 [1994] QB 69.
180 *Ibid*, p 79.

The court 'flinched' from the suggestion that each successive act of appropriation (for example, taking the property and then using it and/or selling it) amounted to a separate theft of the same property by the same defendant.[181] The answer lies in s 3(1) of the TA 1968 which provides that, if a person has come by the property by stealing it (as in this case), then his later dealing with it is, by implication, not included among the assumptions of the right of an owner which amount to an appropriation within the meaning of s 3(1): 'In our judgment, if goods have once been stolen, even if stolen abroad, they cannot be stolen again by the same thief exercising the same or other rights of ownership over the property.'

So far as concerned the duration of theft, the court was less certain. They stated that on a strict reading of *Gomez*, any dishonest assumption of the rights of the owner made with the necessary intention constituted theft, which left little room for a continuous course of action. However, such restriction and rigidity may lead to technical anomalies and injustice so the court preferred, 'to leave it for the common sense of the jury to decide that the appropriation can continue for so long as the thief can sensibly be regarded as in the act of stealing or, in more understandable words, so long as he is "on the job"'. However, the Court of Appeal did not decide the issue as the matter was not strictly necessary for their decision. On the facts of the case, the defendants had clearly committed the theft when they hired the cars in Germany and Belgium and could not be said to be still stealing them when days later, following their pre-arranged plan, they brought the cars to England to dispose of.[182]

It seems, therefore, that the matter of the exact duration of theft – that is, whether it could be a continuous offence – was specifically left open in *Atakpu and Abrahams*. It may still be possible to state that appropriation is neither a series of thefts, nor a continuous act, although, when it suits their purposes, the courts have been inclined to say that it is.[183] But, it must be remembered, that the appropriation is an act which takes places in relation to the property itself, so it is at least arguable that it may continue as long as the defendant is engaged in that act. Professor Smith believes that this is the better view and to treat appropriation simply as an instantaneous act would be inconsistent with the provisions of the Act relating to robbery and handling, which pre-suppose that there can be a course of stealing.[184]

So what does *Atakpu and Abrahams* decide? It is possible to summarise three issues. First, if property is appropriated outside the jurisdiction, no offence is

---

181 A view shared by Williams, G, 'Appropriation: a single or continuous act?' [1978] Crim LR 69, where he concluded that any argument in favour of a continuous appropriation rule would turn on policy rather than authority. If there were to be in law a continuous appropriation rule, then: 'This might enable handling, with all its complexities to be abolished.'

182 They therefore did not commit theft within the jurisdiction.

183 See Smith, ATH, para 5-63.

184 Smith, JC, para 2-49.

committed within the jurisdiction. Secondly, a thief cannot steal the same goods over and over again, because the same goods cannot be appropriated once stolen. In this respect, the case is an important illustration of the implications of *Gomez* because it is no longer necessary to wait for an act which is against the wishes of the owner, as it had been in *Morris*. If that had been the situation, then the appropriation would not have taken place until they attempted to sell the cars in England – a view taken by the trial judge, following the Court of Appeal in *Gomez*. Lastly, the decision in *Atakpu and Abrahams* leaves open the issue of continuous theft. Would it have been different if the appropriation had taken place in Germany, but the *mens rea* – that is the dishonest intention permanently to deprive the owner of the cars – had only occurred later? It might then be possible to treat the appropriation as a continuous act, but regarding it as one 'transaction', with the *mens rea* later superimposed on the *actus reus*.

2-59    Finally, it is worth noting that, according to Sullivan and Warbrick, the whole tortuous rigmarole could have been avoided and a different outcome to the case reached, if the Court of Appeal had not been misled by the words 'theft abroad is not triable in England'.[185] They contend that, whatever the defendants did in Germany and Belgium, it could not be theft under English law because it is outside the jurisdiction. Therefore, the defendants had come by the cars *without* stealing them and the first appropriation took place in England where the cars were stolen for the first time. In fact, the problem in *Atakpu and Abrahams* may now be overcome as Pt 1 of the CJA 1993 at last came into force on 1 June 1999. This extends the jurisdiction of the courts in England and Wales, so that they will have jurisdiction over, for example, theft, handling stolen goods, blackmail and obtaining goods and services by deception, as well as offences of inciting, conspiring or attempting to commit the same. Implications of this Act are further discussed in Chapter 14.

# 4 PROPERTY

2-60    **Section 4 of the TA 1968**

(1) 'Property' includes money and all other property, real or personal including things in action and other intangible property.

(2) A person cannot steal land, or things forming part of land and severed from it by him or his directions, except in the following cases, that is to say –

    (a) when he is a trustee or personal representative, or is authorised by power of attorney, or as a liquidator of a company, or otherwise, to sell or dispose of land belonging to another, and he appropriates the land or anything forming part of it by dealing with it in breach of the confidence reposed in him; or

---

185 [1994] Crim LR 650, p 659.

(b) when he is not in possession of the land and appropriates anything forming part of the land by severing it or causing it to be severed, or after it has been severed; or

(c) when, being in possession of the land under a tenancy, he appropriates the whole or part of any fixture or structure let to be used with the land.

For purposes of this sub-section 'and' does not include incorporeal hereditaments; 'tenancy' means a tenancy for years or any less period and includes an agreement for such a tenancy, but a person who after the end of a tenancy remains in possession as statutory tenant or otherwise is to be treated as having possession under the tenancy, and 'let' shall be construed accordingly.

(3) A person who picks mushrooms growing wild on any land, or who picks flowers, fruit or foliage from a plant growing wild on any land, does not (although not in possession of the land) steal what he picks, unless he does it for reward or for sale or other commercial purpose.

For the purposes of this sub-section 'mushroom' includes any fungus, and 'plant' includes any shrub or tree.

(4) Wild creatures, tamed or untamed, shall be regarded as property; but a person cannot steal a wild creature not tamed nor ordinarily kept in captivity, or the carcass of any such creature, unless it has been reduced into possession by or on behalf of another person and possession of it has not since been lost or abandoned, or another person is in course of reducing it into possession.

## *Background*

2-61 'The great end for which men entered into society was to secure their property'.[186] Although, in more modern times, the power of that 'society' to formalise a person's rights in property are more clearly defined, the sentiment remains the same, so that the Art 1, First Protocol of the ECHR states that a person is:

> ... entitled to the peaceful enjoyment of his possessions. No one shall be deprived of his possessions except in the public interest and subject to the conditions provided for by law and the general principles of international law.

> The preceding provisions shall not, however, in any way impair the right of a State to enforce such laws as it deems necessary to control the use of property in accordance with the general interest, or to secure the payment of taxes or other contributions or penalties.

Thus, censoring dishonest interference with another's rights of ownership in property is a high priority of the State and is, consequently, the very essence of the law of theft. So what is this valuable thing 'property', by which society sets

---

186 *Entick v Carrington* (1765) 19 State Tr 1029, p 1060, 95 ER 807, *per* Lord Camden CJ; Locke, J *Two Treatises of Government*, Bk 11, s 123: 'The Quiet and Chief end therefore, of Mens uniting into Commonwealth, and putting themselves under Government, is the preservation of their Property.'

such store for its protection? Nothing that is not defined as property in s 4 of the Act can be the subject of theft, so an adequate definition is essential,

Not everything we value is regarded as 'property' and, under the old Larceny Acts and at common law, there were restrictions on what property was capable of being stolen. Because the old law was concerned with what could be picked up and taken away out of the possession of the true owner, it meant that land, intangible assets and wild animals were all incapable of being stolen. However, under the TA 1968, almost anything can be stolen because s 4 includes both tangible and intangible property, as well as land (subject to certain restrictions). There is no specific definition of property in the Act, but gas,[187] water, debts,[188] credit balances, company shares and export quotas[189] have all been regarded as property for the purposes of s 4, so it is not confined to that which can be taken into possession. However, there are important exclusions in sub-ss (2)–(4). Sub-section (2) severely restricts situations in which land may be stolen; sub-s (3) excludes plants and mushrooms growing wild and sub-s (4) excludes wild creatures from being regarded as property, unless they have been tamed, or are ordinarily kept in captivity. There are other problems of definition of, for example, things in action and intangible property.

The rights in property which the criminal law is concerned to protect stem from those rights in property recognised by civil law. This may be the reason why information, for example, is not regarded as property for the law of theft (although it is intangible), as it is not generally recognised by the civil law as having the characteristics of property.[190] Nevertheless, the meaning of 'property' as defined in s 4 is very broad, possibly because Parliament was anxious to avoid the limitations imposed by the old Larceny Acts and the common law, so 'property includes money and all other property, real or personal, including things in action and other intangible property'. Each of these will be examined in more detail below.

## Things that can be stolen: the meaning of property

### A thing (chose) in action

2-62 A 'thing in action' (frequently called a 'chose in action') is a known legal expression used to describe all personal rights in property which can only be enforced against another person by an action in law and not by taking physical

---

187 But not electricity.

188 The debt must be in existence at the time of the appropriation.

189 *AG of Hong Kong v Nai-Keung* [1987] 1 WLR 1339.

190 Cornish, WR, *Intellectual Property: Patents, Copyright, Trademarks and Allied Rights*, 4th edn, 1999, Sweet & Maxwell, paras 8-49–53.

possession.[191] It is this very *right* to bring an action in law that is the 'thing in action' and is regarded as property within the meaning of s 4 of the TA 1968 and, therefore, capable of being stolen. Some examples of 'things in action' include negotiable instruments, insurance policies, shares in a company,[192] debts and copyright (but not patents),[193] or a right under a trust.

The right of one party to enforce a contract against the other party to the contract is an example of a 'thing in action'. If student A owes student B £50, A has the right to sue B for the £50. This right to sue is the thing in action, not the £50 itself. The concept is nicely illustrated by the 'ticket' case of *Marshall et al*,[194] where the defendants collected unexpired London Underground tickets and Travelcards from members of the public leaving the underground and then sold them on at a reduced rate to other potential travellers. The tickets were still valid and marked as non-transferable and the defendants were charged with theft. In acquiring and reselling the tickets, it was submitted that the appellants had intended to treat the tickets as their own to dispose of regardless of London Underground's rights within the meaning of s 6(1) of the TA 1968,[195] and, accordingly, depriving London Underground of revenue which it might have expected to receive from those persons who bought the tickets. It was on this basis the defendants had their convictions for theft upheld by the Court of Appeal. It is important to note that the charges were in relation to the tickets and travel cards themselves (as *pieces of paper*) which, of course, were not things in action but tangible property. The case is interesting on that point alone as it appears to be in conflict with part of the rationale in *Preddy*,[196] where it was thought inappropriate to charge theft of the actual cheque form itself (that is, the piece of paper) because there will be no intention to permanently deprive the drawer of the actual cheque form, which would, on presentation for payment, be returned to the drawer via his bank.[197] Be that as it may, the Court of Appeal also suggested that the customer's right to travel was a thing in action enforceable against London Underground and, furthermore, London Underground itself had a thing in action against the customer, that is the *right to prevent transfer* of the tickets to other persons, both rights being created by the contract between the parties made on purchase of the tickets. The Court of Appeal tentatively concluded that the defendants may also have appropriated that right (as well as the actual ticket) by selling the tickets on to other travellers.

---

191 See *Talkington v Magoo* [1902] 2 KB 427, p 430, *per* Channel J.

192 *Grubb* [1915] 2 KB 683.

193 PA 1977, s 30(1).

194 [1998] 2 Cr App R 282.

195 See *Fernandes* [1996] 1 Cr App R 175, p 188. For further explanation of s 6(1), see para 2-119 below.

196 [1996] AC 815 and para 8-29, below.

197 It is submitted by Smith and Hogan, *Criminal Law*, 9th edn, 1999, Butterworths, p 516, that *Preddy* [1996] AC 815 is wrong on this point.

In order to uphold the conviction, the Court of Appeal must have thought the tickets 'belonged' to London Underground. However, was it realistic to regard these tickets as belonging to another? Surely, a person who purchases a ticket believes himself to be the true owner of it, with an owner's right to dispose of it as he would like. Is it satisfactory to regard such a ticket as property of the London Underground, simply because of terms printed on the back of it? True, in civil law the purchase of the ticket creates a contract between the two parties, but a person cannot be bound by any terms of the contract printed on a ticket unless reasonable steps have been taken to bring it to his attention.[198] In addition, every law student knows that, where a ticket is obtained from a machine, any conditions must be brought to the attention of the purchaser *before* he inserts his money: if the term is printed on the ticket issued by the machine it is too late – the contract has already been made.[199]

Even if one were to accept that the tickets did belong to London Underground, then surely it would be best to allow the decision to be decided on the issue of dishonesty.[200] Arguably, there would be situations where a person might not think others would regard his conduct, in passing on his ticket, as dishonest. If that person is charged with theft, it would then be open to a jury to find whether such a person is dishonest, depending on the circumstances. It is small wonder that the Court of Appeal in *Marshall* warned that the decision could have implications for all ticket touts, and even for the ordinary motorist who passes on the benefit of an unexpired parking ticket.

### Bank credits

2-63    Another good illustration of a thing in action is to examine the way in which bank accounts work. Contrary to popular belief, when a customer deposits money in a bank account, he is no longer the owner of the actual money – that ownership has passed to the bank, which is now in the position of a debtor to the customer, that is, the bank owes the customer a debt equal to the amount he has deposited in the bank.[201] It is the right of the customer to enforce the 'debt' against the bank which is the thing in action. As long as the account remains in credit, then the bank will owe the customer that debt and is under an obligation to meet the cheque which can be enforced by an action in law – that is, there is a thing in action which is property capable of being stolen. So, if D tries to debit money from V's account, it is not the actual money which is stolen, but V's right to it. In *Williams (Roy)*,[202] the defendant was a builder who used his business to target and cheat elderly householders over a period of years. Having gained

---

198 *Parker v South Eastern Railway Co* (1877) 2 CPD 416.
199 *Thornton v Shoe Lane Parking Ltd* [1971] 2 QB 163.
200 See, further, Smith, JC, 'Stealing tickets' [1998] Crim LR 723.
201 See *Foley v Hill* (1848) HLC 28 and Lord Goddard CJ in *Davenport* [1954] 1 WLR 569.
202 (2000) *The Times*, 25 October; cf *Burke* [2000] Crim LR 413.

their trust with charging modest prices, he then overbilled them for work he undertook. The victims paid their cheques into his bank account, on which he later drew. He was convicted of theft of a thing in action belonging to the victims. The appropriation took place on presentation of the victim's cheque by (or on behalf of) the defendant, thereby causing a reduction of the victim's credit balance in their bank account.

2-64    It is possible to extend this principle beyond bank balances that are in credit. If the bank account becomes overdrawn, the bank will still owe a duty to the customer to honour the customer's cheque up to his authorised overdraft limit. If it is unauthorised, then the customer ceases to have a thing in action against the bank and thus there is no property capable of being stolen.[203] That is why in Kohn,[204] where the defendant company director drew cheques on his company account for his own benefit, he was not convicted of all the theft charges against him. The theft convictions were upheld for those drawings that were made when the account was in credit and for those made when it was overdrawn but within the credit limits of an agreed overdraft. However, the conviction was quashed in regard to that drawing which related to a period when the account already exceeded the agreed limit.[205] The reason seems to be that, during this latter period, there ceased to be a relationship between the bank and the customer of debtor and creditor; the bank was no longer under an obligation to the customer to honour the cheques. Even if the bank felt compelled to do so as a matter of courtesy, no property rights could be created retrospectively in the customer.[206]

A doubtful distinction has been drawn between the situation as described in Kohn and one where an apparent credit balance on a bank account is created by fraud. It has been held in Thompson (Michael)[207] that such a credit balance will not be regarded as a thing in action (and, therefore, not property within the meaning of s 4(1)), because any attempt to enforce the apparent liability would be capable of immediate denial as soon as the fraud came to light. It is submitted that such a situation is now best covered by s 15A of the TA 1968 (obtaining a money transfer by deception) rather than theft,[208] or s 3 of the Computer Misuse Act (CMA) 1990, if the fraud is effected by means of a computer.

---

203 See Navvabi [1986] 1 WLR 1311, para 2-48, above.

204 (1979) 69 Cr App R 395; Hallam [1995] Cr App R 323.

205 Although, of course, it would have been possible to convict him of an attempt if D believed that the cheque was within the company's overdraft limit.

206 Note that, the part of the decision in Kohn (1979) 69 Cr App R 395 in relation to the charges of theft of the cheque forms themselves (as bills of exchange) has impliedly been overruled by the decision in Preddy [1996] AC 815 (HL); but cf Marshall [1998] 2 Cr App R 282 However, the principle in Kohn survives Preddy; see Graham, Ali and Others [1997] Cr App R 302.

207 [1984] 1 WLR 962.

208 In any case 'appropriation of property 'in the context of bank accounts is something of a legal fiction since nine times out of 10 the 'victim', owner of the bank account, loses nothing. It is the bank which usually loses out because it is forced to honour the cheque. C Thomas [1985] QB 604; Hamilton [1990] Crim LR 806.

## Other intangible property

2-65  Things in action are intangible property, but not all intangible property is a thing in action, as we shall see below. It is not absolutely clear what falls into this category of 'other intangible property' – it certainly does not include all such property as being the subject of theft. For example, if D was to ride on a bus without paying for a ticket, he would have obtained a free ride on a bus but the ride itself is not regarded as property and thus cannot be stolen.[209] However, the ticket itself is property (tangible) and it is arguable that the right to take that ride expressed by the ticket may be property (intangible).[210] By the same token, the giving of a service, such as a hair cut or a car wash, is not regarded as property. D certainly intends to deprive the giver of the service of something of value, but he is not depriving him of any intangible property and it is not theft to contract a debt dishonestly.[211] In this respect, the modern law of theft gives rise to more uncertainty than in pre-1968 days when the law simply excluded all intangible property from the ambit of larceny.

We shall see below that there are other, seemingly arbitrary, categories of things of value which are incapable of being stolen, such as confidential information. On the other hand, it seems that the law is prepared to allow the word 'other' to encompass unexpected categories when the courts are of a mind to do so. In *AG of Hong Kong v Chan Nai-Keung*,[212] the defendant was an exporter of textiles from Hong Kong where the export of textiles was prohibited except under licence. Exports were regulated by a quota system, and since many exporters were unable to meet their target quota, there was a lucrative internal market in selling these surplus quotas. The wording of the law of theft in Hong Kong was virtually identical to s 4 of the TA 1968 and D was convicted of theft when he sold his company's surplus export quotas at a gross undervalue to another company in which he had a personal interest. It was held that the quotas were not 'things in action', but were, nevertheless, transferable for value and could be regarded as 'other intangible property'.

### *Copyright*

2-66  Copyright (conferred by the Copyright, Designs and Patents Act (CDPA) 1988) refers to the exclusive right to do, and to authorise others to do, certain acts such as reproduction and publication in relation to original works which may be either literary, dramatic, musical or artistic.[213] It is a criminal offence knowingly

---

209 *Beecham* (1851) 5 Cox 181.

210 *Marshall* [1998] 2 Cr App R 282, para 2-62, above.

211 See Smith, ATH, para 3-12. He may have committed an offence under the TA 1978, s 1, if he obtains the service by deception, see para 9-01, below.

212 [1987] 1 WLR 1339 (PC).

213 CDPA 1988, s 1; (copyright also protects films, sound recordings, broadcasts and cable programme services and typographical works).

to make or deal in articles that infringe a copyright.[214] In theory, there seems no reason why copyright cannot be stolen because it is regarded as a thing in action, but it is not that simple. D would have to appropriate dishonestly the actual copyright right or licence from V. Although there seems no reason in principle why this could not be regarded as property and so D commit theft when he intends permanently to deprive V of it, in practice it is hard to envisage how he could obtain this right from V, as there is no registration for a fraudulent diversion of the grant to D.[215]

A more common occurrence will be where D photocopies and publishes V's work without his permission, thus infringing the owner's rights in copyright but not depriving him of it. In this situation, popular opinion would surely regard D as having 'stolen' the benefit of all V's hard work. However, notwithstanding whether such a 'benefit' comes within the definition of property, it will not be theft in law.[216] There may be said to have been an appropriation in assuming one of the owner's exclusive rights in the work; D may even be dishonest, but the conduct is still not theftuous because D does not act with either the effect or the intention of permanently depriving V of the actual copyright. V may have had his rights infringed, there will undoubtedly be a breach of copyright which is unlawful, but he does not lose the right to his copyright and, therefore, D cannot be said to have stolen it from him. The same rationale can be applied to trade marks below.

## Trade marks

2-67    Registered trade marks may be dishonestly used by D on goods of a nature similar to the ones for which the trade mark was designed and, as above, there may be an appropriation of the true owner's rights to make use of the trade mark. Yet, once again, it cannot be said that there is an intention permanently to deprive the owner of the actual trade mark itself, as he can make no disposition of it in accordance with s 6(1).[217] Therefore, a dishonest action of this nature cannot be theft, although it would be an offence of unauthorised use of a trade mark under s 92 of the Trademarks Act 1994.

## Patents

2-68    Patents are granted by the Crown through the Patent Office in order to limit the rights of others to interfere with an exclusive right to exploit an invention. Such

---

214 CDPA 1988, s 107.

215 It has been suggested that where Lord Fraser, in *Rank Film Distributors Ltd v Video Information Centre* [1982] AC 380, p 445, expressed the view that copyright was not property for the purpose of the TA 1968, in context he appears to have meant that breach of copyright is not theft, see Smith, ATH, para 3-20.

216 *Lloyd* [1985] QB 829.

217 See para 2-119 below.

protection was limited until the Patents Act (PA) 1977 introduced various measures to protect its integrity. Unlike copyrights, patents and applications for patents are not 'things in action',[218] but they are personal property and are, therefore, capable of being stolen as 'other intangible property', under the TA 1968. Furthermore, an invention for which no patent has yet been granted or applied for, may also be treated as intangible property[219] and so can also be stolen – some may say, perversely so, considering that, as we shall see below, confidential information is not regarded as property for the purposes of theft. If an invention can be property, why cannot information? What is an invention, if not information of a sort? It can be argued that, by reading the information concerning the invention, one is appropriating it since you are assuming the right of the owner in determining who should have access to it.[220]

## Things that cannot be stolen – or probably cannot be stolen

2-69    Nothing which is not defined as property under s 4 can be stolen in law and, although generally the category 'other intangible property' is included in the definition, uncertainties remain as to whether certain types of intangible property will be considered as property.

### *Confidential information and trade secrets*[221]

2-70    This does not come within the ambit of 'other' intangible property, even though it undoubtedly has a value and can be owned, bought and sold and is thus arguably worthy of protection. In the leading case of *Oxford v Moss*,[222] a university student was convicted of theft when he took an examination paper prior to the examination and read it before returning the paper to its original place, retaining the information for his own use. The civil law has had difficulty recognising confidential information as having the characteristics of property,[223] so the Divisional Court took a cautious approach to extending the criminal law to include protection of something which the civil law had not: it quashed his conviction for theft. Even though the information on the examination paper was undoubtedly no longer secret and had therefore been rendered useless, the university had not been deprived of any property defined in s 4. The Court confirmed that confidential information does not come within the category of

---

218 PA 1977, s 30(1).

219 *Ibid*, s 7(2)(b).

220 Although it is admitted that it is part of the application process that the specification is published and published before any eventual patent is granted.

221 See, further, Hammond, RG, 'Theft of information' (1984) 100 LQR 252.

222 (1978) 68 Cr App R 183 (DC).

223 See, *op cit*, Cornish, fn 190.

'other intangible property'; and the piece of paper on which the information was written, though tangible, had been returned.

2-71     It follows that wrongfully acquiring trade secrets generally cannot be theft either, even though the acquisition of them may be flagrantly dishonest. This is strikingly illustrated by *Absolom*,[224] which followed *Oxford and Moss*. The defendant was a geologist who obtained details of a leading oil company's exploration for oil off the Irish coast and then tried to sell them to a rival company. The information, which was contained in a 'graphalog' (a record of geological data and an indication of the likelihood of finding oil) was unique because the oil company was the only one exploring that area. Moreover, the company had invested £13 m in drilling operation and it was attested that the information could have been sold for between £50,000 and £100,000. The judge told the jury that the defendant had acted in the 'utmost bad faith', but directed them to acquit him of theft, on the grounds that the information contained in the graphalog was not capable of founding such a charge. Does this mean that trade and business secrets can be pillaged at will by unscrupulous persons who obtain and exchange them for profit? Industrial espionage and the consequent 'theft' of valuable information is a serious problem in modern times and it seems something of an anomaly that the criminal law of theft is powerless to disapprove it. Are not owners who go to the expense of gathering such information and then preventing access to it by wrongdoers entitled to the protection of the criminal law? The actual decision in *Oxford v Moss* turned on the meaning of property, but even if the information had been recognised as such, there would still have remained the difficulty of establishing an intention permanently to deprive, since the 'information' was returned. Hence, D only deprives his victim of the exclusive nature of his knowledge not the knowledge itself: 'It is difficult to see how there is any question of deprivation where someone has, in breach of confidence, forced the original holder to share, but not forget his secret.'[225]

Normally, the information amounting to the trade secret will be recorded on a physical medium such as, in the case of *Oxford v Moss*, the paper. So there is some comfort in the suggestion[226] that, irrespective of the issue above, D could have been convicted of theft of the piece of paper on the ground that the 'virtue' had gone out of it when he put it back and, thus, there had been an intention permanently to deprive the University of the piece of paper. It has also been pointed out[227] that, if the taker of information is so unwise as to use his employer's duplicating materials and facilities, the resulting copy would belong

---

224 (1983) *The Times*, 14 September.
225 Palmer, N and Kohler, N, 'Information as property', in Palmer, N and McKendrick, E (eds), *Interests in Goods*, 1993, Lloyd's, p 203.
226 Smith, JC, 'Commentary' [1979] Crim LR 119.
227 Smith, ATH, para 3-19.

to the employer,[228] so the taker could technically be charged with theft of the materials. However, none of these charges really reflect the serious nature of the defendant's conduct in *Absolom*.

Presumably, there would be potential for a conspiracy charge. For example, if the student had conspired with a disgruntled member of the university administration to obtain the examination paper, then they could both be found guilty of a conspiracy to defraud, since it has now been accepted in *Welham v DPP*,[229] that there is no need for the fraud to be confined to causing a pecuniary loss. Even this is not a complete solution, however, as a conspiracy would not apply to a lone operator. Nevertheless, it certainly seems strange that there may be the possibility of protecting information under the criminal law of conspiracy, but not under the criminal law of theft.[230] On the other hand, even if it were to be accepted that confidential information be included within the meaning of property, some questions would still remain unanswered. For example, there would still be the attendant problem of what types of confidential information would be included. Should it be confined to trade secrets? What if it is a matter of public interest that the information is 'stolen'? It may simply be best to accept, as Professor Griew suggests, that the TA 1968 is not the appropriate instrument to deal with this specialised kind of mischief.[231]

### Gas, water and electricity

2-72     At common law, a thing could not be larcenable, unless (a) it was tangible, (b) it was movable, (c) it was of some value and (d) it had an owner.[232] Nevertheless, even under common law, it was recognised that there was nothing in the nature of water to prevent it being the subject of larceny,[233] provided that it is placed in a pipe or a reservoir and not in a lake or pond. If in the latter, it becomes a severable part of the land on which it stands[234] and is subject to the restrictions concerning theft of land which will be discussed below. The same can be said of gas.[235] There was never any reason to suppose either would be treated any

---

228 *Secretary of State for Defence v Guardian Newspapers* [1985] AC 339.

229 [1961] AC 103, *per* Lord Radcliffe.

230 Where the information is obtained by intercepting post or by telephone tapping, there may be an offence under the Interception of Communications Act 1985, s 1. Where a computer is used in the process there may be a charge under the CMA 1990.

231 Griew, para 2-25. In 1997, the Law Commission recommended making the unauthorised use or disclosure of confidential information a separate offence, but left open the question whether unauthorised acquisition should be: No 150, *Legislating the Criminal Code: Misuse of Trade Secrets*, 1997, para 5.3.

232 *Archbold*, para 21-52.

233 *Ferens v O'Brien* (1883) 11 QBD 21.

234 Burn, EH, *Cheshire and Burn's Modern Law of Real Property*, 16th edn, 2000, Butterworths, p 176.

235 *Firth* (1869) 11 Cox 234; there are other statutory offences to do with dishonest use of gas under the Gas Act 1995.

differently under the TA 1968. However, electricity is regarded differently. Thus, in *Low v Blease*,[236] it was held that electricity was not appropriated by switching on a current and could not be described as 'property' within the meaning of s 4 of the TA 1968. The court seemed satisfied to accept the simple rationale that Parliament had recognised the difficulty inherent in the concept that electricity could be 'appropriated' and so had provided a specific statutory offence of dishonestly using electricity under s 13 of the Act.[237] This offence will be discussed in more detail in Chapter 7.

There seems little logic in the different treatment accorded to electricity compared with gas and water under the TAs. It was easy to see why electricity was regarded differently under the old LAs because of the concepts of 'taking and carrying away', but that does not apply to the idea of appropriation under the TA 1968 which requires only an assumption of any of the rights of an owner. This is surely something which can occur in relation to electricity as much as to gas or water – particularly as all three are now expensive commodities that are bought and sold.[238] Perhaps it is because only the *effects* of electricity can be experienced through the human senses, and not the thing itself. Nevertheless, it is odd that the law as it now stands has the effect of making the trespasser who warms himself by lighting the gas fire guilty of burglary, while the trespasser who prefers the electric fire is not.[239]

## Corpses and body parts

2-73    It is generally accepted at common law that there is no property in a corpse.[240] The origin of the rule is obscure, but seems to be based on the assumption that since there is no ownership in a live human body, none can exist in a dead one. Therefore, as larceny could only be committed in respect of recognised property belonging to another, it was impossible to have larceny of a corpse, or even portions thereof. There is a limited interim right to possession (but not ownership) in a body which vests in those persons charged with the duty of burying it, such as undertakers, or other personal representatives[241] of the

---

236 [1975] Crim LR 513 (DC).

237 For dishonest use of a telecommunications system, see the Telecommunications Act 1984, s 42.

238 Part of the reasoning in *AG for Hong Kong v Nai Keung* [1987] 1 WLR 1339 was that the export quotas were transferable for value.

239 Smith, para 9-02.

240 *Handyside's* case (1749) 2 East PC 652. For criticism, see Matthews, P, 'Whose body? People as property' [1983] CLP 193.

241 *Williams v Williams* (1880) 20 Ch D 659.

deceased and this right is actionable in law[242] – but it cannot be stolen from them as it is not 'property'.[243]

In addition to common law, there are also statutory regulations which govern many of the circumstances where a corpse or its parts are retained for medical research, or for teaching purposes in a university medical school, namely the Human Tissues Act (HTA) 1961 and the Anatomy Act 1984.[244] Similarly, the procedures to be followed for post mortem examinations are also governed by statute: both the HTA 1961 and the Coroner's Act 1988 require that authorisation be given by the person lawfully in possession of the body; this does not include the person entrusted with the body solely for the purpose of interment or cremation.[245] Body parts and tissue may be removed and retained at post mortem, but only for a particular purpose on instruction of the coroner who may require the 'preservation of material which in his opinion bears upon the cause of death for such a period as the coroner sees fit'.[246]

However, none of these statutory regulations does anything to undermine the common law principle that there can be no property in a dead body. It seems puzzling that such limited possessory rights as exist, though admittedly not the same as ownership, are excluded from protection by the law of theft. If D goes into a post mortem room and removes the body, or removes a cadaver from a dissection room at a university, it seems illogical to suggest that, simply because the body is not 'owned' by the medical school or pathology laboratory, then it is incapable of being stolen and D cannot be guilty of theft because the cadaver is not regarded as property. Does this mean, as Professor Griew suggests, that property within the TA is probably limited to that which is capable of being owned, or of indefinite lawful possession?[247] Surely, even if, for example, a university does not 'own' the cadaver according to the rules of property law, it does have a bailment of the corpse, or, at least, control of it (which is sufficient for the purposes of theft) and the corpse surely possesses all the other necessary characteristics to be classified as property capable of being stolen.[248]

2-74 However, be that as it may, once parts of the body have been removed, they may more readily be seen as property which can belong to someone, if they are altered in some way so that they acquire value. In limited circumstances, there

---

242 Clerk, JF, *Clerk & Lindsell on Tort*, 18th edn, 2000, Sweet & Maxwell, p 746, para 14-45. An earlier edition was relied on with approval in *Dobson v North Tyneside HA* [1977] 1 WLR 596, although Peter Gibson LJ was 'not aware that there is any authority that there is such a duty on the next of kin as such'.

243 Although there seems no reason why the ashes following cremation cannot be regarded as tangible property.

244 See, generally, Montgomery, J, *Health Care Law*, 1997, Oxford: OUP.

245 HTA 1961, ss 1(6), 2(2).

246 Coroner's Rules 1984 (SI 1984/552), r 9.

247 Griew, para 2-22. But, see now, *Kelly* [1999] QB 621 (para 2-75, below).

248 See Smith, ATH, 'Stealing the body and its parts' (1976) Crim LR 622; Dworkin, R, 'Human tissue: rights in the body and its parts' [1993] 1 MLR 291, p 294.

seems no reason why this should not be extended to apply to a whole corpse. For example, if the body has been stuffed, or embalmed, it may be the subject of property. In civil law, *Clerk & Lindsell* are prepared to submit that 'conversion will lie for a skeleton or cadaver used for research or exhibition'[249] and, in *Doodeward v Spence*,[250] the High Court of Australia was prepared to allow the appellant to succeed in an action for detinue[251] for the return of a stillborn two-headed child, preserved in spirits some 40 years before and which the appellant had purchased with a view to exhibiting. Griffiths CJ expressed the view (p 414) that:

> ... when a person has by the lawful exercise of work or skill so dealt with a human body or part of a human body in his lawful possession that it has acquired some attributes differentiating it from a mere corpse awaiting burial, he acquires a right to retain possession of it, at least as against any person not entitled to have it delivered to him for the purpose of burial ...

As some work had been performed in preserving the foetus and it had acquired some pecuniary value, it was held to be property with rights vested in the appellant as its present owner. Barton J was prepared to agree that an action did lie, but only in relation to such stillborn foetus which had become an exhibition piece. He was at pains to emphasise that he did not want to cast the slightest doubt on the general rule that an unburied corpse was not considered property. This, together with a strong dissenting judgment from Higgins J stating that no one could have property in another human being, live or dead, means that the case does nothing to alter the general common law rule.

2-75 Nevertheless, the principle in *Doodeward* was applied in *Kelly*,[252] where the appellant, an artist, together with his friend Lindsay, a laboratory technician, was convicted of theft of a number of assorted body parts that they removed from the Royal College of Surgeons where they had been lawfully stored. Kelly made plaster casts of the parts (some of which were exhibited in an art gallery) and then disposed of the remains, either by burying them or storing them in his flat. The Court of Appeal then had the grisly task of deciding whether these particular body parts, having been dissected, preserved and exhibited for teaching purposes, had thus acquired sufficient attributes that they could be regarded as property under s 4 of the TA 1968. They decided that they had. But in so doing, Rose LJ was adamant that the general principle that neither a corpse, nor parts of a corpse, are in themselves capable of being stolen was still good law and could only be changed by Parliament. However, the parts are capable of being property within the meaning of s 4, if they have acquired different attributes by virtue of the application of skill, such as dissection or

249 *Op cit, Clerk & Lindsell on Tort*, fn 242, p 746, para 14-45.

250 [1908] 6 CLR 406.

251 Detinue was abolished by the Torts (Interference with Goods) Act 1977; recovery of goods is now governed by the provisions of the 1977 Act.

252 [1999] QB 621.

preservation techniques for exhibition or teaching purposes. With regard to the future, however, he also recognised that even the common law does not stand still and it may be that there will be circumstances in which, eventually, the courts will hold that human body parts are capable of being property for the purposes of s 4: '... even without the acquisition of different attributes, if they have a use beyond their mere existence. This may be so if, for example, they are intended for use in an organ transplant operation, for the extraction of DNA or, for that matter, as an exhibit in a trial.'[253]

Despite the robust approach taken in *Kelly*, it remains questionable in civil law whether there can be property in a body (or its parts) which has not acquired sufficient attributes to differentiate it from a corpse awaiting burial.[254] Since this is an area where the criminal law takes its lead directly from the civil, doubt remains as to whether, for example, bodies or body parts which are retained and stored in hospital archives, or whether organs which are removed for one purpose and then used for a different purpose, can be said to have been 'stolen' from the original 'owners'. In *Dobson v North Tyneside HA*,[255] it was held that no actual ownership in property can arise in such cases and it may simply become a question of which party has the better possessory right. In *Dobson*, the deceased's brain was removed at post mortem and preserved in paraffin for use at inquest. The body was later returned to the family for burial, but the brain was retained and stored in the hospital until such time as it was lost or disposed of. For a variety of reasons, not least their own distress at burying an incomplete body, the next of kin sued for conversion but failed. Peter Gibson LJ stated that mere preservation of the brain was not the equivalent of stuffing or embalming a corpse and, as the brain was lawfully in the possession of the hospital, they therefore had a right of possession vested in them. The relatives had no right to possession of, or property in, the deceased's brain at the time the brain was disposed of and therefore no cause of action: '... even if the hospital laboratory protocols were not followed ... I cannot see how that breach of internal rules could help the plaintiffs.' This may mean that a hospital can retain such tissue and organs indefinitely, provided that they have been lawfully[256] removed from the deceased's body, without being convicted of theft.[257]

Modern advances in medical science, resulting in the ability to remove, store and preserve indefinitely various human organs, body parts and even, perhaps, whole human bodies may call for a reappraisal of questions concerning property

---

253 [1999] QB 621, p 631.

254 It has been held in the US that a university hospital owned a patient's spleen and other body substances once they had been removed, *Moore v Regents of the University of California* [1990] 271 Cal Rptr 146.

255 [1997] 1 WLR 596 and discussed in *Kelly* [1999] QB 621 (above).

256 Any unauthorised post-mortem would breach the HTA 1961, s 2.

257 Cf *Lennox-Wright* [1973] Crim LR 529, where eyes were removed from a dead body by someone who was later discovered not to be medically qualified. He was charged not with theft but with 'disobedience to a statute'.

rights in terms of the meaning of ownership. In theory, there seems no reason why such parts, once removed and stored cannot be 'owned' and thus property which can be stolen. Indeed, it has been held that human substances such as blood, urine and human hair taken from living persons are all capable of being owned for the purposes of theft,[258] and so subject to the normal rules of property. But, it remains undecided whether living organs within the body can be the subject of ownership any more than those removed from the dead.[259] So, for example, if a kidney is removed from a living person for the purpose of transplant, and then not used, will it be theft if it is not returned to the body of the donor? The legal status of a human embryo is also unclear in terms of property.

It seems unlikely that any of the draftsmen of s 4 of the TA 1968 had in mind such a case as *Kelly*, and so were content to leave acquisition of body parts from the living to the law of assault and from the dead to the existing common law and other regulatory legislation.[260] The problem is that this is an increasingly emotive area[261] and likely to get more so in the light of BMA proposals to change the presumption on donor organs. If these were implemented, persons would be required to opt out of the donor scheme rather than carry a card to opt in. Would this mean that the State had the power to requisition our organs on death? If so, will the State be declaring 'ownership' of them? In *Kelly*, it was the fact of possession of the parts by the Royal College of Surgeons which was important, which seems to suggest that the Court of Appeal was prepared to recognise a property right (at least for the purpose of theft) which falls short of ownership. It is arguable that modern technology has overtaken the criminal law in this field. There is a clear need for a guiding principle to suit modern bio-technical advances that may be outside the realm of the existing criminal law and is, perhaps, best addressed by Parliament in more specific legislation.[262]

## Real property: limitations on theft of land

2-76   Section 4(2) means that land, or things forming part of the land and severed from it, are incapable of being stolen,[263] subject to the three exceptions below.

---

258 Respectively, *Rothery* [1976] RTR 550; *Welsh* [1974] RTR 478; *Herbert* (1960) 25 J Crim LR 163. It is submitted that this should also apply to sperms deposited in a sperm bank or storage of eggs/human embryos.

259 But the Human Organ Transplants Act 1989 prohibits commercial dealings in human organs.

260 See, eg, the Human Fertilisation and Embryology Act 1990.

261 See, eg, The Royal Liverpool Children's Inquiry Report, 2001, HMSO: London.

262 Cf the CMA 1990, after House of Lords refused to extend the ambit of theft to cover computer hacking in *Gold & Schifreen* [1988] AC 1063.

263 Note, land is regarded as property capable of being 'obtained by deception' for the purposes of the TA 1968, s 15 – the TA 1968, s 34(1) states: 'Sections 4(1) and 5(1) of this Act shall apply generally for purposes of this Act as they apply for purposes of s 1.'

This means that the classic boundary disputes between neighbours are outside the ambit of the law of theft since, even if N dishonestly moves his fence several metres onto his neighbour's land in order to provide himself with a bigger garden, he will not have stolen that land. 'Land' is defined very widely in English law[264] and includes not only the actual earth, but also things which are attached to it; for example, things growing on the land, permanent structures or buildings, or integral parts of such structures or buildings, are all regarded as part of the 'land'. The civil law relating to land allows such items to be severed (separated) from the land and they can be stolen in the ordinary course of events, but they cannot (apart from the three exceptions below) be stolen by the person who severed them, or on whose directions they were severed. For example, D can steal O's logs, unless it was D who chopped down the trees (or on whose directions the trees were felled) from which the logs were made. Thus, D cannot be guilty of theft of the logs if he is the feller of the trees, unless he falls within s 4(2)(b). Furthermore, for the purposes of s 4(2), 'land' does not include incorporeal hereditaments and so easements, profits and rents are all property capable of being stolen.

The TA 1968 provides three exceptions to the general rule that land cannot be stolen. A person may steal land in the following circumstances.

### Where he is a trustee: s 4(2)(a)

2-77    Where a person is a trustee, or personal representative empowered to deal with land in a particular way, but who then does so in breach of the confidence reposed in him, he will be guilty of theft of that land, provided, of course, that the other ingredients of the offence are present. For example, if D is authorised by the vendor to sell an estate of 100 hectares but only sells 95 hectares, appropriating the remaining five for himself – he will be guilty of theft of that five hectares of land, as long as he has done so dishonestly and with the intention permanently to deprive.

### Where he is a non-possessor of land: s 4(2)(b)

2-78    Where a person is a non-possessor of land and that person appropriates after severance (or by severing, or causing it to be severed), he may be guilty of theft. This sub-section modifies the general rule that land cannot be stolen by those not in possession – it can, as long as there has been severance. The modification only applies to those not in possession of the land, so does not apply to landowners or tenants. It covers situations where a person, who is not in possession of the land, removes something which has originally formed an integral part of that land, for example, a load of topsoil from a field, or a rose bush, or he removes

---

264 See Law of Property Act 1925, s 205(1)(ix).

slates from a shed roof, or even perhaps by allowing cattle to graze the grass.[265] In each case, the thing stolen is severed from the land and becomes property that can be stolen.[266] There are important qualifications to this sub-section, provided in s 4(3), which are examined below. They concern the position of non-possessors and things growing wild on land.

### *Where he is a tenant appropriating fixtures: s 4(2)(c)*

2-79   Where he is a tenant appropriating fixtures, or structures let to him as part of the land under the terms of his tenancy, he may be guilty of theft. Therefore, a tenant who appropriates a fixture, such as a fireplace or fitted kitchen cupboard, will be guilty of theft, provided that the other ingredients of the offence are present. The section defines 'tenancy' as meaning a tenancy for years, or any less period stipulated in the agreement. This sub-section creates certain anomalies, in that it draws a distinction between actual fixtures which a tenant can steal and other items forming part of the land which (because of the general rule) he cannot. Consequently, a tenant could steal a moveable greenhouse, but will not be guilty of theft if he removes a rose bush, or topsoil from the garden, because these are not fixtures but form part of the land of which he is lawfully in possession as tenant. It is submitted that there are also anomalies between s 4(2)(c) and (b). If D cuts down a tree on O's land and removes it, he has severed that tree from the land and may be guilty of theft under s 4(2)(b) – unless, that is, he is a tenant, in which case he may not be guilty of theft (provided that the tree is not part of the fixtures under the terms of his let). However, if D dismantles part of the garage or shed and gives it to V, he will be guilty under s 4(2)(b) if he is not in possession of the land, and guilty under s 4(2)(c) if he is a tenant in possession of the land.[267] Note that there is no need for the tenant actually to remove the garage or shed before being guilty of theft, it is enough that he has dishonestly appropriated it. Thus, it will be theft when he sells the garage to V with a promise to dismantle it later: s 4(2)(c) makes no requirement that the fixture be severed.

## Mushroom and plants: s 4(3)

2-80   We have seen that, in accordance with s 4(2)(b), a person who is not in possession of land can be guilty of theft if he appropriates anything forming part

---

265 *McGill v Shepherd* (unreported), Williams and Weinberg, *The Australian Law of Theft*, 2nd edn, 94.

266 *Op cit*, Smith and Hogan, fn 197, remind us that in 1972 a man was prosecuted at Leeds Crown Court for stealing Cleckheaton railway station by dismantling and removing it. He was acquitted on the merits, the jury accepting that, on this bold enterprise, he was acting under a claim of right and, therefore, not dishonest. But, as Smith and Hogan point out, it would appear that railway stations are stealable by severance (p 518)!

267 Provided neither are of a temporary nature and not fixed to the ground, in which case they will be regarded as ordinary items of tangible property capable of theft.

of the land by severing it. This would appear to include things growing wild, since at common law they form part of the land on which they grow. However, there would be no sense in making a thief out of every blackberry picker or mushroom gatherer and so an exception is made in s 4(3). Nevertheless, although flowers, fruit, foliage or mushrooms are all excluded from the definition of property capable of being stolen,[268] the section uses the word 'picks' from the plant (which includes shrub or tree). Therefore, it can be theft to pull out a whole plant (with the exception of mushrooms), or cut down an entire bush as neither could be described as picking.

It will also be theft if the 'picking' is done for reward or commercial gain. Professor Smith suggests that a single isolated sale by a person such as a schoolboy who picks mushrooms, intending to sell them to his mother or the neighbours, might not be theft because the section appears to be aimed at those who are making a 'commercial' business out of such activity.[269] However, it is submitted that the use of the words 'for reward or for sale or for other commercial purpose' seems to suggest differently. Consequently, those restauranteurs who promise to pay members of the public for any wild mushrooms they may gather on their Sunday walks may be guilty of incitement to commit theft, or handling once they have received them. Note too that the section only gives exemption to that which 'grows wild' and not to cultivated plants. It will be theft to pick a single cultivated flower, or piece of holly from a tree grown for commercial purposes, however 'wild' its position in a forest might seem.[270]

## Wild creatures: s 4(4)

2-81   At common law wild animals (*ferae naturae*, including fish, birds, insects and reptiles) were owned by no one, not even the landowner, and, therefore, could not be stolen. This was largely because of the impracticalities of establishing ownership of wild creatures, such as rabbits or birds, that repeatedly crossed and recrossed land boundaries. However, as soon as these creatures were killed, or tamed, they became the property of the owner of the land on which that event occurred. Therefore, although the killing or capture in itself is not theft, a subsequent appropriation by another would be.[271] It was thought that animals too young to roam freely across boundaries were the property of the owner of

---

268 But, it is an offence to pick, uproot or destroy certain wild plants under the Wildlife and Countryside Act (WCA) 1981.

269 Smith, JC, para 2-98.

270 Provided the requisite dishonesty is present.

271 In fact, most situations of appropriation of creatures on another's land were, and are, dealt with under the laws relating to poaching rather than theft; eg, poaching of deer and related offences are covered by the Deer Act 1991.

the land on which they were, until they were old enough to 'gain their natural liberty'.[272]

The situation is only slightly modified by s 4(4) of the TA 1968. A wild animal (or its carcass) cannot be stolen, unless it is (a) tamed or ordinarily kept in captivity, or (b) it has been reduced into the possession (or is in the course of being reduced into possession) and there is sufficient evidence that it has been so reduced. Thus, in *Howlett and Howlett*,[273] it was held that the mere act of raking over an existing natural mussel bed and occasionally moving some mussels from one place to another did not amount to the reduction into possession of the mussels. On the other hand, bees that return to a hive will have been reduced into possession and belong to the person who hives them.[274] They are thus capable of being stolen, provided that possession has not been 'lost or abandoned' by, for example, the bees swarming on land where their 'owner' cannot lawfully follow. A person who then destroyed them, or took them for himself, would not normally commit theft.

The TA 1968 refers to the animal being taken into possession by 'another person' and this need not necessarily be the owner of the land. For example, if P, a poacher, takes or is in the course of taking a rabbit on O's land, this is not an offence under the Act, but if D takes the rabbit from P, then this is theft from both P and O.[275]

Wild animals that have been tamed, or are ordinarily kept in captivity, are regarded as property and can be stolen. So if D takes a tiger from London Zoo, he has stolen it (assuming he has the requisite dishonesty and intention permanently to deprive). D may also commit theft if he appropriates a tiger that has escaped from the Zoo, as the tiger is an animal that is normally kept in captivity. Any wild animal which has been tamed as a pet may be stolen.

## The property stolen must be identified[276]

2-82    Having established what is included in the definition of property for the purposes of s 4, it is important to note that there must be some specific property belonging to another which is alleged to have been stolen.[277] That is, the property, or at least part of the specified property, must be identified in the

---

272  *Case of Swans* (1592) 7 Co Rep 15b, 77 ER 435; *Blades v Higgs* (1865) 1X HLC 621, 11 ER 1474; the taking of such animals or their eggs is now covered by statute, cf the WCA 1981.

273  [1968] Crim LR 222.

274  *Kearry v Pattinson* [1939] 1 KB 471.

275  Smith, JC, para 2-100. Note that this is an extension of the common law which demanded that reduction of the animal into possession be complete before the animal or carcass could be stolen; cf *Roe* (1870) 11 Cox 554.

276  The matter of ensuring that the indictment is framed correctly is discussed in more detail in Chapter 1.

277  See, again, *Navvabi* [1986] 1 WLR 1311, para 2-48, above.

indictment. It would be no good, for example, alleging that D stole money, when in fact he had stolen shoes. Furthermore, where D is charged with stealing several specific items, there may be a conviction for stealing some of them, even if theft of all of them is not proved;[278] the same principle applies if what is charged is theft of a whole and only theft of part of it is proved.[279] For example, if D is entitled to take £100 from his employer's desk, but actually takes £120, is he to be charged with theft of the entire £120, or simply with the balance of £20? According to *Tideswell*,[280] in principle, it would seem that D is only guilty of stealing £20 since that is the amount for which no ownership in property was intended to pass. However, it would not matter if D was charged with theft of the whole £120 – he could be convicted of theft as long as it was proven he had stolen part of it. The principle in *Tideswell* was applied in *Pilgrim v Rice-Smith*, where D, a shop assistant, sold corned beef to her friend at 83.5p below the proper price. D was charged with theft of the meat valued at 83.5p. The Divisional Court held that D's lack of authority thus to price and sell the meat at an undervalue meant that the whole sale was a nullity. Since no contract of sale had been entered into in respect of the meat, it would have been unobjectionable if D had been charged and convicted in respect of the whole of the meat, not just a part of it. However, this fact did not prevent a conviction for theft for simply part of the meat.[281]

## 5 BELONGING TO ANOTHER

**Section 5 of the TA 1968**

(1) Property shall be regarded as belonging to any person having possession or control of it, or having in it any proprietary right or interest (not being an equitable interest arising only from an agreement to transfer or grant an interest).

(2) Where property is subject to a trust, the persons to whom it belongs shall be regarded as including any person having a right to enforce the trust, and an intention to defeat the trust shall be regarded accordingly as an intention to deprive of the property any person having that right.

(3) Where a person receives property from or on account of another, and is under an obligation to the other to retain it and deal with that property or its proceeds in a particular way, the property or proceeds shall be regarded (as against him) as belonging to the other.

---

278 *Tomlin* [1954] 2 QB 274; *Machent v Quinn* [1970] 2 All ER 255.
279 See Smith, JC, para 2-110.
280 [1905] 2 KB 273 CCR.
281 Cf *contra dictum* in *Lacis v Cashmarts* [1969] 2 QB 400 (DC), decided before the TA 1968 came into force.

(4) Where a person gets property by another's mistake, and is under an obligation to make restoration (in whole or in part) of the property or its proceeds or of the value thereof, then to the extent of that obligation the property or proceeds shall be regarded (as against him) as belonging to the person entitled to restoration, and an intention not to make restoration shall be regarded accordingly as an intention to deprive that person of the property or proceeds.

(5) Property of a corporation sole shall be regarded as belonging to the corporation notwithstanding a vacancy in the corporation.

## Introduction

2-84    It is self evident that property must belong to another person in order for it to be stolen, and for the purposes of the TA 1968, property 'belongs' to any person who has any proprietary right or interest in it. If D sets out to steal O's umbrella, but on arriving home discovers that he has in fact picked up his own umbrella, he will not be guilty of theft, even though all the other ingredients of theft are present.[282] But, where D picks up a handbag belonging to V and runs away with it, we would have no difficulty in recognising it as theft because D has comprehensively assumed V's proprietary rights in the handbag. Such conduct would also have been larceny, as the old law of larceny was mainly concerned with punishing those who carried away goods that were in the possession of the owner. The TA 1968 goes much further because it recognises that there are many ways of assuming the rights of an owner, other than by simply taking his goods into possession. This area of theft is inevitably bound up with civil law principles as to when property will pass from one owner to another. The essence of theft is that the property must, at the time of the appropriation, 'belong to another' within the extended meaning of 'belonging to another' given by s 5.[283]

With the wide interpretation given to 'appropriation' by the decision in *Gomez*, considerations as to whether actual ownership has passed from the victim to the defendant are usually irrelevant: it is whether the property belonged to someone else at the moment of appropriation which is important. Consequently, in *Edwards v Ddin*,[284] where the defendant drove off without paying after a garage attendant had filled his car with petrol, the Court of Appeal quashed his conviction for theft because the appropriation only took place when he drove away from the garage; that is, after property in the petrol

---

282 Though there may be circumstances where he is guilty of attempted theft. See 'attempting the impossible', para 14-16, below.

283 See Viscount Dilhorne in *Lawrence v Metropolitan Police Comr* [1972] AC 626, p 632ff.

284 [1976] 1 WLR 942 (DC).

had passed to the defendant.[285] Similarly, in *Corcoran v Whent*,[286] where a meal had been consumed in a restaurant, there could be no theft *after* the meal had been consumed as the food no longer belonged to another for the purposes of s 5.[287]

2-85    The case of *Marshall*[288] involved a different scenario, where arguably the issue of whether the property belonged to another should have been considered. We have seen that the conviction in that case for theft of London Underground tickets was upheld on the basis that there was an intention permanently to deprive London Underground of the tickets. It is arguable that the issue of whether the property belonged to another should have been considered. The Court of Appeal did not specifically address the issue of whether the tickets ever belonged to another person, that is, London Underground. Their Lordships seem to have accepted, without question, the trial judge's ruling that '... although the tickets had passed into the possession and control of the customers, London Underground retained a proprietary right or interest in the tickets which were to be regarded therefore as the property of London Underground pursuant to s 5(1) of the Act'.

## Section 5(1) 'belonging to' includes possession or control

2-86    The law of theft gives protection from interference with the proprietary rights of another – but who has sufficient rights to be protected by the criminal law? The extended meaning given to 'belonging to another' in s 5(1) does not confine itself to ownership. It means that the Act protects 'another' who does not have a proprietary *right* or interest in the property, but who is merely in *possession* or *control*, such as a dry cleaner or a cobbler who has temporary possession of an owner's clothes or shoes. Section 5(1) allows property to be treated as belonging to X, even though technically it may be 'owned' by Y – it may 'belong' simultaneously to several persons for the purposes of theft.

Hence, the definition in s 5(1) is wide enough to include the possibility of theft from those who have a lesser interest in the property than outright ownership: it is possible to steal, not just from the owner, but also from a person who is in possession or control. This has the added advantage that there is no need to establish exactly who the legal owner is at the moment of appropriation.

---

285 Property in the petrol (ownership) passes to the customer as the petrol comes out of the petrol pump and into the tank of the customer's vehicle. That is so in the case both of a manned forecourt and of a self-service petrol station. Cf *McHugh* (1976) 64 Cr App R 92: in the case of a self-service station, the appropriation takes place as soon as D helps himself to the petrol. Provided there is a dishonest intent when he does so, such conduct amounts to theft. It is the very act of appropriation that causes property to pass to the customer. That is no bar to a successful charge of theft: *Lawrence* [1972] AC 626.

286 [1977] Crim LR 52 (DC).

287 This form of conduct may now be covered by the TA 1978, s 3.

288 See para 2-62 above.

Of course, more often than not a person who owns property will also be in possession of it, but the following example may help to illustrate the wide ambit of the section. If student A buys a car, he owns it absolutely; but he may then decide to lend it to student B; student A still owns the car, but he has relinquished possession of it to B; B then drives the car to visit his friend C and parks it overnight in C's garage, thus relinquishing control of the car to C, although B will usually be treated as having retained possession of it. If student D comes along and steals the car from C's garage, he has stolen the car from C who has 'control' of it at time of the dishonest appropriation.[289] But the section goes even further: consider what would be the position if it had been, not D, but A who had turned up and, seeing the car in C's garage, decided to drive it away without telling either C or D. Has A committed theft? It seems absurd to suggest that he could be guilty of stealing his own car, as this would imply that it is possible for a 'true' owner to be a thief, simply by removing his own property from someone to whom he had lent it. Yet that is the conclusion reached by the Court of Appeal in *Turner (No 2)*.[290]

## *Theft by the owner*

2-87   In *Turner (No 2)*, the Court of Appeal affirmed Mr Turner's conviction for theft after he had taken his own car back (without paying and without permission) from a garage which had parked it in the street once repairs had been completed: he had apparently deprived the garage of its possessory right to the car – even though Mr Turner obviously had a better right as the true owner. Unbeknown to the garage, Mr Turner had a spare set of keys to the car and there is no doubt that he dishonestly intended to avoid paying for the repairs. There is also no doubt that, as unpaid repairers, the garage had a lien over the car which they could have enforced to prevent return of the car until the bill was paid, and the decision could be understood on this basis. However, because of the way the matter had been dealt with in the court below, the Court of Appeal disregarded the existence of the lien and came to a decision which was expressly not based on it. If there was no lien, then it was argued that the garage had merely a bailment at will which Mr Turner was free to terminate at any time and which, by implication, gave the garage no possessory right against the wishes of the bailor. However, Lord Parker LJ, delivering the judgment of the court, stated that the words 'possession or control' were not to be qualified in any way: it is enough that the person from whom the property is appropriated, was at the time *in fact* in possession.

Admittedly, the Court of Appeal rather had its hands bound by the fact that the trial judge had instructed the jury not to concern themselves with whether there was a lien, but even so, the decision results in rather an unsatisfactory

---

289 He has also stolen it from A and B.
290 [1971] 1 WLR 901.

position for bailors. Can it really be that a bailee can enforce his position against the wishes of a bailor? Can a person who lends another a book really run the risk of a conviction for theft, if he takes it back again without telling the lendee? He would be entitled to demand its return in civil law, and the bailee would be powerless to stop him. So long as a bailee remains in possession, he does have a proprietary right or interest against third parties, but it is surely rather odd to think that he has it against the bailor himself. Presumably, it follows that a thief can steal property which has been stolen already and is in the possession of another thief. Rather than dismissing the decision as absurd,[291] Professor JC Smith poses a probable explanation that a bailor has no right, even in civil law, to take back the chattel bailed, without notice to the bailee at will[292] – and herein lies the key. The decision serves to illustrate once again the importance of dishonesty: no bailor, perhaps a lender, will be guilty of theft unless it can be shown that his removal of the property was done dishonestly.[293]

The decision in *Turner (No 2)* can be contrasted with *Meredith*,[294] where the defendant secretly removed his car from a police pound, it having been placed there after being towed away from where it was causing an obstruction. He did not pay the required payment for its release and removed the police 'Krooklok' from the steering wheel before driving the car away. Judge Da Cunha allowed his submission that he had no case to answer on a charge of theft of the car. The police had no right to retain the car against that right of the owner to remove it. The decision is hard to reconcile with *Turner (No 2)*, but seems a more feasible response.

It may be that the extended meaning of s 5(1) denotes that it will often be a question of deciding who has the better title to the property in order to ascertain whether it belongs to another. If only *Turner (No 2)* had been decided on the issue of a lien, it would have been a more acceptable decision, but if the lien issue is disregarded there really seems little to choose between the two cases. If no lien existed, then the car belonged to Mr Turner absolutely – as Mr Meredith's did to him – and if the essence of theft is interference with the property rights of another person, then he did not commit theft: the car was his to take when he wished.

## *Theft of things on the land*

2-88 There is no necessity for a person who is in 'control' of the property to be aware of the fact. In general, a householder or an owner of land will be in 'control' of any property in his house, or on his land, and he may frequently be unaware

---

291 See Smith, ATH, para 4-43.
292 Smith, JC, para 2-58.
293 See para 2-10 above.
294 [1973] Crim LR 253.

that the property is there. It was enough in *Woodman*,[295] that, where a person had control of a site (demonstrated by the fact he had excluded others from it), it followed that he was also *prima facie* in control of any articles on that site. It made no difference that he was ignorant that those articles were present.

## Any proprietary right or interest

### *Partners and co-owners*

2-89    The clearest example of a proprietary interest is that of ownership. But it is possible that more than one person may have a proprietary right or interest in the same property; for example, where property is co-owned, or where it is property belonging to a partnership. It is easy to envisage a situation where an errant part-owner or a partner appropriates such property from his unsuspecting fellow owners. The wording of s 5(1) is wide enough to mean that a partner who deprives another partner of his share in the property has appropriated property 'belonging to another' and can be guilty of theft, provided he is dishonest and intends permanently to deprive. Accordingly, a partner who dishonestly sells co-owned property without the other's consent will be guilty of theft.[296] However, this seems more logical than the decision in *Turner (No 2)*, because the person who is deprived of his rights in the property is also a part-owner, or in partnership and therefore thief and victim originally had the same rights in the property.

By the same token, s 5 is also of relevance to company assets. A company is regarded as a separate legal entity, quite separate from those who are in control of it. Consequently, its property 'belongs to another', that is the company itself, and can be stolen by those in sole control of the company, assuming that the requisite *mens rea* is present. The argument that such persons cannot be guilty of theft from the company because that would effectively mean that they had stolen their own property, was rejected.[297]

### *Secret profits and equitable proprietary interests*

2-90    Section 5(1) specifically excludes from the meaning of property 'an equitable interest arising only from an agreement to transfer or grant an interest'. This means that the law of theft does not protect certain types of equitable interest. For example, where P has contracted to buy land or shares, he holds an

---

295 [1974] QB 754.
296 *Bonner* [1970] 1 WLR 838 (and para 2-51, above).
297 *AG Ref (No 2 of 1982)* [1984] QB 624; *Phillipou* (1989) 89 Cr App R 290; for more on the subject of company theft see Elliot, DW, 'Directors' theft and dishonesty' [1991] Crim LR 732, and the reply, Sullivan, GR [1991] Crim LR 732. See, also, para 2-51 above.

equitable interest in that property before the transfer is concluded. If, in the meantime, the transferor sells the property to a third party, he will not be guilty of theft because P's equitable right arises solely out of 'an agreement to transfer' and is not regarded as property 'belonging to another'.

In general, however, if a trustee dishonestly appropriates trust property he will be guilty of theft from the beneficiaries who are the persons having an equitable proprietary right in the property, such property being regarded as 'belonging to another'. Problems can arise for the criminal law when the civil law is prepared to impose a constructive trust and thus create a proprietary interest in property which will then come within the ambit of s 5(1). A constructive trust is one imposed by the principles of equity in order to satisfy the demands of justice and good conscience without reference to any presumed intention of the parties. So for example, if D has acquired by fraud P's property and then seeks to retain it, it may be said that he holds it on trust for P and P retains an equitable interest in it. If D refuses to return the property, he may be guilty of theft. A constructive trust can also arise where a person in a fiduciary position derives a profit from the unauthorised use of trust property.

2-91 In *AG Ref (No 1 of 1985)*,[298] the manager of a tied public house was employed by the brewers to sell only goods which were supplied by them. He obtained beer from a different wholesaler and was caught selling it to the customers with the intention of making a secret profit for himself. The Court of Appeal upheld his acquittal for theft of the sums of money he had secretly made. It was not money 'belonging to another': even if (as was supposed) the manager was doubtless under a contractual obligation to account for the profit from the sale of the beer to his employer, the brewers had never had any proprietary interest in this money. No constructive trust had been formed, as the manager did not hold the proceeds of sale on trust for his employer, but on his own account. In any case, Lord Lane CJ said that the whole concept of theft by importing the equitable doctrine of constructive trust is so abstruse and so far removed from ordinary people's understanding of what constitutes stealing, that it should not amount to it. Furthermore, the brewers would not have been able to sue the customers for the price of the beer because the customers did not hand over the money with the specific purpose of it going to the employer – they handed it over in contractual exchange for the beer that they had in fact received.

Similarly, it has been held in *Powell v Macrea*[299] that a bribe received by an employee does not 'belong to' his employer either. Here the employee, a turnstile operator, had taken bribes in order to allow spectators to get into Wembley stadium without a ticket. It was held that he had no fiduciary relationship with his employer who consequently had no proprietary right in the money. Therefore, retention of the bribe, which was given to *him*, could not

---

298 [1986] QB 491.
299 [1997] Crim LR 571.

be theft from his employer because it was not property belonging to another within the meaning of s 5(1).

Both these decisions are based on the long established decision in *Lister v Stubbs*,[300] that liability to account for profits secretly made, creates a relationship of 'debtor' and 'creditor', not one by which the 'debtor' holds that money on trust for another. The Court of Appeal regarded the duty to account for a bribe to be personal not proprietary. However, it may be that the ambit of the criminal law of theft has been extended by recent developments in the civil law in regard to constructive trusts.[301] It is hard to see how either of these cases will stand in the face of the civil case of *AG for Hong Kong v Reid*.[302] Disapproving *Lister v Stubbs*, the Privy Council ruled that where a person in a fiduciary position receives a bribe or commission, he holds the bribe (and its proceeds) on constructive trust and not solely as a debtor for the amount of the bribe. A person who used his employer's property for his own purposes would now be regarded as a trustee of that property and, consequently, be guilty of theft if he stole it. It might be that the decision in *Powell v Macrea* is no longer correct. If so, doubt, too, must be cast on *AG Ref (No 1 of 1985)*. However, it is arguable that the pub manager in *AG Ref (No 1 of 1985)* would still not be guilty of theft, as he was not using his employer's property to make a profit, but his own. Accordingly even if a constructive trust was imposed, it would not come into existence until the money was identifiable as a separate fund and that was not the case here.

2-92    If the criminal law is to protect recognised principles of property rights, then it seems logical that it must follow the decision of the civil courts as to what those principles are – or else be content to adopt different paradigms. But the circumstances in which a constructive trust will be imposed involve complex (and some would say unresolved) issues of civil law which, once again, may bring about conflict with the criminal law. In his dissenting judgment in *Hinks*,[303] Lord Hobhouse sees no difficulty in the criminal law following civil law concepts:

> Section 5 and, particularly s 5(4) demonstrate that the TA 1968 has been drafted so as to take account of and require reference to the civil law of property, contract and restitution. The same applies to many other sections of the Act. For example, s 6 is drafted by reference to 'regardless of the other's rights' – that is to say rights under the civil law. Section 28, dealing with the restoration of stolen goods, clearly can only work if the law of theft recognises and respects transfers of

---

300 [1890] 45 Ch 1.
301 The possibility that property may 'belong to another' because a person has retained an equitable proprietary interest in it has already been recognised by the criminal law in respect of a person receiving property by mistake in *Shadrokh-Cigari* [1988] Crim LR 465 applying the civil law principle in *Chase Manhattan Bank NA v Israel-British Bank Ltd* [1981] Ch 105. See para 2-112 below.
302 [1994] 1 AC 324.
303 See para 2-42 above.

property valid under the civil law, otherwise it would be giving the criminal courts the power to deprive citizens of their property otherwise than in accordance with the law.

Be that as it may, as Professor Smith has noted, if the decision in *AG for Hong Kong v Reid* is followed, it would be 'an odd situation when an extension to the criminal law which Parliament has declined to make is made ... by the decision of a civil court; but that court cannot be criticised for stating what it believes the civil law to be'.[304]

On the other hand, *AG for Hong Kong v Reid* is a Privy Council decision and unless and until adopted by the English courts it remains only of persuasive authority. Nevertheless, the status of *Lister v Stubbs* remains in doubt.

## The problem of *Preddy*

2-93     We have already seen that there is an appropriation of property when D acquires part or the whole of V's bank balance, the property being V's right to draw on the account.[305] However, the effect of the House of Lords' decision in *Preddy*[306] is that, when the transaction is effected by electronic transfer, D may have appropriated property but apparently he does not *obtain* any property which *belongs to another*. This is because, when D's account was credited, he did not obtain V's thing in action (V's right to sue his bank for the relevant amount), but a completely new thing in action created especially for him, giving D the right to sue his own bank for the relevant amount. Therefore, the property D obtains for himself did not 'belonging to another'. *Preddy* concerned an appeal against a conviction for s 15 of the TA 1968, obtaining property by deception, but the requirement that property 'belongs to another' is the same for the offence of theft.[307]

2-94     However, two recent decisions of the Court of Appeal may have the effect that a charge of theft might resolve the lacuna in the law left as a result of *Preddy*. In *Burke*,[308] the defendant presented a forged cheque at the bank and some days later tried to make a cash withdrawal of funds derived from that cheque. The Court of Appeal quashed his conviction for attempting to obtain property by deception on the basis of *Preddy*, but they saw no reason why they could not substitute a conviction for attempted theft of a thing in action, namely the victim's bank account. The issue was explored further in *Williams (Roy)*,[309] where, on similar facts, the appellant argued that, in the light of *Preddy*, he could

---

304  Smith, JC, '*Lister v Stubbs* and the criminal law' (1994) 110 LQR 180, p 184.
305  *Kohn* (1979) 69 Cr App R 395 (see para 2-48 above).
306  [1996] AC 815.
307  For further discussion of *Preddy* [1996] AC 815 and the TA 1968, s 15, see paras 8-29–8-31.
308  [2000] Crim LR 413.
309  For the facts, see para 2-63 above.

not be said to have appropriated property belonging to another. In dismissing his appeal against a conviction for theft, the court was at pains to point out that *Preddy* concerned the offence of obtaining property by deception and occurred in circumstances where it was difficult to discover any property in existence at the time of the obtaining. Theft, on the other hand, required an appropriation not an obtaining. The court was of the opinion that *Preddy* had not changed the basic principle in *Kohn*: the act of reducing the credit balance on a victim's account amounted to an appropriation within the meaning of s 1 of the TA 1968.[310] A defendant clearly appropriated the balance of another by presenting a cheque from the other person, which was then honoured. Therefore, Williams had appropriated (though he had not obtained) property belonging to another and the principle in *Preddy* did not apply on a charge of theft.[311]

## Abandoned property

2-95    It follows from all that has been said before that, if property does not belong to anyone, it cannot be stolen. Thus if D finds a diamond necklace which has been truly abandoned by its owner, he cannot be guilty of theft from that owner when later he decides to keep it. The question thus becomes: when is property truly abandoned?

The answer seems to be: only when the true owner has given up all rights to the property, when he has no further use for it. But it is not quite so straightforward as it sounds because property usually remains in the possession of somebody and we have already seen that a thief can steal, not only from the true owner, but also from a third person who may be in possession or control. Thus, in general, the courts have been reluctant to find that the property is abandoned rather than merely lost and a person who loses property does not necessarily abandon it just because he has given up all hope of finding it. In *Hibbert v McKiernan*,[312] the defendant was in the habit of trespassing on a golf course in order to pick up golf balls which had been 'lost' by the players. The Divisional Court held that he could be convicted of larceny from the golf club itself. It may be that the original owners had never given up their claims to the balls – but, in any case, presumably the club had a better possessory right to the balls than did a trespasser or, were at least 'in control' of them at the time they were appropriated.

---

310 *Graham, Ali and Others* [1997] Crim LR 341, applying *Preddy* [1996] AC 815, endorsed the principle that 'theft of a chose in action may be committed when a chose in action belonging to another person was destroyed by the defendant's act of appropriation as defined in s 3(1) of the Act'.

311 Cf treatment of the tickets in *Marshall* [1998] 2 Cr App R 282 and see para 8-29 for comparison of this point in *Preddy* [1996] AC 815.

312 [1948] 2 KB 142.

Simply throwing away the property does not necessarily mean that all interest in the property has been abandoned. Where O puts his rubbish out to be collected by the Local Authority refuse collectors, the rubbish is not abandoned but remains in possession of O until it has been collected, when it then becomes the property of the local authority. Refuse collectors (or anyone else for that matter) who take items from the bins have, therefore, stolen property 'belonging to another'.[313] In that scenario, the property has either been picked up and is in the possession of the local authority, in which case the refuse collector has stolen the property from the local authority, or it remains in the possession of the householder, in which case they have stolen from him. This is because, even where the owner has to all intents and purposes disposed of property, he might still be exercising control over it by excluding others from it. So, in *Edwards*,[314] the defendant stole three pigs which the owner had buried underground because they were diseased: it was the owner's right to bury them and he was exercising his right as owner to keep them buried, they were not abandoned property.

There is, thus, no blanket immunity from a charge of theft by invoking the popular maxim 'finders keepers'. However, a *bona fide* belief that the property has been abandoned, may well mean that the finder is not dishonest;[315] for the finder may well fall within one of the limbs of s 2(1), whereby a person is not dishonest if he has a belief that he has in law the right to take the property, or if he believes that the owner cannot be found. Such a claim was not available to the defendant in *Hibbert v McKiernan*, because he knew that the golf club had informed the police to be on the lookout for trespassers collecting balls, thus demonstrating their disapproval of the practice.

### Treasure trove

2-96 Treasure trove is a particular type of lost property deemed to belong to the Crown. It originally meant 'when any gold or silver, in coin, plate, or bullyon hath been of ancient time hidden, wheresoever it be found, whereof no person can prove any property, it doth belong to the king, or to some lord or other by the king's grant, or prescription'. The object had to be composed of a substantial amount of gold or silver to amount to treasure trove, and it also had to be demonstrated that the original owner (long since dead and unknown) had had every intention of recovering his property at some time in the future – in other words it was not truly abandoned but an *animus revertendi* must have existed. If such treasure trove was found, property reverted to the Crown if successors to title could not be found; it did not lie with the 'finder'. However, if the original owner deliberately abandoned the property, or had accidentally lost it, it was

---

313 *William v Phillips* (1957) 41 Cr App R 5 (DC).
314 (1877) 12 Cox CC 384; cf *Woodman* [1974] QB 754 (above).
315 *White* (1912) 7 Cr App R 266.

not regarded as treasure trove. Single items found were usually deemed to be lost and abandoned by their original owner and hence became the property of those who found them rather than the Crown, and a charge of theft avoided.[316]

It is hard to say why long lost items of gold and silver have been left in a particular place. Were they lost, abandoned or stored away with the hope of recovery? The invention of electronic metal detectors has made it easier for members of the public to 'find' such items and, in most cases, it is almost impossible for a jury to establish that the items had been deposited with an *animus revertendi*. The Treasure Act 1996 abolishes the old law of treasure trove and replaces it with statutory provisions for the protection of treasure. The Act aims to give greater protection to items of antiquity by defining treasure in rather wider terms. Treasure is now defined as any object which is at least 300 years old when found and, if not a coin, has a metallic content of which at least 10% by weight is silver or gold.[317] Amongst other provisions, objects found as part of the same find are to be regarded as part of the same haul of treasure; for example, the pot in which the coins are found – thus preserving archaeologically associated remains. Ownership of treasure will still vest in the Crown, subject to the rights of the original owner, or his successors, but applies regardless of where the treasure is left, or in what circumstances; thus, the problem of establishing *animus revertendi* is dispensed with.

It may be, of course, that the article found, ancient though it is, is declared not to be treasure, in which case the question arises as to who may keep it? The 'finder' who is in possession, or the owner of the land who may have a proprietary interest in the property? In *Waverley BC v Fletcher*,[318] Mr Fletcher using a metal detector, found a medieval gold brooch buried nine inches below the surface of a public park owned by the Council. It was declared not to be treasure trove, so the Crown had no proprietary right in the brooch and it was returned to him. However, the Court of Appeal, applying the principle that an owner, or lawful possessor, of land owns all that was in or attached to it, upheld the Council's claim that they had a better right to the brooch than Mr Fletcher who was a mere 'finder' and had become a trespasser by digging up the brooch. This is a civil case, but clearly has implications for the law of theft, as it implies D can be guilty of theft from the landowner if, for example, he digs up and keeps items he finds buried in a field while out for a picnic.

---

316 As well as, perhaps, a national treasure lost to a private collector? See *Hancock* [1990] 2 QB 242, where a conviction for theft failed because the Crown had no proprietary right in the property *before* it was declared treasure trove.

317 Treasure Act 1996, ss 1 and 3(3).

318 [1996] QB 334. The case was decided before the Treasure Act 1996 came into force, but would still be of relevance in determining whether property which is 'found' on another's land 'belongs to another'.

### *Where the owner is unknown*

2-97    It is not necessary to call (as a witness) the owner of the property alleged to have been stolen; circumstantial evidence that the property is stolen is sufficient.[319]

## Trust property: s 5(2)

2-98    Most cases of theft from a trust by a trustee will be covered by s 5(1), because any beneficiary under a trust will have an equitable interest, which is a proprietary interest within that section. However, where a trust does not have identifiable beneficiaries, for example, beneficiaries under a charitable trust, s 5(2) ensures that any property appropriated by the trustees will still be regarded as 'belonging to another', that is, any person who has a right to enforce the trust. In the case of a charitable trust, it will be the Attorney General.

## An obligation to retain and deal with property or proceeds as property belonging to another: s 5(3)

2-99    By this sub-section, the criminal law deems that property 'belongs to another' when in fact, in civil law, legal ownership may have passed to someone else. Section 5(3) deals with situations where D receives property from (or on account of) P and gains, not only possession and control of the property, but also ownership of it (although, it also covers situations where legal ownership remains with P and only possession passes to D).[320] In some circumstances, it may be that D holds that property on trust for P, so that P retains an equitable interest in the property, in which case there may be overlap between s 5(1) and (3). But it will be easier to invoke s 5(3), as it operates in a less complex way, dispensing with the need to establish that P did, in fact, retain an equitable interest. The sub-section would apply where D receives property from P and, although he becomes the legal owner of the property, P has attached particular conditions as to how he is to use it, which D is under an obligation to fulfil. If D fails to use the property in the particular way that P has specified, then he may be guilty of theft, even though technically he is the legal owner – the property 'belongs to another'. A classic example would be where P, a householder, gives D, a builder, £100 to buy some building materials in order to repair P's house. D becomes the legal owner of the £100, but is under an obligation to P to spend the money on the required materials. If he uses the money to buy presents for his wife, then he is guilty of theft. If he uses the money to buy building materials, but then uses them to repair his own or someone else's house, he is guilty of

---

319 *Burton* (1854) Dears 282; *Fuschillo* [1940] 2 All ER 489; *Sbarra* (1919) 13 Cr App R 118.
320 *Arnold* [1997] 4 All ER 1.

theft. He is only the legal owner of that money as long as he is using it in the particular way that P requires. On the other hand, if P gives D £100 on account towards paying the final bill, D not only becomes the legal owner of that money but is free to put it towards whatever purpose he desires: s 5(3) will not apply in that situation.[321]

The sub-section is wide enough to include the 'proceeds' of the property given him by P. Thus, if our householder had given the builder a cheque for the materials, then he would be under an obligation to use the proceeds of that cheque, once cashed, in the particular way specified. Similarly, if P gives D a painting to sell for him, D becomes the legal owner of the painting, but is under an obligation to sell it and retain the proceeds, that is the money, to return to P. Potentially, s 5(3) places a heavy obligation on D, so its parameters are limited by certain requirements: the obligation must be a legal one and not merely a social or moral one; D must be aware that he is under an obligation to deal with the property (or its proceeds) in a particular way; and he must receive the property from (or on account of) the person to whom the obligation is owed.

### There must be a legal obligation

2-100　One of the difficulties with this sub-section is that it is not always easy to ascertain whether D is under an obligation 'to retain and deal with that property or proceeds in a particular way', or if he is free to do whatever he likes with the property. However, it is settled that the 'obligation' must be a legal one; that is legal at civil law.[322] It is insufficient for the obligation to be merely a social or moral one. Whether there is a legal obligation, is a question of law for the judge to decide. However, as a legal obligation will only arise in certain circumstances and in many cases, the circumstances cannot be known until the facts have been established, it is for the jury, not the judge, to establish those facts where they are in dispute. The functions of the judge and jury were described in *Mainwaring and Madders*:[323]

> Whether or not an obligation arises is a matter of law, because an obligation must be a legal obligation. But a legal obligation arises only in certain circumstances, and in many cases the circumstances cannot be known until the facts have been established. It is for the jury, not the judge, to establish the facts, if they are in dispute.

> What, in our judgment, a judge ought to do is this: if the facts relied upon by the prosecution are in dispute he should direct the jury to make their findings on the facts, and then say to them: 'If you find the facts to be such and such, then I direct you as a matter of law that a legal obligation arose to which s 5(3) applies.

---

321 If he had *never intended* to do the building work for P he may be guilty of theft, or under s 15, obtaining property by deception.

322 *Gilks* (1972) 56 Cr App R 734; *Klineberg and Marsden* [1999] 1 Cr App R 427; *Floyd v DPP* [2000] Crim LR 411.

323 (1982) 74 Cr App R 99, p 107, *per* Lawton LJ, approved in *Dubar* [1994] 1 WLR 1484.

Thus, in *Breaks and Huggan*,[324] the judge was held to be in error when he told the jury that the purpose of s 5(3) was to avoid provisions of the civil law.

### The property must be received for a particular purpose

2-101 Section s 5(3) does not usually apply in situations where a simple remedy for breach of contract would suffice. For example, where D merely fails to repay a debt. The relationship between the parties would then be one of creditor and debtor, rather than based on a legal obligation to use the property in a particular way. This can lead to some seemingly bizarre, or at least arbitrary results. For example, in *Hall*,[325] the defendant was a travel agent who took deposits and payments for holidays from clients, which he then paid into the general office account. Unfortunately, his business collapsed before he had paid for the holidays and he was unable to repay the deposits. In allowing his appeal against conviction for theft, the Court of Appeal had to consider whether this was a situation in which s 5(3) should apply, that is, was he under a legal obligation to retain the clients' money for the particular purpose of booking the holidays. They decided he was not. The money had not been held for a particular purpose, it was part of the general trading account and, whereas he might have been in breach of contract, he was not under a legal obligation to repay the unidentified sum; the monies were merely an advance payment, no special arrangements had been made.

It was an important part of the decision in *Hall* that the monies had not been held in a separate account. By comparison with *Hall*, the defendant in *McHugh*[326] was under an obligation to retain the investment money from his clients in a particular way. The court said that s 5(3) only applies (in the absence of a written agreement) if both parties clearly understood that the investment or its proceeds was to be kept in a separate account and not mixed with D's own money, or that of his business. Whether a legal obligation exists will depend on the facts of each case, but the crux of the matter is whether there is evidence that both parties clearly understood the exact nature of the transaction: it must be clear (either expressly or implicitly) that the defendant and the client understood that the client's money was to be kept separate and retained for a particular purpose. That is why the Divisional Court upheld a conviction for theft in *Davidge v Bunnett*,[327] in which a group of people sharing a flat appointed one of their number to collect sufficient cash and cheques from them all to pay their joint gas bill. In fact, the defendant spent it on her Christmas shopping. Despite

---

324 [1998] Crim LR 349.

325 [1973] QB 126.

326 (1993) 97 Cr App R 335; cf *Re Kumar* [2000] Crim LR 504, where the travel agent was under 'an agreed trustee relationship' to use his clients' monies in a particular way and was therefore guilty of theft.

327 [1984] Crim LR 297; cf *Cullen* (1974) unreported, No 968/c/74 and *op cit*, Smith and Hogan, fn 197, p 591.

the fact that domestic arrangements do not usually give rise to legal relationships, there was a clear understanding between the defendant and her flatmates that the monies received were to be kept for a particular purpose. The understanding existed, even though there was never an expectation that she would use any of the actual banknotes received to pay the gas bill.

2-102    The defendant must know of the obligation that he is under, but it is not necessary that he *understands* that an obligation exists, simply that he must appreciate the necessary facts which (as a matter of law) amount to an obligation. Proof that the property was not dealt with in conformity with the obligation is not sufficient in itself. Neither can that knowledge be imputed to him by his agents, even though that would be possible in civil law.[328]

The obligation must also be an obligation owed to the person from whom the property is alleged to have been stolen. In *Huskinson*,[329] the defendant applied for housing benefit from the housing services department in order to pay his rent. When the cheque arrived, he paid only a small amount to his landlord and kept the rest for himself. It was held that he was not guilty of theft as there was nothing in the statutory regulations governing housing benefit to say that the defendant was under any legal obligation to the housing department to pass on the benefit to the landlord. Whereas he might have been under an obligation to the landlord to pay his rent, it was not necessarily to be paid out of the benefit he had received.

### Where D receives 'on account of another'

2-103    Section 5(3) also covers situations where D receives money 'on account of another'; in other words, he receives money from P which is 'in transit' to be given to B, typically where D collects rents from P on property owned by B, in order to give them to B. As in *Hall*, the key is often whether, when D received the money, he was under an obligation to maintain a separate client account for it. If so, he will be guilty of theft when, for example, he spends it on a holiday for himself. On the other hand, if he is under no such obligation and merely pays the rents into a general fund – perhaps he is a rent collector for several Ps – it is hard to see that he will be guilty of theft if he absconds with the money. He will merely be a debtor for the sum of money owed to B. However, matters are not always so simple. A similar transaction, but involving funds collected for a charity, arose in *Lewis v Lethbridge* and the case illustrates the difficulties inherent in such an approach. The defendant collected sponsorship money for his friend who was running the London marathon. The money was to be paid to a certain charity, that is, it was collected 'on account', but he never paid it over. It was held that there was no legal obligation on D to account for the money, or its

---

328 *Wills* (1990) 92 Cr App R 297.
329 [1988] Crim LR 620.

proceeds: the defendant was merely a debtor, rather than a thief. In *Wain*,[330] on similar facts, the Court of Appeal disapproved the narrow basis on which *Lewis v Lethbridge* had been decided, referring to criticism of that case made by Professor Smith in *The Law of Theft* (6th edn) where he stated that it is hard to imagine that the sponsors would be indifferent as to whether the money was paid over to the charity or not: 'Is there not an overwhelming inference (or at least, evidence on which a jury might find) that the sponsors intend to give the money to the charity, imposing an obligation in the nature of a trust on the collector?' Consequently, the modern approach is that, when D collects money for charity, he is under an obligation to the sponsors in respect of the money, or its proceeds, because it is the sponsors' intention to give that money to the charity. In these circumstances, the obligation is sufficient to impose a trust so that the money is to be regarded as belonging to the beneficiaries, that is the charity. D will be guilty of theft if he appropriates the funds for his own use. Furthermore, McCowan LJ was at pains to stress: 'Whether a person in the position of the appellant is a trustee is to be judged on an objective basis. It is an obligation imposed on him by law. It is not essential that he should have realised that he is a trustee ...'[331]

The approach in *Wain* is to be welcomed and we have seen that, if the Privy Council decision in *AG for Hong Kong v Reid* is widely adopted, many hitherto cases where s 5(3) did not apply, will now come within its ambit by virtue of the imposition of a constructive trust.[332] A person receiving property on account will, generally be a fiduciary (having legal title to the property) and capable of stealing it from the equitable owner. It is then at least arguable that the property may 'belong to another' by virtue of s 5(1) without the necessity of recourse to s 5(3). However, the overriding principle is that, as long as the property does 'belong to another' at the time of the appropriation, a theft conviction is possible and it does not seem to matter whether the property 'belongs to another' under s 5(1) or (3). Either way, it may be possible to establish that the person to whom the obligation is owed, that is either the person from whom D receives the property or the person on whose account he receives it, retains an equitable interest in the property or its proceeds.[333] That is not to say that a person to whom an obligation is owed always retains either an equitable or legal interest in the property, although he may do so more often than not.[334]

---

330 [1995] 2 Cr App R 660.

331 *Ibid*, p 666.

332 Despite Lord Lane's disapproval in *AG Ref (No 1 of 1985)* [1986] QB 491 that a lay person's understanding of the criminal law should not be confused by complex civil principles; see para 2-91, above.

333 Cf *Hallam* [1995] Crim LR 323.

334 The Court of Appeal in *Klineberg and Marsden* [1999] 1 Cr App R 427 (below) was critical of earlier statements to the contrary in *op cit*, Smith and Hogan, fn 197, 8th edn, p 538 which was conceded in later editions; but see, now, *Floyd* [2000] Crim LR 411 and 'Commentary'.

### No need for another to have an equitable interest

2-104 In *Klineberg and Marsden*,[335] the Court of Appeal found s 5(3) a useful tool to avoid any potential problems arising from the decision in *Preddy*.[336] The appellants were involved in a timeshare fraud whereby intending purchasers of timeshares in Lanzarote entered into a complex agreement whereby they paid money to a company, PCL, which was run by the appellants, and would eventually receive their timeshare properties. The money was paid to the appellants in the expectation that it would be transmitted to stakeholders to protect the purchasers until their properties were ready for occupation. Needless to say, only a fraction of the money was ever paid to the stakeholders and the purchasers never acquired any timeshares. The appellants contended, *inter alia*, that they had not, according to the House of Lords in *Preddy*, stolen property 'belonging to another'. This was because, once the timeshare purchasers paid monies to PCL, by whatever means, which were then paid into PCL's bank account, such monies ceased to be property belonging to the purchasers and were replaced by a thing in action in the form of a credit balance belonging to PCL. This was a 'new' credit balance that had never belonged to anyone else. However, this argument was rejected and the appellants' convictions for theft upheld (in part) by the Court of Appeal because the prosecution were entitled to rely on s 5(3). There was an established obligation on the appellants to retain and deal with the purchaser's 'property or its proceeds' in a particular way and they had breached that obligation. Both parties understood that the clients were handing over money on the clear understanding (evidenced by documents and oral representations by the defendants) that the money would be held in independent trusteeship until their timeshare apartments were ready.[337] Speaking on behalf of the court, Maurice Kay J stated:

> Section 5(3) ... is essentially a deeming provision by which property or its proceeds 'shall be regarded' as belonging to another, even though, on a strict civil law analysis, it does not. Moreover, it applies not only to property in its original form but also to 'its proceeds' ... Where, as in the present case, people are induced to contract or do contract (by virtue of implied terms or otherwise) on the basis that their money will be safeguarded by trusteeship, there is clearly an obligation within the meaning of s 5(3).[338]

Interestingly, the Court of Appeal made no distinction between the money which was paid by cash, cheque or bank transfer: the increased credit was new property but it was the proceeds of property held on trust for the beneficiaries. I

---

335 [1999] 1 Cr App R 427.

336 [1996] AC 815; for further discussion of *Preddy* [1996] AC 815 and the TA 1968, s 15, see paras 8-29–8-31.

337 Note, that the essence of the charge was not that the defendants had committed a crime when they received the money, but what they did with it subsequently.

338 [1999] 1 Cr App R 427, pp 432, 434.

has been argued[339] that s 5(3) should only be applicable to those clients who paid in cash or by cheque, but not to those who paid by electronic bank transfer. In that situation, s 5(3) should not apply because the appellants had not 'received' either property or proceeds. Accordingly, D can only be guilty of theft if the person whose bank account has been debited retains an equitable interest – in which case s 5(1) is sufficient and there is no need to rely on s 5(3). Of course, just what the particular circumstances are that might give rise to a constructive trust will depend on individual facts and involve difficult questions of civil law.

Nevertheless, it may be that the decision in *Klineberg and Marsden* has led to a new approach and is to be applauded as a valiant attempt to overcome any potential difficulties that *Preddy* may present for the law of theft by relying on s 5(3). It will always be easier to invoke s 5(3) rather than s 5(1) because there is no need to prove that anyone else has an equitable interest in the property, merely that he must deal with it or its proceeds in a particular way.

### *Where it is impossible to perform the obligation*

2-105    Although there must be a legal obligation (at the time D dishonestly appropriates the property or proceeds), it is settled that this does not have to be legally enforceable in civil law at the time the appropriation occurs. After all, it may have become impossible to perform the obligation for reasons of illegality or public policy; such excuses will be irrelevant. In *Meech*,[340] the person to whom the obligation was owed would not have been able to enforce performance of the obligation due to his own fraud (he had acquired the property illegally in the first place), but the defendant was still convicted of theft when he failed to fulfil his obligation to the fraudulent obligee. It is uncertain from the decision whether the outcome would have been the same if the defendant had been aware of the fraud at the time he accepted the obligation.

## Property got by another's mistake may be property belonging to another: s 5(4)

2-106    Like s 5(3), this sub-section is really a 'top up' provision to be used when s 5(1) is inappropriate. It extends the meaning of 'belonging to another' to situations where ownership passes to the defendant as a result of another's mistake. The section uses the words 'gets property' and so the possible means of acquisition are very wide,[341] but that is not enough to come within the section: the defendant must also be under a legal obligation to restore either the property or its proceeds *or the value thereof*, the latter words notably absent from s 5(3).

---

339 Professor Smith's 'Commentary' [1997] Crim LR 417.

340 [1974] QB 549.

341 'The word "get" is about as wide a word as could possibly have been adopted by the draftsmen of the Act.' *AG's Ref (No 1 of 1983)* [1985] QB 182, *per* Lord Lane CJ.

Once again, it is principles of civil law which cause complication for the criminal law. If the mistake is a fundamental mistake, then, at civil law, ownership will be prevented from passing. The property remains belonging to another under s 5(1), and so reliance on s 5(4) becomes unnecessary. Even if the mistake is not so fundamental as to prevent property passing, it must still be established that the defendant is under a legal obligation to make restoration of the property. This will be governed according to the complex principles of the law of restitution. The first part of the section is, thus, governed by the civil law and only the second part is recognisable as attaching criminal liability, that is, 'an intention not to make restoration shall be regarded as an intention to deprive that person of the property or proceeds'.

### Reason for inclusion of s 5(4)

2-107　The sub-section was specifically included to combat the problem that arose in *Moynes v Cooper*.[342] Moynes, an employee, was given too much money in his wage packet at the end of the week. The wages clerk had made a mistake, not realising that the workman had already been paid some of his wages in advance. Moynes did not realise until later that his packet included an overpayment. When he did discover it, he dishonestly kept the extra money. He was charged with stealing it. However, he was acquitted of larceny, as there was no *mens rea* at the moment of taking and he had become the legal owner of the money. He may have been accountable to repay the debt under a contractual obligation, but the criminal law did not make a criminal out of a dishonest debtor. If the facts of this case were to occur today, Moynes would be guilty of theft by virtue of s 5(4): even though ownership of the extra wages might have passed to him when the wages were handed over, he would have dishonestly appropriated property 'belonging to another' by virtue of s 5(4) because he had 'got' the money by mistake and was under an obligation to make restoration.[343]

### Application of s 5(4)

2-108　A typical way in which the sub-section operates is illustrated by *AG Ref (No 1 of 1983)*.[344] The respondent was a policewoman whose salary was paid by direct debit into her bank account. One month she was overpaid by some £74 that her employers mistakenly believed she was due in respect of overtime. When she discovered the mistake, she treated the money as a welcome windfall and decided to keep it. On an *AG Reference*, Lord Lane CJ held that she had 'got' property by another's mistake, the property being the debt owed to her by the

---

342 [1956] 1 QB 439.

343 Note that, where a mistake is induced by fraud or deception, then it may be better to proceed under the deception offences. See Chapter 8.

344 [1985] QB 182.

bank. It had not been so fundamental a mistake as to prevent ownership of the money from passing, but Lord Lane went on to explain that, as a result of the provisions of s 5(4), the respondent was under an obligation to restore not the property or its proceeds, but *the value thereof* – an equivalent sum of money to her employers.

Lord Lane is clear that, in the opinion of the court, the word 'restoration' in s 5(4) has the same meaning as 'making restitution'. The quality of the mistake made in order to invoke a legal obligation to make restoration is thus a complex matter of civil law and it is arguable whether it should not be possible to resolve this type of situation without resorting to the criminal law. However, there may well be occasions where a prosecution is necessary, and this is the purpose of s 5(4).

### *Restoration of the 'proceeds or the value thereof'*

2-109    The fact that the sub-section is wide enough to include an obligation to restore the 'proceeds or the value thereof' of the property received by mistake and not simply the property itself is a useful extension. It means that it is of no consequence that the defendant may not be able to make restoration of the exact property that he has received by mistake. For example, it is not necessary that D must restore the exact coins that he received from V, an equivalent sum will do. But the obligation will not have ceased simply because the defendant has already spent the overpayment on other items of property. However, the wording is deceptively simple and the words 'or the value thereof' are not included in the second part of the section, which criminalises an intention not to make restoration as an intention to deprive that person of 'the property or proceeds'. This means that, if D has dissipated any overpayment on drink and drugs before realising he had acquired it by mistake, then he is not guilty of theft because there would no longer be identifiable property (or proceeds) to be appropriated. But if he spends it on identifiable goods, then they would represent the proceeds of the overpayment, which proceeds would be capable of being stolen by D.

2-110    This issue was partially addressed in *Davis*,[345] where the defendant was entitled to housing benefit from the Local Authority. Due to computer error, he was sent duplicate cheques by mistake. Even after he ceased to be entitled to housing benefit the computer only cancelled one set of payments and he continued to receive one cheque. He kept the cheques and exchanged some for cash, and the rest he endorsed for accommodation. He could have been charged with theft of the cheques, but instead, he was charged with theft of the money he received when he cashed the cheques. In upholding his conviction for theft of the money (but not the endorsed cheque as they were not cash), the Court of Appeal recognised that, by the time a defendant comes to commit his dishonest

---

345 (1989) 88 Cr App R 347.

appropriation, the article may be in one of three conditions: (a) it may still exist, in which case it can be returned; (b) it may have been exchanged for money or goods, in which case D should be able to account for the goods; and (c) it may have ceased to exist altogether, or gone beyond recovery, in which case he may be obliged to 'restore' the value. Where he is under an obligation to restore, he will be guilty of theft of the article or its proceeds, but not its value, as there is no reference to value in the second part of the section. However, the cash Mr Davis got in exchange for the cheques did represent the proceeds of the cheques he had received and, applying s 5(4), he was under an obligation to make restoration of all the cheques paid after his entitlement to benefit had ceased, in addition to the amount by which he was overpaid beforehand.

Implicit in the reasoning in *Davis* is that the property alleged to have been appropriated must be identified. That is why there can be no conviction for theft if the property or its proceeds are dissipated beyond recovery and, in those circumstances, Davis would simply have been a debtor. However, the prosecution was not required to identify the exact cheque to which the charge related. Davis was entitled to one of each pair of cheques and there was no need to identify which one was sent by mistake. Accordingly, it is sufficient identification of the property if it is an unascertained part of an identifiable whole.[346]

### The obligation must be a legal one

2-111 It follows from all that has been said that the obligation in s 5(4) must be a legal one imposed by the civil law of restitution.[347] It is submitted that there seems no reason why directions given to juries should not be couched in the same terms as that to be used when directing them in regard to s 5(3): that is, the jury must be clear that if they are satisfied certain facts exist, then an obligation to restore has been established.[348]

The principle that the obligation must be a legal, rather than a social or moral one, is confirmed in *Gilks*.[349] Gilks placed a bet on several horses in a betting shop. When he went to collect his winnings, the bookmaker made a mistake and, thinking Gilks had placed a bet on a winning horse when he had not, handed him £100 more than he ought. Realising straight away that the bookmaker had made a mistake, Gilks accepted the money and kept it, refusing to consider that he should repay it. He was charged with theft. Initially, the trial judge held that ownership in the money had passed to Gilks, but s 5(4) meant

---

346 Smith, JC, para 2-85; see 'Commentary' on *Davis* [1988] Crim LR 762.

347 Although, note that in *Davis* [1988] Crim LR 762, it was said that 'the language of quasi-contract and of other parts of the civil law' are 'unwelcome visitors to a statute which is supposed to furnish lay juries with tests which they can readily grasp and apply'.

348 See para 2-102, above.

349 [1972] 1 WLR 1341.

that he was under an 'obligation' to repay it. The Court of Appeal upheld his conviction but, it is submitted, on rather spurious grounds which had little to do with s 5(4). Nevertheless, the decision is important because the court confirmed that it would be quite wrong to construe the word 'obligation' in s 5(4) so as to cover a moral or social obligation as distinct from a legal one. As this was a gaming transaction, Gilks would be under no legal obligation to repay the money because contracts with bookmakers were unenforceable under the Gaming Act 1845. However, the court went on to uphold the conviction for theft on the ground that ownership of the money did not pass to Gilks when the money was handed to him. Where a mistake resulted in overpayment of a sum of money, the person accepting the overpayment with knowledge of the mistake was guilty of theft. So when Gilks decided to keep the money it was still property 'belonging to another', namely, the betting shop. In so deciding, the court relied on the decision in *Middleton*,[350] a case which Professor JC Smith calls 'an antique and questionable authority', where the mistake had been one of identity, either of the recipient or of what was being paid. It is arguable that this part of the decision is wrongly decided as there was no such mistake in *Gilks*, as the bookmaker had every intention of giving the money to him. Consequently, the bookmaker's mistake was not sufficiently fundamental to prevent property passing in civil law.

### *Sections 5(4) and 5(1) compared*

2-112 It may be that since the decision in *Gomez*, Gilks might be guilty of theft without reliance on *Middleton* or falling back on s 5(4). Since consent is now irrelevant to the issue of appropriation, it is possible that Gilks dishonestly appropriated property belonging to another when he took it from the bookmaker's hand, irrespective of whether ownership had passed. But there is another reason, too, why the money can be regarded as belonging to another and one which illustrates that s 5(4) may be of limited use. It may be that the bookmaker retained an equitable interest in the property due to his mistake of fact. In *Shadrokh-Cigari*,[351] the appellant acted as guardian to his nephew who was in receipt of funds from his father in Iran. Due to a banking error in the US, the child's account in England was mistakenly credited with $286,000 instead of $286. In full knowledge of what had happened, the appellant made arrangements to have the money spent or transferred by banker's draft to accounts in his own name. By the time he was arrested and charged with theft, only a fraction of the money remained. The Court of Appeal upheld his conviction for theft of the banker's drafts by applying the civil law principle in *Chase Manhattan Bank NA v Israel-British Bank Ltd*.[352] In that case, Goulding J was

350 (1893) LR 2 CCR 38; see criticism of reliance on the decision in 'Commentary' on *Gilks* in [1972] Crim LR 585 and Smith, JC, para 2-28, 88.
351 [1988] Crim LR 465 (and below).
352 [1981] Ch 105.

of the opinion that where an action lies to recover money paid under a mistake of fact, the payer retains an equitable interest in that property and therefore it is property 'belonging to another'. The bank had made a fundamental mistake which had prevented Shadrokh-Cigari from acquiring the entire legal and equitable interest in the property in question. He may have acquired legal ownership, but the bank retained an equitable interest in the property or its proceeds which was considered sufficient to be a proprietary interest for the purpose of s 5(1).

Of course, reliance on s 5(4) was an alternative in the case and the court recognised this would achieve the same result.[353] But, it may be that the whole reason why the draftsman of the TA 1968 felt it necessary to incorporate s 5(4) has become superfluous. It was done to get around the problem of the dishonest debtor in *Moynes v Cooper*, but that employee may now be regarded as a thief on the basis that he dishonestly appropriated property which belonged to his employers in equity. However, it remains to be seen to what extent the courts will be prepared to extend the reasoning in *Shadrokh-Cigari* to mistakes other than those where the victim believes he has no option but to transfer large sums of money to the defendant. Furthermore, it may be that the decision is of doubtful authority now that doubt has been cast on *Chase Manhattan* itself by the House of Lords in *Westdeutche v Islington LBC*.[354] The problem is that the decision, presumably, relies on the creation of a constructive trust and the civil courts have shown themselves less willing to impose such a trust in the absence of a pre-existing fiduciary relationship[355] – but the complexities of the civil law of constructive trusts are beyond the scope of this book, or that of the criminal courts.

## 6 WITH THE INTENTION OF PERMANENTLY DEPRIVING THE OTHER OF IT

2-113    **Section 6 of the TA 1968**

(1) A person appropriating property belonging to another without meaning the other permanently to lose the thing itself is nevertheless to be regarded as having the intention of permanently depriving the other of it if his intention is to treat the thing as his own to dispose of regardless of the other's rights; and a borrowing or lending of it may amount to so treating it if, but only if, the borrowing or lending is for a period and in circumstances making it equivalent to an outright taking or disposal.

---

353 He may also now be guilty under TA 1968, s 24A, dishonestly retaining a wrongful credit.
354 [1996] 2 All ER 961 (HL).
355 See, eg, *Halifax Building Society v Thomas* [1996] Ch 217.

(2) Without prejudice to the generality of sub-section (1) above, where a person, having possession or control (lawfully or not) of property belonging to another, parts with the property under a condition as to its return which he may not be able to perform, this (if done for the purposes of his own and without the other's authority) amounts to treating the property as his own to dispose of regardless of the other's rights.

## Intention permanently to deprive

2-114 The TA 1968 does not define 'intention permanently to deprive'. It must be proved that D intended his victim to be deprived of his property permanently and usually this is self-evident from the circumstances, so that the wording of s 1 is sufficient. If D snatches an ice cream from a child and immediately eats it, or takes V's wallet and spends the money, or rides off on D's bicycle and sells it, there will be little difficulty in proving an intention permanently to deprive. However, there is no requirement that the victim be actually permanently deprived of his property, as long as there is an intention on behalf of the defendant that he should do so. It is assumed that 'intention' has the same meaning as elsewhere in the criminal law, so it may include situations where D knows that it is virtually certain that V will not get his property back as a result of his appropriation. If D takes V's handbag, removes the wallet and then abandons the handbag, the handbag will probably be restored to V and if D knows this, he will not be guilty of theft of the handbag. But what if D takes V's bicycle in order to get home late one night and then leaves it on the side of the road where V later accidentally discovers it? We cannot say that D merely 'borrowed' the bicycle, as he did not have permission and he has not returned it. Yet it will be hard to prove that D had the intention that V would be deprived permanently of his property just because he was uncertain as to whether V would get the bicycle back.

It may be different if D abandons the property, being totally indifferent as to whether V gets it back or not. Whether there is an intention permanently to deprive in such circumstances will often depend on the nature of the property that is appropriated. It is more likely, for example, that a suitcase marked with its owner's name and address will find its way home, than a wallet full of cash, or an egg timer. At common law, there was no intention permanently to deprive where D took a horse and then turned it loose at a distance from where he took it.[356] Presumably, this was because there was every expectation that the horse would eventually be restored to its true owner. The modern equivalent is the 'stolen' car: s 12 of the TA 1968 recognises the potential difficulties of proving an intention permanently to deprive by providing a specific offence of taking a car without its owner's consent which does not require proof of an intention

---

356 *Phillips & Strong* (1801) 2 East PC 662; *Crump* (1825) 1 C&P 658; *Addis* (1844) 1 Cox CC 78.

permanently to deprive the owner of it. Similarly, s 11 criminalises the removal of articles from public places without the need to prove an intention permanently to deprive. It would be different if D sold or destroyed the car or article, because then there is no prospect of its return and D would be guilty of theft.

## V must be deprived of his entire interest

2-115　The intention of the defendant must be to deprive his victim of his entire interest in the property. It is immaterial whether D receives any benefit as a result. If V has only a limited interest in the property which does not amount to full ownership, for example, if he is in temporary possession, it is enough that D intends to deprive him of the whole of that limited interest. To use an example of Professor Smith's:[357] if, as D knows, P has hired a car from Q for a month and D takes it from P intending to return it to him after the month is up, D will have stolen the car from P because he is permanently deprived of his whole – albeit limited – interest in the property. However, it will not be theft from Q because he has not been permanently deprived of his interest as owner of the car. The defendant's intention is paramount, so if he believed P to be the owner of the car when he took it, returning the car at the end of the month, he will not be guilty of theft even though P was, in fact, deprived of his entire interest.

## Section 6 is not to be given a restricted meaning

2-116　What happens if D takes an article from V, for example a book, and then returns the same book to him later on? Provided he has simply 'borrowed' the book and returned it he will not be guilty of theft. But suppose he tells V that he can only have his book back if V pays him for it? Or if D spoils the book in some way, for example, by spilling coffee on the book, or underlining passages of the script, or tearing out some of the pages before he returns it to V, so that, in effect, the book is no longer of any value? Even though V has not been permanently deprived of his book, it can still be said that D is deemed to have the intention to so do. Although the phrase is not actually defined in the TA 1968, s 6 extends the meaning of 'intention permanently to deprive' to cover situations where V may get his property back eventually, but only after such a time or in such a way, or in so altered a form, that it is no longer of any use to him. D may not have set out to deprive V permanently, but he is 'to be regarded' as having done so.

Section 6(1) contains two limbs: D will be deemed to have the intention permanently to deprive V of the property if his intention is, first 'to treat the thing as his own to dispose of regardless of the other's rights' and, secondly, if he borrows the property in circumstances which make it 'equivalent to an

---

357 Smith, JC, para 2-126.

outright taking or disposal'. A third element is to be found in s 6(2), which covers those circumstances where D may be legally in possession or control of V's goods, but puts himself in such a position that he may be unable to return the goods to V at all, for example, if he pawns them.

The section has been accused of being poorly and hurriedly drafted,[358] leading to overlap between the sub-sections and inconsistency in the wording. At one time, it was felt helpful of Lord Lane CJ to restrict the application of s 6(1) to specific examples. In *Lloyd*,[359] he said that the first part of s 6(1) is aimed at what might be called 'ransom' type cases, where a defendant takes something and then offers it back to the owner to buy if he wishes, and the second part is aimed at cases where D borrows or lends V's property in circumstances equivalent to an outright taking or disposal. In doing so, he approved Edmund Davis LJ in *Warner*,[360] who said that: 'Section 6 ... gives illustrations, as it were, of what can amount to the dishonest intention demanded by s 1(1). But it is a misconception to interpret it as watering down s 1.' This led Lord Lane to recommend that s 6 need only be referred to in exceptional cases, s 1 being quite sufficient in the vast majority of cases. He then concluded, 'we would try to interpret s 6 in such a way as to ensure that nothing is construed as an intention permanently to deprive which would not prior to the 1968 Act have been so construed'. In other words, s 6 should be restricted to those situations recognised at common law and under the Larceny Acts where the phrase 'intention of permanently depriving' meant much as his Lordship had described it.

2-117    Subsequent cases have not been so restrictive and have tended to give the words of s 6 a wider meaning. For example, in *Bagshaw*,[361] the Court of Appeal said that the restrictive view taken in *Lloyd* was *obiter* and that 'there may be other occasions on which s 6 applies'. The current opinion is expressed in *Fernandes*, where Auld LJ stated:

> In our view, s 6(1), which is expressed in general terms, is not limited in its application to the illustrations given by Lord Lane CJ in *Lloyd*. Nor, in saying that in most cases it would be unnecessary to refer to the provision, did Lord Lane suggest that it should be so limited. The critical notion, stated expressly in the first limb and incorporated by reference in the second, is whether the defendant intended to 'treat the thing as his own regardless of the other's rights'. The second limb of sub-s (1), and also sub-s (2), are merely specific illustrations of the application of that notion. *We consider that s 6 may apply to a person in possession or control of another's property who, dishonestly and for his own purpose, deals with that property in such a manner as he is risking its loss* [emphasis added].[362]

---

358 Eg, Spencer, JR, 'The metamorphosis of s 6 of the TA' [1977] Crim LR 653. Section 6 was not in the original draft Bill produced by the CLRC (*op cit*, CLRC, fn 12), but was added by a Government amendment.

359 [1985] QB 829 (and para 2-126 below).

360 (1971) 55 Cr App R 93, pp 96, 97.

361 [1988] Crim LR 321.

362 [1996] Cr App R 175, p 188.

In this case, Fernandes was a disreputable solicitor who transferred his client's money to his bookkeeper, R, for investment in a firm of licensed backstreet moneylenders of which R was a partner. Fernandes knew this was a risky business and, needless to say, the money disappeared. His conviction for theft was upheld by the Court of Appeal because someone who 'deals' with property, knowing that he is doing so in such a way that he is risking its loss, is intending to 'treat the thing as his own to dispose of regardless of the other's rights'. By implication, the second and third elements in s 6 are simply specific illustrations of the first. Bearing in mind that s 6 is expressed in general terms, it is still convenient to examine the wording of the section in its component parts.

## Section 6(1): 'to treat the thing as his own to dispose of regardless of the other's right'

2-118   We have seen that the wording is to be interpreted widely, but it is essential for the prosecution to prove that, at the time of the appropriation, the defendant intends 'to treat the thing as his own to dispose of regardless of the other's right'. It must be his intention to exclude the owner's rights, even though there is no requirement that the victim be physically deprived of his property permanently. For example, in *Downes*,[363] D was in lawful possession of vouchers from the Inland Revenue which could be used to gain certain tax advantages. It was held that he committed theft when he sold the vouchers to a third party. The court was of the opinion that the wording of the first part of s 6(1) 'seems quite literally and clearly to cover the admitted facts of the present case'. Although he knew that the vouchers would eventually find their way back to the Inland Revenue, he was treating them as his own regardless of the Revenue's rights by selling them. In *Chan Man-sin v AG of Hong Kong*,[364] the appellant was a company accountant who drew a forged cheque on the company account. He was charged with theft of the chose in action, namely the debt owed by the bank to the companies. His appeal, on the ground that the company had not lost anything as the bank had no authority to honour a forged cheque, was dismissed. Lord Oliver, speaking on behalf of the Board, found 'ample evidence' that an intention permanently to deprive the company of its credit balance could be inferred because, 'quite clearly he had intended to deal with the company's property without regard to their rights'. It is submitted that a similar argument could be used where D offers V's property for sale to a third party. His motive is not seeking to deprive V of his property, but to gain benefit for himself through obtaining money from the third party by deception. Nevertheless, he will be deemed to have an intention permanently to deprive V of the property by virtue of s 6(1).[365]

---

363  (1983) 77 Cr App R 260.
364  [1988] 1 WLR 196.
365  Cf *Pitham & Hehl* (1976) 65 Cr App R 45, para 2-25 above.

## *Importance of 'to dispose of'*

2-119    These words are crucial. It is evidence of a disposition that illustrates D's intention to 'treat the thing as his own'. Yet, there has been some confusion over the precise meaning of the words 'dispose of'. In *Marshall*,[366] the Court of Appeal, following *Fernandes*, emphasised the need for s 6(1) not to be given a restricted interpretation. It was held that the section had wide enough application to cover circumstances where the defendant had acquired and resold London Underground tickets to potential travellers. The appellants submitted that they had no intention permanently to deprive because the tickets would eventually find their way back to the London Underground (as analogous to the treatment of cheques in *Preddy*).[367] However, it was held that by acquiring and reselling the tickets, the appellants had not only demonstrated an intention to treat the tickets as if they were their own, but also 'to dispose' of them regardless of London Underground's exclusive right to sell the tickets. The fact that the tickets would eventually find their way back into London Underground's possession (albeit with all their usefulness exhausted) was irrelevant.

2-120    In *Cahill*,[368] the Court of Appeal approved the dictionary meaning of 'dispose of' and, accordingly, allowed the defendant's appeal against a conviction for theft on the basis of a misdirection. It was not enough to tell the jury that the defendant must treat the property as his own. By omitting the words 'to dispose of' from his direction, the recorder had materially altered the sense of s 6(1). The court found it helpful to refer to Professor Smith's *The Law of Theft* (6th edn, p 73):[369]

> The attribution of an ordinary meaning to the language of s 6 presents some difficulties. It is submitted, however, that an intention merely to use the thing as one's own is not enough and that 'dispose of' is not used in the sense in which a general might 'dispose of' his forces but rather in the meaning given by the *Shorter Oxford Dictionary*: 'To deal with definitely: to get rid of; to get done with, finish. To make over by way of sale or bargain, sell.'

In his commentary on the case, Professor Smith elucidates the reason for this being that the words 'treating the thing as one's own, regardless of the other's rights' add nothing to the meaning of 'appropriates' in s 3(1), since an appropriation consists of an assumption of any of the rights of an owner. The words 'to dispose of' are, therefore, vital in order to establish the defendant's intention permanently to deprive.

---

366 [1998] 2 Cr App R 282, see para 2-62, above, for facts and further discussion.
367 For a discussion of *Preddy* [1996] AC 815 and the TA 1968, s 15, see para 8-29, below.
368 [1993] Crim LR 141.
369 Now 8th edn, 1997, para 2-132.

2-121      Unfortunately, the clarity of this judgment was somewhat marred by an even wider interpretation of the same words being adopted in *Lavender*.[370] The respondent had taken two good doors from a council property undergoing repair and used them to replace two damaged doors on another council property where his girlfriend was the tenant. With arguably some justification, he submitted that he had not had the intention permanently to deprive the council of its doors. However, on a case remitted to the justices with a direction to convict for theft, the Divisional Court, without reference to *Cahill*, thought the dictionary meaning of 'dispose of' was too narrow. The court appeared to say that the words 'disposing of' the doors could also mean 'dealing with' the doors. The proper question was whether the respondent had 'dealt' with the doors regardless of the council's rights not to have them removed and, in so doing, had manifested an intention to treat the doors as his own. But had he really 'disposed of' the doors? They remained in the possession of the council throughout. If I swap my office chair for a better one in a different room of the same university building, surely all I have done is rearrange the furniture? It would come as a nasty shock to be convicted of theft. Of course, if I threw the old chair away onto a tip, then I would have stolen that chair. It is submitted that *Cahill* is the better authority, but *Lavender* illustrates just how the courts may be prepared to overextend the meaning of s 6 in circumstances where they feel it is appropriate.

*There may be a particular problem with bank accounts*

2-122   Where a person wrongfully obtains a cheque from another, intending to cash the cheque, the cheque form will eventually find its way back to the victim's bank and there will be no intention permanently to deprive the victim of his property – that is the cheque form. Therefore, neither a charge of theft or of obtaining property by deception will succeed. There was an attempt, in *Duru*,[371] to get round this problem by saying that there would be an intention permanently to deprive the victim of the thing in action represented by the cheque. However, *Duru* was overruled in *Preddy*, where the House of Lords preferred to rely on the long overlooked case of *Danger*.[372] They decided that the thing in action was not property belonging to another and reaffirmed that there could be no intention permanently to deprive the victim of the actual cheque form.[373]

However, there may still be ways round the problem. While the courts accept there has been no 'obtaining' in such circumstances, there has been an 'appropriation' of the other's bank balance on presentation of the cheque[374] and,

---

370 [1994] Crim LR 297 (DC).
371 (1973) 58 Cr App R 151.
372 (1857) 7 Cox CC 303.
373 See, now, the TA 1968, s 15A, para 8-36, below.
374 *Burke* [2000] Crim LR 413; *Williams (Roy)* (2000) *The Times*, 25 October; see para 2-94 above.

as long as the account is in credit, an intention permanently to deprive was accepted in *Chan Man-sin v AG of Hong Kong*.[375] A further way round the problem has been promulgated by Professor Smith in that, when receiving the cheque, the defendant could be regarded as appropriating a piece of paper with special qualities, that is, the right to sue the bank for the required sum.[376] But it is this very 'special quality' which is the thing in action denied in *Preddy* as belonging to another.

Nevertheless, such an argument seems to have been accepted in *Arnold*,[377] where Potter LJ was prepared to distinguish *Danger* on its facts and stated: 'There was good reason, where the factual situation permits, to give effect to the rationale behind *Duru* that the "substance" of a cheque or valuable security lies in the right to present it and obtain the benefit of its proceeds, rather than in its character as a mere piece of paper with a message on it.' The 'factual situation' in *Arnold* was that the property belonged to another by virtue of s 5(3). In that case, Arnold devised a franchise plan in order to expand his business. Prospective agents were required to deposit with him a 180 day bill of exchange which they believed would be held by the appellant as security until the 180 day maturity date, when the proceeds would be repaid to them against their delivery of another bill. In breach of his obligation to retain the bills on behalf of the agents, the appellant used them to ease his own cash flow problems. Rather predictably, this resulted in him being unable to recredit the agents at the end of the 180 day period. He was charged with, *inter alia*, two counts of theft of a valuable security, that is the bills of exchange. The Court of Appeal upheld his convictions, regarding the bills of exchange as property belonging to another under s 5(3), and holding that the appellant had the intention permanently to deprive the agents of them. Even though the bills would eventually find their way back to the agents via their banks, by the time of their return they would have lost all their value and identity as a valuable security. Therefore, the appellant had intended to treat the bills as his own 'to dispose of regardless of the other's rights'. Submissions by the appellant that his case was analogous to *Preddy* were rejected; in these circumstances, an intention that 'the document should find its way back to the transferor only after all the benefit to the transferor has been lost or removed as a result of its use in breach of such obligation', can amount to an intention permanently to deprive the other of his valuable security, or cheque.[378]

### The 'ransom' principle

2-123    At common law and under the Larceny Acts, the phrase 'intention of permanently depriving' included cases where D takes V's property and only

---

375 See para 2-48 above.
376 Smith, JC, 'Obtaining cheques by deception or theft' [1997] Crim LR 396.
377 [1997] 4 All ER 1.
378 Cf arguments put forward in *Marshall* [1998] 2 Cr App R 282.

returns it to V when he pays the asking price.[379] So, if D takes V's bicycle and, pretending it is his own bicycle, sells it back to V, he has the intention of permanently depriving V of his bicycle, even though in reality V gets it back again. After the passing of the TA 1968, Lord Lane CJ in *Lloyd* used these 'ransom' cases as an example of how the first part of s 6(1) operates: where D takes things and then offers them back to the owner for the owner to buy if he wishes. Consequently, as far as the bicycle is concerned, D has treated it 'as his own to dispose of regardless of the other's rights'; this is because he is effectively bargaining with the owner to sell it back. Only an owner can attach conditions as to the use or sale of his own property. Once again the words 'dispose of' are crucial in terms of indicating D's intention. So in *Scott*,[380] where the defendant took a pair of curtains from a department store without paying for them, only to return them the next day demanding a 'refund', he had 'disposed' of the curtains having regarded himself as free to treat them as his own.

Arguably, the principle must also be applicable to more straightforward 'ransoms'. For example, where D takes V's property and then tells V that he cannot have it back until V has performed some condition which D has no right to impose.[381] Neither does there seem any reason why the condition should be restricted to payment of money. It was envisaged by Professor Smith that the principle could cover cases where D takes V's property and then says, for example: 'I will return the picture when E (who is imprisoned) is given a free pardon.' This should be sufficient evidence of an intent permanently to deprive.[382]

Section 6 may, therefore, be of limited application in that it all depends on what the intentions of the defendant are. If he knows that he will return the goods in a short space of time whether the conditions have been fulfilled or not, then the prosecution may be unable to establish that he has intended 'to dispose' of the goods. In that case, he will not have intended permanently to deprive V of them. The jury must be satisfied that D really did intend to hang onto the goods until he got what he wanted for there to be sufficient evidence to convict.

2-124    A good example of how the principle operates is demonstrated by the Court of Appeal in *Coffey*,[383] where the appellant was convicted of obtaining machinery by use of a worthless cheque. The charge was brought under s 15 of the TA 1968, but the requirement that the defendant had the intention of

---

379 *Hall* (1849) 1 Den 381, 169 ER 291.

380 [1987] Crim LR 235.

381 If the refusal to return is accompanied by threats, D may be charged with blackmail, see Chapter 11; also *Hare* [1910] 29 NZLR 641 where D obtained money from V by threatening to publish an important letter that he had found, unless he was paid. He was convicted of theft, as well as extortion of the money.

382 Smith, JC para 2-133; there may be a conditional intent, in which case there is no need to have recourse to s 6; see below.

383 [1987] Crim LR 498.

permanently depriving the victim of his property is identical to that of theft. At his trial, he explained that he had obtained the machinery in order to put pressure on the victim who was refusing to negotiate over a long running dispute between them. It was not clear what he would do with the machinery if he failed to achieve his purpose. His conviction was quashed because the importance of s 6 had not been brought to the attention of the jury. They should have been told that the defendant's guilt depended on the quality of his intended detention by looking at all the circumstances of the case. In particular, it was important to consider the defendant's own assessment at the time of the appropriation as to the likelihood of the victim's agreement to come to terms and of the length of time he was prepared to retain the machinery. By implication, it seems that, if Mr Coffey believed his victim would come to terms quickly, then it would be difficult to prove he intended to hang on to the machinery for such a time as to be equivalent to an outright disposal. Furthermore, the jury needs to be given the opportunity to consider whether he might have returned the machinery, even though his demands were not complied with. If they concluded that he might have done so, then they would not be entitled to convict unless his taking of the machinery was, 'in circumstances making it equivalent to an outright taking or disposal' – the words used in the second limb of s 6(1) to do with 'borrowing'. It seems that the Court of Appeal accepts that in some circumstances, the interpretation of s 6(1) is broad enough to encompass both limbs of the section. Of course, where D believes that he has a right to retain the property until he is paid, perhaps as security against a debt, he may not be guilty of theft, as he is not dishonest according to s 2(1)(a).[384]

## 'Borrowing' or 'lending'

2-125   There is considerable overlap (some might say overkill) between the two limbs of s 6(1), and it is probably best to regard this second element as simply a specific example of treating property as your own 'to dispose of regardless of the other's rights'. Borrowing is, by definition, not something that is done with an intention permanently to deprive. The owner only loses temporary possession and both parties have every intention that the property be restored. So in what circumstances can an intended borrowing amount to an intention permanently to deprive? According to the latter part of s 6(1), only if the 'borrowing' is for such a period of time and in such circumstances as to make it 'equivalent to an outright taking or disposal'. These words have the potential to be restrictive. For example, if D borrows a law book from his fellow student, V, for one week, but, in fact, keeps it for one month before returning it, there is no intention permanently to deprive if he returns the book in an unchanged state, because it is not equivalent to an outright taking or disposal. Irritating though such a

---

384 See para 2-09 above.

friend is, he is not a thief. The same will be true if D departs the university leaving the book with a third party in the hope that it will eventually be returned to V. But, supposing he keeps it until the end of term, thus depriving V of the use of it during the final examinations? V no longer has any use for the book and D appears to have deprived V of its value and 'virtue'. Yet, arguably, it is still a book and is not useless to anyone other than V. Thus, D's action may not come within the ambit of s 6. It might be different if D were to keep the book so long that it becomes an old edition and of no use to anyone at all.

2-126    The leading authority is *Lloyd*,[385] where Lord Lane stated: 'a mere borrowing is never enough to constitute the necessary guilty mind unless the intention is to return the "thing" in such a changed state that it can truly be said that all its goodness or virtue has gone.'[386] In that case, a cinema projectionist was in the habit of removing, or 'borrowing', films from the cinema for a few hours so that others could make master copies of them with a view to selling 'pirate' videotapes of the films. The originals were always returned in an undamaged state. The Court of Appeal quashed his conviction for conspiracy to steal on the basis that the original films had not diminished in value. The goodness, the virtue, the practical value of the films had not been destroyed and they could still be shown to paying audiences. Consequently, the 'borrowing' had not been 'for a period and in circumstances making it equivalent to an outright taking or disposal'. By contrast, the trial judge gave the example of D borrowing V's battery (not a rechargeable one) and using it, only returning it to V once its power is exhausted. Similarly, if D 'borrows' V's football season ticket and then returns it to him at the end of the season when all the matches have been played – the season ticket is useless, it has no value or 'virtue' left in it and D can be said to have intended permanently to deprive V of it. However, suppose D returns the ticket when there is one match left to play? It has *some* value left in it and Lord Lane refers only to situations where '*all*' the virtue has gone. This may mean that very few borrowings will be regarded as theft. Even though it was stressed in *Fernandes* that s 6(1) is not limited in its application to the illustrations given by Lord Lane in *Lloyd*, unless emphasis is placed on the words 'in circumstances making it *equivalent* to an outright taking', it seems that, only where D returns the 'thing' in a totally useless state or completely changed in substance,[387] will he be regarded as having an intention permanently to deprive.[388]

2-127    The sub-section appears to treat 'lending' in the same way, so the principle will apply to situations where D is in lawful possession of V's property and he

385 [1985] QB 829.

386 *Ibid*, p 836.

387 Such as, where D takes a horse intending to kill it and return the carcass; cf *Cabbage* (1815) Russ & Ry 292.

388 The sub-section must not be used too enthusiastically; see *Bagshaw* [1988] Crim LR 321, where the principle seems to have been misapplied.

lends it to a third party who then uses it in such a way that all its 'goodness and virtue' is gone by the time it is returned to V.

## Where D returns similar goods

2-128　Particular problems can arise where a person takes another's goods intending to replace them with similar goods before he notices. For example, D may take money from V's wallet, or tins of soup from his larder. If he later replaces the equivalent goods, has he stolen them? Strange as it may seem, an intention to return equivalent money or goods is not inconsistent with an intention permanently to deprive. In *Velumyl*,[389] the defendant had borrowed money from his employer's safe (even though he knew this was against company rules), intending to repay it the following day after a debt had been repaid to him. It was held that intending to return coins of an equivalent value is not the same as intending to return the identical ones that were taken. Therefore, although such an intention may be relevant to the issue of dishonesty, it does not negative the intention permanently to deprive the owner of the original notes and coins. The same would presumably be true of our tin of soup. The reason for so seemingly bizarre a decision is that, in the court's opinion, taking someone else's property in these circumstances means that the owner is forced to accept a substitution to which he has not freely consented; there is, after all, a difference between being a true owner and merely a creditor. Of course, the matter will usually be settled within the context of dishonesty.[390]

## Dishonest 'borrowings'

2-129　Except where 'borrowings' are deemed to be the equivalent of an outright taking, the TA 1968 does not criminalise dishonest borrowings. But it would certainly make the law simpler if someone who dishonestly borrows another's property could be convicted of an offence without the need to prove an intention permanently to deprive. However, the CLRC[391] thought that an intention to return property, even after a long time, makes the conduct essentially different from stealing, quite apart from the undesirable social consequences which would result from criminalising such behaviour in terms of, for example, quarrelling neighbours and overstretching of police and court resources. Yet there are good reasons for doing so.[392] For example, consider the anti-social flatmate who habitually 'borrows' his friend's latest CD, or fashionable jumper, and then keeps them so long that, by the time he gives them back, they have gone out of fashion. There may be a greater loss involved for the victim here

---

389 [1989] Crim LR 299.

390 *Feely* [1973] QB 530 and para 2-17, above.

391 *Op cit*, CLRC, fn 12, para 56.

392 See Williams, G, 'Temporary appropriation should be theft' [1981] Crim LR 129; Smith, ATH, para 6-06.

than in many cases of theft with all the requisite intention permanently to deprive. So far, the TA 1968 has only been prepared to recognise unauthorised 'borrowing' of a car, or 'borrowing' articles from public places as warranting specific criminalisation, in ss 12 and 11 of the TA 1968, respectively. There may well be a case for criminalising the 'borrowing' of other items of property by enacting a crime of unlawful temporary deprivation of property belonging to another.

## Section 6(2): parting with property under a condition as to its return

2-130   This sub-section covers situations where D puts himself in a position where he is no longer able to return V's property to him. He may even be in lawful possession of V's property, but then parts with it to a third party under a condition as to its return which he may not be able to fulfil. The obvious example is where he pawns the goods, hoping to redeem them before V finds out, or pledges them as security for a loan. He is running the risk that he may lose them and so be unable to return them to V. Such an action, according to s 6(2), will 'amount to treating the property as his own to dispose of regardless of the other's rights' and consequently he will be deemed to have the intention permanently to deprive V of his property. It is arguable that to pawn or pledge goods should count as a disposition under s 6(1), in which case, s 6(2) is overkill. However, the better view may be that a person who is convinced that he will be able to redeem the property does not come within the meaning of s 6(2), because he intends to dispose of the property under a condition that he honestly believes he will be able to perform.[393]

## Conditional intention to deprive

2-131   Suppose a person only has a 'conditional intention' permanently to deprive another of his property; that is, he only intends permanently to keep something if he finds it to be valuable after he has examined the property to see whether it is worth taking. Will this be sufficient *mens rea* to be guilty of theft? In theory, there seems no reason why he cannot be convicted, in that any intention permanently to deprive will involve a conditional element – if only when he has a good look round first to see if he can get away with it. But it may be more difficult where he decides not to take the thing after all. For example, where D rummages in a handbag to see if there is anything worth stealing and, deciding that there is not, departs the scene leaving the handbag ready to hand to be repossessed by the owner. It is hard, in such circumstances, to convict him of

393 Smith, JC, para 2-138.

theft because he has no intention of permanently depriving the owner of either the handbag or the contents – although he would have done if he had found anything worth stealing. In such circumstances, it has been held that 'a conditional appropriation will not do'.[394] Such situations are best dealt with as an attempt to steal on a correctly worded indictment and will be dealt with in Chapter 14.

394 *Easom* [1971] 2 QB 315. See para 14-13 below.

# CHAPTER 3

# ROBBERY

3-01

**Section 8 of the Theft Act (TA) 1968 – Robbery**

(1) A person is guilty of robbery if he steals, and immediately before or at the time of doing so, and in order to do so, he uses force on any person or puts or seeks to put any person in fear of being there and then subjected to force.

(2) A person guilty of robbery, or an assault with intent to rob, shall on conviction on indictment be liable to imprisonment for life.

## Introduction

3-02    Robbery was originally dealt with under the common law. A possible reason for this may have been that the combination of a property offence with that of violence put it outside the ambit of the Larceny Act (LA) 1916. The current relevance of the cases decided under the common law, when interpreting the provisions of s 8, arose for discussion in *R v Dawson and James*.[1] In relation to the definition to be attached to the word 'force' in s 3(1), argument was presented that this was a matter of an ordinary English word that was to be given its ordinary meaning. The Court of Appeal, in agreeing with this contention, considered that the old common law distinctions and refinements had no relevance under the TA.

3-03    The offence of robbery is essentially an aggravated form of stealing. As such, the elements which the prosecution are required to prove may also be sufficient to make out other offences such as theft, assault, or the offences that may arise under the statutes relating to possession and use of firearms and offensive weapons. Consequently, the possibility of adding other counts to the indictment, or of alternative verdicts need to be considered. As far as alternative verdicts are concerned, reference must be made to s 6(3) of the Criminal Law Act (CLA) 1967, which provides:

> Where on a person's trial on indictment for any offence ... the jury find him not guilty of the offence specifically charged in the indictment, but the allegations in the indictment amount to or include (expressly or by implication) an allegation of another offence falling within the jurisdiction of the court of trial, the jury may find him guilty of that other offence or of an offence of which he could be found guilty on an indictment specifically charging that other offence.

---

1    (1976) 64 Cr App R 170.

3-04    One effect of this is that, if the prosecution fails in proving robbery, it is possible for the jury to convict, instead, for theft. It would appear that there is no specific requirement on the trial judge to direct the jury as to the 'lesser' alternative verdict. He may do so, however, if he considers that this should be done in the interests of justice.[2] If the prosecution is unable to satisfy the jury as far as robbery is concerned, but there is ample evidence that the force used amounted to an assault, would an alternative verdict of assault be possible? This would depend on the degree of assault involved. If the use of force amounts only to common assault, the matter has been resolved through the Criminal Justice Act (CJA) 1988. Under s 39 of the CJA 1988, assault is classified as a summary offence and, therefore, does not come within the words of s 6(3) of the CLA 1967 as 'another offence falling within the jurisdiction of the court of trial', robbery being an indictable only offence. However, provided the rules of criminal procedure are adhered to, there is nothing to prevent the indictment specifically containing a count for an assault which amounts to grievous bodily harm.

3-05    There are, in effect, two offences contained within the section: (a) robbery and (b) assault with intent to rob. The particular offence must be specified in the indictment.

## Mode of trial and sentence

3-06    As indicated above, both offences under s 8 are indictable only, reflecting the seriousness of the offence.[3] As a consequence of the classification in the *Practice Direction (Crown Court: Allocation of Business) 1995*,[4] the offences are class 4 offences. The maximum sentence, as stated in s 8(2), is imprisonment for life.

3-07    The degree of violence used in cases of robbery and assault with intent to rob may vary from extremely serious cases of armed robbery to instances of street robbery, or 'mugging'.[5] Whatever the degree of seriousness, however, the combination of violence and theft means that there is a high likelihood of a convicted defendant receiving a custodial sentence:

> Partly, this is because the introduction of force makes theft more likely to succeed and, conversely, the object of theft makes the assault more highly motivated, arguably exposing the victim to a greater risk of injury. More importantly, however, the use of force to complete a theft changes the moral character of D's

---

2    See *Maxwell* [1990] 1 WLR 401.

3    Magistrates' Courts Act 1980, Sched 1, para 28(a).

4    [1995] 1 WLR 1083; as amended by *Practice Direction (Crown Court: Allocation of Business (No 2)* [1998] 1 WLR 1244.

5    *Archbold*, 2000 (paras 21-91–94), provides four general classifications: (a) armed robbery (b) robbery in the course of burglary; (c) street robbery; (d) robbery of small shops.

action, such that it is legitimate to criminalise D's wrong specifically by the 'combined' offence of robbery.[6]

3-08    A number of cases may be cited as illustrative of sentencing practice. In *Turner*,[7] 19 defendants, over a period of four years, carried out 20 armed robberies on banks and security vans. Firearms and ammonia were carried, although the injuries inflicted were slight. The Court of Appeal ruled that a 'benchmark' of 15 years was a suitable starting point. This has been confirmed in subsequent cases.[8] In *O'Driscoll*,[9] the Court of Appeal refused to entertain an appeal against a 15 year prison sentence on the basis of the need to protect elderly people living alone who were preyed upon in savage and sadistic attacks. It may be that, in some cases, no (or very little) actual violence was used. Although this is a factor to be taken into account, it can have only minimal effect in mitigating the sentence.[10] Similarly, even where the defendant is young, has a clean record and pleads guilty, the seriousness attached to this offence means that a custodial sentence would still be considered appropriate.[11]

Nonetheless, it remains the fact that some instances of robbery may be relatively minor in the calendar of criminal activity. An example of this might arise in the case of the juvenile delinquent who snatches a purse and runs off with it. As Professor Ashworth puts it, this raises the question of fair labelling: 'A major armed robbery falls into the same legal category as a sudden, impulsive bag-snatching.'[12]

## Elements of robbery

### *Steals*

3-09    Robbery is essentially a species of theft which is aggravated by the use of violence. The crucial word, in s 8(1), is the word 'steals', which brings into play s 1(1) and (3). If, therefore, a defendant is not guilty of theft, he cannot be guilty of robbery, that is, all the essential elements of theft must be proved by the prosecution. The doubts on this point, expressed in the case of *Forrester*, cannot be correct.[13] Consequently, if there is no dishonest (s 2) appropriation (s 3) of property (s 4) belonging to another (s 5), with an intention to permanently to

---

6    Simester, AP and Sullivan, GR, *Criminal Law: Theory and Doctrine*, 2000, Hart, pp 493–494.

7    (1975) 61 Cr App R 67.

8    See, eg, *Daly* (1981) 3 Cr App R(S) 340; *Gould* (1983) 5 Cr App R(S) 72.

9    (1986) 8 Cr App R(S) 121.

10   See, eg, *Stanford* (1988) 10 Cr App R(S) 222.

11   *Golding* (1992) 13 Cr App R(S) 142. Conversely, if the charge in this case had been for theft rather than robbery, a custodial sentence would have been unusual.

12   Ashworth, p 401.

13   [1992] Crim LR 792 and the accompanying 'Commentary'.

deprive (s 6), no conviction of robbery can be sustained.[14] In addition to the cases dealing with theft, two other cases may be dealt with here.

3-10     In *Robinson*, for instance, there was no appropriation by dishonesty and accordingly, it was not possible to convict for robbery.[15] The defendant, in this case, ran a clothing club. The victim and the victim's wife were contributors to the club and owed the defendant £7. The defendant had confronted the victim brandishing a knife, and a fight had ensued. In the course of the fight, a £5 note had fallen from the victim's pocket; the defendant had grabbed the note and demanded the balance of £2 still owing to him. The defendant's defence to robbery, reduced to theft by the jury, was that he had not acted dishonestly. The jury were directed that, for the defence to succeed, it was necessary for the defendant to have had an honest belief that he was entitled to the money, but also, that he was entitled to take it in the manner that he did. This was held to be misdirection and the conviction was quashed.

3-11     In *Corcoran v Anderton*,[16] two youths, the defendant and his co-accused acting in pursuance of an agreed plan, attacked a woman in the street. The co-accused hit her and tugged at her bag in an effort to get her to release it. The defendant participated. Their victim screamed, fell to the ground and released the bag. The two youths ran away and the victim regained control of the bag. The defendant was arrested and charged with robbery. The issue that arose was whether the tugging of the bag, accompanied by force, could amount to robbery, despite the fact that the youths did not obtain sole control over the bag at any point in time. The Divisional Court had no hesitation in broadening the concept of appropriation for the purposes of robbery. An appropriation sufficient for the purposes of s 3(1) could be located in the forcible tugging of the bag. The youths were seeking to exercise the rights of the owner and, in doing so, were using force. The requirements of robbery were satisfied. At least one commentator has pointed out that the 'decisive factor was that the victim had been made to lose control, if only momentarily'.[17] This, it is submitted, is not entirely correct in the light of the broadening of the concept of appropriation in *Gomez*: the two youths had, using force, usurped the rights of the lawful owner of the bag by tugging at it.[18] The fact that she, momentarily, may have lost control of the bag is simply evidence of their appropriation. It must be noted, however, that the particular problem could have been avoided if the defendant had been charged, instead, with the second offence under s 8: an assault with intent to rob.[19]

---

14  See the previous discussion of these issues in Chapter 2.
15  [1977] Crim LR 173.
16  (1980) 71 Cr App R 104.
17  Griew, para 2-74.
18  [1993] AC 442 and the discussion of this issue in Chapter 2.
19  Needless to say, a further alternative would have been attempted theft. Further, depending upon the evidence of the plan to attack the victim, there may have been a conspiracy to rob.

## Use of force or fear of force

3-12 Stealing without the use of force, or putting the victim to the fear of being subjected to force, cannot amount to robbery, although it may be theft. This is a point that has to be specifically addressed in any direction to the jury. Moreover, it is essential that the force must be used 'in order to' steal. For instance, where a defendant attempted to rape a woman and she gave him money to stop, this would not be robbery; the force was not used in order to steal.[20] This point was made in *Shendley*.[21] The trial judge directed the jury that:

> The allegation is that immediately before taking the property, or at the time of taking it, or immediately after, force was used towards [the complainant] to put him fear ... If you come to the conclusion that the violence was unconnected with the stealing, but you were satisfied there was a stealing, it does not mean that is an acquittal because it would be open to you to find [him] guilty of robbery, that is, robbery without violence.

The Court of Appeal held that this amounted to a misdirection. There could not be robbery without violence. What the trial judge obviously intended was that, if the jury were satisfied that the defendant stole the property, but were not satisfied that he used violence for this purpose, then they should find him not guilty of robbery, but guilty of theft.

3-13 Both the trial judge and the Court of Appeal, in the *Shendley* case (above), used the term 'violence' instead of 'force', the term actually used in s 8. There is a very real difference between these two words, not least because violence raises implications of unlawfulness and culpability *per se*. This issue was explored in a number of subsequent cases.

3-14 In *Dawson*,[22] the essential facts were that the defendant and his accomplices approached a man in the street. One of them nudged him, in such a way that he lost his balance, while another stole his wallet. The defence, relying on pre-1968 cases, contended that their actions could not be said to amount to violence. This contention was decisively rejected. The Court of Appeal ruled that the words of the TA 1968 had been purposely chosen in order to rid the law of the old, unnecessary, technicalities. It was true that the LA 1916 and the common law cases had used the terminology of 'violence', but this was no longer relevant. The word 'force' was an ordinary word in ordinary use which any jury would understand. The Court of Appeal went on to rule that the trial judge had been correct in leaving it to the jury to decide whether the nudging, or jostling, amounted to the use of force. However, it was not necessary for the trial judge to go further and direct the jury that the force had to be 'substantial': this was a matter entirely for the jury.

---

20  See *Archbold*, para 21-100, relying on the old case of *Blackham* (1787) 2 East PC 711.
21  [1970] Crim LR 49.
22  (1976) 64 Cr App R 170.

3-15 It is arguable whether this approach is justified. It should not automatically follow that the mere laying of a hand on the victim will amount to the use of force under s 8. The *Dawson* approach, however, which requires that the matter be left to the jury, may produce exactly that result. Similar facts may produce dissimilar verdicts, depending on individual juries. Further, minor variations in the facts (for instance, that in one case the victim touched was male whilst, in other the victim was female) may have a disproportionate effect on the outcome. It may be argued that public policy requires that, even a relatively slight application of force, may merit the condemnation of being classified as robbery but, surely, this is casting the net of criminal culpability too wide, bearing in mind the, always available, alternative verdict of theft. It may be true that 'no jury could reasonably find that the slight physical contact which might be involved where D picks P's pocket would amount to a use of force',[23] but this is not a matter that ought to be left to the vagaries of jury decisions.

3-16 It is clear also that *Dawson* does not reflect the views of the Criminal Law Revision Committee which sought a distinction between degrees of force:

> We should not regard mere snatching of property, such as a handbag, from an unresisting owner, as using force for the purpose of the definition, though it might be so if the owner resisted.[24]

3-17 If the 'mere snatching' of a handbag was not to be considered sufficient for robbery, then neither could the jostling that occurred in *Dawson*. However, the matter appears to be settled as result of the decision in *Clouden*.[25] The defendant followed and then wrenched a shopping basket out of the hands of his victim, running off with it. He was convicted of robbery. He appealed on the grounds that there was insufficient evidence of any resistance on the part of the victim which might have amounted to the kind of force required under s 8. Moreover, the old common law cases had drawn a distinction between force directed to the property and force directed to the person.[26] It was submitted that, since s 8(1) uses the words 'uses force on any person', no conviction could stand where the force that was used was on the property. The Court of Appeal dismissed the appeal and followed its previous decision in *Dawson*: first, it would not entertain such fine distinctions and, secondly, whether the defendant had used force on his victim in order to steal was an issue that was for the jury to decide.

3-18 A further issue that arose in *Dawson* was whether the force that was used had been used for distracting the victim's attention, or for overcoming the

---

23 Smith and Hogan, *Criminal Law*, 9th edn, 1999, Butterworths, p 549.
24 Criminal Law Revision Committee, *Eighth Report*, Cmnd 2977, 1966, HMSO: London, para 65.
25 [1987] Crim LR 56.
26 The case often cited as authority for this is *Gnosil* (1824) 1 C & P 304, where the charge was that of highway robbery. It was held that the force used had to be of such a nature as to overpower the victim and prevent his resisting, not merely to get possession of the property.

victim's resistance. The Court of Appeal rejected the attempt to draw such a distinction by ruling that, while such a distinction might have been relevant under the old law, under the 1968 Act the only issue was whether force had been used *in order to* steal.

## Immediately before or at the time of the theft

3-19     The specific words used in s 8(1) indicate that, as with burglary, an appropriation can be a continuing act as far as robbery is concerned. This is illustrated by cases such as *Hale*.[27] The defendant and an accomplice had forced their way into the house of the victim. He put his hand over her mouth to stop her screaming, while the accomplice went upstairs, returned with her jewellery box and demanded further property. Before leaving the house they tied her up and told her that they would harm her son if she informed the police within five minutes of their leaving. The jury convicted of robbery. On appeal, it was argued that a conviction for robbery was not possible where a defendant used force in order to effect an escape with the stolen goods. Also, as the theft was completed as soon as the jewellery was seized, any further force could not be 'in order to' steal. The Court of Appeal rejected these contentions. Eveleigh LJ held that the necessary appropriation of the property did not come to an end at the point at which the defendant and his accomplice had physical control of the property: the act of appropriation did not suddenly cease. Appropriation could be a continuous act and it was a matter for the jury to decide when the appropriation was finally accomplished. As to robbery, if the jury were satisfied (as they clearly were) that the act of tying her up in order to effect their escape was force used in order to successfully accomplish their theft, then they were perfectly entitled to convict for robbery. Any submission that the force used was intended merely to facilitate escape, and not to steal, could not be sustained. In any case, there was sufficient application of force at the point at which the defendant placed his hand over his victim's mouth.

3-20     Consequently, the fact that s 8(1) does not specifically refer to force used after the stealing is of no consequence. However, a limitation in terms of time is imposed by the requirement that the victim must be 'there and then' subjected to the fear of force. As such, it is submitted that any force used *after* the stealing, must be used *immediately after*. There are two issues for the jury to decide: first, whether on the facts, the force was 'in order to' steal and, secondly, whether the force was used before, during or after the appropriation was completed. In the latter case, it would still be open to the jury to convict of the 'lesser' offence of theft.

---

27   (1978) 68 Cr App R 415.

## *Any person*

3-21    It is clear that the force need not be directed to the actual victim of the robbery The robber could well accomplish his purpose by applying force to a third party The position is slightly more complicated where the prosecution alleges the defendant used threats of force against a third party in order to steal. In Hale the defendants had, as a parting shot, threatened the victim's young son. This raises the question as to whether the third party, who was being threatened, had to be aware of the threat. It is submitted that this is immaterial. The threat is made to the victim that force will be used against someone else. This should be sufficient. However, the use of the words 'there and then subjected to force indicate a necessary degree of immediacy.

## *There and then subjected to force*

3-22    In situations where the defendant threatens either the actual victim or a third party with some future force, then the appropriate charge would be for blackmail, in that it might well constitute an unwarranted demand with menaces under s 21(1).[28]

## Assault with intent to rob

3-23    The second offence under s 8 is that of an assault with intent to rob. This, too, is an aggravated form of theft. However, it seems to have been introduced into the section almost as an aforethought, included as it is in the sub-section dealing with sentence. It is submitted that, rather than conceptualising the offence as an aggravated form of *theft*, it would be more appropriate to think of it as an aggravated form of *assault*. In a similar vein, the offence has not been the subject of much case law and has not been subjected to any form of critical scrutiny in the established texts on the law of theft.[29] It submitted that the approach taken by *Archbold* is to be preferred: 'It is submitted that the better view is that this is a common law offence, the penalty only being provided by the statute.'[30]

3-24    A few points may be noted. First, it is necessary for the prosecution to prove all the elements of an assault.[31] Consequently, the question arises as to whether assault may be an alternative verdict. It would appear that an alternative verdict for common assault is not available. This is because this form of robbery is an indictable only offence, while common assault is summary only: therefore, the

---

28   See the discussion at para 11-10 below.
29   Neither Smith nor Griew devote any attention to this offence in their texts.
30   *Archbold*, para 21-103.
31   It should be noted that, an assault may be either the application of force or a threat of it.

terms of s 6(3) would not be applicable.[32] On the other hand, in the appropriate circumstances, there is nothing to prevent a charge for assault being specifically included in the indictment. Secondly, while it is true that assault may be satisfied upon proof of recklessness, for the present offence, this would not be sufficient. The sub-section spells out that there must be an 'assault with intent to rob' and it is difficult to see how a reckless assault could be committed with the requisite intention.

## Mens rea

3-25   In common with some other offences under the TA 1968 (for instance, the offence of going equipped, under s 12), the *mens rea* required to prove robbery is not automatically obvious. It is clear, however, that since robbery is an aggravated form of theft, the *mens rea* for theft must be read into this section. Similarly, since the force or threat of force must be in order to steal, there must have been an intention to use force or to threaten force; it would not be sufficient to prove negligence or even recklessness.[33] An accidental use of force would clearly be ruled out.

A further reason for doubting the correctness of the decisions in *Dawson* and *Clouden*,[34] (discussed above) lies in the fact that in neither of those cases was the necessary *mens rea* made clear.

---

32   *Mearns* [1991] QB 82.

33   Prof JC Smith is of the view that recklessness may be sufficient. It is submitted, with all respect, that this cannot be right: Smith, JC, para 3-07.

34   See paras 3-14 and 3-17 above.

# CHAPTER 4

# BURGLARY AND AGGRAVATED BURGLARY

## 1 BURGLARY

4-01 **Section 9 of the Theft Act (TA) 1968 – Burglary (as amended by s 26(2) of the Criminal Justice Act (CJA) 1991)**

(1) A person is guilty of burglary if –

    (a) he enters any building or part of a building as a trespasser and with intent to commit any such offence as is mentioned in sub-s (2) below; or

    (b) having entered any building or part of a building as a trespasser he steals or attempts to steal anything in the building or that part of it or inflicts or attempts to inflict on any person therein any grievous bodily harm.

(2) The offences referred to in sub-s (1)(a) above are offences of stealing anything in the building or part of a building in question, of inflicting on any person therein any grievous bodily harm or raping any person therein, and of doing unlawful damage to the building or anything therein.

(3) A person guilty of burglary shall on conviction on indictment be liable to imprisonment for a term not exceeding –

    (a) where the offence was committed in respect of a building or part of a building which is a dwelling, 14 years;

    (b) in any other case, 10 years.

(4) References in sub-ss (1) and (2) above to a building, and the reference in sub-s (3) above to a building which is a dwelling, shall apply also to an inhabited vehicle or vessel, and shall apply to any such vehicle or vessel at times when the person having a habitation in it is not there as well as at times when he is.

## Introduction

4-02 It would not be an exaggeration to say that the previous law on this point was in an impossibly complicated state. The provisions in the TA 1968 relating to burglary, therefore, represent a whole scale rewriting of the provisions in the Larceny Act 1916. The concept of 'breaking' has been eliminated entirely. Similarly, some quite unnecessary distinctions that were drawn between, for instance, breaking in the day as opposed to breaking in the night, have been removed. The previous case law, therefore, has little role to play. However, the laudable attempt to provide simplicity in this area of the law has been frustrated by the language actually employed in s 9. Subsequent statutory amendments, in the form of the CJA 1991, have re-introduced the old distinctions applying to dwellings (as opposed to other premises), while some of the decisions made under s 9 have introduced unnecessary difficulty.

4-03    It is clear enough that s 9(1) contains two separate offences: one under paragraph (a) and the other under paragraph (b). These may be roughly (even if not precisely) summarised as:

(a) under s 9(1)(a) – entry with intent to commit one of the specified offences (the offence is completed as soon as the defendant has entered with the requisite intent, that is, even when one of these offences is not actually committed). The specified offences are theft, inflicting grievous bodily harm and rape; and

(b) under s 9(1)(b) – committing one of the specified offences after having gained entry. The specified offences are theft (or attempted theft) and inflicting (or attempting to inflict) grievous bodily harm.

4-04    However, one consequence of the amendments made by the CJA 1991, in reducing the maximum penalty for non-residential premises to 10 years and retaining the maximum penalty of 14 years in relation to a 'dwelling', is to create four separate offences:[1]

(a) an offence under s 9(1)(a) – maximum sentence of 10 years;

(b) an offence under s 9(1)(a) read together with sub-s (3) – maximum sentence of 14 years;

(c) an offence under s 9(1)(b) – maximum sentence of 10 years; and

(d) an offence under s 9(1)(b) read together with sub-s (3) – maximum sentence of 14 years.

Accordingly, it is necessary that the indictment should make clear to the defendant which of the above offences he is facing.[2]

## Alternative verdicts

4-05    At the same time, case law has made it clear that alternative verdicts are possible. A number of options exist:

(a) Where the charge is of burglary contrary to s 9(1)(b), the court or jury is entitled to convict for the underlying offences specified in sub-s (2), provided the provisions of s 6(3) of the Criminal Law Act (CLA) 1967 are satisfied. The effect of this is that an alternative verdict is possible for theft, or criminal damage, or (provided the defendant is being proceeded against on an indictment), grievous bodily harm or rape.

---

1    *Courtie* [1984] AC 463.

2    The fact that there are four, as opposed to two, offences has sometimes been overlooked in the existing literature.

(b) Where the charge is of burglary under s 9(1)(b), and the offence is being tried as a summary offence, an alternative verdict for assault is no longer possible. The decision often cited for the proposition that it is possible is the decision of the House of Lords, in *Wilson*.[3] In that case, Lord Roskill had ruled that the words 'another offence falling within the jurisdiction of the court of trial' in s 6(3) could be ignored.[4] However, this decision cannot stand as a result of ss 39 and 40 of the CJA 1988 and the decision in *Mearns*.[5]

(c) On a charge for burglary under s 9(1)(b), an alternative verdict is possible for the offence under s 9(1)(a). This is so because an allegation under s 9(1)(b) includes an allegation under s 9(1)(a). The authority for this is *Whiting*,[6] where the Court of Appeal followed the approach taken in *Wilson*. However, it is submitted that this is incorrect. Apart from the fact that *Wilson* may no longer be good law, these two offences are different in certain crucial respects. The best that can be said is that an alternative verdict is possible for some, but not all, cases.

(d) When a defendant is charged with burglary in respect of a dwelling, it is open to the court to convict, instead, of burglary in respect of a building, or part of a building.

4-06    Much time and effort is frequently expended on an unnecessary exposition of the terms used in s 9. Instances of this include questions as to whether a holiday caravan is an 'inhabited vehicle'; or when 'a part of a building' is properly within the section; or whether entry of a part of the body is 'entry' under the section. The pragmatic approach taken by the courts has often been to resort to the resolution of such matters by holding that these are questions of fact to be left to the jury. Such an approach may be justifiably criticised on grounds of principle: too much 'law' is left to the vagaries of jury decisions. Nonetheless, it is submitted that this remains the only acceptable solution when dealing with the wide and imprecise drafting of this particular section, further complicated as it is by statutory amendments.[7]

## Mode of trial and sentence

4-07    Burglary is an offence triable either way. However, burglary becomes indictable only where its commission involves an intent to commit an offence which is, in itself, indictable. For instance, if the burglary involves an intent to rape under s 9(2), then the offence must be tried on indictment only. Further, if the burglary

---

3    [1984] AC 242.

4    *Ibid*, p 451, j.

5    [1991] 1 QB 82.

6    (1987) 85 Cr App R 78.

7    There are occasions when the attempt to make sense out of certain statutory provisions may be entirely futile, see para 1-15 above.

comes within the terms of sub-s (3)(a) – is committed in respect of dwelling – and any person in the dwelling has been subjected to either violence or the threat of violence, the offence, thus, constituted is treated as indictable only.[8] If triable on indictment only, it is a class 3 offence; where triable either way, it is a class 4 offence.[9]

4-08    Under s 9(3), where the indictable offence is committed in relation to dwellings, the maximum sentence is 14 years, whereas in all other cases the maximum sentence is 10 years. Comparisons may be made with the offences of robbery and aggravated burglary where the maximum sentence is imprisonment for life. The different approach taken between robbery and burglary is illustrated by the case of *Brewster*.[10] Lord Bingham CJ, in issuing sentencing guidance, stated that although burglary is a serious offence, it is not so serious that a non-custodial sentence could never be justified.[11] Nonetheless, Lord Bingham acknowledged that the particular abhorrence attached to domestic burglaries, especially if occurring at night and involving violence, is something the courts must take into account when considering sentence.

4-09    There is an extremely wide variety of factual circumstances which may be encompassed by the offences under s 9. These range from 'ram raiding' (for instance, in *Hunter*)[12] to the burglary of doctors' premises in order to obtain drugs (*Larcher*),[13] through to the merely 'opportunistic' offence committed by a 19 year old looking for money to pay his taxi fare home in the early hours of the morning (*Suker*).[14] These cases all fall within s 9, and rightly so, but any generalised guidance is unlikely to be of great assistance.

## Elements of the offence

### Entry

4-10    The element of an entry is a fundamental element that has to be proved in relation to all the offences under s 9. In most cases, it will be clear enough that the defendant has 'entered' the building or dwelling. This would be a question of fact that the prosecution must prove. However, much time and effort had been expended on dealing with three possible situations:

---

8    Magistrates' Courts Act (MCA) 1980, Sched 1, para 28(c).
9    MCA 1980, s 17(1) and Sched 1.
10   [1998] 1 Cr App R 220.
11   Compare this with the case of *Golding* (1992) 13 Cr App R(S) 142, where the view expressed was that a non-custodial sentence for robbery could *not* be justified.
12   (1994) 15 Cr App R(S) 530.
13   (1979) 1 Cr App R(S) 137.
14   (1990) 12 Cr App R(S) 290.

(a) where it can be proved that only a part of the defendant's body has entered the premises;

(b) where the defendant is outside the premises, but has inserted some manner of instrument; and

(c) where the defendant has relied on an innocent agent to enter.

4-11    Under the common law, the insertion of any part of the defendant's body was enough to constitute the necessary entry.[15] The question as to whether the common law position was to be followed arose in the case of *Collins*.[16] One issue before the court concerned the question as to when the defendant had 'entered' the bedroom of his victim. Edmund Davies LJ held that it was unnecessary to consider the old common law authorities; what had to be proved was 'an effective and substantial entry'.[17] Unfortunately, apart from the fact that this could properly be regarded only as *obiter dictum*, no further explanation of this phrase was forthcoming. Much criticism has been levelled at this turn of phrase. For instance, it has been argued that it seems to indicate that the insertion of a small part of the body could never be enough.[18] However, the point that may be made is that, whether an entry has been effected is, essentially, one of fact and degree. The insertion of one arm is 'an effective and substantial entry', if the defendant's purpose is to snatch an item of jewellery from a shelf just inside the window.

4-12    This issue was further raised in *Brown*, where the defendant's feet were still on the ground outside a shop window, while the upper part of his body had been inserted through the shop window.[19] The Court of Appeal rejected the contention that 'entry' required the entry of the whole body and went on to consider what had been said on this point in *Collins*. The court concluded that while the word 'substantial' was not of much assistance, the entry here had been sufficiently 'effective'; it had put the defendant in a position to steal. This, however, is not entirely problem free. It suggests that the test of what constitutes 'entry' is whether it is sufficient to enable the defendant to accomplish his unlawful purpose. Following on from this, if the defendant is arrested at the point when only one arm is inside the dwelling, it will be impossible to convict him of burglary with intent to rape. This would, in effect, frustrate the legislative purpose of creating the ulterior offence in the first place. On the other hand, if the prosecution proves that he had inserted his hand in order to undo a latch so that he might, thereby, insert the rest of his body in order to commit the rape, then the offence *is* made out. Such distinctions are clearly untenable.

---

15  *Davies* (1823) R & R 499.
16  [1973] QB 100.
17  *Ibid*, p 106.
18  This criticism is made by Smith, JC, para 11-03.
19  [1985] Crim LR 212.

4-13    A number of alternatives might be suggested. First, there could be a return to the original common law rule that the insertion of even a small part of the body is sufficient to constitute entry. Secondly, if that approach is not to be followed, that the courts should provide adequate guidelines. This might involve a judicial rewriting of the statutory language. Thirdly, that the pragmatic approach be adopted of leaving this as a question of fact to be determined by the jury. The word 'entry' should be seen as an ordinary English word and it will be up to the jury to determine whether, on the facts before them, the defendant has entered the premises.[20]

4-14    One other point raised in *Collins* can usefully be noted at this stage. It was held there that any entry must be deliberate (or at least reckless). Consequently, if the entry is accidental then this essential element cannot be proved.[21]

4-15    It is submitted that a similar approach be taken with regard to the insertion of some instrument in situations where no part of the defendant's body is within the premises. Under the old law, the insertion of such an instrument for the purpose of committing one of the specified offences amounted to an entry. However, if the insertion of the instrument was merely to facilitate access to the premises, this was not sufficient. Should this distinction be perpetuated? Two lines of argument may be suggested. First, the language of *Brown*, above, could be employed here: has the defendant used the instrument in order to accomplish an effective entry? If it is an effective entry (with the necessary ulterior intent), the defendant could be charged with burglary. Secondly, in the alternative, it could be argued that, if the defendant has inserted the instrument in order to gain or to facilitate access and is then apprehended before anything further occurs, the insertion can only constitute an attempted burglary. It is submitted that the legislative purpose underlying s 9 would be better served if the former approach were to be followed.[22]

4-16    Situations may arise where it is not the defendant who has entered, but an innocent agent.[23] In such cases, the general principle in criminal law should be applied. The *actus reus* of a crime may be committed by an innocent agent but attributed to the defendant: 'Where a statute uses a verb like "enters" ... conduct by an innocent agent coming within the verb is attributed to the principal.'[24] This point is well made in the old authorities:

> If A, being a man of full age take a child of seven or eight years old well instructed by him in this villainous art, as some such there be, and the child goes

---

20    This is the position adopted in *Ryan* [1996] Crim LR 320.

21    See the discussion of this issue with regard to the requirement that there has to be a trespass, para 4-17.

22    Griew takes the contrary view: para 4-21. The Smith view is to, reluctantly, accept the common law approach: Smith, JC, para 11-03.

23    The label 'innocent agent' is used in its very general sense; there is no reason that the 'agent' should even be human, as, for instance, where a well trained monkey is employed.

24    Williams, G, *Criminal Law: The General Part*, 2nd edn, 1961, Stevens, p 351.

in at the window, takes goods out, and delivers them to A who carries them away, this is burglary in A [although] the child that made the entry, be not guilty by reason of his infancy.[25]

In *Wheelhouse*,[26] the defendant had persuaded an innocent dupe to gain entry to the garage of a house in order to steal a car. It was held that there was nothing to prevent the defendant being convicted of burglary even upon the acquittal of the innocent dupe: the defendant had, through the agency of this man, 'entered' the garage. Consequently, if the defendant sends in his dog to steal something from a room, while he remains outside, he commits burglary through its agency.

### As a trespasser

4-17 It is necessary for all the offences under s 9 that the defendant is a 'trespasser', thus utilising another concept of civil law that is not defined in the Act. Under the civil law, specifically the law of tort, trespass is entry without the consent of the lawful possessor. Accordingly, it follows that there can be no conviction for burglary without a finding that civil trespass has taken place. In *Laing*,[27] the defendant was convicted of burglary, under s 9(1)(a), after being found in the stock area of a department store after it had shut. The point at issue was whether a conviction was proper in a situation where the defendant had lawfully entered, even though he may have become a trespasser at the time he was arrested. The Court of Appeal was clear on this point: there was no evidence he was a trespasser when he entered the store and, accordingly, the conviction was quashed.[28]

For criminal culpability, moreover, something more is required. This point is adequately explained in one of the more infamous, even if slightly bizarre, cases in the annals of the law on theft: *Collins*.[29] The facts of this case were that the defendant had climbed, naked, up to the open window of a young woman. She awoke and, thinking that it was her boyfriend paying her a nocturnal visit, sat up in bed and indicated that he should enter. He did so. Sexual intercourse took place. She then, suspecting something was amiss, turned on the bedside light and discovered that he was not, after all, her boyfriend. She slapped and bit him and when she went to the bathroom, he made his escape. On the evidence, there was some doubt that he possessed the necessary *mens rea* for rape: he admitted

---

25  *Hale* (1736) 1 PC 555, quoted in the 'Commentary' to *R v Wheelhouse* [1994] Crim LR 756. The commentary rightly points out that there is nothing in the TA 1968 to affect this principle.

26  *R v Wheelhouse* [1994] Crim LR 756.

27  [1995] Crim LR 395.

28  It may have been the case that he became a trespasser when he moved from one part of the building to another, but this point was not canvassed by the prosecution.

29  [1973] QB 100; as Edmund Davies LJ put it, p 102: '... if the facts had been put into a novel, or portrayed on the stage, they would be regarded as being so improbable as to be unworthy of serious consideration and as verging at times on farce.'

that he was prepared to have sexual intercourse with her whether she consented or not, but, on the facts, he may have honestly believed that she was consenting. The real issue was whether, for the purpose of s 9, he had entered the room 'as a trespasser'. In order to deal with this issue, it was necessary to establish clearly where the defendant was at the precise moment in time when the young woman had awoken and invited him into her bedroom. Was he on the outside of the windowsill, or was he on that part of the sill which was inside the room? This was crucial because, if he were already in the room before she invited him in, then he would be a trespasser. On the other hand, there would be no trespass if he were *outside* the window at that crucial point. The facts were unclear and the jury had not been directed to consider the vital question as to whether the defendant 'had entered as a trespasser'. On that basis his conviction for burglary with intent to rape was quashed.

4-18    Section 9 does not specify the necessary state of mind that must exist before the defendant can be said to trespass. On the basis of *Collins*, it is necessary that:

> There cannot be a conviction for entering premises 'as a trespasser' within the meaning of s 9 of the TA 1968 unless the person entering does so knowing that he is a trespasser and nevertheless deliberately enters, or at the very least, is reckless as to whether or not he is entering the premises of another without the other party's consent.[30]

Accordingly, the prosecution should prove that the person entering does so intentionally or deliberately or, at the very least, is subjectively reckless as to whether or not he is entering the premises without consent. Quite clearly, an accidental trespass would not be sufficient. What about a negligent trespass, or trespass which is objectively reckless? It is submitted that negligence or objective recklessness cannot be enough. To hold otherwise would be inconsistent with the general scheme of culpability under the TA 1968, as well as with the concept of ulterior intent utilised in s 9.

4-19    In the *Collins* case itself, giving the defendant the benefit of the doubt, the invitation to enter had been based on a mistake of identity, but the defendant may not have been aware of this. Implausible as it may sound, the defendant contended that he approached the bedroom window and was then invited to enter. It was not the defendant who was mistaken. What about situation in which the defendant relies on mistake as his answer to trespass? This may occur where the defendant enters the wrong building by mistake, thinking it to be the one he has been given permission to enter. Similarly, the defendant may genuinely believe that he has, under the civil law, a right to enter the building. These cases can be dealt with by the application of the general principle that, in cases of serious offences such as burglary, the defendant should be judged on the basis of the facts as he believed them to be. An objection may be raised as to

---

30   [1973] QB 100, p 105. Later, p 107, Edmund Davies LJ pointed out that 'the common law doctrine of trespass *ab initio* has no application to burglary'.

whether this would also hold true when the mistake is one made while intoxicated. It is submitted that, on the *ratio* of *Collins*, the same result should follow.

4-20    If the defendant has a legal right to enter the premises he cannot be a trespasser. It is immaterial, on the authority of *Collins*, that after lawfully entering, he then commits one of the specified offences. The same analysis will apply to anyone who has a licence to enter. The entry granted is limited to the terms, either express or implied, under that licence. If the defendant has entered with the intention to commit one of the specified offences, then quite clearly he has exceeded the scope of that licence and is, thereby, a trespasser. This is illustrated by the case of *Jones and Smith*.[31] Both defendants had entered the house of Smith's father for the purpose of stealing two television sets. The defence contended that they could not be regarded in law as trespassers, since Smith's father had given the son general permission to enter the house. The Court of Appeal rejected this contention. Their entry into the house was clearly in excess of any licence that had been granted by the father to the son. James LJ referred to the civil law decision in *Hillen and Pettigrew v ICI (Alkali) Ltd* where Lord Atkin had ruled that:

> [The invitation] extends so long as and so far as the invitee is making what can reasonably be contemplated as an ordinary and reasonable use of the premises by the invitee for the purpose for which he has been invited.[32]

4-21    James LJ cited the decision in *Collins* with approval and proceeded to elaborate it for the purposes of the instant appeal:

> It is our view that a person is a trespasser for the purpose of s 9(1)(b) of the TA 1968, if he enters premises of another knowing that he is *entering in excess of the permission* that has been given to him ... providing the facts are known to the accused which enable him to realise that he is acting in excess of the permission given ... then that is sufficient for the jury to decide that he is in fact a trespasser.[33]

4-22    The impact of the decision in *Jones and Smith* may be tested against the case of a shopper who enters a shop intending to steal. While there is a general licence to genuine shoppers, the defendant-shopper has entered in excess of this licence and is, therefore, a trespasser. At first sight, this may appear to be inconsistent with the decision in *Collins*, as it may be argued that the crucial point is that, at the time that the defendant-shopper enters the shop, he has permission to do so. The response to this is that, in *Collins*, the defendant may have genuinely believed that he himself (rather than the victim's boyfriend) was being invited in. The defendants in *Jones and Smith* could not be said to be in the same position.

---

31   (1976) 63 Cr App R 47.
32   [1936] AC 65, p 69.
33   Emphasis added.

4-23   What, however, of the later decision in *Laing*?[34] Here, the conviction of the defendant-shopper was quashed, as he had not entered the store as a trespasser, even though he was found in the store after it had shut. On the basis of *Jones and Smith*, it could be argued that the defendant had exceeded his invitation to enter and, therefore, was, in fact, a trespasser. This would be especially so, as the only likely purpose for his presence in the store was to steal.[35] It is submitted, however, that the Laing decision is not sufficiently authoritative as this issue was not properly addressed either at first instance, or by the Court of Appeal.[36] It is also worth noting that the CLRC postulated a very similar example and concluded that there would be a trespassory intent.[37] Moreover, on policy grounds, the view taken of this issue in Jones and Smith is to be preferred.[38]

## *The building*

4-24   Any building, or part of a building, may be the subject of burglary. At the same time, special provision has been made under s 9(3) for buildings which are dwellings, and a further extension under s 9(4) for inhabited vehicles and vessels. There is considerable discussion in the authorities as to the meaning to be ascribed to 'building' and, especially, to 'part of a building'.[39] It is submitted that much of this discussion is unnecessary. The words 'building' and 'part of a building' are ordinary English words and their meaning is to be determined by the jury on the facts of each particular case. Byles J recognised the difficulty of attempting any definition, either statutory or judicial, in the old case of *Stevens v Gurley*:

> The imperfection of human language renders it not only difficult, but absolutely impossible, to define the word 'building' with any approach to accuracy. One may say of this or that structure, this or that is not a building; but no general definition can be given.[40]

---

34   See para 4-17.

35   If this is so, then the view of both Smith (para 11-09) and Griew (para 4-12) to the effect that such a defendant-shopper could be a burglar, would be incorrect.

36   It is possible that, in this case, the defendant may not have entered the store with the intention to steal, but formed that intent at a later point.

37   Criminal Law Revision Committee, *Eighth Report*, Cmnd 2977, 1966, HMSO: London, para 75.

38   Reference may be made to the decision of the High Court of Australia in *Barker v The Queen* (1983) 153 CLR 338. Here, the view was expressed that entry does not amount to trespass merely because the defendant's purpose is one of which the person giving consent would not have approved. Griew comments (para 4-12) that 'account will have to be taken of this case in any future consideration of the relationship between licence and unlawful purpose'. It is submitted that account should only be taken of this decision to the extent of rejecting it.

39   See Smith, JC, paras 11-13–21; Griew, paras 4-22–26.

40   (1859) 7 CB (NS) 99, p 112.

The learned judge made the same point when a similar issue arose with regard to the definition of 'building' under s 6 of the old Malicious Damage Act 1861: 'Such words as those used in the section must be interpreted in their ordinary sense.'[41] At the same time, however, there would be situations where a dividing line needs to be drawn and it would not be feasible to leave this entirely to the jury. In *Stevens v Gurley*, it had was held that a building in its ordinary sense is '... a structure of considerable size and intended to be permanent or at least to endure for a considerable time',[42] Accordingly, it would be perfectly proper for a trial judge to direct a jury that a tent was not a building.[43]

4-25    A number of cases are illustrative. In *B and S v Leathley*,[44] the defendants had stolen some meat from a freezer container in a farmyard. On the facts, the freezer was 25 ft long with a 7 ft cross-section, weighing about three tons. Moreover, it had been in place for a number of years and was clearly intended to remain in that place for the foreseeable future. Accordingly, it could be classed as a building within the terms of *Stevens v Gurley*. On the other hand, in *Norfolk Constabulary v Seekings*,[45] it was decided that a disconnected freezer trailer was not a building. It is important to note, however, that cases such as these cannot be entirely decisive. There is always a grey area of uncertainty where the issue must be left for jury determination. It is tempting to regard cases such as *Stevens v Gurley* as laying down a test to be followed; this is a temptation to be resisted.

## *Parts of buildings*

4-26    The same approach should also be utilised when dealing with the definition of 'part of a building'.[46] In *Walkington*,[47] the defendant had gone into a counter area of a department store. This counter area was made up of a movable three-sided counter containing a cash till. Only staff were permitted to be within this area. The defendant was observed to have opened the drawer of the till and, discovering that it was empty, slamming it shut. He was detained as he left the store and was, subsequently, charged with burglary, under s 9(1)(a), in that he had entered 'part of a building' as a trespasser with intent to steal. The defence contention was that he had lawfully entered the store and had not realised that he was not allowed into the counter area. It was only when he was there that he decided to open the drawer to see if there was anything worth stealing. It was

---

41    *R v Manning* (1871) LR 1 CCR 338, p 340, *per* Byles J. In the same case, Lush J stated (p 341): 'I do not think four walls erected a foot high would be a building.'

42    (1859) 7 CB (NS) 99, p 112.

43    It is submitted that such a direction would be on an issue of law and, therefore, revisable by an appellate court.

44    [1979] Crim LR 314.

45    [1986] Crim LR 167.

46    The older cases show that this was a vexed issue in civil cases as well. See, for instance, *Hedley v Webb* [1901] 2 Ch 126; *Birch v Wigan Corp* [1953] 1 QB 136.

47    [1979] 1 WLR 1169.

submitted that there was no case to answer and that the case should be withdrawn from the jury. The trial judge refused and directed the jury, *inter alia*, that it was for them to decide whether the counter area constituted a 'part of a building'. The defendant was convicted and appealed. Lane LJ considered that the situations in which shoppers could be charged with burglary could be divided into two categories. The first related to cases where a part of the building is shut off physically to prevent shoppers gaining admittance. This may be by a door with perhaps a notice on it. The second related to situations where there was no such physical demarcation, such as, for example, a table placed in the middle of the shop floor, where it would be virtually impossible for a shopper to know whether he was allowed beyond a particular point. Lane LJ further concluded that the facts of this particular case came within the former category. The three-sided counter was clearly a physical demarcation. Whether it was sufficient to amount to an area from which the public was excluded was a matter for the jury and the trial judge had been right to leave it to them. On the facts, there was ample evidence that the defendant knew he was not allowed into this area and he had entered it with intent to steal. The appeal was dismissed. The court also considered the legislative intent that lay behind the inclusion of the words 'part of a building' and approved the opinion of Professor JC Smith on this point:

> It would seem that the whole reason for the words 'or part of a building', is that D may enter or be in part of a building without trespass and it is desirable that he should be liable as a burglar if he trespasses in the remainder of the building with the necessary intent. It is submitted that building need not be physically divided into 'parts'. It ought to be sufficient if a notice in the middle of a hall stated, 'No customers beyond this point'. These considerations suggest that, for present purposes, a building falls into two parts only: first, that part in which D was lawfully present and, second, the remainder of the building. This interpretation avoids anomalies, which arise if physical divisions within a building are held to create 'parts'.[48]

4-27 This approach has the merit of dealing with the difficult problems that arose under the old law where the entry had to be into a particular dwelling house or building. Consequently, if the defendant broke into Flat 1 with intent to pass through it and enter Flat 2, then the entry into Flat 1 was neither burglary nor the old offence of house breaking. If the word building is to be given its ordinary, natural meaning (as it is submitted it should be), then the block of flats, as a single whole, would constitute a building and the defendant will have entered a part of it with trepassory intent. This would also apply to terraced houses, as well as to a shopping mall with individual retail outlets within it.

---

48   Smith, JC, para 11-17 (of the current edition).

## Dwellings

4-28    The old law contained various special distinctions, which applied to domestic burglaries. Some element of those distinctions was re-introduced by the CJA 1991. The consequential amendment, in s 9(3), provides for higher penalties where the offences are committed in respect of dwellings. The rationale for this is adequately set out in the judgment of Lord Bingham CJ in *Brewster*:

> Domestic burglary is, and always has been, regarded as a very serious offence. It may involve considerable loss to the victim. Even where it does not, the victim may lose possessions of particular value to him or to her. To those who are insured, the receipt of financial compensation does not replace what is lost. But many victims are uninsured; because they may have fewer possessions, they are the more seriously injured by the loss of those they do have.

> The loss of material possessions is, however, only part (and often a minor part) of the reason why domestic burglary is a serious offence. Most people, perfectly legitimately, attach importance to the privacy and security of their own homes. That an intruder should break in or enter, for his own dishonest purposes, leaves the victim with a sense of violation and insecurity.[49]

4-29    What amounts to a dwelling must be considered as a question of fact and presumably must refer to a building, vehicle or vessel, which is being used as a home or residence. In this context, reference may usefully be made to the definition of dwelling provided in s 8 of the Public Order Act (POA) 1986:

> ... 'dwelling' means any structure or part of a structure occupied as a person's home or as other living accommodation (whether the occupation is separate or shared with others) but does not include any part not so occupied ...

What then of a victim who lives in a tent? On grounds of policy, it could be argued that the statement of Lord Bingham CJ, in *Brewster*, should apply equally to protect such a person. The problem with such a submission is that s 9(3) speaks of 'a building or part of a building which is a dwelling'. Since it could be argued that a tent is not a building in the first place, it cannot be a dwelling, even though it is inhabited. On the other hand, the definition of dwelling in s 8 of the POA 1986 goes on to say that 'for this purpose "structure" includes a tent, caravan, vehicle, vessel or other temporary or movable structure'.

An important issue arises in relation to *mens rea* when dealing with the entry into dwellings (and, equally, into inhabited vessels and vehicles). While the defendant must have deliberately entered as a trespasser, is it necessary that he must know that he is entering a dwelling? There may be circumstances where this only becomes apparent to the defendant *after* he has entered. The argument in favour of requiring prior knowledge (intention, or even recklessness) rests on the fact that this relates to an aggravating factor that results in a more severe sentence. This would not be merited if the defendant thought that he was

---

49    [1998] 1 Cr App R 220, p 224.

entering business premises and, consequently, an alternative charge for the 'lesser' offence would be preferable.[50]

## *Inhabited vehicles and vessels*

4-30 The protection afforded to those who dwell in buildings has been extended to those who dwell in vehicles and vessels. There is legislative sense in this. A burglary is committed just as much when the building is a house or flat, as when it is a caravan or a houseboat. On the other hand, if a tent is not to be protected, why should a holiday caravan? Moreover, sub-s (4) introduces unnecessary complications by insisting that the vehicles and vessels should be 'inhabited'. This has given rise to interesting speculation as to when a vehicle or vessel used for occasional visits is properly to be regarded as 'inhabited'.[51] There is an absence of any reported case law. Should the courts be called upon to deal with such an issue the only solution is to treat the issue as one entirely dependent on the individual facts. There are some factual situations where a caravan will properly be considered to be an 'inhabited vehicle' and there are some situations where it will not: the words of s 9(4) do not provide an answer. Similarly, if the victim of a burglary has been made homeless and has been 'living rough' in his motorcar, it is also conceivable that the motorcar in question might be viewed as an 'inhabited' vehicle.[52]

## Ulterior intent: the offence under s 9(1)(a)

4-31 The offence under s 9(1)(a) is a crime of specific intent. It is also a crime of ulterior intent: the offence of burglary contains a classic example of the use of this concept in the criminal law. Generally, the prosecution must prove the *actus reus* and the accompanying *mens rea*, for each offence and each element of the offence. On occasion, however, a crime may be defined in such a way that its *mens rea* goes beyond the *actus reus* actually committed by the defendant:

> It is not enough that D intended to enter a building as a trespasser, that is, to achieve the *actus reus* of burglary. It is necessary to go further and to show that D had the intention of committing one of a number of specified offences in the building. The actual commission of one of those offences is no part of the *actus reus* of burglary which is complete as soon as D enters.[53]

---

50 There are a number of other statutory provisions, which seek to protect the 'integrity' of the home from intrusions. These include the Protection from Eviction Act 1977 (in particular, s 1) and the CLA 1977 (in particular, ss 6–8).

51 See Griew, para 4-27.

52 See the discussion surrounding a similar issue in *Bundy* [1977] 2 All ER 382, para 13-06, above, dealing with the issue of the 'place of abode'.

53 Smith and Hogan, *Criminal Law*, 9th edn, 1999, London: Butterworths, p 70.

4-32   The defendant's trespassory entry onto premises must be proved to be with the ulterior intent to commit one of the offences specified in sub-s (2): stealing, inflicting grievous bodily harm, rape, or unlawful damage. It should be noted that the intent must exist at the time of entry (not before and not after): the offence is complete as soon as the defendant enters with the necessary intention: As far as attempts are concerned, where a defendant attempts to enter the premises as a trespasser with ulterior intent, this is sufficient to constitute the offence of attempted burglary. It is not necessary for the prosecution to prove an attempt to commit the specified offence:[54]

> This illustrates the considerable reach of s 9(1)(a) burglary, going beyond that of an attempt to commit the substantive crime (for example, rape). If it can be justified, it is on the ground that entering a building as a trespasser is a non-innocent act which should be sufficient (when combined with evidence of a proscribed intent, often inferred from surroundings circumstances or from the absence of any other plausible explanation) to warrant criminal liability. D has crossed the threshold between conceiving an intent and taking steps to translate the intent into action.[55]

## *Stealing*

4-33   The stealing must satisfy the definition of theft as contained in s 1 of the Act.[56] If the defendant's intention is to commit a non-theft offence, such as blackmail or abstracting electricity, then he cannot be charged with burglary.[57] However, in the light of the decision in *Gomez*, this would include the obtaining of property by deception.[58] An issue that has arisen concerns the defendant who argues that he only intended to steal, if he could find something worth stealing – a concept sometimes referred to as conditional intent. In *Husseyn*, the Court of Appeal had concluded that this would not be sufficient in dealing with an attempt to steal.[59] Lord Scarman had stated: 'It cannot be said that one who has it in mind to steal, only if what he finds is worth stealing, has a present intention to steal.'[60] Unfortunately, this single sentence was then applied as a general principle to burglary. In *Greenhof*, the defendant had been found late at night in a house and admitted he was looking for money to steal. He was, however, acquitted of burglary on the grounds that the prosecution had not proved that there was money in the house and that he knew this.[61] In the subsequent case of *Walkington*, on the other hand, the Court of Appeal ruled that a defendant could

---

54   *R v Toothill* [1998] Crim LR 876; see the discussion in Chapter 14, para 13-10.
55   Ashworth, p 408.
56   See Chapter 2.
57   *Low v Blease* [1975] Crim LR; see para 7-03.
58   [1993] AC 442; see Chapter 2, para 2-31.
59   (1977) 67 Cr App R 131; see the discussion of this case in Chapter 14, para 14-15.
60   *Ibid*, p 132.
61   [1979] Crim LR 108.

have the requisite intent to steal where his stated aim is to do so, only if there is something worth stealing.[62]

Any remaining dispute appears to have been settled in *AG's Refs (Nos 1 and 2 of 1979)*.[63] Two questions were posed in the conjoined references:

*Question one*

Whether a man who has entered a house as a trespasser with the intention of stealing money therein is entitled to be acquitted of an offence against s 9(1)(a) of the TA 1968 on the grounds that his intention to steal is conditional on his finding money in the house.

*Question two*

Whether a man who is attempting to enter a house as a trespasser with the intention of stealing anything of value which he may find therein is entitled to be acquitted of the offence of attempted burglary on the ground that at the time of the attempt his said intention was insufficient to amount to 'the intention of stealing anything' necessary for conviction under s 9 of the TA 1968.

The Court of Appeal had no hesitation in giving a negative answer to both of these questions. Lord Roskill, however, refused to either specifically find the *Husseyn* ruling to be wrong, or to declare that the statement of Lord Scarman had been *obiter*. The solution lies in considering the particulars of the indictment under which the defendant in *Husseyn* had been charged. In that indictment, the goods had been specifically identified. Therefore, when the prosecution failed to prove that he had an intention to steal those *specific* goods, the charge could not be sustained. As to the practice to be adopted in the future, it was the view of Lord Roskill, in the present appeal, that it would be sufficient to frame indictments without reference to specific objects. It is submitted that, if this advice is followed, no further difficulties are likely to arise.

### Inflicting grievous bodily harm

4-34    Section 9(1)(a) read with sub-s (2) specifically refers to the offence of inflicting grievous bodily harm with intent to do so. This is clearly the offence under s 18 (but not s 20) of the Offences Against the Person Act (OAPA) 1861.[64] It is necessary that there should be evidence on which the jury could infer that there was the requisite intention and it must be proved that the intention existed at the time of entry. In the absence of such proof, it is submitted that there would not be a case to answer. However, the only authority that appears to exist for this view is the unreported case of *O'Neill, McMullen and Kelly*.[65] The defendants had carried no weapons, no grievous bodily harm had actually been committed and

---

62    [1979] 1 WLR 1169.

63    [1980] QB 180.

64    Note, the view of Smith and Hogan (*op cit*, fn 53, p 621) that this would also include the OAPA 1861, s 23.

65    (1986) *The Times*, 17 October.

there was no evidence of any such intent. It was held that the case should have been withdrawn from the jury.

## *Rape*

4-35    The offence of rape is contained within s 1 of the Sexual Offences Act 1956 (as amended by s 142 of the Criminal Justice and Public Order Act 1994).[66] A defendant may be charged with the offence of burglary with intent to rape if he enters a building, or dwelling, intending to have non-consensual sexual intercourse. The offence is complete as soon as the defendant enters the premises with this intention. Consequently, if the defendant enters the premises not knowing whether his victim will consent or not, but prepared to carry on even where no consent is forthcoming, then the offence is made out. If, *after* entering the premises, his intended victim does, in fact, consent, he cannot be charged with rape, but he may be charged with burglary with intent to rape. On the facts of *Collins*,[67] the charge of burglary with intent to rape would have succeeded, but for the inability of the prosecution to prove that he had entered his victim's bedroom as a trespasser. It should be noted that rape, or attempted rape, is not included in the offence under s 9(1)(b).

## *Unlawful damage*

4-36    The issue here is whether the defendant intends to commit an offence covered by the Criminal Damage Act 1971. This might be either the 'basic' s 1 offence, or any of the other offences dealt with by that Act.[68] The offence under s 9(1)(b) does not extend to committing or attempting to commit unlawful damage.

## The offence under s 9(1)(b)

4-37    While the offence under s 9(1)(b) is also an offence of specific intent, it is not an offence of ulterior intent. The prosecution must prove that the defendant has entered the premises and then committed, or attempted to commit, the two specified offences of stealing and inflicting grievous bodily harm. No additional issues arise in relation to the element of stealing. However, in relation to grievous bodily harm, there is no specific mention in s 9(1)(b) of the 'offence'. It

---

66  Rape may be summarised as: an offence committed by a man who has non-consensual sexual intercourse (either vaginal or anal) with a woman or a man and, at the time, he either knows that there is no consent, or is reckless as to whether there is consent.

67  See above, para 4-16.

68  The basic offence in s 1(1) deals with a person who, either intentionally or recklessly, and without lawful excuse, destroys or damages property belonging to another; under s 1(3) committing criminal damage or destruction by fire constitutes the offence of arson; under s 1(2) the criminal damage may be charged as endangering life; s 2 deals with threats to destroy or damage property; and s 4 deals with possessing anything with intent to destroy or damage property.

has been suggested that this was merely a drafting error.[69] Nonetheless, it has led to decisions which have drawn a distinction between grievous bodily harm under s 9(1)(a) and under s 9(1)(b). A case in point is the decision of the Court of Appeal in *Jenkins*.[70] The defendants were charged under s 9(1)(b) and it was alleged that they had entered the house of their victim and had inflicted grievous bodily harm upon him. One issue that arose concerned the effect of the omission of the word 'offence' from s 9(1)(b). The conclusion arrived at was that the offence of burglary was made out where there had been an 'assault', even if that assault did not constitute an 'offence'. This would mean that a defendant who entered a building as a trespasser and, whilst there, accidentally assaulted the victim, could, nevertheless, be guilty of burglary under s 9(1)(b). This is clearly incorrect. It is submitted, however, that this need not be the only interpretation of the *ratio* in this case. Purchas LJ did go on to rule that:

> In enacting s 9(1)(b), Parliament clearly had in mind the commission of an offence under s 20 of the 1861 Act. Although the strict wording of s 9(1)(b) would not necessarily confine the court to an exactly equivalent interpretation, it is clearly convenient that this should be so.[71]

Consequently, it was held in this case that it was not open to the jury to acquit the defendants on the s 9(1)(b) charge but to substitute a verdict for assault occasioning actual bodily harm. While not expressly referred to in the judgment, this would, of course, leave open the possibility of a substitution of a conviction under s 20 of the OAPA 1861.

## 2 AGGRAVATED BURGLARY

4-38 **Section 10 of the TA 1968 – Aggravated burglary**

(1) A person is guilty of aggravated burglary if he commits any burglary and at the time has with him any firearm or imitation firearm, any weapon of offence, or any explosive; and for this purpose –

    (a) 'firearm' includes an airgun or air pistol, and 'imitation firearm' means anything which has the appearance of being a firearm, whether capable of being discharged or not; and

    (b) 'weapon of offence' means any article made or adapted for use for causing injury to or incapacitating a person, or intended by the person having it with him for such use; and

    (c) 'explosive' means any article manufactured for the purpose of producing a practical effect by explosion, or intended by the person having it with him for that purpose.

---

69  Smith, 'Burglary under the Theft Bill' [1968] Crim LR 367.
70  [1983] 1 All ER 1000.
71  *Ibid*, p 1005.

(2) A person guilty of aggravated burglary shall on conviction on indictment be liable to imprisonment for life.

## Introduction

4-39    When charging a defendant under s 10, it is necessary for the prosecution to specify which particular offence of burglary under s 9 is being aggravated. This is crucial for the reason that, on a charge under s 9(1)(a) for one of the ulterior intent offences, the defendant must have entered with the specified aggravating object (the firearm, weapon, or explosive). On the other hand, where the charge is under s 9(1)(b), aggravated burglary is possible when he acquires the aggravated object while committing the specified offences.[72]

## Mode of trial and sentence

4-40    Like many other offences under the TA 1968, burglary may also take an aggravated form. If the circumstances covered by s 10(1) are proved, the maximum sentence that may be awarded is imprisonment for life. Consequently, the offence of burglary is tribal on indictment only. With regard to alternative verdicts, it would be open to a jury to acquit of the s 10 offence and substitute a conviction for the appropriate offence under s 9.

## Possession and the relevant time

4-41    Section 10(1) indicates that the prosecution must prove that the defendant 'at the time [of the burglary] has with him the specified firearm, weapon of explosive'. No problem would arise in those situations where the defendant is holding, or has on his person, the firearm, weapon or explosive at the time he enters the premises with trespassory intent. What, however, would be the situation where the aggravating object is not directly in his possession? In other similar offences, it has been held that the prosecution must show a degree of actual physical control by the defendant. In *Kelt*,[73] the defendant had been charged under s 18(1) of the Firearms Act (FA) 1968 which provides that: It is an offence for a person to have with him a firearm ... with intent to commit an indictable offence ...' The issue that arose on appeal was the interpretation to be given to the words 'to have with him'. It was held, firstly, that a distinction must be drawn between those offences where a mere possession was sufficient and those offences where the prosecution had to go further and prove that the defendant was in control of the weapon and, at the time, had an intention to use it. According to Scarman LJ,

---

72    This point is further explained below, para 4-43.
73    [1977] 1 WLR 1365.

there had to be a very close physical link and a degree of immediate control over the weapon. Secondly, it was held that this was a matter of fact to be determined by the jury.

4-42     Would such an interpretation apply equally to the offence under s 10 of the TA 1968? This may be viewed in the light of the decision in *Pawlicki and Swindell*.[74] The defendants had been convicted with the offence, under s 18 of the FA 1968 (above). They had entered a building, it would seem, for the purpose of reconnoitring it prior to a robbery. Evidence was given that they had left three sawn-off shotguns in a car parked outside the premises. Despite the fact that the defendants were some 50 yards away from their weapons, it was held, on appeal, that there was sufficient evidence on which the jury could find that the terms of the section were satisfied. What would have been the result if the defendants had been charged, instead, with aggravated burglary under s 10 of the TA 1968? It has been suggested that there could not be a conviction in such circumstances.[75] This must be correct: the defendants must have had the firearms with them at the time of their trespassory entry onto the premises.

4-43     Situations may arise where the defendant, who is perhaps surprised during the commission of a burglary, picks up an object and uses it as a weapon against his victim. It could be argued that he has not entered the premises with the weapon. This point was raised in the case of *O'Leary*.[76] The defendant had broken into a house. He picked up a knife from the kitchen and used it to confront the occupants of the house and forced them to hand over property. He appealed against his conviction for aggravated burglary on the grounds that the offence of burglary was complete at the time he entered the premises and, at that point in time, he was unarmed. The Court of Appeal rejected this argument. The crucial point was that the defendant had been charged with the aggravation of the offence under s 9(1)(b), rather than s 9(1)(a). Accordingly, the relevant point in time was not the time he entered, but the time at which he stole. At this time, he had armed himself and the conviction was, therefore, proper. This decision has been subsequently affirmed in *Kelly*.[77] Here, the defendant had used a screwdriver in order to facilitate his entry onto the premises. It was held that he could properly be convicted for aggravated burglary when he then used it to prod his victim in the stomach.

4-44     A further issue may be raised. What if the aggravating object is used in order to facilitate the burglar's escape? It would be argued that the burglary is complete as soon as the theft (or grievous bodily harm, rape, or criminal damage) has taken place, so that the aggravating factor comes after the burglary

74   [1992] 1 WLR 827.
75   Smith, ATH, para 28-54. Griew (para 4-43) agrees although, Smith, JC (para 11-38) appear to take a contrary view.
76   (1986) 82 Cr App R 341.
77   (1992) 97 Cr App R 245.

and not at the time of it. The answer to this would depend on whether the courts would be prepared to treat burglary, in this context, as a continuing offence. Support for such an approach may be gleaned from the case of *Watson*.[78] The defendant, in this case, had entered the home of an elderly man late at night with the intent to commit burglary. His victim was awoken and verbally abused. The defendant then made off. Shortly after the burglary, the victim had a heart attack and died. The defendant was convicted of burglary and manslaughter. He appealed against the manslaughter conviction. The Court of Appeal had no difficulty in coming to the conclusion that, for the purposes of involuntary manslaughter,[79] the burglarious intrusion (as Lord Lane CJ put it) had to be considered as a continuing one.

4-45    A final point to be mentioned here is that, on the authority of *Klass*, where the aggravating object is in the possession of an accessory, neither he nor the principal party can be convicted of aggravated burglary.[80]

### Firearm – imitation firearm

4-46    Paragraph (a) of s 10(1) provides only that a 'firearm' includes an airgun or air pistol. A much more extensive definition is provided in s 57 of the FA 1968.[81] Section 57(1) begins by defining firearm as meaning 'a lethal barrelled weapon of any description from which any shot, bullet or other missile can be discharged,' and then goes on to further extensions of this basic definition. While, strictly speaking, this definition cannot be applied to aggravated burglary, it does provide a measure of guidance. In any case, in those situations where there may be doubt as to whether the object is or is not a firearm, an alternative would be to deal with it as a 'weapon of offence' under s 10(1)(b). In relation to imitation firearms, this is defined under s 10(1)(a) in exactly the same terms employed in s 57(4) of the FA 1968 as 'anything which has the appearance of being a firearm'. Consequently, this is a matter of fact to be determined by the jury

### Weapon of offence

4-47    This is defined as any article made or adapted for use for causing injury to or incapacitating a person, or intended for such a use. This definition appears to be based on the similar wording used in s 1(4) of the Prevention of Crime Act 1953.[82] This definition incorporates two categories of weapons; those which are

---

78   (1989) 89 Cr App R 211.

79   In this case, manslaughter by an unlawful act (constructive manslaughter).

80   [1998] 1 Cr App R 453.

81   See, also, the Firearms (Amendment) Acts 1988 and 1997.

82   See, also, the definition of 'dangerous weapons' in the Restriction of Offensive Weapons Act 1959, s 1; the kinds of weapons referred to in the Criminal Justice Act 1988, s 139 and the definition of 'knife' in the Knives Act 1997, s 10.

weapons *per se* (a knife, for instance) and those objects which have some other function, but which are intended to be used for the offensive purpose (for instance, the screwdriver used in *Kelly*). It is possible for the court to take judicial notice that some objects are offensive weapons per se and this would relieve the prosecution of the obligation of proving this fact.[83] On the other hand, when dealing with those offensive objects which the prosecution claims have been adapted for offensive use, it will be necessary for this to be proved to the jury's satisfaction.

## *Explosive*

4-48    The definition of 'explosive' for the purposes of aggravated burglary is narrower than that to be found in the Explosive Substances Act 1883, but that Act may still be of assistance.

---

83  Examples include flick knives and stilettos (*Simpson* (1983) 78 Cr App R 115); coshes, knuckle-dusters and revolvers (*Petrie* (1961) 45 Cr App R 72); and swordsticks (*Davis v Alexander* (1970) 54 Cr App R 398) .

# CHAPTER 5

# REMOVAL OF ARTICLES FROM PLACES OPEN TO THE PUBLIC

5-01 **Section 11 of the Theft Act (TA) 1968**

(1) Subject to sub-ss (2) and (3) below, where the public have access to a building in order to view the building or part of it, or a collection or part of a collection housed in it, any person who without lawful authority removes from the building or its grounds the whole or part of any article displayed or kept for display to the public in the building or that part of it or in its grounds shall be guilty of an offence.

For this purpose 'collection' includes a collection got together for a temporary purpose, but references in this section to a collection do not apply to a collection made or exhibited for the purpose of effecting sales or other commercial dealings.

(2) It is immaterial for purposes of sub-s (1) above that the public's access to a building is limited to a particular period or particular occasion; but where anything removed from a building or its grounds is there otherwise than as forming part of, or being on loan for exhibition with, a collection intended for permanent exhibition to the public, the person removing it does not thereby commit an offence under this section unless he removes it on a day when the public have access to the building as mentioned in sub-s (1) above.

(3) A person does not commit an offence under this section if he believes that he has lawful authority for the removal of the thing in question or that he would have it if the person entitled to give it knew of the removal and the circumstances of it.

(4) A person guilty of an offence under this section shall, on conviction on indictment, be liable to imprisonment for a term not exceeding five years.

## Mode of trial and sentence

5-02 The offence is triable either way.[1] If tried on indictment, it is a class 4 offence with a maximum penalty of imprisonment for five years.[2] Following summary trial, the magistrates can sentence to imprisonment for up to six months, a fine up to the statutory maximum, or both.[3] There is no provision for s 11 to be an alternative charge to a charge of theft, so if an article is removed from a place, and there is any doubt as to the accused's intention permanently to deprive on a

---

1  Magistrates' Courts Act (MCA) 1980, s 17(1) and Sched 1, para 28.
2  TA 1968, s 11(4).
3  MCA 1980, s 32(1) and Sched 1, para 28. The statutory maximum is currently £5,000.

charge of theft, it is advisable to include in the indictment a second count charging an offence under s 11.

## Introduction and purpose of the offence

5-03 This is a 'brand new' offence created by the TA 1968, in response to a handful of high profile 'removals' of valuable items from places open to the public. Section 11 is sometimes referred to as the 'Goya offence', since the removal from the National Gallery of Goya's portrait of the Duke of Wellington by a man who kept it for four years before eventually returning it, was part of the impetus behind the Criminal Law Revision Committee (CLRC)'s recommendation that there should be special provision made to penalise the temporary taking of such articles.[4] Since the intention permanently to deprive could not be proved, he could not be convicted of theft of the picture, although he was convicted of theft of the frame which was never recovered.[5] The result is the very wordy s 11, described by Professor Griew as being drafted 'with a complexity disproportionate to the importance of the offence'.[6]

The objective of the offence is to protect works of art which are put on public display, without the need to prove an intention permanently to deprive. Such items may be irreplaceable and are at greater risk than those held in private collections. But the section actually protects 'any article' kept for the purpose of display to the public, there is no need for it to be of great value. Even a saucepan would warrant the protection of s 11 if it were displayed for the purpose of exhibition in a place to which the public have access in order to come and view it.[7] Section 11, together with ss 12 and 12A,[8] are all that emerge from the CLRC's lengthy deliberations about whether to extend the offence of theft to include temporary deprivations, or to create an entirely new general offence of temporary deprivation of property.[9] In the end, they decided to recommend neither and settled on confining protection from temporary deprivation to the removal of articles from places open to the public, which is the subject of this chapter, and the taking of conveyances, which is the subject of the next.

---

4  CLRC, *Eighth Report*, Cmnd 2977, 1966, London: HMSO, para 57(ii); another instance discussed by the Committee was the removal of the Stone of Scone from Westminster Abbey.

5  On the facts, there seems ample evidence that an intention permanently to deprive could now be established, since he held the picture 'to ransom' by trying to make the Gallery buy the portrait back by paying a large sum of money to charity. See para 2-123 above.

6  Griew, para 5-02.

7  But not if it were on sale in a shop, as s 11(1) excludes items displayed for commercial purposes.

8  See Chapter 6, below.

9  *Op cit*, CLRC, fn 4.

## *Actus reus* of the offence

5-04 The following elements of the *actus reus* must be proved in order to gain a conviction: (a) there has been a removal, (b) from a building or the grounds of a building, (c) to which building the public have access, (d) in order to view it or part of it or a collection or part of a collection housed in it, (e) of the whole or part of any article, (f) displayed or kept for display to the public, (g) in the building or that part of it or the grounds of the building.

### *Removal from building or grounds*

5-05 The article, or part of the article, must be removed from where it is displayed, either from the building, or from the grounds. It is not enough that it is removed from one part of the building to another, or from one part of the grounds to another. However, it will be sufficient if it is removed from the building to the grounds. A complicated distinction is drawn between removal from permanent and temporary exhibitions as a result of s 11(2). Where the exhibition is a permanent one, that is one for an indefinite period, even though the entire collection may not be on view at one time[10] (as in most museums or art galleries), removal need not take place exclusively during the times at which the public are granted access. It can take place at any time, even when the gallery is closed. This also extends to any item which has been temporarily lent to be exhibited alongside the permanent collection. On the other hand, where the exhibition is only temporary, the removal must take place on a day when the public are allowed access to view it. There seems little justification for the distinction. It results in a situation where, if D enters a stately home on a day it is open to the public and takes a painting, he is guilty of the offence, but if he enters on that same day and hides in a cupboard until the building is closed and then takes the painting he is not guilty. It seems that, any time he takes a painting from the National Gallery, he will be guilty of the offence.

### *From a building to which the public have access in order to view the building or part of it*

5-06 The offence is confined to removal from those buildings, or parts of buildings, to which the public have access in order to view the building (or part of it) or a collection (or part of it). It is not sufficient that the public have access to the buildings' grounds in order to visit, for example, the botanical gardens, or a funfair, or an outdoor theatrical performance, if they are denied access to the house. In these circumstances, if a person were to surreptitiously creep into the house and remove some article, he cannot be guilty of the offence. Furthermore, if the public do not have access to the building where the article or collection is

---

10    *Durkin* [1973] QB 786 (and, below, para 5-09).

housed, then no articles in its grounds are protected by s 11. This would be so even if the grounds contained, for example, valuable sculptures which visitors incidentally saw on their visit to the gardens. It is not uncommon in such circumstances to have access to the building in order to visit the lavatories, or the café, or a souvenir shop, but this still does not come within the requirement of the section, since it is the use for which access is permitted that is of paramount importance. So if D entered the building in order to get a cup of tea this would not be an entry for the purpose of viewing the building or articles collected there. Similarly, if a theatre exhibits pictures in its foyer, removal of such articles will not be covered by s 11 because the prime reason for visiting the theatre building is in order to watch the performance. A person's purpose in visiting a building is irrelevant, it is the purpose for which they are allowed access that is important.

5-07     This requirement can pose difficulties in buildings which are of historic interest, such as historic town halls or cathedrals. These buildings may contain valuable items which the public may have access to view, but for which entry is usually for a different purpose, namely prayer in the case of cathedrals. However, in *Barr*,[11] there was no case to answer when the defendant removed a crucifix and ewer from a Victorian parish church and put them in the churchyard: the vicar gave evidence that the prime purpose for access to the church was devotional.

Once it is established that the building is one which is open to the public in order to view it, or a collection, then any article which is displayed (or kept for display) in the grounds of the building will also be protected. In these circumstances, it is possible that one sculpture inside the house will give protection to 50 more in the gardens. This will be so, even if it is only part of the building for which access is granted in order to view the sculpture. It is submitted by Professor Griew that a 'building' must probably have a roof, and if so, an exhibition staged in the ruins of Tintern Abbey or Coventry Cathedral would not be protected.[12] It follows that a statue exhibited in a public park is not protected by the section.

## To view a collection or part of a collection

5-08     The section protects single articles, or parts of articles, or whole collections or parts of collections and includes a collection which is got together for a temporary purpose. However, s 11(1) states that it does not apply to a collection gathered together in order to admit the public to view it when that collection is 'made or exhibited for the purpose of effecting sales or other commercial dealings'. This is often a fine distinction. If, for example, paintings are displayed

---

11   [1978] Crim LR 244 (Bristol Crown Court).
12   Griew, para 5-03.

to the public in a gallery, but are at the same time also on sale by the individual artists, this, it is submitted, will not be regarded as the exhibitor exhibiting for commercial purposes and so the paintings would be protected by the section. An example of such an exhibition is the Summer Exhibition at the Royal Academy, but the principle should apply equally to an exhibition at the local art college. The same would be true where a local artist exhibits for sale in the public library.[13]

*The article must be displayed or kept for display*

5-09    Very few galleries and museums have room to display all their artefacts all of the time. The offence thus gives protection to those items which are not displayed, but are kept in store. Once again, it is the purpose for which the article is kept which is important.[14] Those articles in store must be kept there with the purpose that they will be exhibited in the future. The requirement is to exempt any personal belongings of those who may live in the stately home, or work in the galleries; it makes no difference if, as is often the case, those belongings are valuable. Therefore, a Chippendale chair which is being repaired in the workshops ready to exhibit at some future date would be protected by the section, but not any old chair which is used to sit on by the gallery watchman. In *Barr*, it was important for the decision that the crucifix and ewer were said to be displayed as an aid to devotion, rather than as historical exhibits. An interesting situation arose in *Durkin*.[15] The defendant removed a valuable painting by LS Lowry from an art gallery as a protest that it was not being exhibited by the gallery more frequently. The Court of Appeal upheld his conviction under s 11, stating that the words 'a collection intended for permanent exhibition to the public' in s 11(2) meant simply a collection intended to be permanently available for exhibition. That intention was sufficiently manifested by the gallery's settled practice of periodically displaying to the public at the gallery the pictures in their permanent collection.[16] Accordingly, the defendant had been properly convicted. It is submitted that the situation would have been no different, if the painting had been in store at the time he removed it.

---

13    As long as the paintings were exhibited in a part of the building to which the public had access in order to view the paintings, rather than to look at incidentally when they change their library books.

14    *Barr* [1978] Crim LR 244 (Bristol Crown Court); see para 5-07.

15    [1973] QB 786.

16    D had removed the painting on a Sunday when the museum was closed, hence the importance of establishing it was part of the 'permanent exhibition', see, above, para 5-05.

## *Mens rea* of the offence

### *D must intend the removal*

5-10    The defendant must have the intention to remove the article from the building or part of the building, or its grounds. There is a partial defence under s 11(3) if the defendant has the belief that he has either the lawful authority to remove the article, or he believes he would have had the consent of the owner if the owner knew of the removal and its circumstances. Although there is no requirement of dishonesty for this offence, the provision is similar to s 2(1)(a) of the TA 1968 in relation to the offence of theft, and almost identical to the defence in s 12(6) of the TA 1968.[17] Where such an issue is raised, the burden of proof is on the prosecution to prove lack of good faith on the part of the defendant. It is submitted that an honest mistake as to that belief will be an excuse, even if that mistake is based on unreasonable grounds.

---

17  See para 6-12, below, where the defence is discussed at greater length in relation to s 12.

# CHAPTER 6

# TAKING CONVEYANCES WITHOUT AUTHORITY AND AGGRAVATED VEHICLE-TAKING

## 1 THE BASIC OFFENCE

**Section 12 of the Theft Act (TA) 1968 – Taking motor vehicle or other conveyance without authority (as amended by ss 37 and 38 of the Criminal Justice Act (CJA) 1982; and s 37(1) of the CJA 1988)**

(1) Subject to sub-ss (5) and (6) below, a person shall be guilty of an offence if, without having the consent of the owner or other lawful authority, he takes any conveyance for his own or another's use or, knowing that any conveyance has been taken without such authority, drives it or allows himself to be carried in or on it.

(2) A person guilty of an offence under sub-s (1) above, shall be liable on summary conviction to a fine not exceeding level 5 on the standard scale, to imprisonment for a term not exceeding six months or to both.

(3) [Repealed by Sched 7 of the Police and Criminal Evidence Act 1984.]

(4) If on the trial of an indictment for theft the jury are not satisfied that the accused committed theft, but it is proved that the accused committed an offence under s 12(1). The jury may find him guilty of the offence under sub-s (1) and if he is found guilty of it, he shall be liable as he would have been liable under sub-s (2) above on summary conviction.

(5) Sub-section (1) above shall not apply in relation to pedal cycles; but, subject to sub-s (6) below, a person who, without having the consent of the owner or other lawful authority, takes a pedal cycle for his own or another's use, or rides a pedal cycle knowing it to have been taken without such authority, shall on summary conviction be liable to a fine not exceeding level 3 on the standard scale.

(6) A person does not commit an offence under this section by anything done in the belief that he has lawful authority to do it or that he would have the owner's consent if the owner knew of his doing it and the circumstances of it.

(7) For the purposes of this section –

(a) 'conveyance' means any conveyance constructed or adapted for the carriage of a person or persons whether by land, water or air, except that it does not include a conveyance constructed or adapted for use only under the control of a person not carried in or on it, and 'drive' shall be construed accordingly; and

(b) 'owner', in relation to a conveyance which is the subject of a hiring agreement or hire purchase agreement, means the person in possession of the conveyance under that agreement.

## Mode of trial and sentence

6-02    Offences contrary to s 12 are summary offences,[1] but an allegation of an offence contrary to s 12(1) may be included as a count in an indictment in circumstances provided for by s 40 of the CJA 1988.[2] Following summary trial, the magistrates can sentence to a fine not exceeding level 5 (currently £5,000) on the standard scale, to imprisonment for a term not exceeding six months, or both.[3] An offence under s 12 in respect of a motor vehicle, also carries discretionary disqualification from driving.[4]

Where a person is charged with theft of a conveyance, but the jury is not satisfied that an intention permanently to deprive has been established, s 12(4) allows them to return an alternative verdict of the offence under s 12(1), as long as the facts mean that such an offence has indeed been committed.

### *Attempts*

6-03    Where the s 12(1) offences are summary offences, an attempt to commit them cannot be an offence.[5] However, s 9 of the Criminal Attempts Act (CAA) 1981 creates a separate offence of interference with a motor vehicle 'or trailer or with anything carried in or on a motor vehicle or trailer', with the intention of committing theft of any of the same, or an offence under s 12(1). Note, however, that the s 9 offence is limited to motor vehicles and does not extend to cover other conveyances included in s 12(7) of the TA 1968. Section 9 creates a summary offence and, on conviction, the defendant is liable to imprisonment for a term not exceeding three months, or to a fine not exceeding level 2 on the standard scale (currently £500), or to both.[6]

## Introduction

6-04    The requirement of an intention permanently to deprive in order to convict for theft can create difficulties in relation to valuable items such as motor vehicles. If it is proven that the vehicle belongs to another and is dishonestly appropriated driven away and either sold or kept permanently by the person who took it there will be little difficulty in proving a charge of theft. However, it may be that the vehicle will only be taken for a temporary purpose, such as a way of getting

---

1    CJA 1988, s 37; originally s 12(1) was triable either way.
2    *Archbold*, para 21-144. Such an offence may also be committed for trial in conjunction with an either way offence under the CJA 1988, s 41.
3    TA 1968, s 12(2), in line with the Magistrates' Courts Act (MCA) 1980, s 32(1) and Sched 1 para 28.
4    RTOA 1988, ss 34, 97 and Sched 2, Pt II.
5    CAA 1981, s 1(4): see para 14-04 below.
6    CAA 1981, s 9(3); CJA 1982, s 46.

home after a late night party, or for a 'joy ride', in which case, the likelihood is that the vehicle will be abandoned and, if it is properly licensed and registered, eventually returned to the owner. It will thus be difficult to prove an intention permanently to deprive and a theft conviction will be impossible.

Temporary deprivation of motor vehicles was first recognised as a serious social evil and, accordingly, made an offence of 'taking and driving away' by s 23 of the Road Traffic Act (RTA) 1930. The same offence was included in the subsequent RTA 1960, until it was thought more appropriate to include a specific offence within the new TA 1968 of 'taking a motor vehicle or other conveyance without authority', dispensing with the need to prove an intention permanently to deprive. Section 12 of the new TA 1968 was also intended to extend criminalisation to taking forms of conveyances other than motor vehicles.[7] The idea of its inclusion in the TA 1968 seems to be designed to confront the danger, loss and inconvenience resulting from such conduct, rather than loss in financial terms which is usually covered by insurance. In the 1990s, growing public concern over 'joy riding' by young drivers taking cars and racing them in a manner which was likely to, and did, cause harm to other road users and pedestrians resulted in the Aggravated Vehicle-Taking Act (AVTA) 1992. This inserted a new s 12A into the TA 1968,[8] which is basically an aggravated from of s 12 (although, s 12A is confined to mechanically propelled vehicles). Section 12A gives the courts power to impose heavier sentences in cases where the s 12 vehicle-taking was likely to cause injury to others.

## The offence under s 12(1)

6-05    The section appears to create two offences:

(a) *Taking conveyance without authority*: a person commits an offence if, 'without having the consent of the owner or other lawful authority, he takes any conveyance for his own or another's use'.

(b) *Driving conveyance without authority*: 'knowing that any conveyance has been taken without such authority, drives it or allows himself to be carried in or on it.' The latter also includes a third way in which the offence can be committed, simply by 'allowing' oneself to be carried in, or on, such a conveyance as a passenger.

In this way, s 12(1) recognises that taking the car may have been a 'joint effort' and whichever person is driving at the time is immaterial as to the purpose for which the car has been taken. Consequently, the prosecution are spared the task of having to prove which one of the 'gang' was driving in order to gain a conviction.

---

7    Criminal Law Revision Committee, *Eighth Report*, Cmnd 2977, 1966, London: HMSO, para 83.

8    See para 6-20 below.

## The 'primary' offence: taking conveyance without authority

### Conveyance

6-06    The thing taken must be a conveyance. This is defined in s 12(7)(a) as meaning any form of conveyance 'constructed or adapted for the carriage of one or more persons whether by land, water or air'. The meaning is wide enough to include most forms of transportation, including yachts and aircraft. However, it seems important that the transportation can be 'driven'[9] insofar as 'it does not include a conveyance constructed or adapted for use only under the control of a person not carried in or on it'. Thus, the section excludes conveyances which are intended to be controlled externally, so it would not include self-piloted vehicles[10] or anything in, or on, which it is impossible to ride, such as a pram or a supermarket trolley, or presumably the driverless trains that operate on the Docklands Light Railway and the Newcastle-upon-Tyne metro; but it may include wheelchairs which are controlled by a person within them.

The conveyance will usually be mechanical, such as cars, motorcycles, buses, boats, trains, even hang-gliders, but this is not essential. It is enough that the conveyance satisfies the requirement that it is capable of being 'driven'. So, for example, a home made 'soap box' or go-kart, or a rowing boat will presumably fall within the definition, but not skis or roller skates. This may reflect the portable nature of these items which are thus less likely to find their way back to the owner and, therefore, an intention permanently to deprive may be more easily proven with the consequent charge of theft. But, note that, in *Bow*, it was held that for an offence under s 12(1) to be made out, it is not necessary for the conveyance to be propelled by an engine as long as somebody is 'driving' or 'being carried ' in or on it.[11]

It seems that animals, however, are not 'conveyances' even though they are capable of being transportation and of 'giving a ride'. In *Neal v Gribble*,[12] it was held, not only that 'conveyance' must be given its ordinary meaning and did not include a horse, but also that putting a halter on a horse did not 'adapt' it for the purposes of s 12(7)(a). Pedal cycles are not conveyances for the purposes of s 12(1),[13] but mopeds are included within the main offence and a person can be convicted of taking one, even though he rides away on it without using the motor.

---

9    See para 6-17 below.

10    But see Smith, JC, para 8-07, where he supposes that 'any conveyance with accommodation for a passenger or passengers which has no means of self-propulsion and so cannot be driven but must be towed' may be included.

11    See para 6-10 below.

12    (1978) 68 Cr App R 9.

13    Section 12(5) and see para 6-19, below.

## *Meaning of 'takes'*

6-07    The offence requires a 'taking'. Thus driving it, whatever the motive, would probably be enough, but it is not essential. Although the conveyance must be capable of being driven or controlled, there is no need for the defendant to be in or on the conveyance at the time it is taken in order to be guilty under s 12(1), as long as the conveyance itself is moved. For example, in *Pearce*[14] the offence was committed where D loaded an inflatable dinghy onto a trailer and drove it away. The court rejected a submission that such a conveyance should be 'taken' by water. Nevertheless, it must be stressed that some element of movement is implicit in the word 'take'. There is no requirement that the vehicle be *driven* away, but it must be *taken away* from where it was. Therefore, it would be enough to sit in, or on, a punt, untie its mooring and drift downstream. On the other hand, it would be insufficient to sit in it while it is still moored, as this does not amount to its being 'taken'.[15] Therefore, a mere unauthorised taking into possession is not sufficient for a taking under s 12(1). Consequently, merely getting into the vehicle is not enough, although this may be sufficient evidence for an offence under s 9 of the CAA 1981. In *Bogacki*,[16] the three defendants had gone to a bus garage late at night, boarded a bus and tried to start the engine without success. It was held that 'some movement, however small' of the conveyance was necessary before s 12(1) was complete. Whether or not the conveyance has been 'moved' must be examined on the facts of each case. It is the requirement of movement which sets the boundary between an offence under s 9 of the CAA 1981 and the completed offence under s 12(1).

6-08    An offence under s 12(1) occurs each time there is a new 'taking'. In *DPP v Spriggs*,[17] the first 'taker' took the car without consent and then abandoned it. When D came along and drove it away, this was held to be a separate and new offence quite independent of the act of the original offender. It was irrelevant whether the car had reverted back to the possession of the true owner, or whether it was actually abandoned and therefore in the possession of no one.

## *A 'taking' by those already in possession*

6-09    It makes sense that a vehicle can be 'taken' by a person authorised to drive it, if that person deviates significantly from that which he is authorised to do by the owner. In *Phipps & McGill*,[18] the defendant was a bailee in possession of the car. He had been lent it to drive into London, on condition that he returned it by a

---

14   [1973] Crim LR 321.

15   *Miller* [1976] Crim LR 147; *Diggin* (1980) 72 Cr App R 204 (and below).

16   [1973] QB 832: in fact, the defendant's conviction for an attempt was quashed on the basis of a misdirection.

17   [1993] Crim LR 622.

18   (1970) 54 Cr App R 301, convicted under the RTA 1960, s 217, before enactment of the TA 1968 (see below); cf *Peart* [1970] 2 QB 672 (below).

certain time that same evening. He did not return the car for several days. It was held that the offence took place as soon as he decided not to return the car and use it for his own purposes. Furthermore, his passenger would be guilty too, if he knew of the circumstances in which D had been lent the car. In *McKnight v Davies*,[19] the Divisional Court had the opportunity to discuss *Phipps & McGill* and its application to s 12, with reference to employees who deviate from their authorised activities. Lord Widgery CJ observed that it is not always easy to define the exact type of unauthorised activity which would give rise to a conviction in such circumstances: 'Not every brief, unauthorised diversion from his proper route by an employee in the course of his working day will necessarily involve a "taking" of the vehicle.'[20] However, in that case, where the defendant had not returned his employer's lorry to the depot at the end of the day, but used it for going on a pub crawl with his friends instead, he was clearly guilty of an offence under s 12. Similarly, if in the course of his working day, or otherwise while his authority to use the vehicle is unexpired, he will commit the offence if he uses it in a manner which 'repudiates the rights of the true owner' and shows that he has assumed control of the vehicle for his own purposes.[21] It is submitted that whether an employee has so repudiated his employer's rights will usually be a matter of the terms of the contract between them.

### For his own or another's use

6-10 The conveyance taken must be for the use of D or another, and it has been held that D must intend the 'use' to be one of transportation.[22] In *Bow*,[23] the appellant together with his brother, father and their air rifles had driven to a country estate in the brother's car. It was assumed they were on a poaching expedition and when challenged by gamekeepers they refused to give their names and addresses. The head gamekeeper called the police and parked his Land Rover so as to obstruct the appellant's only escape route, whereupon the appellant got into it, released the handbrake and allowed it to coast some 200 yds in order that his brother could drive his own car away. He appealed against his conviction contrary to s 12(1) on the basis that he had not taken the Land Rover 'for his own use'. He also submitted that this issue should have been left to the jury to determine as a matter of fact. In dismissing his appeal, the Court of Appeal were at pains to say that it was immaterial whether the engine of the Land Rover was switched on, as 'coasting' or 'driving' both involve the required element of movement. The relevant question was the 'use' to which the appellant had put

---

19  [1974] RTR 4.
20  *Ibid*, p 8.
21  But cf *Peart* (para 6-11), where D got permission for one journey but, in fact, went on a completely different one.
22  Although this point seems to have been overlooked in *Pearce* [1973] Crim LR 321 (above).
23  (1976) 64 Cr App R 54.

the vehicle. In reaching this decision, Bridge LJ considered examples relevant to the meaning of 'for his own use or another's,' from Smith and Hogan's *Criminal Law* (3rd edn, 1973),[24] and came to the conclusion that there would be no offence in circumstances where D releases the handbrake of a car so that it runs down an incline, or releases a boat from its moorings so that it is carried off by the tide. This is because, although the conveyance had been moved, it would not have been 'used as a conveyance'. It would be different had D been in the boat at the time, because then there would be, not only movement, but it would be in circumstances where D was using the boat as a conveyance, that is, as a means of transporting him downstream. He was willing to admit that, if an obstructing vehicle was merely pushed a few yards out of the way, it would clearly not be being used as a conveyance, 'but where the vehicle is necessarily used as a conveyance, the taker cannot be heard to say that the taking was not for that use'.

The decision in *Bow* seems to contravene the spirit of the offence, that is, to tackle the inconvenience of having your conveyance 'taken', and this is not what appeared to happen in *Bow*. Presumably, if the vehicle really is causing an obstruction (in different circumstances from *Bow*), then a person would be authorised in removing it without running the risk of a conviction under s 12.[25] Be that as it may, it seems that the Court of Appeal are prepared to give a narrow interpretation of the word 'use': that is, is 'use as a conveyance'. So, in *Dunn and Derby*,[26] there was no case to answer when the defendants pushed a motor bike a distance of some 40 yards to look at it under a light. There was not enough evidence to prove that they intended to use it as a conveyance rather than just to admire it. Obviously, it would have been different if they had been moving it to a place where they could more easily start it. Similarly, in *Stokes*,[27] it was held that merely pushing a car round a corner as a practical joke in order to make the owner think his car had been stolen would not amount to an offence under s 12(1), because the car was not taken for D's own use or another's *as a conveyance*.

Proof of the defendant's intention to 'use' the thing 'as a conveyance' includes where it can be demonstrated that it is his intention to do so in the future and even if the conveyance has not been moved very far. In *Marchant and McCallister*,[28] it was enough to have moved the car two or three feet for there to

---

24  Now Smith and Hogan, *Criminal Law*, 9th edn, 1999, London: Butterworths, p 597.

25  Despite being cited with approval by the Court of Appeal in *Bow*, later editions of Smith and Hogan point out that D did not actually use the vehicle as a conveyance and, if all D is doing is removing an obstruction, it is hard to see why the actual distance should make a difference, *ibid*, p 598; see, also, Smith, ATH, para 9-13.

26  [1984] Crim LR 367.

27  [1982] Crim LR 695.

28  (1985) 80 Cr App R 361: in fact, they were convicted of an attempt, but the principle is the same.

be sufficient evidence for a jury to find that the defendants had intended to use it as a conveyance, that is, as a means of transport, even though they had not yet done so.

### *Without the owner's consent or lawful authority*

6-11    The taking of the conveyance must be without the consent of the owner or other lawful authority. Having lawful authority to take a conveyance covers situations where the emergency services or local authority have statutory powers to do so. For example, where a vehicle has been parked in a dangerous situation, or where it appears to have been abandoned, it can be removed under reg 20 of the Removal and Disposal of Vehicles Regulations 1986.

It is for the prosecution to prove that the defendant took the conveyance 'without the consent of the owner'. The word 'owner' is to have its ordinary meaning, but s 12(7)(b) extends the meaning to include a person in possession of the conveyance under a hiring or hire purchase agreement. It is no answer to a charge under s 12(1) that the owner would have given consent had he been asked – even where the owner agrees to testify to this.[29] Most situations are fairly clear cut. For example, we have seen in *Phipps & McGill*[30] that the defendant had specific instructions as to when he was to return the car. In those circumstances, it was not difficult to prove he did not have the consent of the owner when he used it for other purposes. However, in that case, he had been lent the car and so, initially, had the consent of the owner and was in legal possession of it; his unauthorised use was simply a straightforward deviation from that authorised use. It may be different when D initially obtains possession of the car by exercising a deception. For example, by pretending he wants it for one purpose but, in fact, uses it for another. There is no general principle that fraud vitiates consent in either criminal or civil law (unless it is as to the nature of the act or identity of the person), so it seems that an owner's consent gained by deception is nevertheless a valid consent.[31] There is nothing in the wording of s 12 to say otherwise. But can this really be so?

It seems that it can. In *Peart*,[32] the defendant obtained the loan of a car from V by deceiving him into thinking he was going to drive 30 miles from Newcastle to Alnwick and would return the car by 7.30 pm, when in fact he intended all along to drive 100 miles to Burnley where he was discovered at 9 pm. His conviction under s 12 was quashed as there was no 'taking' of a conveyance because he had the owner's consent – not vitiated by fraud. It seems a fragile distinction that a person should be guilty if he starts on a permitted journey but

---

29    *Ambler* [1979] RTR 217. Unless, of course D believed that the owner would have given his consent: s 12(6), see para 6-14 below.

30    See para 6-09 above.

31    Unless, of course, it is achieved by force or threats: *Hogdon* [1962] Crim LR 563.

32    [1970] 2 QB 673.

then deviates into a frolic of his own (as in *Phipps & McGill*), and not guilty if he obtained permission for one journey but, in fact, goes on another (as in *Peart*). It would appear that, if Mr Peart had originally been lent the car and later decided to go to Burnley, he would have been guilty, too.

6-12 However uneasily the decision in *Peart* may sit with that in *Phipps & McGill*, it was applied *Whittaker v Campbell*[33] which settles any doubts as to its authority. The defendant managed to hire a van using a driving licence that did not belong to him, but representing to the hirer that it did. The hirer said that, if he had known the defendant was not the real owner of the licence, he would not have consented to him taking the van. However, his conviction under s 12 was quashed by the Divisional Court, approving the decision in *Peart*. It had been argued by the appellants that the misrepresentations as to the identity of the name on the driving licence were not so fundamental as to make the hiring contract void, but merely misrepresentations as to the defendant's attributes that might make it voidable. While Robert Goff LJ accepted that this might be so, he preferred to decide the case on the broader principle that fraud did not vitiate consent in relation to s 12. Even if there had been a mistake of identity so fundamental as to make a contract void in contract law, it did not vitiate the owner's consent for the purposes of s 12. The reason for the decision seems to be based in the mischief which s 12 was designed to confront. Goff LJ thought that it was intended to deal with the situation where persons simply took another person's vehicle for their own purposes, for example, for use in the commission of a crime, or for a joy ride, or just to get home, without any attempt to obtain the owner's consent and where, in the vast majority of cases, the owner was not even consulted at all. This was not the case here, even if that consent had been obtained by fraud. It seems that, as a matter of policy, fraudulent obtaining of temporary possession of a vehicle should not be punishable under s 12.[34]

An interesting postscript is provided by the civil case of *Singh v Rathour (Northern Star Insurance Co Ltd, Third Party)*,[35] where the fraud was as to the use to which the defendant put the vehicle. The Court of Appeal distinguished both *Whittaker v Campbell* and *Peart* and held that, where D borrowed a vehicle subject to certain implied limitations about the purpose for which it was to be driven, and he knew about those implied limitations, then he did not have 'the consent of the owner' to drive the vehicle for a purpose outside the implied limitations.

## Mens rea

6-13 There is a required mental element to s 12(1), in that the defendant must have knowledge that he is taking a car without the owner's consent. In addition, some

---

33 [1984] QB 318; see 'Commentary' [1983] Crim LR 812.

34 The decision is warmly welcomed by Smith, ATH, para 9-22 post; and treated with caution by Smith, JC, para 8-09 who submits that *Phipps & McGill* is to be preferred to *Peart*.

35 [1988] 1 WLR 422.

mental element is implicit in the act of 'taking'. There must be an intention to possess, and the movement of the conveyance must be intentionally brought about.[36] In *Blayney v Knight*,[37] the defendant was found not guilty of s 12(1) when he sat in the front seat of an automatic car with the intention of talking to the passengers who were sitting in the back but, accidentally, pressed the accelerator in the course of a struggle with the owner.

6-14     There is a partial defence under s 12(6) providing that a person does not commit the offence if he has *'the belief* that he has lawful authority to do it or that he would have the owner's consent if the owner knew of his doing it and the circumstances of it [emphasis added]'. Although there is no requirement that a person be dishonest for s 12(1), the provision is similar to s 2(1)(a) of the TA 1968 in relation to theft. Where the issue is raised under s 12(6) that the defendant might have taken the conveyance because he believed he had lawful authority to take it, or that he would have had the owner's consent if the owner had known of the taking and the circumstances of it, the burden is on the prosecution to prove that he did not so believe.[38] The defendant's belief is based on a subjective appraisal. So, if D honestly believed that he would have had the owner's consent if the owner had known of the circumstances of the taking, it is not necessary to enquire whether the owner really did consent, or whether he would have done so had he known more about D; for example, if he had insurance to drive.[39] The statute only requires that there be a 'belief' in consent and since this is to be judged subjectively, an honest mistake as to that belief will be an excuse, even if that mistake is based on unreasonable grounds.

It may be different if he makes this mistake because he is drunk. The most usual situation is where the defendant's intoxication means that he fails to consider whether the owner consents or not. In *Macpherson*,[40] the trial judge refused to consider the excuse that the defendant was drunk, ruling that s 12 is a crime of basic intent, so evidence of intoxication is not relevant in determining the defendant's *mens rea* under s 12. This was affirmed on appeal and the defendant's conviction upheld. It is interesting to note that MacPherson did not attempt to rely on s 12(6) – presumably because, in failing to consider the consent of the owner at all, he did not have that belief required by the sub-section. The situation is different where the defendant claims he did have such a belief because he was drunk and there seems no reason, in principle, why this cannot be a defence under s 12(6). *MacPherson* was considered in *Gannon*,[41] where the trial judge ruled that, if a belief in lawful authority arises as a result of self-induced intoxication, it is not a belief that affords a defence under s 12(6).

---

36  Smith, ATH, para 9-35.
37  (1975) 60 Cr App R 269.
38  *Macpherson* [1973] RTR 157 (below); *Gannon (Kevin)* (1988) 87 Cr App R 254 (below).
39  *Clotworthy* [1981] RTR 477.
40  [1973] RTR 157.
41  (1988) 87 Cr App R 254.

However, the matter of whether this would always be the case was left open by the Court of Appeal because, by his own admission, the defendant was so drunk at the time of the 'taking' that he was incapable of forming any such belief. There is support in *Jaggard v Dickinson*[42] (to which the court was referred in argument) to suggest that the judge's ruling in *MacPherson* was wrong. That case concerned a similar provision to s 12(6), in s 5(3) of the Criminal Damage Act (CDA) 1971; it was held that where a person drunkenly forms a belief that falls within s 5(3), he is entitled to an acquittal, as he was entitled to rely on his mistake for which that section allows. If the same reasoning were applied under s 12(6) of the TA 1968, it would mean that a belief mistakenly held would be a defence, whether made while sober or drunk.

Note, that in some circumstances it will not be necessary to rely on s 12(6). If a person makes a genuine mistake and takes home the wrong car, he will not be guilty of the offence because he lacks the basic *mens rea*, that is, knowledge that he is taking a car without the owner's consent. There is no need for him to rely on s 12(6).[43]

## The 'secondary' offence: driving or allowing oneself to be carried in a conveyance

6-15    This is a separate offence from the 'primary' offence of 'taking' the conveyance without authority and must be charged separately. It covers passengers in the conveyance and those who are not involved in the initial 'taking', but drive the car later on. Of course, it will still be possible to charge D with being an accessory to the 'primary' offence of taking, but only if there is sufficient evidence of encouragement on his part. Consequently, the advantage of this second offence under s 12 is that the prosecution is spared the trouble of proving D has aided and abetted; neither do they have to identify which one of the persons in the conveyance was driving at the time it was taken without the owner's consent. For example, if D is offered a lift by C in a car which D knows C has taken without authority, it will be too late to convict him as a secondary party to the 'taking', but he can be convicted of an offence under s 12(1).

### *Mens rea*

6-16    The *mens rea* requirement is fairly minimal, but it must be proved that the defendant knew that the conveyance had been taken without authority (either contrary to s 12(1), or stolen contrary to s 1), when he 'drove' it, or 'allowed himself to be carried' in or on it. There is no need for the defendant to be the

---

42   [1981] QB 527.

43   In reality, he could not do so anyway; his mistaken belief that it is his own car means that he could not possibly believe that the owner (by definition someone other than himself) would have consented to him taking it.

'taker' of the conveyance, but he must know that it has been taken without the owner's consent or lawful authority. If D knows this and then takes his turn at driving the conveyance, or allows himself to be carried in or on it as a passenger, then he is guilty of this 'second' offence under s 12(1). But, if D is offered a lift by C and D does not know that C has no authority to drive the car, he cannot be guilty of an offence. It is thought that 'wilful blindness' would be enough to denote knowledge, as is the case in other statutes. Such a state of mind is tantamount to saying that the defendant had the belief 'that the conveyance had been taken without authority'.[44]

## Meaning of 'driving'

6-17   There is no specific definition of 'drive' in the Act, but s 12(7)(a), which describes the meaning of conveyance, ends with the words 'and "drive" shall be construed accordingly'. So for the purposes of s 12(1), a person can 'drive' a soap box or a rowing boat. There is no need for the conveyance to have an engine or, if it has, that it be switched on, before a person can be said to be 'driving it'. Although there is little guidance in the statute itself, the word 'drives' has been considered in many cases under the various RTAs.[45] In *Roberts*,[46] it was held that a person cannot be said to be the driver of a vehicle unless he is in the driving seat, or in control of the steering wheel and has something to do with making it move. This was approved in *MacDonagh*,[47] where the defendant was pushing the car from the outside and steering at the same time, it was held that he was 'driving' the vehicle, even though he was not in a position to apply braking force and the vehicle was incapable of propelling itself. The test of whether a person is 'driving' a vehicle was said to be whether he has, in a substantial sense, 'use of the controls for the purpose of directing the movement of the vehicle ... and ... his activities are ... not to be held to amount to driving unless they come within the ordinary meaning of that word'.[48] Therefore, propelling skis or roller-skates would not be included under s 12(1), as they would not be capable of being 'driven' in the ordinary sense of the word. Neither is a mere accidental setting in motion to be regarded as an act of 'driving',[49] but steering a vehicle which was being towed by another vehicle would be, as he had directional control of it.[50] Whether a person is driving is a

---

44   See Smith, JC, para 8-18, where he sees no reason why this principle should be affected by the wording of the TA 1968, s 22, which includes the words 'knowing *or* believing' (emphasis added).

45   See, currently, RTA 1988, s 192(1).

46   [1965] QB 85.

47   [1974] QB 448, a decision in relation to the offence of driving whilst disqualified.

48   *Ibid*, p 452.

49   See again, *Blayney v Knight* (1975) 60 Cr App R 269 (above).

50   Noted in *Whitefield v DPP* [1998] Crim LR 349.

matter of fact and degree for the jury to decide, so in *Hastings*,[51] where a passenger intentionally grabbed the steering wheel so as to direct the vehicle at a pedestrian, it was held that he was not 'driving', but interfering with the driving of the vehicle.

### *Allowing oneself to be carried*

6-18    The offence is wide enough to include those who are merely passengers in the conveyance. However, the inclusion of the words 'to be carried' mean that the conveyance must have been set in motion when the defendant is in or on it before he can be convicted.[52] It is not enough that he is merely present in it. In *Miller*,[53] some persons took a motor launch without authority, moving it from one wharf to another. The defendant got on board the launch while it was moored, in anticipation of a ride. He was held not guilty of an offence under s 12(1) because he was not being 'carried in it', even though the launch was moving up and down in the water under its own momentum. If Parliament had intended that mere presence in or on a conveyance was sufficient, this could have been done by leaving out the word 'carried'. However, some problems may arise as to the exact point at which a person begins to 'be carried'. In *Boldizsar v Knight*,[54] the defendant pleaded guilty to 'allowing himself to be carried' when he entered the car innocently enough but, on later discovering that it had been taken without authority, did not get out of the car but continued to remain in it. It was from this point onwards that he 'allowed himself to be carried'. Accordingly, he was guilty of the offence. It is submitted that this seems too severe. It imposes an unwarranted burden on a person to extricate himself from a situation that was none of his making and may expose him to danger in order to avoid that situation.

## Taking a pedal cycle

6-19    Pedal cycles are excluded from the offence of s 12(1). Presumably, this is because when bicycles are taken and abandoned, it is less likely that they will be returned to their owners and so their being taken and abandoned will come within the definition of theft, because an intention permanently to deprive will be easier to infer. However, it is recognised that this may not always be the case, so s 12(5) deals with 'pedal cycles' expressly, in a separate offence under this section. It is considered a less serious offence than taking other conveyances, so on summary conviction is punishable only by a fine, not exceeding level 3 on the

---

51    [1993] RTR 205, where the charge was reckless driving contrary to the RTA 1988, s 2.

52    Cf *Bogacki* [1973] QB 832 (above), re a 'taking'.

53    [1976] Crim LR 147, applied in *Diggin* (1980) 72 Cr App R 204, where it was held to be a misdirection that 'being carried' started before the driver even turns on the ignition switch.

54    [1980] Crim LR 653.

standard scale (£1,000). It is submitted, as many pedal bicycles now cost very much more than a cheap motor car, that the distinction is no longer valid. The defence of belief in consent provided for in s 12(6) also applies to pedal cycles.

A person who 'allows himself to be carried' on a pedal cycle is not committing any offence under this section. Section 12(5) includes only those 'taking' or 'riding' as coming within the s 12(5) offence. However, he may be convicted under s 24 of the RTA 1988, which forbids more than one person to ride a cycle not made or adapted for that purpose.

## 2 THE AGGRAVATED OFFENCE

6-20     **Section 12A of the TA 1968 – Aggravated vehicle-taking (inserted by s 1(1) of the Aggravated Vehicle-Taking Act (AVTA) 1992)**

(1) Subject to sub-s (3) below, a person is guilty of aggravated taking of a vehicle if –

    (a) he commits an offence under s 12(1) above (in this section referred to as a 'basic offence') in relation to a mechanically propelled vehicle; and

    (b) it is proved that, at any time after the vehicle was unlawfully taken (whether by him or another) and before it was recovered, the vehicle was driven, or injury or damage was caused, in one or more of the circumstances set out in paras (a)–(d) of sub-s (2) below.

(2) The circumstances referred to in sub-s (1)(b) above are –

    (a) that the vehicle was driven dangerously on a road or other public place;

    (b) that, owing to the driving of the vehicle, an accident occurred by which injury was caused to any person;

    (c) that, owing to the driving of the vehicle, an accident occurred by which damage was caused to any property, other than the vehicle;

    (d) that damage was caused to the vehicle.

(3) A person is not guilty of an offence under this section if he proves that, as regards any such person driving, injury or damage as is referred to in sub-s (1)(b) above, either –

    (a) the driving, accident or damage referred to in sub-s (2) above occurred before he committed the basic offence; or

    (b) he was neither in or on or in the immediate vicinity of the vehicle when that driving, accident or damage occurred.

(4) A person guilty of an offence under this section shall be liable on conviction on indictment to imprisonment for a term not exceeding two years or, if it is proved that, in circumstances falling within sub-s (2)(b) above, the accident caused the death of the person concerned, five years.

(5) If a person who is charged with an offence under this section is found not guilty of that offence but it is proved that he committed a basic offence, he may be convicted of the basic offence.

(6) If by virtue of sub-s (5) above a person is convicted of a basic offence before the Crown Court, that court shall have the same powers and duties as a magistrate's court would have had on convicting him of such an offence.

(7) For the purposes of this section a vehicle is driven dangerously if –

(a) it is driven in a way which falls far below what would be expected of a competent and careful driver, and

(b) it would be obvious to a competent and careful driver that driving the vehicle in that way would be dangerous.

(8) For the purposes of this section a vehicle is recovered when it is restored to its owner or to other lawful possession or custody; and in this sub-section 'owner' has the same meaning as in s 12 above.

## Mode of trial and penalties

6-21    The offence is triable either way.[55] However, if the only damage is to the vehicle and it is considered slight (currently set at £5,000) then the offence is triable summarily only.[56] There is provision to allow two persons who are involved in the same incident to be tried jointly, for example, where one has been charged with taking the vehicle and the other (on separate information) is charged with allowing himself to be carried in it.[57] Following summary trial, the magistrates can sentence to imprisonment up to six months, or a fine of the statutory maximum, or both.

6-22    In reality, there are two offences committed under s 12A in view of their different maximum penalties.[58] The punishments, on indictment, are set out in s 12A(4). First, an offence under s 12A(1) with a maximum penalty of two years' imprisonment. Secondly, an offence under s 12A(2)(b), where the additional facts of that sub-section are proved and death results, with a maximum penalty of five years' imprisonment. It is essential that the indictment makes it clear which offence is being alleged.[59] Note that a person cannot be charged with the more serious offence simply as a result of death occurring: s 12A(2)(b) specifies that the death must be as a result of an accident 'owing to the driving of the vehicle'. In addition, the offences under s 12A (unlike s 12) carry automatic disqualification from driving for 12 months and endorsement of between 3–11 points,[60] and the fact that a person did not actually drive the vehicle is not to be

---

55    AVTA 1992, s 1(2)(b), confirming application of the MCA 1980, Sched 1, para 28.

56    MCA 1980, s 22(1). The criteria by which the value of the damage is to be assessed is set out in the MCA 1980, Sched 2, para 3. The lower maximum penalties for similar criminal damage cases do not apply and maximum sentence remains as for other either way offences tried summarily, ie, six months imprisonment, or a fine up to the statutory maximum, or both: the MCA 1980, s 33(3), added by the AVTA 1992, s 2(3).

57    MCA 1980, s 24.

58    The procedural point emerging from *Courtie* [1984] AC 463.

59    *Button; Sherwood* [1995] RTR 60, applying *Courtie* [1984] AC 463.

60    AVTA 1992, s 3(1).

regarded as a special reason why a defendant should not be disqualified under s 34 of the Road Traffic Offenders Act (RTOA) 1988. However, it was held in *Bradshaw*,[61] that it is inappropriate to order a passenger to take an extended driving test at the end of his period of disqualification. Furthermore, in *Wiggins*,[62] it was held that, when sentencing for an offence under s 12A, if there is evidence to suggest that the passenger had made attempts to prevent the driver driving in the manner complained of, then the judge should differentiate between the driver and the passenger when passing sentence.

There is also an alternative verdict. A person found not guilty of an offence under s 12A, but is proved to have committed a basic offence under s 12, can be convicted of that offence, according to s 12A(5).

## Introduction

6-23    This is the so called 'joy riding' offence, inserted into the TA 1968 by the AVTA 1992, in response to what was perceived as an 'epidemic' of offences under s 12, referred to in the Act as 'the basic offence'. Fast cars, police chases, severe injuries to members of the public and the joy riders themselves all played their part in a perceived social evil which was responded to by the 1992 Act. Dangerous driving, or causing death by dangerous driving are already criminalised under the RTA 1988, and criminal damage under the CDA 1971, but joy riding is usually a group activity and there are problems of proof associated with those particular offences which have been mostly eliminated in the new s 12A. For example, there is no need to prove which person was driving, or who caused the damage to the vehicle. In fact, the offence contains draconian measures which it is questionable are justified, such as dispensing with the need to prove the driving was dangerous when an accident occurs with the consequential damage or injury.

## The offence under s 12A[63]

6-24    The offence is set out in s 12A and is confined to the taking of mechanically propelled vehicles (unlike s 12 which applies to all kinds of conveyances), which include not only motor cars but, for example, scrambling bikes, dumper trucks and motor mowers. First, it must be proven that the defendant has committed an offence under s 12, that is, the 'basic offence', and then, secondly, after the vehicle has been taken and before it was recovered,[64] it must be proved that one

---

61    (1994) TLR, 31 December.
62    [2001] RTR 37.
63    See, generally, Spencer, JN, 'The Aggravated Vehicle-Taking Act 1992' [1992] Crim LR 699.
64    A vehicle is recovered when it is restored to the owner or lawful custody: s 12A(8).

of the four aggravating circumstances came about. These are set out in s 12A(2) and are:

(a) that the vehicle was driven dangerously on a road or public place;

(b) that, owing to the driving of the vehicle, an accident occurred by which injury was caused to any person;

(c) that, owing to the driving of the vehicle, an accident occurred by which damage was caused to any property, other than the vehicle;

(d) that damage was caused to the vehicle.

## *The fault element*

6-25 It will be noticed immediately that only the first circumstance requires a fault element, that is, that the car be driven dangerously. This is defined in s 12A(7), which mirrors the definition used in the RTA 1991 amendment to the 1988 Act. That is, it is driven in a way which falls far below what would be expected of a competent and careful driver, and it would be obvious to such a driver that driving the vehicle in that way would be dangerous. Note, too, that this first aggravating act can only take place on a road or other public place whereas the 'basic offence' can take place anywhere.

All the other circumstances, in (b), (c) and (d), depend on strict liability. This means that, even if the driver is not driving dangerously, he will be culpable if, as a result of an accident, injury is caused to any person or damage to property. The mere fact of death resulting from the circumstance of s 12A(2)(b) is sufficient to attract the maximum penalty, there is no need to prove it was brought about by dangerous driving.[65] Culpability for any damage to the vehicle itself, in s 12A(2)(d), does not even depend on its being in an accident, although the vehicle does have to have been 'taken'.

## *Passengers*

6-26 The Act is particularly draconian in that strict liability extends to all the participants in the basic offence,[66] whether or not they were involved in the original 'taking', and after the vehicle was taken, whether or not they were driving and whether or not they were the member of the group who caused the damage to the vehicle or injury to a person. So if B and C commit the basic offence, each is liable if either one of them causes damage or injury. If they pick up E later on and he accepts a ride knowing the vehicle has been unlawfully taken, he is guilty of s 12A if an accident occurs which causes damage to another vehicle or injury to any person, even if he never touched the steering wheel. In other words, there is guilt by association. Furthermore, s 12A(3) allows the

---

65 Although, of course, there is need to prove that it was brought about by the driving.

66 Section 12A(1)(b) includes the words 'by him or another'.

burden of proof to be reversed where a defendant claims that the damage or injury occurred before he committed the basic offence, or he was not 'in the immediate vicinity' when such injury or damage occurred – but it is up to him to prove that this was the case.[67] How far the defendant has been able to dissociate himself from the events will be a matter of degree, depending on the circumstances of the case. But it could be envisaged that when D, as a passenger having committed the basic offence, decides to leave the vehicle only a short while before his friends decide to set it alight, he will be guilty of the aggravated offence, if he is still within the 'immediate vicinity'. It is submitted that this makes the possibility of withdrawal almost impossible.

## Owing to the driving of the vehicle

6-27    For circumstances (b) and (c), no fault element is required as to the driving. It seems that it is what happens to the vehicle itself after it has been taken which is the deciding factor in culpability and not the way in which it was driven. In *Marsh*,[68] the defendant had given his girlfriend a lift home to change her clothing, using her landlord's car without permission. He had, therefore, committed the 'basic offence', but was driving competently when a pedestrian ran into the road and was knocked down by the car. She was not seriously injured, but he was convicted of aggravated vehicle-taking under s 12A(2)(b). It was contended on appeal that no liability could attach under that sub-section, unless it was proved that the accident had been caused by the culpable driving of the appellant. In upholding his conviction, Laws J held that the words of the Act were plain and simple and it was unhelpful to gloss the statute by referring to the manner or mode of driving.[69] There was only one question to be asked: was the driving of the vehicle the cause of the accident? Any other approach would require the court to read in words which are not there. He went on to explain that there is no requirement of fault, because that was not the policy behind the statute. The purpose of the Act is to impose heavier sentences on those who take vehicles unlawfully and then cause an accident, whether or not the accident involves any fault in the driving.

## Damage to the vehicle

6-28    The provision in (d) allows prosecution when there is any damage at all to the vehicle which has been taken and, as we have seen, applies to all participants. It is not dependent on the damage having been caused in an accident and, so, will include situations where the defendant damages the locks or immobilising

---

67  The standard of proof is the civil standard, that D must establish the defence on the balance of probabilities.

68  [1997] 1 Cr App R 67.

69  *Ibid*, p 70.

systems of the car when committing the basic offence. In *Dawes v DPP*,[70] the defendant took a vehicle which had been specially adapted so as to cut out the engine and to lock the doors after only a few yards. In an attempt to escape before the police arrived, the defendant broke a window. It was held that this fell within s 12(2)(d) and so he was guilty of the aggravated offence.

---

70   [1995] 1 Cr App R 65 (DC); see 'Commentary' [1994] Crim LR 604.

# CHAPTER 7

# ABSTRACTING OF ELECTRICITY AND THEFT FROM MAILS

## 1 ELECTRICITY

7-01 **Section 13 of the Theft Act (TA) 1968 – Abstracting of electricity**

A person who dishonestly uses without due authority, or dishonestly causes to be wasted or diverted, any electricity shall on conviction on indictment be liable to imprisonment for a term not exceeding five years.

### Introduction

7-02 If electricity could be treated as 'property belonging to another', it would not have been necessary for special provision to have been made in the Act. At common law, however, a thing could not be larcenable unless (a) it was tangible, (b) it was movable, (c) it was of some value and (d) it had an owner.[1] Would any special difficulties have arisen if electricity had been treated as property capable of appropriation? After all, the objection that electricity could not be taken and carried away could be met by the concept of intangible property utilised in s 4(1). Further, no difficulty arises with the notion of 'appropriation'; one can assume the rights of an owner over electricity, as well as over any tangible property. Moreover, water and gas had been treated as property in a number of cases.[2]

7-03 Nonetheless, it was felt that electricity belonged in a special category, indicating Parliament's intention that abstracting electricity was not be construed as theft under s 1. Consequently, the practice contained in the Larceny Act 1916 of separate statutory treatment was continued. The case of *Low v Blease* [1975] Crim LR 513 is illustrative of the reasoning behind this. Here the offender was a trespasser who made a telephone call and was charged with stealing electricity while using the telephone, contrary to s 9(1)(b). The magistrates accepted the prosecution submission that electricity was property under s 4 and convicted. The conviction was quashed on appeal on the ground, *inter alia*, that electricity could not properly be described as property. One consequence of this ruling is that, since electricity cannot be 'stolen', abstracting electricity cannot come within the scope of the offence of burglary, under s 9.

---

1    *Archbold*, para 21-53.
2    *R v White* (1853) 3 C&K 363, in relation to gas; *Ferens v O'Brien* (1883) 11 QBD 21, in relation to water.

## Mode of trial and sentence

7-04    The offence is triable either way by virtue of the Magistrates' Courts Act 1980, s 17(1) (read together with Sched 1). If tried on indictment, it is a class 4 offence with a maximum penalty of five years. For summary offences, it is six months, a fine, or both. The view taken by the courts of this offence is reflected in *Hodkinson* (1980) 2 Cr App R(S) 331. Here, the offender had fitted a device to an electricity meter, which caused a false reading to be given. In dealing with the appropriate sentence, Bristow J ruled:

> Deliberately stealing electricity in this way is an offence which calls for deterrent treatment when caught. In the circumstances of this case, this court has come to the conclusion that the necessary deterrent element would be sufficiently dealt with by a sentence of one month's immediate imprisonment, accompanied by a fine of £750.

This may be seen as unnecessarily harsh in the light of the fact that the offence took place in a domestic setting and, so, the value of the electricity 'stolen' could not have been high. It may be that the judicial view was based on the fact that, at this time, the 'owner' was a publicly owned (in other words, State owned) utility. Whether a different view needs to be taken of the deterrence when the owner is simply a private company remains to be seen.

## Elements of the offence

### *Electricity*

7-05    An interesting issue that has been raised relates to the interpretation to be accorded to the term 'electricity'. Should this be taken to refer only to electricity supplied though a mains system?:

> There is nothing in the section to suggest that the electricity must come from the mains. Therefore, it is probable that D commits the offence if he borrows my flashlight or portable radio and uses the dry battery.[3]

Whether this view is correct remains to be seen; it is unsupported by authority and, if similar facts were to occur, it may be that it will more properly be dealt with as theft, in the sense that it would amount to a dishonest appropriation of property belonging to another without consent. The existing case law is confined to the use of electricity from a mains supply.

### *Use without authority; waste or diversion*

7-06    Any form of use, waste or diversion will suffice. In situations such as occurred in *R v Hoar and Hoar* [1982] Crim LR 606, where there has been tampering with a

---

3    Smith, JC, *The Law of Theft*, 8th ed, 1997, London: Butterworths, para 9-03.

meter, 'use' is easily made out. However, it is not always necessary for there to be proof that a meter had been tampered with. This was made clear in *McCreadie* (1992) 96 Cr App R 143. Here, the offenders had contended that, since they themselves had not actually touched the fuse box or equipment, the prosecution had failed to make out a case against them. This was decisively rejected by Lord Taylor CJ who ruled that the word 'use' implies 'some consumption of electricity which would not occur but for the accused's act'.[4] Similarly, as in *Boggeln v Williams* (1978) 67 Cr App R 50, where the supply of electricity has been disconnected, any reconnection will amount to 'use'.

7-07 The requirement that the use must be unauthorised is relatively straightforward. As *Low v Blease* indicates, it will be 'use without authority' to make a call from a telephone belonging to another person without the necessary consent. Nonetheless, a problem may arise where the defendant tampers with the electricity supply but, at the same time, informs the supplier of what he has done. It is submitted that this can only be dealt with through asking if dishonesty was present. In most cases, use without authority would be *prima facie* evidence of dishonesty. That this will not always be the case is illustrated by *Boggeln v Williams* (see below).

## Dishonesty

7-08 The partial definition of dishonesty provided in s 2 of the Act applies only to the basic theft offence, by virtue of s 1(3), and, therefore, has no application to the offence of abstracting electricity. The particular problem that this causes relates to the central issue of whether the test for dishonesty, applied in *R v Ghosh* [1982] QB 1053, to the basic theft offence should be applied to the offence under s 13. Previous cases arising out of the s 13 offence had indicated that a subjective test is appropriate. In *Boggeln v Williams*, the electricity company disconnected the supply of electricity to the appellant's home for non-payment of bills.[5] However, the appellant then informed the company of his intention to reconnect the supply. He was told that if he did this, it would be disconnected again. Nevertheless, the appellant went ahead and reconnected the supply himself. The court accepted that the appellant believed that he was not acting dishonestly as he had given the company notice of his intention. This was especially the case since he had reconnected the supply to ensure that any consumption was properly recorded by the meter, even though he knew how to reconnect the supply in such a way that it would not be recorded. The question certified for appeal was:

> Is an intention to pay for electricity knowingly used without authority of the Electricity Board capable of affording a defence to a charge under s 13 of the TA

---

4   Page 146.
5   (1978) 67 Cr App R 50.

1968 if that intention is based on a genuine belief that the user will be able to pay at the due time for payment?

7-09 The Divisional Court ruled that although s 2(2) of the Act provided that dishonesty might exist despite a willingness to pay, dishonesty was nevertheless, a question of fact to be decided in each case. Moreover, the test had to be subjective. According to Lloyd J:

> [Dishonesty] is a question which relates to the defendant's state of mind, and must, in my judgment be answered subjectively: Did the defendant have a honest mind or not? That being the question, it seems to me that it is answered for us in the present case by the finding [that:] 'The defendant nevertheless did believe that, by giving notice of his intention and by ensuring that consumption was duly recorded through the meter, he was not acting dishonestly in reconnecting ... [T]he prosecution argues that the finding does not really help the defendant because a man's belief as to his own honesty or dishonesty must, he says, be irrelevant. In my judgment, that finding is not only relevant, but crucial.'[6]

7-10 The main objection against the approach taken in this case is that it cannot be reconciled with the decision of the Court of Appeal in *Ghosh* [1982] QB 1053,[7] which requires the objective element of 'whether according to the ordinary standards of reasonable and honest people what was done was dishonest'. If the *Ghosh* ruling is to apply generally, then this part of the decision in *Boggeln v Williams* must be regarded as no longer good law.

## Associated offences

7-11 A number of offences exist under the Telecommunications Act 1984 of dishonestly obtaining services provided by means of a telecommunication system. Such offences may provide better alternatives to the kind of charges utilised in cases such as *Low v Blease* (see above). This point is illustrated by *R v Nadiq* (1993) 14 Cr App R(S) 49, where the offender was convicted after using a tone dialling device to make unauthorised use of a telephone without paying.

A similar offence exists under the Copyright, Designs and Patents Act 1988 of dishonestly receiving programmes provided by a broadcasting or cable programme service. Consequently, it would not be necessary, as in *Low v Blease*, to charge an offender with abstracting electricity while unlawfully receiving such a programme.

---

6  (1978) 67 Cr App R 50, p 54; the words quoted by Lloyd J are from the case stated by the Crown Court.

7  See para 2-18, above.

# 2 THEFTS FROM MAILS

**7-12**   **Section 14 of the TA 1968 – Extension to thefts from mails outside England and Wales, and robbery, etc, on such a theft**

(1) Where a person –

(a) steals or attempts to steal any mail bag or postal packet in the course of transmission as such between places in different jurisdictions in the British postal area, or any of the contents of such a mail bag or postal packet; or

(b) in stealing or with intent to steal any such mail bag or postal packet or any of its contents, commits any robbery, attempted robbery or assaults with intent to rob;

then, notwithstanding that he does so outside England and Wales, he shall be guilty of committing or attempting to commit the offence against this Act as if he had done so in England or Wales, and he shall accordingly be liable to be prosecuted, tired and punished in England and Wales without proof that the offence was committed there

(2) In sub-s (1) above the reference to different jurisdictions in the British postal area is to be construed as referring to the several jurisdictions of England and Wales, of Scotland, of Northern Ireland, of the Isle of Man and of the Channel Islands.

(3) For purposes of this section 'mail bag' includes any article serving the purpose of a mail bag.

**7-13**   This is not an offence that has required the attention of the courts. Further, it could be argued that its proper place lies within the Post Office Act 1953, which contains the other mail theft offences. Three of these offences under the 1953 Act may be mentioned:

(a) unlawfully to take away or open a mail bag – s 53;

(b) wilfully and maliciously, with intent to injure any other person, to open or divert postal packets – s 56; and

(c) to secrete a postal packet – s 57.

Section 14 adds two other offences to this range:

(a) to steal or attempt to steal any mailbag or postal packet, or any of their contents, during transmission between the several jurisdictions of England and Wales, Scotland, Northern Ireland, the Isle of Man or the Channel Islands; or

(b) whilst stealing or attempting to steal, to commit robbery, attempted robbery or assault with intent to rob.

**7-14**   The main issue that arises here is that of jurisdiction. Section 14(1) makes quite clear that a prosecution is possible within England and Wales despite the fact that the offences in paras (d) and (f) above have, in fact, occurred outside the jurisdiction. This is an exception to the general rule that the courts of England and Wales do not have any extraterritorial jurisdiction. Nonetheless, the section applies only to the specified offences occurring within the 'British postal area' as defined in s 14(2) and, accordingly, does not cover an offence committed while mail is being transmitted from or to a foreign country.

# CHAPTER 8

# DECEPTION OFFENCES IN THE 1968 ACT

## 1 OBTAINING PROPERTY BY DECEPTION

8-01 **Section 15 of the Theft Act (TA) 1968 – Obtaining property by deception**

(1) A person who by any deception dishonestly obtains property belonging to another, with the intention of permanently depriving the other of it, shall on conviction on indictment be liable to imprisonment for a term not exceeding 10 years.

(2) For the purposes of this section a person is to be treated as obtaining property if he obtains ownership, possession or control of it, and 'obtain' includes obtaining for another or enabling another to obtain or to retain.

(3) Section 6 above shall apply for purposes of this section, with the necessary adaptation of the reference to appropriating, as it applies for purposes of s 1.

(4) For purposes of this section 'deception' means any deception (whether deliberate or reckless) by words or conduct as to fact or as to law, including a deception as to the present intentions of the person using the deception or any other person.

### Mode of trial and sentence

8-02 The offence is triable either way.[1] If tried on indictment, it is a class 4 offence with a maximum penalty of imprisonment for 10 years. Following summary trial, the magistrates can sentence to imprisonment for up to six months, a fine up to the statutory maximum, or both.[2]

### Introduction

8-03 This offence of obtaining property by deception replaced the offence, formerly in the Larceny Act (LA) 1916, of obtaining by false pretences.

---

1 Magistrates' Courts Act (MCA) 1980, s 17(1) and Sched 1, para 28.
2 *Ibid*, s 32(1) and Sched 1, para 28. The statutory maximum is currently £5,000.

## Deception

8-04    To deceive is, I apprehend, to induce a man to believe that a thing is true which is false, and which the person practising the deceit knows or believes to be false. *per* Buckley J in *Re London and Globe Finance Corp Ltd*.[3]

The closing words of this quotation deal with the mental state required for guil which will be dealt with a little later.

### *Deceiving a person*

8-05    The earlier part of the quotation states the, perhaps obvious, fact that fo deception to take place, it is not sufficient that a deceptive statement is made One can make a false statement, or, as it was put in the LA 1916, a false pretence without actually deceiving anyone. There is no deception unless someone i thereby deceived. Thus, if an untrue statement never reaches the consciousnes of the person to whom it is addressed, the latter is not deceived by it. Equally, he is not deceived by it, if he hears it but does not believe it. In *Hensler*,[4] the defendant sent a begging letter containing lies. The recipient saw through the lies but, nevertheless, sent the beggar some money. The beggar was held no guilty of obtaining by false pretences.[5] This was because the false pretence wa not the cause of his obtaining the money. Today, the reason he would not be guilty, under s 15, is that there was no deception. He would, however, be guilty of attempting to obtain property by deception – as, indeed, in the actual case he was convicted of attempting to obtain by false pretences.[6]

The requirement that there must be someone (a person) who is deceived, mean that fooling a machine will not amount to deception. Operating a vending machine by inserting a foreign coin, or a button, or mere metal disk, is almos certainly dishonest, but it does not amount to deception. Whereas, such ar activity might well amount to theft (of the item obtained from the machine), o (if the machine fails to yield anything) attempted theft, it will not amount to obtaining by deception, nor even of attempting to do so. As Lord Morris said, ir a different context in *DPP v Ray*: 'There must be some person, or persons who will have been deceived.'

### *Deceiving a company*

8-06    A company is a person and is, thus, capable of being the victim of a deception. A company being a fictitious person, there has to be some natural person acting or behalf of the company who is shown to have been deceived, before it can be saic

---

3    [1903] 1 Ch 728, approved by the House of Lords in *DPP v Ray* [1974] AC 370.

4    (1870) Cox CC 570.

5    The offence which was effectively replaced by the offence of obtaining by deceptior contrary to the TA 1968, s 15.

6    For attempts, see Chapter 14, below.

the company has been deceived. The relevant natural person is normally the person in the company who is responsible for the transaction in question. If, however, that person is shown to have been a party to the fraud, then the prosecution will need to show that there was deception of some other company employee from whom the property could properly be said to have been obtained. These propositions derive from *Rozeik*.[7] In *Rozeik*, D obtained a number of loans from two finance companies on the strength of false representations. In each case, the branch manager's direct endorsement or approval was required for each transaction and, in each case, it was the branch manager who had agreed D's credit limit and who had conducted the relevant transactions. D was charged with a number of similar offences of obtaining a cheque from the finance company dishonestly by deception. The judge directed the jury to assume that the branch managers had known of the falsity of D's representations. Allowing the appeal, the Court of Appeal held that it had not been established either that the branch managers were deceived, or that they had been a party to the fraud. Furthermore, in relation to the latter possibility, the judge had directed the jury too widely in asking them to consider whether 'any' employee of the company had been deceived into doing something that resulted in the cheques being obtained. The deception had to be proved to have acted on the mind of the person (within the company) from whom the cheque could properly be said to have been obtained – and that did not include the person who merely typed it out.[8]

## *Section 15(4)*

3-07    The definition of deception in s 15(4) applies, not only to the offence in s 15, but also to the offences in ss 15A, 15B, 16 and 22 of the TA 1968 and to ss 1 and 2 of the TA 1978.[9] The *mens rea* requirement mentioned in s 15(4) will be considered a little later.[10] The rest of s 15(4) makes it clear that:

(a) a deception can be effected by conduct (or words);

(b) a deception can be a deception as to someone's present intention.

## *Deception by conduct*

3-08    Where deception is effected by conduct, it is because the conduct *implies* a statement. In *Barnard*,[11] where the defendant had entered an Oxford bookshop

---

7    [1996] 1 WLR 159 (CA).

8    Since the later decision of the House of Lords in *Preddy* [1996] AC 815, we now know that s 15 was entirely the wrong charge to bring. An appropriate charge would now be: dishonestly obtaining a money transfer by deception, contrary to s 15A, see para 8-36, below.

9    TA 1978, s 5(1).

10    Para 8-19, below.

11    (1837) 7 C & P 784.

wearing a university cap and gown, that conduct implied that he was a member of the university. Even if he had not said anything, that would have been enough to deceive the shopkeeper into believing the defendant to be a member of the university. A customer who orders a pint of beer at a bar whilst having no intention of paying for it, is another example. His conduct in ordering the drink implies that he has, at the time of ordering the drink, the intention that the barman will be paid. If: (i) the barman who serves him believes him to have that intention; and (ii) the barman would not have served him with the beer if he had known that the customer had no intention of paying; and (iii) the customer was dishonest; and (iv) the customer intended to deprive the barman permanently of the beer, then the customer is guilty of obtaining the beer by deception.[12] The customer will not, however, have obtained the beer by deception, if he had the intention of paying for the beer when he was served and only afterwards decided not to pay.[13] It is not the breaking of his (implied) promise to pay which makes him guilty. Rather, it is the making of an untrue statement of fact - namely, that he (the customer) has, at the time he orders the drink, a certain intention (that is, that the barman will be paid). Presumably, the act of ordering the drink, or of ordering a meal in a restaurant, implies (unless there has been an agreement that he can have credit) that the customer has – or at least believes himself to have – the means of paying.

The act of filling a rotten car with filler and spraying the affected area is capable of causing the car to tell a lie about itself (that is, that it is bodily sound) and, thus, is capable of causing a deception. Similarly, the act of 'clocking' a car by turning back the odometer reading is also capable of causing a deception. Although these practices are usually prosecuted as offences under s 1 of the the Trade Descriptions Act (TDA) 1968, nevertheless, if a buyer is, thus, deceived as to the amount of miles covered and if that deception causes the buyer to make the purchase, then the seller could be charged with obtaining property (the purchase price) dishonestly by deception. Just as the act of 'clocking' can give rise to a deception as to the mileage covered by the vehicle, so, equally, can the act of displaying for sale a vehicle which someone else has 'clocked'. In the latter case, however, the displayer could not be guilty under s 15, if he did not know the vehicle had been 'clocked', because s 15 requires proof of dishonesty, as well as deception.

---

12  See *Hickmott v Curd* [1971] 2 All ER 1399, where the decision was complicated by the fact that the offence charged was obtaining a pecuniary advantage (namely, evasion of a debt contrary to s 16(1) and (2)(a). Section 16(2)(a) has since been repealed by the TA 1978; see para 9-03, below.

13  Though he may be guilty of evading liability by deception or making off without payment, see paras 9-09 and 9-25, below.

## Deception by omission/silence

3-09 As a general rule, a failure to speak or to act will not imply any statement and, thus, will be incapable of giving rise to a deception. There is, however, an exception to this which can apply where a statement already made by the defendant becomes untrue and the defendant fails to correct it. In *DPP v Ray*,[14] D ordered a meal in a restaurant, thereby making an implied statement that he intended to pay. This statement was true. However, after finishing his meal, he changed his mind and decided not to pay and sat at the table until the waiter left the room, whereupon the defendant then left without paying. The House of Lords upheld his conviction for obtaining a pecuniary advantage (evading liability) by deception on two alternative bases:

(a) his initial representation made on ordering the meal (that he had the intention of paying) was a continuing representation which remained alive and active and which became false when he changed his mind;

(b) by remaining at the table after deciding not to pay, he repeated the representation that he had an intention of paying.

That decision was taken a step further in *Rai*.[15] D had applied to the council for a grant to provide a bathroom downstairs in his house for the use of his elderly and infirm mother. On 29 July, he was notified that his application was approved. On 31 July, his mother died. He was living in the house himself, but remained silent and did not inform the council of his mother's death until after the contractors (on behalf of the council) had completed the work. He was charged with obtaining services (the building work) dishonestly by deception. The Court of Appeal held that his acquiescence in, knowingly, letting the work proceed was conduct capable of amounting to a deception of the council that his mother was still alive.

3-10 Neither *DPP v Ray* nor *Rai* was an example of pure omission. In each, there was a prior statement by D which became untrue and which his later silence failed to correct. In the absence of some such other statement, it is difficult to imagine a situation where silence/inaction could be held to give rise to any deception. It is submitted that, unless there is some act (or statement) to which D's silence is related, that silence cannot be construed as amounting to a deception. It is not enough that the law (civil or criminal) imposes a duty to inform. Failing to send in a tax return may be a breach of the law. It does not amount to a deception of the tax inspector. Nor does the decision of the Court of Appeal in *Firth*[16] provide much assistance. D, a consultant gynaecologist, had failed to tell a hospital that certain of his patients were private patients, with the result that he or they were not charged for their treatment. He was convicted of evading liability by deception. He appealed, arguing that there had to be some act of commission for

14  [1974] AC 370.
15  [2000] 1 Cr App R 242.
16  (1990) 91 Cr App R 217.

the offence to be established. It was held (but without any reference to s 15(4) that, if it was incumbent upon D to inform the hospital and he deliberately and dishonestly refrained from doing so, with the result that no charge was levied, then the offence was established. Again, however, it is submitted, that this was not a case of deception purely by omission. Rather, the omission to inform the hospital was merely part of a larger course of conduct:[17]

> But the deception was not *just* his omission to disclose what he should have disclosed: it lay in the act of referring the patient, plus his failure to ensure that the hospital did not draw the usual inference from that act.[18]

### Failing to undeceive

8-11    *DPP v Ray* and *Rai* were cases where D, in carrying out further conduct, failed to do anything to undeceive the victim (P). They were cases where the need to undeceive arose from an earlier statement by D. What, then, is position where D remains silent and, thus, fails to undeceive P, in the situation where P's mistake has not arisen from anything said or done by D? This might arise where P makes clear to D that he assumes some fact to be true which is material to a negotiation between them. Suppose that D knows the assumption to be false, but completes the negotiations without doing anything to disabuse P. Both Griew[19] and Smith[20] consider this not to be conduct amounting to a deception. Smith relies on the fact that D's positive acquiescence in P's self-deception does no invalidate the contract, to conclude that, *a fortiori*, it cannot amount to a criminal offence. The matter is not quite as straightforward as that makes it appear. True D has no duty to undeceive P from his self-deception. If, however, there is anything in D's subsequent conduct of the negotiations which can be construed as confirming P's mistaken assumption, D will have moved from silence/inaction to making a positive statement. The question will then no longer be one of whether D is liable for silence/inaction. Rather, it will become one of whether it is deception to confirm P in a mistaken belief which P already holds. Can D be said to have deceived P when P was already mistaken and all D has done is to confirm P in his mistaken belief?

### Implied statements in relation to cheques, etc

8-12    Professor Kenny[21] summarised the implied statements which are made by someone presenting a cheque as follows:

---

17    Just as a driver's failure to apply the brakes (perhaps resulting in a collision with the car in front) can give rise to a charge of careless driving, since it is merely part of the larger activity of driving.

18    Arlidge and Parry, para 4-074.

19    Griew, para 7-34.

20    Smith, JC, para 4-18.

21    Kenny, *Outlines of Criminal Law*, 19th edn, 1966, CUP, p 359.

Similarly the familiar act of drawing a cheque (a document which on the face of it is only a command of a future act) is held to imply at least three statements about the present: (1) that the drawer has an account with that bank; (2) that he has authority to draw on it for that amount; (3) that the cheque, as drawn, is a valid order for the payment of that amount (that is, that the present state of affairs is such that, in the ordinary course of events, the cheque will on its future presentment be duly honoured). It may be well to point out, however, that it does not imply any representation that the drawer now has money in this bank to the amount drawn for, inasmuch as he may well have authority to overdraw, or may intend to pay in (before the cheque can be presented) sufficient money to meet it.

This passage was based on *Hazelton*[22] and approved by the Court of Appeal in *Page*.[23] It was considered again, this time by the House of Lords, in *Metropolitan Police Comr v Charles*,[24] where their Lordships held that the second of Kenny's three implied statements was not correct and that the first can be subsumed within the third. Thus, Lord Edmund Davies[25] said, 'it accordingly appears right to restrict the representation made by the act of drawing and handing over a cheque to that which has been conveniently labelled "Page (3)"'. His Lordship went on to cite, with approval, the following passage from Pollock B, in *Hazelton*:[26]

> I think the real representation made is that the cheque will be paid. It may be said that that is a representation as to a future event. But that is not really so. It means that the existing state of affairs is such that in ordinary course the cheque will be met.

This statement of the law applies equally in the case of a post-dated cheque.[27] Whether or not the cheque is post-dated, the drawer may well expect funds to be credited to his account (either by himself or by someone else) before the cheque is presented. It is, for example, not uncommon for an employee, D, whose monthly salary is paid directly into his bank account to 'anticipate' his salary. D may do this, a day before he expects his monthly salary to be paid into his account, by writing and handing over a cheque for more than the balance currently in his account. Assuming that D's salary payment will provide sufficient funds to enable his cheque to be honoured, his implied statement will not be false. Suppose that, remarkably and unprecedentedly, his employer fails on this occasion to pay his monthly salary into his account until 10 days later than it is due, with the result that the cheque is dishonoured by D's bank. Still D's implied statement is not false. Deception requires a false statement of fact – and a statement of fact can only relate to the present or the past, since the future is not fact, but is mere forecast, prediction, promise or guesswork. The implied

---

22  (1874) LR 2 CCR 134.
23  [1971] 2 QB 330.
24  [1977] AC 177 – for the facts, see para 8-14, below.
25  Page 191.
26  (1874) LR 2 CCR 134, p 140.
27  *Griffiths* [1983] QB 953.

statement made by D upon handing over the cheque was that the present state of affairs (that is, when he handed it over) was such that, in the ordinary course of events, the cheque would on its future presentment be met. That statement was true, because, in the ordinary course of events (that is, if his salary had been paid as it should have been), the cheque would have been honoured.

8-13     The implied statement made by D has been further refined by the addition of the word 'first'. Thus, the implied statement has become 'that the present state of affairs is such that, in the ordinary course of events, the cheque will on its first future presentment be met'.[28] In that case, the defendants had indulged in a process known as 'stagging'. This practice was not itself illegal and became prevalent at a time when new share issues were frequently oversubscribed, with the result that applications for shares in a given issue of shares were scaled down. Thus, someone applying for, say, 10,000 shares would be allocated only 1,000. Stagging involved applying for far more shares than the applicant expected to be allocated – or even could afford to buy, if they were allocated to him. To curb the worst extremes of stagging, issuing houses adopted the practice of requiring each applicant to include, with his application, a cheque for the price of the full number of shares applied for. If the application was scaled down, that cheque was retained and cashed by the issuing house which sent the applicant, together with the letter notifying him of his share allocation, a 'change' cheque for the difference between the cost of the shares allocated to him and the higher cost of the number of shares applied for. Thus, when applying for shares the defendants in this case had not only applied for far more shares than they wished to buy but had included cheques for very large amounts which greatly exceeded the funds available in their bank accounts. They did this on over a 100 occasions. In doing this, each defendant relied on being able to pay the 'change' cheque into his bank account (and arrange for express clearance of it), before the large cheque which he had written was presented to his bank for payment. This meant that there were sufficient funds available for the large cheque to be met. In a small minority of instances, however, (14 out of 130 applications) this system broke down because the defendant was unable to get the change cheque credited to his account before the large cheque was presented for payment. On these occasions, the large cheque was dishonoured when first presented – though it was paid when later re-presented for payment. The defendants were convicted on a number of counts of dishonestly obtaining by deception a letter of acceptance in respect of shares and a return cheque contrary to s 15.[29] In relation to three of the counts on which they were convicted, the defendants' cheques had, in fact, been met on first presentment.

---

28   *Greenstein* [1975] 1 WLR 1353 (CA).

29   The main issue arising on the appeal, whether the defendants were dishonest, will be discussed later; see para 8-34. Also, it is clear that s 15 would not now be an appropriate charge for obtaining the cheque (whether the intangible property rights represented by the cheque or the tangible piece of paper on which it was written) – see *Preddy* [1996] AC 815 para 8-29, below.

(thanks to the return cheques being credited in time). The Court of Appeal, nevertheless, dismissed the appeals. Even in relation to those counts, the defendants had, when sending in their cheque with each application, made a false implied statement that the present state of affairs was such that that cheque would, in the ordinary course of events, on its first future presentment, be met. The only satisfactory explanations of this seem to be, either (i) that use of the 'change' cheque to meet the payment was not part of the 'ordinary' course of events, or (ii) the risks as to whether the return cheque could be credited before the first presentment of the defendant's cheque meant that the implied statement would be accurate only if it were a statement that the defendant's cheque 'might' or 'would probably' be met on first presentment. There are hints of both in the judgment. Certainly, reference is made to the significance of the risk of the return cheque not being credited in time and to the defendants' recklessness towards that risk. Accordingly, it appears to be the law that the implied statement made by someone delivering a cheque is that: the present state of affairs is such that, in the ordinary course of events, the cheque will *definitely* be met on *first* future presentment. If this statement is untrue, then it is deceptive, in which case it is immaterial if, as things turn out, the cheque is, in fact, honoured on first presentment.

### *Implied statements and cheque guarantee cards and credit cards*

8-14    In *Charles*,[30] the House of Lords had to consider the implied statements made by someone who, when presenting a cheque, presents also his cheque guarantee card. When a bank issues its customer with a cheque guarantee card, it authorises the customer to use the card to communicate to the payee an offer from the bank. That offer is a promise that, if the conditions attaching to the card are complied with, the bank will honour the cheque (irrespective of whether there are sufficient funds in the customer's account). The effect of the use of the guarantee card is, thus, to create a contract between the bank and the payee, whereby the bank becomes contractually obliged to honour the cheque. That is so, even if the customer has, unknown to the payee, used the guarantee card beyond any authority which the bank has given the customer. The authority given by the bank to the customer is limited. In giving the customer the guarantee card, the bank does not thereby authorise the customer to issue any cheque (or to use the guarantee card in relation to any cheque) which the bank would not honour if it were issued without the accompaniment of the cheque guarantee card. In *Charles*, D visited a gambling club where he kept losing. He purchased a number of gambling chips on 17 separate occasions during the visit. On each occasion he paid for them with a cheque (for £30) backed by his cheque guarantee card. These cheques were, as he knew, all in excess of the funds available and his agreed overdraft facility. The result was that his bank was

---

30   [1977] AC 177.

contractually bound to the gambling club to honour the cheques, which it duly did, thereby, causing D's account to go £30 further into overdraft in respect of each of the cheques – an unauthorised overdraft. He was convicted, on a number of counts, of dishonestly obtaining a pecuniary advantage (increased borrowing by way of overdraft) by deception, contrary to s 16. D appealed. As already seen above, in presenting each cheque, D made the implied statement that the present state of affairs was such that, in the ordinary course of events, the cheque would be honoured. That statement, however, was true – thanks to D's use of the cheque guarantee card. Their Lordships held that, when someone presents a cheque guarantee card together with a cheque (written in accordance with the conditions of the card), that is conduct from which it normally will be inferred that the drawer represents that he has actual authority from the bank to use the cheque guarantee card to create a direct contractual relationship between the bank and the payee, thereby obliging the bank to honour the cheque. In D's case, this second implied statement was, as he well knew, untrue and was the cause[31] of his obtaining the unauthorised overdraft. Thus, his appeal against conviction was dismissed.

8-15    *Charles* was followed in *Lambie*,[32] where the House of Lords held that, in presenting a credit card in payment for goods, D thereby made an implied statement that she had the authority of the credit card company to use the card to make a contract between the shop and the bank. Since she knew that she was using the card in excess of her credit limit and thus did not have the bank's authority to use the card in relation to that transaction, her conviction for dishonestly obtaining by deception a pecuniary advantage was upheld.[33] The implied statement held by their Lordships to have been made was, however, to some extent inappropriate. A credit card differs from a cheque guarantee card. Use of the latter, undoubtedly, does create a contractual relationship between the bank and the payee of the cheque. In the case of a credit card, however, there already exists a contractual relationship between the bank and the retailer; otherwise payment via the credit card simply would not be accepted by the shop. A simpler and more appropriate statement implied by the customer's use of the card, is that she has the authority of the card issuer (the bank) to use the card on the transaction in question. Either way, there remains, in relation to

---

31  See para 8-22, below.

32  [1982] AC 449.

33  The form of pecuniary advantage with which she was charged (evasion of a debt) has since been repealed; see para 8-44, below. Her activities would now, in all probability amount to obtaining services by deception contrary to the TA 1978, s 1, and, possibly, to obtaining a credit transfer, contrary to s 15A. In the case itself, Lord Roskill expressed the opinion that she could have been successfully charged under s 15 with obtaining property (the goods which she used the card to pay for) by deception. Arguably, however, she was not dishonest in relation to the obtaining of the *goods* because she knew that they would paid for, see Professor Sir John Smith's 'Commentary' to *Nabina* [2000] Crim LR 481, p 483.

*Lambie* as well as *Charles*, a problem of whether the deception caused the obtaining – a problem which is discussed below.[34]

## *Promises, statements of intention and of opinion*

8-16    Statements about the future are by definition not statements of fact and cannot in themselves be either true or false. Such statements can, however, contain an implied statement of fact. In particular, a statement of intention implies that the person said to have that intention does, in fact, presently have it. Section 15(4) expressly allows for such statements to give rise to a deception. Convictions have been secured on that basis – see, for example, *Hickmott v Curd* and *DPP v Ray*.[35] These cases could be regarded as ones where the defendant (ordering a drink or a meal) was making a promise to pay. A promise normally implies that the promisor now has an intention of carrying out that promise. A similar analysis has occurred in prosecutions under the TDA 1968, where the issue has been whether a statement of fact has been made. One such was *British Airways Board v Taylor*,[36] where a traveller was sent a letter saying 'I have pleasure in confirming the following reservations for you' and going on to give dates, times and flights. In fact, when he came to travel the traveller was denied a seat on his booked flight which was full, due to the overbooking policy of the airline. It was held that the letter contained, not just a promise as to a flight, but also a statement of present fact, namely, that the traveller had a definite and certain booking. That statement was false because, due to the overbooking policy, the traveller was exposed to the risk that he might not have a seat on the aircraft. Assuming that the passenger believed that he had a definite and certain booking, then, presumably, a conviction for a deception offence could have been secured provided all the other ingredients, including dishonesty, could have been established.

8-17    Statements of opinion are different, in that they are not statements as to the future, but an opinion ('it an is interesting play' or 'it is a beautiful car'). They are not facts, the truth or falsity of which can be ascertained by objective means. Rather, they are purely subjective matters. Section 15(4) expressly includes within the definition of deception, a deception as to the present intentions of any person. There is no express inclusion of a deception as to the present opinion of any person. Nevertheless, a statement of opinion may contain within it an implied statement of fact. Thus, in an old contract case, the statement by the seller that the premises were let to a 'most desirable tenant', whilst clearly an opinion, also implied that the seller knew of no reason why the tenant should not be desirable, whereas the truth was that the tenant was a very bad payer when it came to the rent. This was held to be an actionable misrepresentation, an

---

34   See para 8-22.

35   Paras 8-08 and 8-09, above.

36   [1976] 1 WLR 13 (HL), affirming a similar approach taken in relation to holiday brochures in *R v Sunair Holidays* [1973] 1 WLR 1105.

untrue statement of fact, which was one of the causes which induced the buyer to buy.[37] There is every reason to suppose that the same approach is taken by the criminal law and that, in a criminal case, the seller could, today, be found to have committed an offence involving criminal dishonest deception.

## Proof of falsity

8-18    A statement of fact can be deceptive only if it is false. The burden of proof, in this respect, as in respect of other elements of the crime, rests on the prosecution. Sometimes, the nature of the deception alleged requires the prosecution to establish a negative which, theoretically, can be done only by bringing evidence of the practices of every one of a vast number of traders. In *Mandry and Wooster*,[38] the defendants were street traders selling perfume of which they claimed: 'You can go down the road and buy it for two guineas in the big stores.' In an attempt to disprove this claim, the prosecution put a policeman in the witness box who testified that he had visited four department stores in the area and found none which was selling the perfume. He had not, however, visited every possible store. It was held that the police officer's testimony was evidence which, in the absence of any positive evidence from the defence to the contrary, the jury were entitled to accept as proof of the falsity of the claim.

## Deliberate or reckless deception

8-19    The wording of s 15(4) requires the deception to be deliberate or reckless. What is referred to here is not the making of a false statement, for that is merely the means by which a deception is achieved. Deception is causing someone else to believe something is true which is not. It is this result which has to have been brought about deliberately or recklessly. This is a requirement as to the *mens rea* of the defendant.[39] Thus, it must be proved either (i) that the defendant intended to deceive, or (ii) that the defendant was reckless as to whether someone was deceived. The defendant who utters a deliberate lie when talking to himself at a time when he believes no one else to be in earshot, cannot have deliberately deceived anybody – even if unknown to the defendant someone was listening at the keyhole and believed the lie. Nor, in that example, did the defendant deceive anyone recklessly, since recklessness in this context must mean *Cunningham*[40] and not *Caldwell*[41] recklessness.[42] *Cunningham* recklessness requires that the

---

37    *Smith v Land & House Property Corp* (1884) 28 Ch D 7.
38    [1973] 1 WLR 1232.
39    For the remaining elements of *mens rea* in this offence, see para 8-32, below.
40    [1957] 2 QB 396.
41    [1982] AC 341.
42    See *Large v Mainprize* [1989] Crim LR 213 where on a charge against a fisherman of recklessly making a false declaration as to the quantity of fish caught, the Divisional Court rejected *Caldwell* [1982] AC 341 recklessness and held that the mental element must be subjectively proved.

defendant must be proved to have foreseen deception as a possible outcome of his action. If the defendant realises that his statement might be false and realises that someone might believe it, then he is reckless as to whether someone is deceived. Of course, since the making of a false statement is a step on the way to deceiving someone, a defendant who utters a false statement, believing it to be true, cannot be either deliberate or reckless in deceiving the hearer. Believing it to be true, the defendant cannot foresee that it will deceive anybody.

The requirement that the defendant has to be deliberate or reckless in deceiving someone is, in practice, not going to present the prosecution with any difficulty. This is because the prosecution has to prove dishonesty[43] and it will be unusual case where, once dishonesty is established, there remains any doubt that the defendant realised that he would or might bring about a deception.

## Causation

8-20 The offence requires not only that the defendant deceived someone and that he obtained property. It requires it to be established that the obtaining was caused by the deception. The requirement for this causal link is also shared by the following offences of obtaining/procuring by deception: a pecuniary advantage (s 16 of the TA 1968); the execution of a valuable security (s 20(3) of the TA 1968); services (s 1 of the TA 1978): evasion of liability (s 2 of the TA 1978). The causal link is important, also, in relation to a charge of going equipped to cheat, contrary to s 25(1) of the TA 1968. In the latter case, the prosecution has to prove that the defendant was equipped to do something which, if he carried it out, would result in him deceiving someone and, thereby, obtaining something 'by' (which means, 'because of') that deception. Thus, the relevant case law has arisen under various of these sections.

It is obvious that, if the obtaining occurred before the deception was practised, the obtaining cannot have been caused by the deception. In *Collis Smith*,[44] D had filled his car with petrol before then asking the attendant to book it to D's employer (thereby implying that he had his employer's authority to do that). That implied statement was false. The Court of Appeal quashed his conviction for obtaining the petrol by that deception, since the obtaining had preceded the deception.

In *Laverty*,[45] D sold a car which had been stolen and on which he had put false number plates. He was convicted of obtaining property (the purchase price) by deception, the deception being that the purchaser was deceived as to the car's correct registration number. D's conviction was quashed because the prosecution had failed to show that the buyer had parted with his money

---

43 See para 8-34, below.
44 [1971] Crim LR 716.
45 [1970] 3 All ER 432.

relying on that falsehood. There was no evidence that the authenticity, or otherwise, of the number plates operated on the buyer's mind. This meant that there was no causal link between the deception alleged and the obtaining of the purchase price. The only evidence as to what induced the buyer to buy the car was that he bought because he believed D to be the owner. The conviction would have been unassailable if the prosecution had relied on a different implied statement, namely that, by agreeing to sell the car, D was stating that he had the right to sell it.

8-21 Some older cases in which it was held that deception was not the cause of the obtaining are now of doubtful authority. In *Lewis*,[46] a schoolmistress was charged with obtaining property (her salary) by false pretences (namely, that she had lied about her qualifications when seeking appointment to the job). It was held that her work (as a schoolteacher) was the cause of her obtaining her pay. In other words, her deception was too remote from the obtaining.[47] Similarly, in *Clucas*,[48] D got a bookmaker to accept a large bet by claiming (falsely) that he was placing the bets for a syndicate. The horse won. It was held that his false claim was not the cause of him obtaining his winnings; the effective cause was his backing the right horse. The court distinguished *Button*[49] where D told lies about his identity (thereby presenting himself as a runner with a poor record), thereby securing a favourable handicap in a race which he then went on to win, thus entitling himself to the winner's prize. It was held in *Button* that, if he had claimed the prize, then he would have been guilty of obtaining it by the false pretence; the pretence was not too remote from the obtaining.[50] *Button* is still good law. *Lewis* and *Clucas* are now, however, of doubtful authority. In *King and Stockwell*,[51] the defendants called at the house of an elderly widow and falsely informed her that they were from a firm of tree surgeons and falsely claimed that four of the trees in her garden were dangerous and needed to be removed. As a result, she agreed to them doing the work for £470 in cash. Subsequently, they were arrested by the police before claiming the £470 and were charged with attempting to obtain property (the cash) by deception. The Court of Appeal dismissed their appeal, holding that, had the attempt succeeded, the money would have been paid over by the victim as a result of the defendants' lies. The court expressly rejected an argument based on *Lewis* and cited, first, the following passage from *Martin*,[52] *per* Bovill CJ:

---

46 (1922) unreported.
47 Today, these facts would amount to the offence of obtaining a pecuniary advantage, contrary to s 16(2)(c) – see para 8-46, below.
48 [1949] 2 KB 226.
49 [1900] 2 QB 597.
50 He had, in fact, not gone up to claim the prize and was, thus, convicted only of attempting to obtain by his false pretence.
51 [1987] QB 547.
52 (1867) LR 1 CCR 56.

What is the test? Surely this, that there must be a direct connection between the pretence and the delivery – that there must be a continuing pretence. Whether there is such a connection or not is a question for the jury.

The court then cited the following passage from *Moreton*,[53] *per* Coleridge LJ:

*Martin* leaves the law in no doubt; it was held there that the fact that the goods were obtained under a contract does not make the goods so obtained goods not obtained by a false pretence, if the false pretence is a continuing one and operates on the mind of the person supplying the goods.

These cases recognise, as perhaps some others do not, that there can be more than one cause of the obtaining and it is sufficient if the deception alleged was one such cause. It does not have to be the dominant, or even the 'effective' cause. The test stated in *King and Stockwell*[54] is: 'Was the deception an operative cause of the obtaining of the property? This question falls to be answered as a question of fact by the jury applying their common sense.' It seems that the criminal law is now in line with the civil law: in civil law there is an actionable misrepresentation if the untrue statement of fact (the deception) was one of the causes which induced the other party to enter the contract.[55] So. in relation to s 15, if the deception is one of the causes which induces the victim to hand over the property, then the property is obtained by that deception.

### Reliance and inducement

8-22    Reliance is related to inducement. If the person deceived places no reliance on the deceptive statement, it is difficult to see how it can have induced him to hand over the property. Suppose that I succeed in persuading you to lend me £10. Suppose that, in the process I make four statements to you, as follows: (i) that I am 50 years old; (ii) that my black hair is naturally black; (iii) that I am in high paid employment; (iv) that I have an intention of repaying you the following evening. Suppose further that statements (i) to (iii) are all lies and that you believe them. If, in fact, you could not have cared less about my age, my natural hair colour or my salary level, then, presumably, you did not rely on those statements and they cannot have induced you to part with the £10. You would have lent me the money anyway. In that case, I am not guilty of obtaining the £10 by deception unless it can be proved that: (a) I did not have the intention of repaying you the following evening; and (b) that statement influenced you to lend me the money. If asked what statements of the borrower you relied upon, you would reply: 'Only that he said he intended to repay me the next evening.' If the only thing upon which you relied was not a deception, then I am not guilty. It was an argument along these lines which the House of Lords had to

---

53    (1913) 8 Cr App R 214.
54    [1987] QB 547, p 553, *per* Neill LJ; [1987] 1 All ER 547, p 550.
55    *Edgington v Fitzmaurice* (1885) 29 Ch D 459.

consider in *Charles*.[56] It will be remembered that D had bought gambling chips and, when paying for them, used his cheque guarantee card when writing cheques which, as he knew, went beyond the funds available in his bank account. By doing so, he impliedly stated that he was authorised to use the cheque guarantee card on those transactions. D's argument was that, in deciding to accept each cheque, the manager of the club had not relied upon that implied statement by D, but had relied only upon ensuring that the terms and conditions of the guarantee card were complied with (thereby ensuring that D's bank would be bound to honour the cheque). Their Lordships found, however, that the manager, in giving evidence, had repeatedly stressed that, if he had been aware that the accused was using his cheque book and card in an unauthorised way, no cheque would have been accepted. Thus, there was, in that case, evidence of reliance upon D's deceptive statement that he was authorised to use the cheque guarantee card. This does, however, suggest that, in the absence of evidence of such reliance, the case must fail.

8-23    In *Lambie*, where the statement implied by D presenting her credit card to the retailer was that D was authorised to use the credit card on that transaction, there was no direct evidence of inducement; there was no direct evidence that the retailer relied upon that (false) statement in deciding to accept the credit card. Nevertheless, the House of Lords held D to have been properly convicted. Their Lordships observed that many credit card transactions might be made by a retailer in the course of a day and held that, where no one could reasonably be expected to remember a particular transaction in detail, it can be left to the jury to infer, upon the evidence in the case as a whole, whether the inference of inducement is irresistible. Their Lordships considered what would have been the answer if the shop assistant, who accepted the credit card, had been asked whether, if she had known D's statement that she was authorised to use the credit card was untrue, she would have completed the transaction and allowed D to take the goods away. Their Lordships assumed that the answer must be 'No'. They, thus, found it an irresistible inference that the individual assistant accepting the credit card was induced to do so by the implied statement by D that she had authority. Thus, if in any given case the relevant shop assistant does give evidence[57] and states that she would have accepted the credit card irrespective of whether the person presenting it was authorised to use it, inducement is not established and the prosecution must fail.[58]

The unfortunate preparedness of the courts to allow inducement to be inferred, without direct evidence from the person said to have been deceived, finds a counterpart in some of the cases where D is charged with going equipped to cheat, contrary to s 25. This offence does not require D to have deceived anyone, or to have obtained anything. It requires him to have gone

---

56  See, generally, paras 8-14 and 8-15, above.
57  As, it is submitted, normally she should.
58  See 'Commentary' to *Nabina* [2000] Crim LR 481, p 482.

equipped to do something which, if he had done it, would have been the offence in s 15. This requires proof, *inter alia*, that his planned deception would have been a cause of him obtaining property. In *Rashid*,[59] where a British Rail steward went equipped to provide his own, and not his employers', tomato sandwiches to customers ordering them on the train, the Court of Appeal, *obiter*, was not prepared to assume that customers would not have bought and paid for the sandwiches if they had known they were not those of British Rail. In *Doukas*,[60] the facts were very similar. D, a hotel waiter had with him bottles of wine and spirits which liquor he was proposing, for his own profit, to supply to hotel customers, instead of supplying his employer's liquor. There the Court of Appeal referred to the test being dependent on the answer to a question put to 'the hypothetical customer', along the lines of: 'If you had been told the truth, would you or would you not have bought the commodity?' Acknowledging that, 'It is, at least in theory, for the jury in the end to decide that question,' the court considered[61] how that question might have been answered and concluded:

> It seems to us the matter can be answered on a much simpler basis. The hypothetical customer must be reasonably honest as well as being reasonably intelligent and it seems to us incredible that any customer, to whom the true situation was made clear, would willingly make himself a party to what was obviously a fraud by the waiter upon his employers. If that conclusion is contrary to the *obiter dicta* in *Rashid*, then we must respectfully disagree with those *dicta*.

8-24    Whilst one can understand the reluctance of an appellate court to quash the conviction of someone who is an out and out rogue, the judicial tendency, evident especially in *Lambie* and in *Doukas*, to assume that the person deceived (s 15), or hypothetically deceived (s 25), is honest or 'reasonably' honest, demonstrates a touching faith in the honesty of their fellow citizens.[62] It would be better to regard this, in practice, and not just in theory, as a jury matter. If the jury has not been asked to consider the issue of inducement, that should be regarded as a misdirection. It is, thus, gratifying to note that in *Cooke*,[63] another British Rail steward case, the House of Lords refused to assume that there would have been a conviction if the jury had been required to consider whether the crime of conspiracy to go equipped had been committed. Lord Mackay stated that whether the necessary ingredients of the offence have been established, 'is one for the jury, and whether they have been will depend on the detail of the evidence, particularly that relating to the attitude and understanding of those

---

59   [1977] 1 WLR 298.

60   [1978] 1 WLR 372.

61   *Ibid*, p 376.

62   In any case, shop assistants dealing with credit card customers may be honest and still not rely on the implied statement that D has authority to use the card: see Law Commission, *Conspiracy to Defraud*, No 228, 1994, para 438, cited in the 'Commentary' to *Nabina* [2000] Crim LR 481, p 483.

63   [1986] AC 909.

receiving the supplies'.[64] And Lord Bridge said: 'Upright citizens as the ordinary run of British Rail passengers may be presumed to be, I am not prepared to assume that they would necessarily refuse to take and pay for refreshments even if they knew perfectly well that the buffet staff were practising the kind of "fiddle" here involved.'[65] So far as evidence is concerned, evidence should be led as to reliance/inducement – that being an ingredient of the offence. Under s 15,[66] that evidence should normally come from the person said to have been deceived. Under s 25, it should come from one or more of the customers at the establishment (hotel or train, etc) who might have been victims of the deception which the defendant is said to have gone equipped to commit. In addition, the jury should be directed to consider whether there was (or under s 25 would have been) a causal connection between the deception and the obtaining. If this is not done, it should be recognised as a misdirection and the appellate court should be very hesitant before substituting its own assumed answer to that question.

Thankfully, this seems to have been the approach of the Court of Appeal in *Nabina* – though, in truth, the issue there was more whether there was a deception than whether, if there was, it was relied upon. D had obtained a number of credit cards by giving false information about his personal circumstances. He used these credit cards to obtain goods from a number of retail outlets and was charged, under s 15, with obtaining those goods by deception, namely, by falsely representing that he was the legitimate holder of the credit card which he presented. His conviction was quashed because there was no evidence in relation to the alleged deception; nor was the alleged deception one which could be said to rest upon any necessary or irresistible inference. It was doubtful whether a jury could properly draw such an inference, since suppliers of goods were generally concerned to ensure that they would receive payment when a credit card was used and there must be doubt as to whether they were interested in how the holder got the card, provided that the transaction would be honoured. In this case, there was no evidence that the transaction would not be honoured. D, probably, was the 'legitimate' holder of the card in the sense that his contract with the credit card issuer was not void, but merely voidable and had not been avoided by the credit card company at the time D's purchases were made. The prosecution might have had a better chance of success, if D had, instead, been charged with obtaining the credit cards by deception or, possibly, with theft of the goods obtained by the use of the card.[67]

---

64   [1986] AC 909, p 934; [1986] 2 All ER 985, p 1000.

65   [1986] AC 909, p 921; [1986] 2 All ER 985, p 990.

66   Or any other offence of actual obtaining by deception.

67   Though, then, there is an argument that D was not dishonest in relation to the purchase of the goods, since D (presumably) knew that they would be paid for by the credit card issuer, see fn 33 (discussing *Lambie*) at para 8-15, above.

*Deception of X and obtaining from Y*

8-25    The requirement for a causal connection between the deception and the obtaining does not mean that the property has to have been obtained from the person who was deceived. D can commit the offence if, by deceiving X, he manages to obtain property from Y. Thus, D by presenting a cheque together with his cheque guarantee card, implies that he has his bank's authority to use the card. If, by thus deceiving the person accepting the cheque, he obtains a pecuniary advantage from his bank, that can be an offence: *Kovacs*.[68]

## Obtaining property belonging to another

*Property*

8-26    Section 34(1) provides that s 4(1) applies to other offences in the TA 1968 (including, therefore, s 15) as it applies to theft.[69] Thus, property includes, for example, intangible property.[70] However, the remaining sub-ss of s 4 apply only to the offence of theft. Thus, land (without the restrictions imposed by s 4(2)–(3)), wild animals and mushrooms, etc, which belong to someone else, are capable of being obtained by deception.

*Belonging to another*

8-27    Section 34(1) provides that s 5(1) applies to other offences in the TA 1968 (including, therefore, s 15) as it applies to theft.[71] Thus, apart from one exception mentioned in s 5(1), property belongs to another, if that other has possession or control of it or any proprietary right or interest in it. It follows that, just as D can steal D's own property, so D can obtain property which belongs to himself, but which is in the possession of someone else. This would have occurred if, in *Turner*,[72] D, instead of simply grabbing possession of his own car from the garage, had obtained it by paying the garage proprietor with a cheque which D knew would bounce.

*Obtain*

8-28    D obtains property if he obtains ownership, possession or control of it.[73] Typically, D will obtain possession by his deception. However, it is perfectly

---

68    [1974] 1 WLR 370, approved and applied in *Charles* [1977] AC 177.

69    See paras 2-60–2-82, above.

70    For problems over whether the property obtained is the same as the property which belonged to the victim, see *Preddy* [1996] AC 815, para 8-29, below.

71    For discussion of s 5(1), see paras 2-85–2-86, above. Section 34(1) provides: '(1) Sections 4(1) and 5(1) apply generally for the purposes of this Act as they apply for the purposes of s 1.'

72    [1971] 1 WLR 901 and see, generally, paras 2-86 and 2-87 above.

73    Section 15(2).

possible for him to obtain ownership as well – as occurred in the well known contract case of *Phillips v Brooks*,[74] where a rogue obtained a ring from a jeweller by lying about his identity and leaving a forged cheque. The resulting contract between the rogue and the jeweller was voidable and gave the rogue a voidable title, which he was able to pass on to an innocent third party. Though much less commonly achieved, it is possible for the offence to be committed by obtaining ownership without possession, for example, by causing a reversionary interest in land to be conveyed to the defendant. Obtaining includes obtaining for another or enabling another to obtain or retain.[75] Thus, in *DPP v Stonehouse*,[76] D was convicted of attempting, by faking his own death, to cause his wife (innocently) to obtain the insurance money payable under his life insurance policies.

## Preddy

8-29    It is a requirement of the offence that D obtains property belonging to another. This means that the property that D obtains must be property which, at the time of the obtaining, belongs to another. The House of Lords applied this requirement logically in a case of mortgage fraud, *Preddy*,[77] a decision which had considerable repercussions. Before considering the case, it helps to grasp what are the property rights involved in a bank account. Put simply, if my bank account is in credit to the tune of £1,000, then the bank is my debtor for that amount. If the bank were to refuse to pay me, I could sue the bank for the money. I have a cause of action (a right to bring a legal claim against the bank). That right, that cause of action, is a piece of property – albeit intangible property. Intangible property is property for the purposes of the TA 1968.[78] It can be stolen. It can, at least in theory, be obtained by deception. In *Preddy*, the defendants had made several applications to building societies for mortgage loans – applications containing various pieces of false information. Some of these applications were successful. In some of them, the same solicitor acted for the defendants (the borrowers) and for the lenders and the mortgage advances were made by means of electronic transfer of funds from the bank accounts of the lenders to the bank account of the solicitor. The defendants were convicted on various counts of obtaining, and of attempting to obtain, property by deception (contrary to s 15 of the TA 1968). These convictions were quashed by the House of Lords. Assuming that the bank account of the lender (the building society) was in credit when the transfer of funds was made and assuming that the bank

---

74    [1919] 2 KB 243.
75    Section 15(2).
76    [1978] AC 55.
77    [1996] AC 815; [1996] 3 WLR 255; [1996] 3 All ER 481.
78    See ss 4(1) and 34(1).

account of the recipient (the defendant or his solicitor) was also in credit at that time, the effect of the transfer of funds was to extinguish a right of action that the lender had against the lender's bank and to create a new right of action of the recipient against the recipient's bank. The property which the recipient obtained was not the lender's right to sue the lender's bank. The property which the recipient obtained was a new piece of property, the right of the recipient to sue the recipient's bank (for the amount transferred). The recipient, thus, did not obtain property belonging to another. The nub of the decision is that an act which destroys a piece of your property and which at the same time creates for me a *different* piece of property does not amount to me obtaining property belonging to another. Nor, their Lordships decided, was the position any different where the transfer of funds was effected by a cheque, instead of by electronic transfer. Certainly, the defendant's (or his solicitor's) obtaining of the cheque was the obtaining of an intangible piece of property, a chose in action, since the payee has the right to sue on a cheque. However, before the cheque was drawn (written) and handed over, the drawer (the building society) did not have that chose in action (the right to sue on the cheque). It was the very act of drawing the cheque and passing it to the payee which created the intangible property. Neither could it be said that the defendant was guilty of obtaining by deception a tangible piece of property, namely, the piece of paper on which the cheque was written. This was because the offence in s 15, requires proof of an intention to deprive the owner permanently of the property and the defendants could not have had that intention, since the piece of paper would, after being presented to the payee's bank for payment, be returned to the drawer (the building society) through the bank's clearing system.[79]

8-30    The House of Lords decision in *Preddy* comprehensively reversed the law as it had previously been understood. It had four particular consequences. First, a number of earlier cases that are authority for propositions which are still valid must now be looked at with the qualification that, after *Preddy*, s 15 would not be an appropriate charge on their facts.[80] Secondly, it left the courts wondering what other offences (already existing at that time) could successfully be used to secure convictions of mortgage fraudsters who had carried out their activities before the decision in *Preddy*, but had yet to be charged. Thirdly, in relation to a number of cases where the defendant had been convicted of the s 15 offence shortly before *Preddy* was decided, it left the Court of Appeal having to quash the convictions and consider what, if any, alternative verdicts could be substituted for them.[81] Fourthly, it led to Parliament amending the TA 1968 to add two new offences and amending s 1 of the TA 1978, all of which amendments were calculated to provide offences capable of catching such

---

79  This aspect of the decision is further discussed, para 8-31, below.

80  For example: *Rozeik* [1996] 1 WLR 159 (CA), para 8-06, above (establishing who in a company must be deceived for the company to be deceived).

81  *Graham (No 1)* [1997] 1 Cr App R 302; [1997] Crim LR 340; *Naviede* [1997] Crim LR 663.

fraudsters. As to the second of these things, the possible charges would appear to include: theft of the lender's intangible right to sue the lender's bank for the amount of the money transferred;[82] false accounting, contrary to s 17 (where the fraudulent application involved the fraudster furnishing a document which was misleading and was made for an accounting purpose);[83] procuring the execution of a valuable security, contrary to s 20(2) (where the building society advanced the loan by means of a cheque); conspiracy to defraud (where the fraudster was acting in concert with at least one other).

Now; let us consider two particular examples in the light of *Preddy*. First, consider the case of W who, knowing that a cheque is forged, presents it and obtains cash for it. Then he has dishonestly by deception obtained property (the cash) belonging to another (the bank paying him the cash) with the intention of permanently depriving the bank of it. Thus, he has committed the s 15 offence. If, on other hand, W pays the cheque into the credit of his own bank account, he does not obtain property belonging to another. By his deception, he has simply: (a) extinguished the right of the person on whose account the cheque was drawn; and (b) created a new right of his own to sue his own bank for the amount of the credit (assuming that his account was already in credit at the time). In this situation, he does not obtain property by deception. However, providing that the account upon which the cheque was drawn was in credit at the time the cheque was honoured, W commits theft of that account holder's right to sue his bank for the amount of the cheque.[84] In the second example, X sells a car knowing that he does not own it and that he lacks the owner's authority to sell it. If he is paid in cash, then he has obtained, by his deception, property (the cash) belonging to another (the buyer). If he is paid by means of a cheque (which he then pays into the credit of his own bank account), then the only property belonging to another which he has obtained is the piece of paper on which the cheque is written. In relation to that tangible piece of paper, he cannot successfully be charged with either theft or obtaining it by deception, since he lacks the intention of permanently depriving the owner of it. Again, however, he could – assuming the cheque is duly presented and honoured and that at that time the buyer's bank account was in credit – be charged with theft of that amount of the buyer's intangible property consisting of the buyer's right to sue his own bank for the amount thus debited from it.[85] It may, incidentally, be that X commits theft of the car, assuming he intended to deprive the owner permanently of it. In each of the examples, where W and X do not obtain cash but, instead, have their accounts credited, there can be no conviction for theft unless the victim's account was in credit when the cheque was honoured. This

---

82  See *Hawkins* [1997] 1 Cr App R 234; *Graham (No 2)* [1997] Crim LR 358, confirming *Kohn* (1979) 69 Cr App R 395; *Burke* [2000] Crim LR 413; *Williams (Roy)* [2001] Cr App R 362.

83  *Hawkins* [1997] 1 Cr App R 234.

84  *Burke* [2000] Crim LR 413.

85  *Williams (Roy)* [2001] Cr App R 362.

problem is now overcome because, in the situation where W or X obtains a cheque and has it credited to his account, there is now the possibility of a conviction for obtaining a money transfer, contrary to s 15A – and that offence is committed irrespective of whether the victim's account or the defendant's account was in credit at the time.[86]

## *An error in Preddy?*

8-31    If, by deception, I get you to draw (write) a cheque payable to me and to give it to me and I then present it to my bank as a credit to my account, do I have an intention to deprive you permanently of the tangible piece of paper (the cheque form) on which the cheque is written? The passages above have all been written on the basis that the answer is 'No'. That was the clear answer given in *Preddy*, by Lord Goff, in his judgment, with which all his brethren agreed. He said 'there can have been no intention on the part of the payee permanently to deprive the owner of the cheque form, which would on presentation of the cheque for payment be returned to the drawer via his bank'.[87]

Professor Sir John Smith has challenged this aspect of the decision[88] arguing that a cheque is not just two things but three: (i) it is a piece of paper; (ii) it creates a chose in action; (iii) it is a valuable security. Referring to the third, he described it as 'not the thing in action, nor a mere piece of paper, but the instrument, the physical thing with certain writing on it'. Later on, he continued: 'But the argument is not that the cheque is intangible property; it is that the tangible thing, the paper with writing on it, is the key to the drawer's bank account ...' He would seem to have it that a cheque comprises two different pieces of physical, *tangible* property: (i) a mere piece of paper; and (ii) a piece of paper which is a metaphorical 'key'. This is too sophisticated. Is my front door key two pieces of property because it: (a) is a mere piece of metal; and also (b) opens my door? If it also happens to be magnetic, is it also yet a third piece of tangible property? If so, how many pieces of *tangible* property are in my hand when I hold my credit card?! It is perhaps realistic to ask a jury to accept that a tangible piece of property can also represent a separate piece of intangible property. It is simply too much to ask them to accept that a single physical tangible item is, nevertheless, two pieces of physical tangible property. A cheque is a valuable security.[89] That does not make it two separate pieces of tangible property.

But were their Lordships in *Preddy* correct to hold that the defendant had no intention permanently to deprive the owner of the tangible property, the cheque

---

86    See para 8-36, below.
87    [1996] AC 815, pp 836–37.
88    [1997] Crim LR 396.
89    See para 10-21, below.

form? In *Marshall*,[90] the defendants had collected London Underground tickets from passengers emerging from the Underground and had sold them to other travellers; they were convicted of theft. On an assumption that the tickets would, upon being used, find their way back to the owner (London Underground), the Court of Appeal held that, nevertheless, the defendants had an intention of permanently depriving the owner of them. They had treated them as their 'own to dispose of regardless of the other's rights' and, thus, applying s 6(1) of the TA 1968, they were to be regarded as having had an intention permanently to deprive the owner of them. *Preddy* was distinguished on the basis that it was concerned with intangible property – an inadequate distinction given that Lord Goff in his speech in *Preddy* made it clear that he was referring to the cheque forms (tangible property). Nevertheless, a different, and valid, distinction is possible. When I obtain a cheque from you, even when I obtain it from you by deception, you expect and authorise me to present it for the credit of my bank account and the corresponding debit of yours. When I do just that, I am not acting 'regardless of your rights', but in accordance with your authority and expectations; s 6(1), accordingly, has no application. The same cannot be said of the defendants in *Marshall*, when they sold the tickets to other travellers.

That part of the judgment in *Preddy* which applies to cheques has been held to be *obiter* by the Supreme Court of Victoria[91] which declined to follow it. It has, however, been followed by the Court of Appeal in England.[92] In *Clark (Brian)*,[93] the Court of Appeal considered it wrong to regard it as *obiter* and applied it, in quashing a conviction for obtaining by deception a cheque, namely, the cheque itself, rather than the sum for which it was drawn; the defendant had no intention to deprive the owner (the drawer) permanently of it. It seems that, if in *Preddy*, the House of Lords was wrong about cheques, only the House of Lords can put the matter right.

## Mens rea

8-32   There are three mental elements required for the offence. The first, that the defendant was deliberate or reckless as to causing a deception, has already been discussed.[94] The second is that the defendant must have had an intention of permanently depriving the owner of the property obtained. The third is that the defendant has to have been dishonest.

---

90   (1992) 2 Cr App R 282, already discussed at paras 2-62 and 2-85, above.
91   *Parsons* [1998] 2 VR 478. The court preferred the views of Professor Smith.
92   *Graham* [1997] 1 Cr App R 302.
93   [2001] EWCA Crim 884. If the matter had been free of authority, the court would have found Professor Smith's views persuasive.
94   See para 8-19, above.

## *Intention of permanently depriving*

8-33    This requirement is the same as the requirement in theft. The expression means the same here as it does in the offence of theft and, by virtue of s 15(3), s 6 applies, just as it does for the purposes of theft. Prior to *Preddy*,[95] there was authority that the act of cashing a cheque indicated an intention of permanently depriving the owner of it because, once paid, it ceased to be in substance the same thing it originally was.[96] That authority has now, however, been comprehensively overruled by *Preddy*.

## *Dishonesty*

8-34    Dishonesty is a requirement common to all the obtaining offences in the TAs. The test for dishonesty is the same as that which applies in the case of theft.[97] Indeed, the leading case, *Ghosh*, was a decision arising out of a prosecution under s 15. That test was discussed in Chapter 2. Here, will be discussed only matters particularly pertinent to s 15. It is clear from the wording of s 15 that the issue is one of whether the defendant obtained dishonestly, not whether his deception was dishonest.

The first part of the *Ghosh* test requires the jury to decide whether what the defendant did was dishonest, according to the standards of ordinary people. It might be thought that, if the prosecution proves, as it must for a conviction under s 15, a deliberate or reckless deception, that a finding of dishonesty would be automatic. How can one obtain by deception without being dishonest? However, the wording of the section is clear. Deception and dishonesty are separate requirements and each must be proved. This was held in *Greenstein*, the 'stagging' case already discussed in relation to deception,[98] where the judge told that jury that, even if they found deception proved, they must not convict unless they also found that the defendant had been dishonest. That was a matter for them to decide.

It is, in fact, with implied statements leading to deception, that the defendant is most likely to be found to have deceived without being dishonest. Thus, someone who draws and presents a cheque impliedly represents that the present state of affairs is such that, in the ordinary course of events, it will be honoured on its first future presentment.[99] It may, however, be that the drawer has simply failed to monitor his own bank account and, therefore, fails to realise that that implied statement is false. Such a person will not be found to be dishonest.[100]

---

95  Paragraph 8-29, above.
96  *Duru* [1974] 1 WLR 2.
97  Except that s 2 applies only to the offence of theft.
98  For the facts, see para 8-13, above.
99  See para 8-13, above.
100 Also, his deception is probably not deliberate or reckless.

8-35     The current definition of dishonesty was developed dramatically in three particular cases, *Feely*,[101] *Greenstein* and *Ghosh*. Certain cases decided before these three are, thus, no longer good law. It is no longer correct to say: that it is no defence that the defendant intended to repay a loan he obtained by deception;[102] or that it is no defence that the defendant intended to repay an overdraft created by his cashing a cheque drawn on an account with insufficient funds.[103] Rather, the defendant is entitled to have the jury consider these claims when applying the *Ghosh* test to determine whether the defendant was dishonest.

Section 2 applies only to the offence of theft. So, it is not absolutely clear that the three beliefs set out in s 2(1) will each automatically negate dishonesty for the purposes of s 15. Suppose the defendant claims that he believed he had a legal right to deprive the other person of the property. If charged with theft,[104] he is entitled, relying on s 2(1)(a), to have the jury directed that, if he had such a belief, he was not dishonest and must be acquitted. If, however, he is charged with obtaining the property by deception, the jury must be directed to make up its own mind whether such a belief meant that the defendant either (a) was not dishonest, according to the standards of ordinary people, or (b) did not realise that ordinary people would regard his actions as dishonest.[105]

## 2 OBTAINING A MONEY TRANSFER

8-36     **Section 15A of the TA 1968 – Obtaining a money transfer by deception**

(1)   A person is guilty of an offence if by any deception he dishonestly obtains a money transfer for himself or another.

(2)   A money transfer occurs when –

(a)   a debit is made to one account,

(b)   a credit is made to another, and

(c)   the credit results from the debit or the debit results from the credit.

(3)   References to a credit and to a debit are to a credit of an amount of money and to a debit of an amount of money.

(4)   It is immaterial (in particular) –

(a)   whether the amount credited is the same as the amount debited;

(b)   whether the money transfer is effected on presentment of a cheque or by another method;

---

101  [1973] QB 530.

102  As was held in *McCall* (1970) 55 Cr App R 175, a decision which cannot survive the decisions in *Feely* [1973] QB 530 and *Ghosh* [1982] QB 1053; see *Melwani* [1989] Crim LR 565.

103  As was held in *Halstead v Patel* [1972] 1 WLR 661.

104  Or, indeed, robbery; see *Robinson* [1977] Crim LR 173.

105  *Woolven* (1983) 77 Cr App R 231.

   (c) whether any delay occurs in the process by which the money transfer is effected;

   (d) whether any intermediate credits or debits are made in the course of the money transfer;

   (e) whether either of the accounts is overdrawn before or after the money transfer is effected.

(5) A person guilty of an offence under this section shall be liable on conviction on indictment to imprisonment for a term not exceeding 10 years.

**8-37** **Section 15B of the TA 1968**

(1) The following provisions have effect for the interpretation of s 15A of this Act.

(2) 'Deception' has the same meaning as in s 15 of this Act.

(3) 'Account' means an account kept with –

   (a) a bank; or

   (b) a person carrying on a business which falls within sub-s (4) below.

(4) A business falls within this sub-section if –

   (a) in the course of the business money received by way of deposit is lent to others; or

   (b) any other activity of the business is financed, wholly or to any material extent, out of the capital of or the interest on money received by way of deposit; and 'deposit' here has the same meaning as in s 35 of the Banking Act 1987 (fraudulent inducement to make a deposit).

(5) For the purposes of sub-s (4) above –

   (a) all the activities which a person carries on by way of business shall be regarded as a single business carried on by him; and

   (b) 'money' includes money expressed in a currency other than sterling or in the European currency unit (as defined in Council Regulation (EC) 3320/94 or any Community instrument replacing it).

(6) Nothing in this section has effect in relation to anything done before the day on which this Act is passed.

## Mode of trial and sentence

**8-38** The offence is triable either way.[106] If tried on indictment, it is a class 4 offence with a maximum penalty of imprisonment for 10 years. Following summary trial, the magistrates can sentence to imprisonment for up to six months, a fine up to the statutory maximum, or both.[107]

---

106 MCA 1980, s 17(1) and Sched 1, para 28.
107 *Ibid*, s 32(1) and Sched 1, para 28. The statutory maximum is currently £5,000.

## Background and scope of the offence

8-39     Sections 15A and 15B, and also s 24A, were added to the TA 1968 by s 1(1) of the Theft (Amendment) Act 1996. The latter Act, which also added sub-s (3) to s 1 of the TA 1978, enacted the recommendations of the Law Commission Report, *Offence of Dishonesty: Money Transfers.*[108] These changes were designed to plug the hole in criminal liability created by the decision of the House of Lords in *Preddy.*[109] The meaning of 'deception' and 'dishonesty' are the same as they are in relation to s 15, as, also, is the requirement that the deception is a cause of the obtaining. The offence in s 15A will catch the mortgage (or loan) fraudster, the person who dishonestly obtains a loan, whether or not it is a mortgage loan, by deception. It is wider than that, however, in that it is not restricted to the obtaining of loans, but applies to any money transfer dishonestly obtained by deception. For example, the defendant might by his deception have induced the victim to make a money transfer for one of the following purposes:

(a) to make a gift of the money to the defendant or anyone else;

(b) to pay a debt which the victim is deceived into believing he owes;

(c) to buy goods or services which he is deceived into buying or to paying for.

8-40     In relation to the last of these, consider D who has lied about goods (or services), thereby inducing the victim to agree to buy them (or at least to pay for them). The appropriate charge will depend upon how the victim pays. If he pays for them by cheque or by any other form of money transfer other than by handing over cash, then D has obtained a money transfer and a charge under s 15A is appropriate. If, however, the victim pays in cash, that (surprising as it may seem) is not a 'money transfer' and the appropriate charge is one of obtaining property by deception under s 15.

A money transfer requires a credit to one account and a debit to another. The offence under s 15A will be complete as soon as the money transfer is made. Assuming that the credit results from the debit, or vice versa, the money transfer will be made (and the offence will be completed) when the second of those two (the debit of one account and the credit of another) occurs. What, then, is the position where D by dishonest deception obtains a cheque, but never presents it, or where he does present it but, perhaps because by then he has been rumbled, it is not honoured? In the latter case, he will be guilty of attempting to commit the offence in s 15A. In the former, he will almost certainly not be, because he has not progressed beyond preparation to commit it. Nor will he be guilty of obtaining property (the cheque) by deception.[110] In that case, it is difficult to see what charge could succeed against D, unless of course D has, by his deception,

---

108 Law Commission No 243.

109 Paragraph 8-29, above.

110 That is true in respect of both the intangible property represented by the cheque and, also, the tangible piece of paper: *Preddy* [1996] AC 815; see paras 8-29–8-31 above.

obtained something else as well as the cheque. If, for example, that other property was a letter agreeing to him having a loan, or a letter allotting him a number of shares, that would be property which (unlike the cheque) D was likely to retain. He might be charged with obtaining that property, the piece of paper on which the letter is written, by deception contrary to s 15 – not, perhaps, a charge entirely reflecting the substance of what D has done.

## 3 OBTAINING A PECUNIARY ADVANTAGE

8-41    **Section 16 of the TA 1968 – Obtaining a pecuniary advantage by deception**

(1) A person who by any deception dishonestly obtains for himself or another any pecuniary advantage shall on conviction on indictment be liable to imprisonment for a term not exceeding five years.

(2) The cases in which a pecuniary advantage within the meaning of this section is to be regarded as obtained for a person are cases where –

(a) [repealed]

(b) he is allowed to borrow by way of overdraft, or to take out any policy of insurance or annuity contract, or obtains an improvement of the terms on which he is allowed to do so; or

(c) he is given the opportunity to earn remuneration or greater remuneration in an office or employment, or to win money by betting.

(3) For the purposes of this section 'deception' has the same meaning as in s 15 of this Act.

## Mode of trial and sentence

8-42    The offence is triable either way.[111] If tried on indictment, it is a class 4 offence with a maximum penalty of imprisonment for five years. Following summary trial, the magistrates can sentence to imprisonment for up to six months, a fine up to the statutory maximum, or both.[112]

## Common expressions

8-43    For the purposes of this offence, concepts of deception, dishonesty and the causal connection between the deception and the obtaining are the same as for s 15.

---

111 MCA 1980, s 17(1) and Sched 1, para 28.
112 *Ibid*, s 32(1) and Sched 1, para 28. The statutory maximum is currently £5,000.

## Scope of the offence

8-44    Sub-section (2) contains an exhaustive list of pecuniary advantages. Thus, the s 16 offence is not committed by someone obtaining something which might be described as a pecuniary advantage, but is not mentioned in sub-s (2). On the other hand, if the defendant obtains something which does fall within sub-s (2) that, for the purposes of the offence, is a pecuniary advantage, even if the defendant gains no benefit (advantage) of a monetary (pecuniary) nature.[113] Sub-section (2)(a) was repealed by the TA 1978, which contains three new offences. The scope of s 16 is, therefore, limited to sub-paras (b) and (c) of sub-s (2).

### *Allowed to borrow by way of overdraft*

8-45    This was the offence of which the defendant in *Charles*[114] was convicted when he used his cheque guarantee card to back his cheques when he bought chips in a gambling club. His deception of one person (the person accepting the cheque) was a cause of him obtaining the pecuniary advantage (the overdraft) from another person (D's bank). D's use of the card effectively bound his bank to honour the cheques, even though there were no funds in D's account and even though the cheques were in excess of any overdraft D was authorised to create. The obligation of the bank to honour the cheques was a contractual obligation arising under the contract made between the payee and the bank. Although the bank was bound to honour the cheque, this was an obligation owed by the bank only to the payee. The bank owed no such duty to the defendant. It is, thus, still true to say that the defendant was 'allowed' to borrow by way of overdraft, since the bank's decision to honour the cheque (thereby honouring its obligation to the payee), is an act of will on the part of the bank and the offence is not complete until the bank makes that act of will.[115]

### *Sub-section 2(c)*

8-46    This was included because of the inability to secure convictions for obtaining property by false pretences in respect of the activities mentioned in the sub-section. The prosecution had failed to secure a conviction, in *Lewis*,[116] of a schoolteacher who had lied about her qualifications and, in the *Clucas* case,[117] of a punter who was allowed to place a bet because of a lie. It had been held,

---

113 *DPP v Turner* [1974] AC 357.

114 [1977] AC 177; see para 8-14 above.

115 *Bevan* (1986) 84 Cr App R 143, applying *Waites* [1982] Crim LR 369. The offence is, thus committed where (at D's bank) and when the cheque is honoured. For criticism of *Bevan* see Smith, ATH, para 18-52.

116 (1922) unreported.

117 [1949] 2 KB 226.

respectively, that the teacher's pay and the punter's winnings were not obtained by the false pretence (the deception). In the light of *King and Stockwell*,[118] it can now be said that, perhaps, sub-s (2)(c) was unnecessary, since *Lewis* and *Clucas* are no longer good law.[119]

The words 'office or employment' appear, at first sight, not to include someone who obtains the opportunity to earn remuneration as an independent contractor, which may account for why, in *King and Stockwell*, the defendant was charged (successfully) under s 15. However, it has since been held, in *Callender*,[120] that in this sub-section 'employment' means work and can include work as an independent contractor – in that case as a self-employed accountant.

---

118 [1987] QB 547.
119 See para 8-21 above.
120 [1993] QB 303 (CA).

# CHAPTER 9

# THE THEFT ACT 1978

## 1 OBTAINING SERVICES BY DECEPTION

9-01    **Section 1 of the Theft Act (TA) 1978 – Obtaining services by deception**

(1) A person who by any deception dishonestly obtains services from another shall be guilty of an offence.

(2) It is an obtaining of services where the other is induced to confer a benefit by doing some act, or causing or permitting some act to be done, on the understanding that the benefit has been or will be paid for.

(3) Without prejudice to the generality of sub-s (2) above, it is an obtaining of services where the other is induced to make a loan, or to cause or permit a loan to be made, on the understanding that any payment (whether by way of interest or otherwise) will be or has been made in respect of the loan.

## Mode of trial and sentence

9-02    The offence is triable either way.[1] If tried on indictment it is a class 4 offence with a maximum penalty of imprisonment for five years. Following summary trial, the magistrates can sentence to imprisonment for up to six months, a fine up to the statutory maximum or both.[2]

## Background and scope of the offence

9-03    The TA 1978 implemented with some modifications the recommendations in the *Thirteenth Report* of the Criminal Law Revision Committee (CLRC).[3] In accordance with those recommendations, it repealed s 16(2)(a) of the TA 1968 and enacted three new offences (in ss 1–3 of the TA 1978). Section 1 is not as in the terms proposed in the draft bill which was attached to the *Thirteenth Report*, but is very differently worded and considerably wider.[4] The requirements for 'deception', 'dishonesty' and for the deception to have been a cause of the

---

1    TA 1978, s 4(1).

2    *Ibid*, s 4(2) and (3), as amended by the Magistrates' Courts Act (MCA) 1980, s 154(1) and Sched 7, para 170. The statutory maximum is currently £5000.

3    Cmnd 6733.

4    For the history of how the clause originally recommended came to be changed to that eventually enacted, see Spencer, JR, 'The Theft Act 1978' [1979] Crim LR 24.

obtaining are the same as they are in s 15 of the TA 1968.[5] The requirement for deception does mean that the person who sneaks into a concert without paying or who climbs over the back fence and, thus, gains entry into a football match without paying does not commit this offence. There is, however, no requirement that the deception must relate to payment. Suppose that a university has a car park, the charge for which is £1 per day and use of which is restricted to its staff and suppose that a student knowing this pays the £1 and gains entry by claiming falsely that he is a member of staff. Assuming, as seems likely, that the student would be found to be dishonest, his actions amount to the offence. His deception does not have to be a deception as to payment, so long as it was a cause of him obtaining the benefit of being allowed in.

## Services

9-04    A very wide number of activities can be described as services. Amongst the most obvious which might be the subject of this offence are: (i) travel, a taxi/train/bus ride; (ii) accommodation, a stay in a hotel room; (iii) leisure, entrance to a concert/theme park/sporting event; (iv) household services, having one's house painted/drains cleared/garden tidied. The definition of services is limited by the requirements: (i) that a benefit is conferred; and (ii) that it is conferred on the understanding that it has been or will be paid for.

## Benefit

9-05    Professor Griew took the view that the word 'benefit' in s 1(2) indicated no such limitation and was no more than a device to enable felicitous drafting.[6] Given that the sub-section could have been perfectly well drafted – even if less elegantly – without the word 'benefit', this does not seem a legitimate interpretation of a penal provision. The limitation seems unlikely, however, to be very much of one, because of the other restriction in the definition in s 1(2) namely, the requirement for an 'understanding that the benefit has been or will be paid for'. It is seldom likely to be the case that something provided on such an understanding would not be clearly something one would call a benefit. It is nevertheless, thought that the service can confer a benefit without it being an economic benefit. Consider F, who dishonestly by deception induces a barber to give him a shave (on the understanding, of course, that the barber will be paid

---

5    See paras 8-04 and 8-34, above. The TA 1978, s 5(1) provides: '(1) For the purposes of ss and 2 above, "deception" has the same meaning as in s 15 of the TA 1968, that is to say, it means any deception (whether deliberate or reckless) by words or conduct as to fact or as to law, including a deception as to the present intentions of the person using the deception or any other person; and s 18 of the that Act (liability of company officers for offences by the company) shall apply in relation to s 1 and 2 above as it applies in relation to s 15 of that Act.'

6    Griew (para 9-06), a view shared by Arlidge and Parry (para 4-149) and also canvassed by Smith, ATH (para 18-23).

for it). It may be that, if the barber had not been induced to provide the shave, F would have shaved himself. F may, thus, have enjoyed no economic benefit. He has, however, clearly had the 'benefit' of being shaved. If, as has been stated above, the word 'benefit' has some meaning, then it must be possible to imagine a situation where all the requirements of the offence are present – or may be present – with the exception of this one. Suppose, as a prank, X tells Y: 'Did you know that if you find a salmon in this river, you will be entitled to a payment of £10 from the Fresh Water Authority?' Assuming this to be a lie and X to be dishonest and that Y, induced by this statement, looks for and finds a salmon in the river, it is frankly impossible to see how this is a benefit to X. It is no answer to say[7] that the doing of an act by Y can be sufficient consideration to support a promise by X. That does not make it a benefit to X. Unless it is a benefit to somebody, it is not a 'service'. In other words, this offence is not capable of catching the likes of X who are simply malicious in dishonestly by deception inducing someone else to do something – not unless it is something which is of benefit to somebody.

It is not necessary, however, for the act to be of benefit to the defendant. D can certainly commit this offence by inducing the victim to confer a benefit on someone else. Although there is, in s 1, no such express extension to the word 'obtain', nevertheless, it is possible to be guilty of obtaining services for another.[8]

9-06 Merely inducing the victim *not* to do something – even if that confers a benefit on D – does not amount to the offence. Thus, if, say, P has been threatening D that P will commence legal proceedings against D and D dishonestly by deception induces P not to do so, that will not fall within the definition of the offence. On the other hand, inducing the victim to cause or permit some act to be done, can do so. This would cover the example given earlier of the university car park attendant who is duped into allowing a student to park in the staff car park. It also covers the situation where a ticket collector is induced to allow D to enter a concert by D's lies that he has already paid and has lost his ticket.

Finally, it is nice question whether an act, such as tattooing, or serving alcohol to, a 17 year old from which it is the policy of the law to protect D is a 'benefit' to him.[9] The 17 year old who obtains such a tattoo or alcoholic drink by deception cannot be guilty as accessory to the tattooing or licensing offence committed by the supplier.[10] It would be consistent with that for the courts to

---

7    As does Professor Sir John Smith: Smith, JC, para 4-83.

8    *Nathan* [1997] Crim LR 835 (CA).

9    Obtaining delivery of goods (here, the drink) is capable of amounting to the obtaining of a service; see para 9-08 below. The tattooing example (*prima facie* an offence contrary to the Tattooing of Minors Act 1969) is given in Smith and Hogan, *Criminal Law*, 9th edn, 1999, Butterworths, p 575. That work, however, would seem to have it that such acts are the only ones incapable of conferring a 'benefit'.

10   *Tyrell* [1894] 1 QB 710. Public policy is, in fact, not the same in relation to all crimes involving supplies to young people. Thus, it is a crime for someone under 18 in licensed premises to buy or attempt to buy intoxicating liquor – Licensing Act 1964, s 169(2).

hold that he is not guilty of this offence either. If the result were to depend however, upon holding that he obtains no 'benefit', why in the case of the alcoholic drink should the 17 year old not be guilty of obtaining property by deception, contrary to s 15 of the 1968 Act? The better view is that, even though it may be a crime for the supplier to provide something (whether a tattoo, alcohol, tobacco, fireworks, an '18' video recording, pornographic pictures, etc) – and irrespective of whether its purchase is a crime by the person supplied – its provision is, nevertheless, a 'benefit'.[11]

### Understanding the benefit will be or has been paid for

9-07    This limitation on the definition of services excludes from the crime any situation where services are provided free of charge – even if they are dishonestly obtained by deception. Thus, if a student by lying gains entry to a staff car park for which there is no charge, it would seem that he does not commit the offence.[12] Similarly, being allowed to open a bank account or a building society account may well involve no charge for the benefit of having the account, in which case the person who, by deception, induces the bank or building society to open the account does not commit the offence.[13] If, however there is an understanding that the benefit will be paid for, it is immaterial that the understanding is unenforceable. D who dishonestly obtains the services of a prostitute by the deception that he intends to pay her for them, commits the offence.[14]

There is no requirement for an understanding that the *defendant* has paid, or will pay, for the service. If, for example, Y dishonestly gains admission to a concert by claiming falsely that Z has already paid for his entrance, that would appear to amount to the offence. Now suppose that a bus company charges old age pensioners (OAPs) half price. Suppose also that W, who is not an OAP boards a bus and shows the driver a document, falsely stating him to be an OAP, whereupon the driver charges him half fare. Certainly, to be allowed to stay on the bus and, thus, to have the journey is to be given a service, since the journey was given on the understanding that it would be paid for. However, has W obtained a service (being allowed to board the bus or being allowed to stay on it for a journey) *by* deception? Arguably he has not, because without the deception he would still have been given the service, albeit he would have been charged the full fare. In such a case, it would be sensible, and more appropriate to charge, instead, the offence in s 2(1)(c) of the TA 1978. The same argument, if correct, would, however, appear also to undermine the case against Y in the example above, where he gained free admission to a concert by lying that Z had

---

11   A view cogently put by Smith, ATH, para 18-28.
12   See, also, Examples 8 and 9, under s 2(1)(c) below.
13   *Halai* [1983] Crim LR 624, disapproved on other grounds; see para 9-08 below.
14   And see Example 7, under s 2(1)(b), para 9-19 below.

already paid for his entrance. At least, it would appear to do so in circumstances where, without the deception, he would have been allowed in upon paying the entrance fee.

## What acts are within the definition?

9-08    In *Halai*,[15] the Court of Appeal held that a mortgage advance was not a service. This decision was heavily criticised by academics[16] and doubted in the Court of Appeal.[17] It was distinguished in *Widdowson*,[18] where the Court of Appeal held that a benefit was conferred and, thus, a service was provided, when D obtained a vehicle on hire purchase terms. This was clearly correct, since it is clearly a benefit to D and there is no doubt that the hire purchase agreement represents an understanding that D will pay for it. The decision in *Halai* was much discussed in a series of cases in which the Court of Appeal either overruled it or, at least, made it clear that it would have done so if necessary.[19] In any event, in respect of acts committed after 18 December 1996, the decision has been reversed by s 1(3). This sub-section was added by the Theft (Amendment) Act 1996 implementing verbatim a recommendation of the Law Commission.[20] As the Law Commission concedes, this means that there is a lot of overlap between this offence and the new offence, in s 15A of the TA 1968, of obtaining a money transfer by deception. A mortgage or loan fraudster who obtains a loan by deception will often be guilty of both offences.

Now that *Halai* has been disposed of, it can be submitted that virtually any act, which confers a benefit on the understanding that it has been or will be paid for, will amount to a service. The act could be giving D the temporary possession of goods, whether that be by way of a loan of them, or under a hiring or hire purchase agreement.[21] It could, equally, be where the goods are sold to D. This would result in a considerable overlap with s 15 of the TA 1968, though for the present offence there is no need to prove that the goods belonged to another, nor that D intended to deprive the owner permanently. In most of these situations, it is clear that there is an understanding that the goods (or their hiring, etc) will be paid for. Provided that there is that understanding, then, if in any of these situations, D has dishonestly by deception induced another to loan, hire, sell or deliver goods to him, D has, it is submitted, committed the offence.

---

15  [1983] Crim LR 624.

16  Smith, JC, *Theft*, 7th edn, para 4-70. Griew, para 9-08.

17  *Teong Sun Chuah* [1991] Crim LR 463.

18  (1986) 82 Cr App R 314.

19  *Graham (No 1)* [1997] 1 Crim App R 302, [1997] Crim LR 340; *Cummings-John* [1997] Crim LR 660; *Naviede* [1997] Crim LR 663.

20  *Offences of Dishonesty: Money Transfers*, Law Commission No 243.

21  See *Widdowson* (1985) 82 Cr App R 314, above.

# 2 EVADING LIABILITY BY DECEPTION

9-09    **Section 2 of the TA 1978 – Evasion of liability by deception**

(1) Subject to sub-s (2) below, where a person by any deception –

   (a) dishonestly secures the remission of the whole or part of any existing liability to make a payment, whether his own liability or another's; or

   (b) with intent to make a permanent default in whole or in part on any existing liability to make a payment, or with intent to let another do so, dishonestly induces the creditor or any person claiming payment on behalf of the creditor to wait for payment (whether or not the due date for payment is deferred) or to forgo payment; or

   (c) dishonestly obtains any exemption from or abatement of liability to make a payment;

   he shall be guilty of an offence.

(2) For the purposes of this section 'liability' means legally enforceable liability; and sub-s (1) shall not apply in relation to a liability that has not been accepted or established to pay compensation for a wrongful act or omission.

(3) For the purposes of sub-s (1)(b) a person induced to take in payment a cheque or other security for money by way of conditional satisfaction of a pre-existing liability is to be treated not as being paid but as being induced to wait for payment.

(4) For the purposes of sub-s (1)(c) 'obtains' includes obtaining for another or enabling another to obtain.

## Mode of trial and sentence

9-10    The offence is triable either way.[22] If tried on indictment, it is a class 4 offence with a maximum penalty of imprisonment for five years. Following summary trial, the magistrates can sentence to imprisonment for up to six months, a fine up to the statutory maximum, or both.[23]

## Introduction

9-11    Section 2 was enacted exactly as proposed in the *Thirteenth Report* of the CLRC.[24] Deception and dishonesty are requirements common to all three sub-paragraphs and were discussed above.[25]

---

22  TA 1978, s 4(1).

23  *Ibid*, s 4(2) and(3), as amended by the MCA 1980, s 154(1) and Sched 7, para 170. The statutory maximum is currently £5,000.

24  Cmnd 6733.

25  Paras 8-04 and 8-34, respectively.

## Scope of the offence

9-12   Common to all sub-paragraphs is the rule that they apply only where the liability in question is a legally enforceable one – s 2(2). Sub-paragraphs 2(1)(a) and (b) require this liability to be an 'existing' liability, whereas sub-para (c) does not. In *Modupe*,[26] D gave material false information on a hire purchase proposal form by which he applied to a finance company for credit to acquire a Mercedes car. Convicted under s 2(1)(a) or (b),[27] he appealed arguing that, because the agreement (which was regulated by the Consumer Credit Act (CCA) 1974) had not been properly executed by the finance company, it was, by virtue of s 65(1) of the CCA 1974, 'enforceable ... on an order of the court only' and, therefore, did not create an 'existing liability'. Dismissing the appeal, the Court of Appeal held that it did create an existing liability, since all that s 65(1) did was to remove the right of the finance company to one particular remedy, namely, the right to help itself to the car. It did not remove the finance company's right to go to court to enforce the agreement.[28] There is, however, a problem with the decision. It overlooks another simpler argument as to why there was no 'existing' liability, namely, that D's deception was the cause of the agreement being made and it was the agreement being made which created the liability. The liability was not an 'existing' liability, but, rather, was one which was created by D's deception. This case appears to have been one, not of an evasion, but of a creation, of liability by deception. Section 2 does not catch a defendant who by deception creates a liability except (possibly) where, under s 2(1)(c), D obtains an 'exemption' or 'abatement' of liability, which in *Modupe* D did not. In any case, in *Modupe*, D was not charged under para 2(1)(c). The proper charge, today, on such facts would be of obtaining services by deception.[29]

The three sub-paras in sub-s 1 create different, though overlapping, offences.[30] Sub-paragraph 2(1)(b) requires, but the other two do not require, D to

---

26   [1991] CCLR 29; [1991] Crim LR 530 (CA).

27   The report in Crim LR states that he was charged under s 2(1)(b), as also does the headnote to the CCLR report. In the judgment, Lord Lane CJ, as reported at [1991] CCLR 32, states that the relevant charge in the case, count 6, was 'laid under s 2(1)(a)'.

28   In fact, when an agreement is improperly executed and, thus, by virtue of the CCA 1974, s 64(1), is unenforceable against the debtor (D) without a court order, it is not automatic that such an order will be granted. The judge has a discretion to refuse to grant such an order, depending on the degree of culpability of the finance company for the improper execution and the amount of prejudice caused by it – the CCA 1974, s 127. In certain circumstances (for example, where the debtor has not signed an agreement containing certain basic prescribed terms), the judge is not allowed to grant an enforcement order – the CCA 1974, s 127(3) and (4). If these circumstances had characterised the facts in *Modupe* [1991] CCLR 29, then there would not have been any 'legally enforceable' liability of D to make any payments under the hire purchase agreement. In that case, the TA 1978, s 2(2), would rule out any chance of a conviction for this offence for any evasion of that liability. A charge of obtaining services by deception under s 1, however, would still be perfectly possible.

29   See *Widdowson* (1986) 82 Cr App R 314, para 9-08, above .

30   See *Holt* [1981] 1 WLR 1000 (CA) and *Jackson* [1983] Crim LR 617 (CA).

have an intention to make permanent default. Apart from that and the requirement for sub-paras (a) and (b) that there be an existing liability, the scope of each sub-paragraph depends, to a large extent, on the correct interpretation of the different words used: (a) 'remission' of a liability, (b) 'waiting for' or 'forgoing' payment, (c) an 'exemption' from or 'abatement' of a liability. The matter can be explained by a series of examples.

## Section 2(1)(a)

### Example 1

9-13    D owes X £100 and when asked for it by X lies, thereby, deceiving X into thinking that D has already repaid the £100. This is not within this sub-paragraph (though it is within s 2(1)(b) below). X has not 'remitted' any liability of D. Being duped into believing that the liability did not exist is not the same as remitting it. Whether or not X ever wakes up to the fact, it is a fact that, in this example, D still has the liability to repay X £100. It is only if X has agreed to waive a liability (that is, to agree that, although it is a liability, X no longer regards it as such) that he remits it.

### Example 2

9-14    D owes X £100. D lies, causing X to believe that D has fallen into financial difficulties and, thereby, gets X to agree to accept £60 in full satisfaction of the debt. This falls within sub-para (a). X has, to the extent of £40, agreed to release to waive or extinguish an existing liability. It is a remission by X of part of D's liability to pay X £100. This is so, even though D's fraud (by definition not rumbled by X at the time) renders unenforceable X's agreement to waive payment of £40 of the debt. Sub-paragraph 2(1)(a), thus, catches a situation where the victim waives all or part of a liability but where – though the victim does not realise it – that waiver is, in fact, not binding on the victim. The essence of this sub-para is that the victim agrees to let off D, to excuse him, from having to pay. Intriguingly, this example also falls within sub-para 2(1)(b) as being a situation where X has agreed to 'forgo' payment of £40. At least, it does so provided D intended permanently to avoid paying the £40.

### Example 3

9-15    D dishonestly presents a stolen credit card in payment for petrol which D has put into the tank of his car at a self-service petrol station. The card is accepted by the cashier. D is guilty under s 2(1)(a). He has tendered a stolen credit card and had it accepted by the trader who, forthwith, will look to the card issuing company for payment and not to D. D has, thereby, secured remission of his liability to pay. These were the facts and the decision in *Jackson*.[31] Unless this decision was wrong, the argument[32] is untenable that remission of a liability describes only the situation where the liability is actually extinguished in law. It is true that where a cardholder (the legitimate cardholder) pays with a credit card, that payment is an unconditional payment and the cardholder's own liability to pay is, thus, extinguished and totally replaced by that of the card issuing company.[33] Where, however, D presents a stolen credit card, it seems incredible that the law is that his own liability to pay for the petrol is extinguished. If the card issuer discovers the deception and refuses to pay the garage proprietor, can it be doubted that D remains legally liable to the proprietor for the price of the petrol? Professor Smith, in his commentary to *Jackson*,[34] finesses this point by describing D's liability as a 'contingent' liability 'which might fairly be regarded as having been remitted, even though it might revive in a certain event'. The better view is that a liability is 'remitted' if the creditor agrees to its extinction, even though D's deception means that that agreement (that extinction) is legally ineffective.

## Section 2(1)(b)

### Example 4

9-16    A restaurant customer, intending to avoid paying the bill, lies to the manager saying that the waitress has already collected the money from the table, thereby causing the manager to forgo collecting payment of the bill. This is caught by s 2(1)(b). These were the facts in *Holt*,[35] except that, in that case, the manager was not duped by the lies and therefore did not forgo collecting payment. It was held that D was correctly convicted of attempting to commit the offence in s 2(1)(b).

### Example 5

9-17    D has milk delivered daily to his house. On Saturday morning, the milkman calls so he can be paid for the week's milk. D lies to the milkman saying that D has no money in the house and asks if it will be all right for him to pay the following week. The milkman agrees. D is not guilty under s 2(1)(b), unless D intended permanently to avoid paying any of the bill. Section 2(1)(b) does not catch someone who merely intends to defer payment. Nor, in this example, is D guilty under s 2(1)(a); the milkman has not agreed to remit any liability (that is to let D off, to excuse him, to release him from any liability to pay).

---

31  [1983] Crim LR 617 (CA).
32  Of Professor Sir John Smith (*The Law of Theft*, 8th edn, para 4-91).
33  *Re Charge Card Services Ltd* [1989] Ch 497 (CA).
34  [1983] Crim LR 617 (CA), p 618.
35  [1981] 1 WLR 1000 (CA).

## Example 6

9-18 Having enjoyed a restaurant meal, D pays the bill with a cheque which D knows will be dishonoured by D's bank. D is guilty under s 2(1)(b), provided he intended permanently to avoid having to pay. The restaurant proprietor (or his agent in the restaurant) is treated as being induced to wait for payment – s 2(3).

## Example 7

9-19 Having enjoyed the favours of a prostitute and intending permanently to avoid having to pay her, D pays her with a cheque which D knows will be dishonoured by D's bank. D is not guilty under s 2(1)(a), (b) or (c). Agreements promoting sexual immorality are unenforceable and s 2 does not apply unless the liability is a legally enforceable liability – s 2(2). Section 3 (making off without payment) similarly does not apply where the payment is not legally enforceable.[36] In this example, D could, however, be guilty of obtaining services by deception contrary to s 1 of the TA 1978, if right from the start it was his intention not to pay.

## Section 2(1)(c)

### Example 8

9-20 A cinema has a concession whereby OAPs are admitted free on Mondays. One Monday D, a 50 year old, dishonestly lies that he is an OAP and gets admitted free. He is guilty under s 2(1)(c). He has obtained an 'exemption' from liability.

### Example 9

9-21 This is the same as Example 8 except that OAPs are charged half price and D's deception gets him admitted for half price. D is guilty under s 2(1)(c). He has not secured an exemption from having to pay, but has obtained an 'abatement' of liability. In this example, though not in Example 8, D is also guilty of obtaining a service contrary to s 1 of the TA 1978, since the benefit (of entry to the cinema) is given on the understanding that it has been, or will be, paid for (albeit at a reduced rate).

### Example 10

9-22 D, a consultant gynaecologist, refers a patient to an NHS hospital dishonestly, without informing the hospital that the patient is a private patient, with the

---

36 See para 9-33, below.

result that he and the patient are not charged for the treatment. On these facts, D was found guilty under s 2(1)(c), in *Firth*.[37]

## *Example 11*

9-23    D dishonestly flashes an irrelevant season ticket at a ticket inspector at a barrier on the London Underground. On these facts, in *Sibartie*,[38] it was held that D had been properly charged with attempting to commit the offence in s 2(1)(c). This clearly implies that, if the ticket collector had been deceived by D's efforts, D would, thereby, have secured an 'exemption' from liability to pay his fare. That is a questionable construction of the word 'exemption', since being exempted means, in ordinary language, being excused from having to pay. D was not, it is submitted, seeking to be excused from having to pay, but was rather trying to cause the ticket collector to think that he had already paid. D should, it is submitted, have been charged with attempting the offence under s 2(1)(b), not s 2(1)(c).[39]

## Evading liability of someone else

9-24    The situation in s 2(1)(a) and (c) appears straightforward. In (a), D can be guilty of securing the remission of an existing liability of his own or of someone else. In (c), D can be guilty of obtaining, either for himself or for someone else, an exemption from or abatement of a liability to make a payment – s 2(4). In addition, D can be guilty of enabling someone else to obtain such an exemption or abatement. Where the prosecution's case is based on one of these alternatives (for example, that D secured the remission of someone else's liability, or an exemption for someone else of a liability to make a payment), this needs to be made clear, since the question of dishonesty might then appear in a quite different light from the situation where D is said to have evaded a liability of his own. That was the *ratio* of the decision in *Attewell-Hughes*,[40] a decision on s 2(1)(b). D, a manager of a hotel, wrote cheques on the hotel bank account which he knew would be dishonoured, thereby inducing the payees to wait for payment. The cheques were in payment of the VAT liability of the hotel owner. The count, charging D under s 2(1)(b), charged him with dishonestly by deception inducing the payees to wait for payment, with intent to make permanent default in an existing liability to make a payment, meaning an existing liability of his own. The trial judge held that it was immaterial whether it was D's own liability or the liability of the hotel owner and that the issue, in

---

37  (1990) 91 Cr App R 217 (CA), discussed at para 8-10. above.

38  [1983] Crim LR 470 (CA).

39  See, to the same effect, Smith, JC, *The Law of Theft*, 7th edn, para 4-89 and Griew, para 10-21.

40  [1991] 1 WLR 955; [1991] 4 All ER 810 (CA).

either case, was one of dishonesty. The Court of Appeal, however, held that the issue of dishonesty might appear in a very different light according to whether, on the one hand, it was D's own liability upon which he intended to make permanent default or, on the other, he intended to let the hotel owner make permanent default on the latter's liability.

# 3 MAKING OFF WITHOUT PAYMENT

9-25    **Section 3 of the TA 1978 – Making off without payment**

(1) Subject to sub-s (3) below, a person who, knowing that payment on the spot for any goods supplied or service done is required or expected from him, dishonestly makes off without having paid as required or expected and with intent to avoid payment of the amount due shall be guilty of an offence.

(2) For the purposes of this section 'payment on the spot' includes payment at the time of collecting goods on which work has been done or in respect of which service has been provided.

(3) Sub-section (1) above shall not apply where the supply of the goods or the doing of the service is contrary to law, or where the service done is such that payment is not legally enforceable.

(4) Any person may arrest without warrant anyone who is, or whom he, with reasonable cause, suspects to be, committing or attempting to commit an offence under this section.

## Mode of trial and sentence

9-26    The offence is triable either way.[41] If tried on indictment, it is a class 4 offence with a maximum penalty of imprisonment for two years. Following summary trial, the magistrates can sentence to imprisonment for up to six months, a fine up to the statutory maximum, or both.[42]

## Introduction

9-27    In *DPP v Ray*,[43] the defendant, once he had decided not to pay for the meal he had eaten at the restaurant, had remained seated at the table until the waiter left the room. By the deception which D thus practised, D induced the waiter to believe that D still intended to pay the bill. D was able, subsequently, to slip out

---

41  TA 1978, s 4(1).

42  *Ibid*, s 4(2) and(3), as amended by the MCA 1980, s 154(1) and Sched 7, para 170. The statutory maximum is currently £5,000.

43  [1974] AC 370 and see para 8-09, above.

when the waiter had temporarily left the room. The real mischief was that D went off without paying, not that, in the process, he practised a deception. Accordingly, the CLRC, in its *Thirteenth Report*,[44] recommended the enactment of what is now s 3. The wording of the offence in s 3 follows exactly the wording in the draft bill attached to the Committee's Report. The section has the advantage that there is no requirement for any deception.

## *Mens rea*

9-28    There are three necessary elements: (i) dishonesty; (ii) knowledge that payment on the spot is expected or required; and (iii) an intention of avoiding payment of the amount due. In relation to intention, an intention to defer payment is not sufficient. In *Allen*,[45] the House of Lords held that only an intention *permanently* to avoid having to pay will suffice. Dishonesty has the same meaning as in ss 1 and 2 of the TA 1978 and s 15 of the TA 1968.[46] Usually, once it is proved that D intended permanently to avoid paying, it will follow that he was acting dishonestly. One situation where that may not occur, is where D considers the charge to be excessive and, thus, not one he is legally obliged to pay. If he tenders or pays an amount which he considers he is liable to pay, making it clear that he has no intention ever of paying the rest, he may well be found not to have been dishonest. It is when he made off from the spot where payment is required or expected, that he has to have been dishonest and to have formed the intention to avoid payment.[47]

## Knowing that payment on the spot ... is required or expected

9-29    Payment is not confined to payment in cash. A restaurant may well accept payment by cheque, credit card or cash. If so, payment by one of those means is payment as expected or required. Well known situations where payment 'on the spot' is required or expected include petrol stations and restaurants. Another situation, identified in the CLRC Report, is that of the guest in a hotel (or boarding house); the guest is expected to pay before he leaves. The service and/or goods may then have been provided over a period of time (say, hours in a restaurant or days at a hotel), but, still, payment on the spot is required or expected. The position may be the same where work (perhaps repair or improvement work) has been carried out on goods. Where a car is left for servicing at a garage, payment on the spot is normally expected or required. It includes 'payment at the time of collecting the goods on which work has been

---

44   Cmnd 6733.
45   [1985] AC 1029.
46   For discussion, see para 8-34, above.
47   *Aziz* [1993] Crim LR 708 (CA); see para 9-30, below.

done or in respect of which service has been provided' – s 3(2). Whether payment on the spot is expected or required is a question of fact in each case. In the petrol station, restaurant and hotel situations mentioned above, it normally will be. The same is true when someone takes a ride in a taxi. Where, on the other hand, credit has been agreed (as where the price is 'put on the slate'), clearly payment on the spot is not expected or required. Even if the agreement to grant credit to the defendant has been obtained dishonestly by deception, that agreement means that payment on the spot is not expected or required: *Vincent*.[48]

## Payment on the spot

9-30   The meaning of 'on the spot' has two elements: place and time. It means 'there and then'. It is question of fact. In a restaurant, it may be impossible to say that payment is expected or required to be made at the table, rather than some other location within the premises. It may be even more difficult to prove that D knew that payment was expected or required to be made at the table. Proof that D left the table without paying is, thus, likely to be insufficient. If, on the other hand, D has left the restaurant altogether without having paid, then that will be sufficient to amount to making off from the spot where payment was expected.[49] Where, on the other hand, D has been stopped when in the process of leaving without paying, he will not have completed the act of making off, in which case a charge of attempting to commit the offence in s 3 would be appropriate.[50]

In *Aziz*,[51] D and one other took a taxi to a destination 13 miles away. On arrival, and still in the taxi, they refused to pay the fare. The driver stated that he would return them to their hotel, used the central locking system to lock the doors and drove off and, on the way, pulled into a petrol station, where he asked the attendant to call the police. It was at that petrol station that the two let themselves out of the taxi and ran off. D was convicted of making off without payment, contrary to s 3. The Court of Appeal dismissed D's appeal, together with his argument that he had not made off from the spot where payment was required, namely, at the end of the journey. It seems that in this situation, the 'spot' or place is as mobile as the taxi. Thus, once the journey demanded by the passenger has been completed,[52] payment is 'required' anywhere the taxi finds itself after it has been made clear to D that payment is required.

---

48   [2001] 1 WLR 1172 (CA).
49   *Brooks and Brooks* (1982) 76 Cr App R 66; [1983] Crim LR 188.
50   *McDavitt* [1981] Crim LR 843.
51   [1993] Crim LR 708 (CA).
52   See *Troughton v Metropolitan Police* [1987] Crim LR 138 (DC); see para 9-33, below.

## Makes off

9-31    The person who, as in *DPP v Ray*, leaves surreptitiously, trying not to be noticed, clearly makes off. After all, the offence was intended to be able to catch someone such as the defendant in *Ray*. Equally, the person, who aggressively pushes staff out of the way and leaves the premises at speed with staff at his heels, also 'makes off'. The mischief at which the offence is aimed (leaving without paying) is exactly the same, whatever the manner or method of the departure. Does the use, nevertheless, of the expression 'makes off' limit the application of the offence to certain kinds of departure? JR Spencer suggests that D does not 'make off' unless he leaves 'in a way that makes it difficult for the debtor [D] to be traced'.[53] According to this view, if, when departing, D leaves his address (or some other means by which he can easily be traced), D does not 'make off'. This is unconvincing. One could well imagine a restaurateur being unhappy with being fobbed off with a note of the customer's address and still insisting that the customer pays there and then. Imagine that the customer, D, thereupon, immediately runs out of the restaurant hotly pursued by an irate restaurateur and his staff. It seems implausible, in those circumstances, to suggest that D's having left a note of his address means that he has not 'made off'. His leaving of a means of being traced may suggest a lack of the necessary intention of permanently avoiding payment, but it surely does not bear on the question of whether he 'made off'.

9-32    Francis Bennion, less implausibly, argues[54] that someone does not 'make off' if he leaves with the creditor's consent. It might, for example, be that the creditor takes details of D's address and agrees to D not paying immediately. In that situation, it is arguable that there is another reason why D is not guilty of the offence, namely, that the creditor's agreement to be paid later has altered what would otherwise have been the requirement or expectation as to payment. Thus, D has not left 'without having paid as required or expected'.[55] Bennion, however, takes matters further and deals with the situation where the creditor's consent to D leaving is obtained by a deception practised by D. D might, for example, pay using counterfeit banknotes or by giving the creditor a cheque which D knows full well will be dishonoured. In this situation, Bennion asserts that D does not 'make off', because he is leaving with the creditor's consent – albeit that consent has been obtained by a deception. If that is correct, it considerably limits the scope of the offence. As a matter of English, is it really impossible to describe D as 'making off' when he dupes the creditor into allowing him to leave? The purpose of the offence was to catch the bilking debtor who was expected to pay on the spot and the examples just given are

---

53  [1983] Crim LR 573.

54  [1983] Crim LR 205 and 574 – an argument adopted, apparently, by HH Judge Morrison in *Hammond* [1982] Crim LR 611 (Lincoln Crown Court).

55  *Vincent* [2001] 1 WLR 1172 (CA) and see para 9-29, above.

certainly examples of bilking debtors. Despite the use of the colourful phrase 'makes off', the better view is that it means nothing more or less than 'leaves' or 'goes away'. The CLRC clearly intended that meaning when they said in their Report,[56] 'where the customer knows that he is expected to pay on the spot for goods supplied to him or services done for him it should be an offence for him dishonestly to *go away* without having paid and intending never to pay. We have developed this proposal into cl 3 of our draft Bill and have given the offence the label "making off without payment"' [italics supplied].

Bennion has a good point[57] when he says that, after payment on the spot, two things can happen. Either the payer, D, can move away, or the payee can move away. If it is the latter, then it cannot be said that D has 'made off'. D has not left . D has not gone away. Where D alights from a taxi, leans through the window and pays the fare with what he knows is counterfeit money (or with a cheque which he knows will be dishonoured) and then stands on the pavement watching the taxi drive off, D has not 'made off'. This is an example of a bilking debtor whom the offence fails to catch.[58]

## Without having paid as required or expected

9-33   Giving counterfeit coins in payment or giving a dud cheque cannot be payment 'as required and expected'. It has been argued[59] that the latter is a payment, albeit a conditional one, and that the words 'as required or expected' refer only to the requirement or expectation that payment be made 'on the spot'. This places a restriction on the meaning of the words which they do not merit. The better view is that where D pays with a cheque which he knows will be dishonoured, he does not pay as required or expected. Admittedly, the matter is largely academic, since, on those facts, D will normally be guilty of the offence in s 2(1)(b) of the 1978 Act. Suppose that a restaurant makes it clear, by prominent notices, that it will not accept cheques or credit cards, but that all bills must be settled in cash. Suppose that, in the restaurant, D leaves a cheque in payment and then leaves the premises (either with or without having heard objections from the waiter/manager that a cheque will not do). In that situation, D has not 'paid as required or expected' – and that is so, irrespective of whether the cheque was a good one or a dud.

The payment required or expected must be one which is legally enforceable and which is not for goods or services the supply of which is contrary to law – s 3(3). Also, if liability to make the payment has not yet accrued, then D cannot

---

56   Paragraph 18.
57   [1983] Crim LR 206.
58   D will be guilty of the offence in the TA 1978, s 2(1)(b).
59   By Syrota, G [1980] Crim LR 413 – another argument adopted, apparently, by HH Judge Morrison in *Hammond* [1982] Crim LR 611 (Lincoln Crown Court).

make off without paying as required or expected. In *Troughton v Metropolitan Police*,[60] a taxi driver had broken away from the route which would have taken D home as he had requested and had driven to a police station. The reason for this was that an argument had developed between the two which included an allegation by D that the taxi driver had made an unnecessary diversion. D was said to have made off at the police station. His conviction for making off was quashed because the taxi journey had not been completed. The breaking of the journey was a breach of contract by the driver who, therefore, was not lawfully entitled to demand the fare. D had not made off without payment as required or expected, since he not legally bound to pay the fare.

---

60   [1987] Crim LR 138 (DC).

# CHAPTER 10

# FALSE ACCOUNTING AND OTHER OFFENCES OF FRAUD

## 1 FALSE ACCOUNTING

10-01 **Section 17 of the Theft Act (TA) 1968 – False accounting**

(1) Where a person dishonestly, with a view to gain for himself or another or with intent to cause loss to another –

(a) destroys, defaces, conceals or falsifies any account or any record or document made or required for any accounting purpose; or

(b) in furnishing information for any purpose produces or makes use of any account, or any such record or document as aforesaid, which to his knowledge is or may be misleading, false or deceptive in a material particular;

he shall, on conviction on indictment, be liable to imprisonment for a term not exceeding seven years.

(2) For the purposes of this section, a person who makes or concurs in making in an account or other document an entry which is or may be misleading, false or deceptive in a material particular or who omits or concurs in omitting a material particular from an account or other document, is to be treated as falsifying the account or document.

## Mode of trial and sentence

10-02 The offence is triable either way.[1] If tried on indictment, it is a class 4 offence with a maximum penalty of imprisonment for seven years. Following summary trial, the magistrates can sentence to imprisonment for up to six months, a fine up to the statutory maximum, or both.[2]

## Introduction

10-03 This offence replaced offences previously in the Larceny Act (LA) 1861 (ss 82 and 83) and the Falsification of Accounts Act 1875. Those earlier offences were intended to deal with employees who falsified documents in order to defraud their employers. The wording of the current offence is exactly that recommended in the *Eighth Report* and is deliberately wider than its

---

1 Magistrates' Courts Act (MCA) 1980, s 17(1) and Sched 1, para 28.
2 *Ibid*, s 32(1) and Sched 1, para 28. The statutory maximum is currently £5,000.

predecessors, in that it is not limited to frauds practised upon employers.[3] Instead, it contains the limitation that the account, record or document which is falsified must be one which is 'made or required for an accounting purpose'. The inclusion in s 17(1) of para (b) means that offence can also be committed by someone who uses a falsified account, record or document.

The general policy behind the offence is to enable someone to be dealt with whose fraudulent activity may not be caught by other provisions. Although, since its enactment, a number of other offences of deception have been created – notably by the TA 1978 – s 17 remains a useful weapon in the prosecution's armoury. In contrast to the deception offences covered in the last chapter, this offence does not require the defendant to have obtained any benefit – simply that he acted 'with a view to gain ... or with intent to cause loss'. Nor does it require that anyone was actually deceived. This offence is committed at the time when the account is destroyed, defaced, concealed or falsified, or (once it has been falsified) when it is produced or used. Thus, it bites at an earlier time in the fraudster's activities and can be seen, in some instances, as an alternative to a charge of attempting one of the deception offences. Although it may be said that the offence in s 25 of 'going equipped' fulfils this function, that offence does not catch anyone for going equipped to commit any deception offence other than obtaining *property* by deception.

## Account, record or document

10-04   The prosecution can, in an appropriate case, secure a conviction for falsifying a document, even though there is no *identifiable* document which has been falsified and even though nothing has been written or marked on any document. An account or document can be falsified, not only by the insertion of false information, but also by *omitting* a material particular: s 17(2). In *Shama*,[4] an international telephone operator was required by his employer to complete a form each time he connected a call to an overseas number – a separate form for each call. The forms were used for accounting purposes. He had a supply of blank forms. He was held to have been properly convicted under s 17 in respect of a number of occasions when, having connected a subscriber to an overseas number, he failed to complete any form. It was not possible, and held not to be necessary, for the prosecution to show which particular blank form he would have completed if he had carried out his duty.

It is not just an *account* or a *document* which can be falsified within the meaning of the section. For example, a turnstile may keep a record of persons passing through it. If the operator admits two people in a single movement of

---

3   CLRC, *Eighth Report*, Cmnd 2977, 1966, London: HMSO. See, generally, para 103 of the Report.

4   [1990] 1 WLR 661.

the turnstile, he falsifies a record, *Edwards v Toombs*.[5] Other devices which keep records, or on which records are kept, include taximeters,[6] tachographs, odometers, electricity meters and, no doubt, many computers. Section 17(2) refers to someone who makes a false entry in, or omits a material particular from, an account or a document. Such a person is to be treated as falsifying the account or document. Although s 17(2) refers only to an account or document and not to a record, it was held, in *Edwards v Toombs*, that it was only a deeming provision and did not prevent the court construing the words of s 17(1)(a) as they appeared and holding that D had, in that case, falsified a *record*. It seems clear then, that this offence is committed by someone who, in order to avoid payment for electricity consumed, constructs an unauthorised bypass to the electricity meter on his premises, so that the meter does not record all the electricity used. The offence is committed as soon as any electricity is consumed without being recorded on the meter. The position appears not to be the same, however, in the case of someone who turns back the odometer on his car, since, although he may do so 'with a view to gain', it seems impossible to argue that the record (of the mileage covered) is 'made or required for any accounting purpose'.

## Made or required for an accounting purpose

10-05    On the one hand, a document (record or account) may be made specifically for an accounting purpose. An example is a set of accounts. On the other hand, it may be made for some other purpose but required, perhaps later, for an accounting purpose. The section applies to both, *AG's Ref (No 1 of 1980)*:[7] '[A] document may fall within the ambit of the section if it is made for some purpose other than an accounting purpose but is required for an accounting purpose as a subsidiary consideration.'[8] A loan proposal is *made* in order for the potential lender to determine whether to agree to make a loan – and that is not an 'accounting' purpose. The loan proposal in the *AG's Ref* case – as is not uncommon – contained figures setting out repayment dates and amounts and the rate and amount of interest. It was held that these details were required for an accounting purpose, since they would, if the loan was agreed, be used by the lender to make up its accounts on a computer. It was also held[9] that it was irrelevant that the part of the form which was falsified was not the part which was required for an accounting purpose. The applicants had given false

---

5    [1983] Crim L R 43 (DC).

6    *Solomons* [1901] 2 KB 980.

7    [1981] 1 WLR 34; [1981] 1 All ER 366.

8    [1981] 1 WLR 34, p 38, *per* Lord Lane CJ.

9    It had already been held, for the purposes of s 17(1)(b), that a document can be false 'in a material particular', even if the false information is not part of the information which is required for an accounting purpose, *Mallett* [1978] 1 WLR 820 (CA).

information about matters which might affect whether their loan applications were accepted. but which were not part of the information required for input to the lender's computer – such matters as the extent of their outstanding financial commitments and the number of their dependants: 'This was one entire document; it was as to part required for an accounting purpose; it was as to part falsified. The fact that these two parts were not the same does not exonerate the man who was responsible for the falsification.'[10] The *AG's Ref* was followed in *Osinuga v DPP*,[11] where a housing benefit claim form, similarly, had a dual function: (i) to enable the local authority to decide if the applicant was entitled to housing benefit; and (ii) if the applicant was entitled to benefit, to enable the amount of that entitlement to be calculated. The latter meant that the form was required for an accounting purpose.

10-06    Although it is common for some documents, such as loan or housing benefit applications, to serve two functions, one of which is that it is required for an accounting purpose, the Court of Appeal in *Okanta* was not prepared to assume, without some evidence to that effect, that the document in that case, a loan application, was required for an accounting purpose.[12] It was equally unprepared to do so in *Sundhers*,[13] where the falsified documents were insurance claim forms. The conclusion that these were required for an accounting purpose could not be drawn without the jury having some knowledge of accounting practice – and no evidence had been led as to that. *Sundhers* was distinguished in *Manning*,[14] where the falsified documents were insurance cover notes in respect of insurance on ships. The distinction was that each cover note set out what the client had to pay and how he had to pay it. By simply looking at the document (and without any other evidence), a reasonable juror could conclude that it was required for an accounting purpose, since it set out what the client owed. The court, nevertheless, pointed out the desirability of the prosecution 'calling evidence, of brief and probably unchallenged nature, as to how documents on which they rely under s 17(1)(a) are in fact used'.[15]

What is the policy behind this restriction in the definition of the offence? There would appear to be two possible rationales for the offence in s 17. First, the intention could be to protect the integrity of accounting processes by deterring people from falsifying (or using already falsified) accounts, records or documents which are made or required for accounting purposes. Secondly, it could simply be to protect the integrity of accounts, records or documents. If it is the latter, then it is difficult to see why the offence should be limited to accounts, records or documents which are made or required for accounting purposes.

---

10   [1981] 1 WLR 34, p 38, *per* Lord Lane CJ.
11   (1997) 162 JP 120.
12   [1997] Crim LR 451.
13   [1998] Crim LR 497.
14   [1998] Cr App R 461 (CA).
15   Page 466.

Why, as matter of policy, should someone who completes and submits a loan application form dishonestly with false information and with a view to obtaining a loan be guilty of the offence, if the form happens to be one which the finance company requires, *inter alia*, for accounting purposes, but not, if the finance company requires the form only for the single purpose of deciding whether to make the loan? It is no answer to say that, in either case, the fraudster is likely to be guilty of other offences. The question is: 'Why is he to be made guilty, if he is made guilty, of this offence?' The ruling[16] that the falsity in the document does not have to relate to any of the information required for an accounting purpose, means that the defendant can be guilty of this offence, even though his activities have not in any way threatened the integrity of any accounting process. His guilt or innocence of this offence depends upon what, thus, appears to be the mere caprice of whether the form happens to be required for an accounting purpose. The rationale of this restriction in the definition of the offence is considered further below, in relation to the *mens rea* required for the offence.

## Mens rea

10-07 There are three or, possibly, four required elements of *mens rea*:

(a) dishonesty;

(b) that the defendant acted with a view to gain or an intent to cause loss;

(c) where the charge is laid under s 17(1)(b), that the defendant knew that the account, record or document was or might be misleading, false or deceptive; and, possibly,

(d) that the defendant knew that the account, record or document was required for an accounting purpose.

As to dishonesty, little more needs to be said than is said in Chapter 8 about dishonesty in relation to deception.[17] Given the rule in this section,[18] that the falsification does not have to relate to that part of the document or record which is required for an accounting purpose, it must follow that the defendant's dishonesty equally need not do so. The third element of *mens rea* just mentioned is spelt out in s 17(1)(b) and, clearly, requires proof of at least recklessness, in the *Cunningham*[19] sense, as to the fact that the information is misleading, false or

---

16  *AG's Ref (No 1 of 1980)* [1981] 1 WLR 34, para 10-05, above. See, also, *Mallett* [1978] 1 WLR 820, where the Court of Appeal held that a document required for an accounting purpose (a hire purchase proposal form) could be false or misleading 'in a material particular' for the purposes of s 17(1)(b), even though the false statement was not material to an accounting purpose.

17  Paragraph 8-34, above.

18  *AG's Ref (No 1 of 1980)* [1981] 1 WLR 34, para 10-05, above.

19  [1957] 2 QB 396.

deceptive. The requirement that the defendant acted with a view to gain or an intent to cause loss will be considered shortly.

## A required element of *mens rea* not spelt out in the section?

10-08    The offence is not committed unless the account, document or record is 'made or required for an accounting purpose'. Clearly, the Criminal Law Revision Committee considered that, without this restriction, the offence would be too wide. Apart from that, the policy behind this restriction is not spelt out in the report. On initial perusal of the section, the objective of the offence would appear to be to protect and preserve the integrity of accounting processes. If it is, a question then arises in relation to a defendant who commits the *actus reus* of this offence and has all the elements of *mens rea* which are spelt out in the section (is dishonest, knows of the falsity and acts with a view to a gain), but who has no idea that the document is required for an accounting purpose. For example, he thinks (erroneously) that his hire purchase proposal form is wanted for just a single purpose, namely, to enable the finance company to decide whether to advance him the credit he wants. In this example, it never crosses his mind that the document might be required for an accounting purpose. In *B v DPP*,[20] the House of Lords confirmed the presumption that, where the statutory words of an offence do not expressly state the necessity for any particular mental element, they are, nevertheless, to be read as subject to the implication that a necessary element in the offence is the absence of a belief, whether or not held on reasonable grounds, in the existence of facts which would make the act innocent. Thus, it was held, a man who commits an act of gross indecency with a girl under 14 is not guilty of that offence[21] unless he knows that she is, or may be, under 14. That presumption has traditionally been stated as applying, and was applied in *B v DPP*, to an offence which does not expressly state any requirement for *mens rea*. The offence of false accounting, on the other hand, does expressly spell out certain *mens rea* requirements (dishonesty and 'with a view to gain'). It would seem odd, however, if an offence, apparently intended to protect the integrity of accounting processes, were to catch someone who had no idea that his action posed any threat at all to any such process.[22] The better view, therefore, is that the defendant is not guilty unless he knows that the document (account or record) is or may be required for an accounting purpose. If that is correct, then the evidence must be such as to enable a reasonable juror to conclude, not only that the document (or account or record) was required for an accounting purpose,[23] but also that the defendant was aware that it was or

---

20    [2000] 2 WLR 452; [2000] 1 All ER 833.

21    Contrary to the Indecency with Children Act 1960, s 1.

22    To the same effect, see Professor Sir John Smith in his 'Commentary' to *Cummings-John* [1997] Crim LR 660, p 662.

23    As was held in *Manning* [1998] Cr App R 461 (CA), para 10-06, above.

might be required for such a purpose. Such authority as there is, however, is contrary to the view just stated. In *Graham*,[24] the Court of Appeal was not persuaded that knowledge of the purpose for which the document or record was created or required was part of the *mens rea* of s 17. If this view and the rulings in *AG's Ref (No 1 of 1980)* and *Mallet*[25] are all correct, then the policy of s 17 as thus interpreted is not to protect the integrity of the accounting process. Rather, it is to protect the integrity of documents, accounts and records – but only those which, whether the defendant realises it or not, are made or required for an accounting purpose and irrespective of whether any accounting function is actually compromised or threatened. What, one wonders, is the purpose of this qualification on the definition of the offence?

## With a view to gain or an intent to cause loss

10-09   The requirement that the defendant acts with a view to gain or an intent to cause loss is the same in the offences of suppression of documents (s 20) and blackmail (s 21). The meaning is the same in each.[26] The wording of each of these offences contains two contrasting expressions – 'with a view to gain' and 'with intent to cause loss'. The latter is unambiguous. It is not enough that D realised that his actions might cause a loss to someone; nothing less than intention to cause loss will suffice. On the other hand, doing something with 'a view to gain' seems to suggests that something less than intention to make a gain will suffice. It suggests anticipation or contemplation of making a gain, without necessarily having a settled intention of making one. Thus, it is suggested that D may have a view to a gain if he has: (i) an intention to make a gain; or (ii) a hope of making a gain; or (iii) merely an intention of creating a chance of making a gain.

Section 34(2)(a) provides:

(2)   For the purposes of this Act –

(a)   'gain' and 'loss' are to be construed as extending only to gain or loss in money or other property, but as extending to any such gain or loss whether temporary or permanent; and

(i)   'gain' includes a gain by keeping what one has, as well as a gain by getting what one has not; and

(ii)   'loss' includes a loss by not getting what one might get, as well as a loss by parting with what one has ...

Section 34(2) was applied in *Eden*,[27] in which a sub-postmaster who was required to send in weekly accounts had sent in false ones. This could have been either to facilitate theft on his part (the retention of money which he ought to

---

24   [1997] 1 Cr App R 302; [1997] Crim LR 340.
25   [1978] 1 WLR 820 (CA) and see fn 9, above.
26   For a discussion in relation to blackmail, see para 11-25 below.
27   (1971) 55 Cr App R 193 (CA).

send to Head Office) or, simply, to cover up an administrative muddle and, thus, to put off the evil day of having to sort it out and to pay up money which may have been kept in error. Either of these purposes was held to be sufficient for the section, the latter being a form of temporary gain within s 34(2) and sufficient to support a conviction under s 17. It would, of course, be a separate question for the jury whether such a purpose was dishonest within the *Ghosh*[28] test.

10-10    It is impossible, frankly, to see that the decision of the Court of Appeal in *Golechha*[29] can be correct. It was held that, where the defendant's purpose was to secure the forbearance of his creditor to enforce a debt owed by the defendant, he was not acting 'with a view to gain'. How is that not, to quote from s 34(2)(a), 'keeping what one has'?[30] If you sue me for a debt, secure judgment and enforce that judgment against me, then you obtain something from me, property, which otherwise I would keep.

In *Lee Cheung Wing v R*,[31] the defendants were employed as securities dealers dealing in futures contracts. It was a term of their employment that they were not allowed, themselves, to have dealings accounts with their employer. To circumvent this rule, they opened a dealings account with their employer in the name of a friend of theirs. They used this account to trade extensively and profitably. In order to withdraw their profits, they presented falsified documents. This was held to have been done 'with a view to gain' of the money. This was because, without the falsification, their employer would have known of the bogus account and, thus, would have known that he (the employer) was entitled to withhold the money under the principle[32] which entitles the employer/principal to retain secret profits made by its agents/employees.

## 2 LIABILITY OF COMPANY OFFICERS FOR DECEPTION OFFENCE

10-11    **Section 18 of the TA 1968 – Liability of company officers for corporate deception offences**

(1) Where an offence committed by a body corporate under ss 15, 16 or 17 of this Act is proved to have been committed with the consent or connivance of any director, manager, secretary or other similar officer of the body corporate, or any person who was purporting to act in any such capacity, he as well as the body corporate shall be guilty of that offence, and shall be liable to be proceeded against and punished accordingly.

---

28  See para 2-18, above.
29  [1989] 1 WLR 1050.
30  For similar doubts, see: Smith, JC, para 6-08; Griew, para 12-07; Arlidge and Parry, para 4-182; Smith, ATH, para 24-12.
31  (1991) 94 Cr App R 355 (PC).
32  *Reading v AG* [1951] AC 507.

(2) Where the affairs of a body corporate are managed by its members, this section shall apply in relation to the acts and defaults of a member in connection with his functions of management as if he were a director of the body corporate.

## Mode of trial and sentence

10-12  The offence is triable either way.[33] If tried on indictment, it is a class 4 offence with a maximum penalty of imprisonment for five years. Following summary trial, the magistrates can sentence to imprisonment for up to six months, a fine up to the statutory maximum, or both.[34]

## Scope of the offence

10-13  This section applies in relation to offences under ss 15, 16 and 17 of the TA 1968. By virtue of s 5(1) of the TA 1978, it also applies in relation to offences under ss 1 and 2 of the TA 1978.[35] The wording of the section has some similarity to that of a number of other enactments which are also designed to catch company (or corporate) officers who consent to, or connive in the commission of, an offence committed by the corporation, including s 733 of the Companies Act 1985. In *Boal*, it was held that another similarly worded provision, s 23 of the Fire Precautions Act 1971, was intended 'to fix with criminal liability only those who are in a position of real authority, the decision makers within the company who have both the power and the responsibility to decide corporate policy and strategy'.[36] Accordingly, the Court of Appeal quashed D's conviction. As assistant general manager of the company's bookshop (the company's only business), he was responsible only for the day to day running of the bookshop, rather than enjoying any sort of governing role in respect of the affairs of the company itself. That meant he was not a 'director, manager, secretary or other similar officer'.

Unlike some other statutory provisions, s 18 does not catch the officer for mere neglect or omission. It requires proof that the officer 'consented to' or 'connived at' the commission of the offence. This is, however, easier to prove than it would be to establish the officer's guilt as a secondary party, on the ordinary principles of aiding or abetting. Those would require proof that D had done some positive act of one of the following: assistance, encouragement,

---

33  MCA 1980, s 17(1) and Sched 1, para 28.

34  *Ibid*, s 32(1) and Sched 1, para 28. The statutory maximum is currently £5,000.

35  The relevant part of the TA 1978, s 5(1) reads: '... and s 18 of that Act [the TA 1968] (liability of company officers for offences by the company) shall apply in relation to ss 1 and 2 above as it applies in relation to s 15 of that Act.'

36  [1992] 1 QB 591, p 597.

counselling, or that he produced the crime by endeavour. *Mens rea* does have to be proved for a conviction under s 18, since one cannot consent to, or connive at, something, unless one has knowledge of it.

Section 18 cannot apply unless the corporation has itself committed an offence. In order to prove that the corporation has committed the relevant offence, it will, thus, in practice be necessary to establish that at least one person with whom the company can be identified (director, company secretary or equivalent senior officer) had the necessary *mens rea* for the deception or false accounting offence in question.[37] In relation to all the offences to which s 18 relates, that involves establishing that at least one director (or similar officer) acted dishonestly.

## 3 FALSE STATEMENTS BY COMPANY DIRECTORS, ETC

**10-14** **Section 19 of the TA 1968 – False statements by company directors, etc**

(1) Where an officer of a body corporate or unincorporated association (or person purporting to act as such), with intent to deceive members or creditors of the body corporate or association about its affairs, publishes or concurs in publishing a written statement or account which to his knowledge is or may be misleading, false or deceptive in a material particular, he shall on conviction on indictment be liable to imprisonment for a term not exceeding seven years.

(2) For purposes of this section a person who has entered into a security for the benefit of a body corporate or association is to be treated as a creditor of it.

(3) Where the affairs of a body corporate or association are managed by its members, this section shall apply to any statement which a member publishes or concurs in publishing in connection with his functions of management as if he were an officer of the body corporate or association.

## Mode of trial and sentence

**10-15** The offence is triable either way.[38] If tried on indictment, it is a class 4 offence with a maximum penalty of imprisonment for seven years. Following summary

---

37 *Tesco Supermarkets v Nattrass* [1972] AC 153 (supermarket manager was not a director or senior officer); *AG's Ref (No 2 of 1999)* [2000] 3 All ER 182 (no conviction of corporation for manslaughter without evidence that a director or other senior officer also guilty). In *Tesco v London Borough of Brent* [1993] 1 WLR 1037 and *Meridian Global Funds Management Ltd v Securities Commission* [1995] 2 AC 500, it was held that companies could be convicted upon proof of the existence of *mens rea* in the company official carrying out the transaction in question, an official more lowly than someone such as a director, company secretary or equivalent. Those two cases turned, however, upon the construction of the particular statutory provisions which enacted the offences there charged.

38 MCA 1980, s 17(1) and Sched 1, para 28.

trial, the magistrates can sentence to imprisonment for up to six months, a fine up to the statutory maximum, or both.[39]

## Scope of the offence

10-16   This provision is not confined to statements about financial matters but extends to those which are misleading, false or deceptive 'in a material particular'. The required *mens rea* is an 'intent to deceive members or creditors', which means that D can be guilty without having acted with a view to gain or an intent to cause any loss. Section 19 replaced s 84 of the LA 1861. That section was concerned primarily with fraudulent statements in prospectuses. Under s 19, however, the *mens rea* required is proof of an intent to deceive members or creditors, which must mean existing members and creditors. Unlike its predecessor, s 19 does not catch statements made with intent to induce someone to become a shareholder, or to lend money to the company. Proof of the necessary intent to deceive, will normally, without more, establish also the other required element of *mens rea* – that D knew that the statement was or might be misleading, false or deceptive in a material particular.

The expression 'officer' obviously includes any director or company secretary. In *Shacter*,[40] it was held, for the purposes of s 84 of the LA 1861, that a company's auditor is also an officer of the company. The expression also includes officers of unincorporated associations.

## 4 SUPPRESSION OF DOCUMENTS

10-17   **Section 20(1) of the TA 1968 – Suppression of documents**

(1) A person who dishonestly, with a view to gain for himself or another or with intent to cause loss to another, destroys, defaces or conceals any valuable security, any will or other testamentary document or any original document of or belonging to, or filed or deposited in, any court of justice or any government department shall on conviction on indictment be liable to imprisonment for a term not exceeding seven years.

(2) A person who dishonestly, with a view to gain for himself or another or with intent to cause loss to another, by any deception procures the execution of a valuable security shall on conviction on indictment be liable to imprisonment for a term not exceeding seven years; and this sub-section shall apply in relation to the making, acceptance, indorsement, alteration, cancellation or destruction in whole or in part of a valuable security, as if that were the execution of a valuable security.

---

39   MCA 1980, s 32(1) and Sched 1, para 28. The statutory maximum is currently £5,000.
40   [1960] 2 QB 252.

(3) For the purposes of this section 'deception' has the same meaning as in s 15 of this Act, and 'valuable security' means any document creating, transferring, surrendering or releasing any right to, in or over property, or authorising the payment of money or delivery of any property or evidencing the creation, transfer, surrender or release of any such right, or the payment of money or delivery of any property, or the satisfaction of any obligation.

## Mode of trial and sentence

10-18 The offence is triable either way.[41] If tried on indictment, it is a class 4 offence with a maximum penalty of imprisonment for seven years. Following summary trial, the magistrates can sentence to imprisonment for up to six months, a fine up to the statutory maximum, or both.[42]

## Introduction

10-19 This section creates two offences: sub-s (1) an offence of destroying, defacing or concealing valuable securities; sub-s (2) an offence of procuring the execution of a valuable security (which term includes having it altered or destroyed, etc).[43] Sub-section (1) does, but sub-s (2) does not, extend to destruction, etc, of certain documents other than valuable securities. Sub-section (1) replaced, with a more limited offence, offences originally in ss 27–30 of the LA 1861.

## Sub-section (1)

10-20 This offence may be useful in providing 'the only way of dealing with a person who, for example, suppressed a public document as a first step towards committing a fraud but did not get so far as attempting to commit the fraud'.[44] There are certain concepts which this sub-section has in common with sub-s (2), namely, 'dishonestly', 'with a view to gain ... or with intent to cause loss' and 'valuable security'. These are considered under sub-s (2), below.

The words 'destroys', 'defaces' and 'conceals' all appear, also, in the offence of false accounting, though that offence is confined to documents (accounts and records) required for an accounting purpose.[45] Where D's activity involves destruction or defacement, it would usually amount to the offence of criminal

---

41 MCA 1980, s 17(1) and Sched 1, para 28.

42 *Ibid*, s 32(1) and Sched 1, para 28. The statutory maximum is currently £5,000.

43 For the legislative history of s 20(2), see the speech of Lord Ackner in *Kassim* [1992] 1 AC 9 p 14.

44 *Eighth Report*, para 106.

45 See s 17, above.

damage,[46] which does not require dishonesty or any proof of any aim to gain or intent to cause loss. However, concealment of a document such as a will, or a valuable security, could well be done dishonestly with a view to gain or an intent to cause loss and would not necessarily amount to another offence or attempted offence. Apparently, the offence in s 20(1) is not committed by the destruction, defacement or concealment of a photocopy of any document, whether or not done with a view to gain or an intent to cause loss – though again destruction or defacement of it will usually amount to criminal damage if the photocopy belongs to someone other than the defendant.

## Valuable security

10-21  'Valuable security' is defined in sub-s (3) and the following documents are clearly within the definition: cheques, bills of exchange, receipts for money paid, conveyances of property, pawn receipts and other receipts for goods deposited. In *Benstead and Taylor*,[47] an irrevocable credit was held to be a valuable security, since it created a right of property. A clearing house automated payment system order (a CHAPS order) has also been held to be a valuable security: *King*.[48] In *King*, the Court of Appeal held that a CHAPS order, once it has been processed and bears the signatures of bank officials signifying that it has been processed, is a document which has *transferred* a right over property, namely, the bank credit which has been created by the CHAPS order. This part of the reasoning in *King* rests upon the notion that property, or a right over property, is transferred by a money transfer. Such reasoning seems unsustainable after *Preddy*,[49] where the House of Lords held that a 'transfer' of funds between bank accounts is not a *transfer* of property. Such a payment, or transfer of funds, does not transfer either property or a right over property. Rather, it extinguishes property of the first account holder and creates a new piece of property in the recipient account holder. The decision in *King* may, however, be sustainable on at least one of several other explanations, each based on the wording of s 20(3): (i) a CHAPS order authorises the payment of money; (ii) it authorises the delivery of property; (iii) it evidences the creation of a right over property; (iv) it evidences the satisfaction of an obligation. Whether the first two of these were accurate, the Court of Appeal, in *King*, found it unnecessary to decide. It did, however, expressly support the third and fourth, holding that 'once the necessary signatures have been appended to show that the transfer has been effected, [a CHAPS order] does evidence the creation ... of a right over property. In our view, it also evidences the satisfaction of an obligation, namely the obligation of

---

46  Contrary to the Criminal Damage Act 1971, s 1(1).
47  (1982) 75 Cr App R 276.
48  [1992] 1 QB 20.
49  [1996] AC 815, see para 8-29, above.

the bank to act upon the instructions of its paying customer to effect the transfer'.[50]

10-22     Where a document creates rights in or over property, or where it evidences the creation of a right in or over property, is that document capable of amounting to a valuable security if the property did not exist prior to the document? Professor Sir John Smith argues that: 'The words [in s 20(3)] "any right to, in or over property", seem to assume some existing property, a right to in or over which is created, transferred, surrendered or released.'[51] He argues that this point must be right 'because otherwise every contract in writing becomes a valuable security'.[52] It may be, however, that Professor Sir John Smith is wrong. Perhaps every contract in writing is, indeed, a valuable security. Would it be undesirable for example, for someone to be guilty (under s 20(2)) who, with a view to gain for himself, dishonestly by deception procures someone else to execute such a contract? It certainly seems pretty clear that the crime is committed if, with that intent, D dishonestly procures someone to execute a document releasing D from a contract.

If Professor Smith's argument is correct, then it removes one of the remaining explanations of the decision in *King* (item (iii) in the discussion above, as well as removing the basis of the decision in *Benstead and Taylor*,[53] since the document in question in each of these cases did not create (or transfer, etc) a right in an already existing item of property. Rather, it created the property in question. In the case of the CHAPS order, the decision that it is a valuable security can still be sustained on the final basis mentioned in the above discussion of *King*, namely, that it evidenced the satisfaction of an obligation. There is an alternative basis, however, for the finding in *Benstead and Taylor* that an irrevocable credit is a valuable security, namely, that it is (as it seems it is) a document 'authorising the payment of money'. On any view, cheques and bills of exchange are valuable securities, since it is beyond doubt that each of these authorises the payment of money.

Only a document can be a valuable security. Where a document authorises or evidences the payment of money, that document is capable of being a valuable security.[54] It is not the transfer of money, but the document itself which is the valuable security. Thus, the crime, in s 20(2), is committed, not by procuring the transfer (telegraphic or otherwise) of money, but by procuring the execution of the document.

---

50   [1992] 1 QB 20, pp 28–29.
51   Smith, JC, para 6-19.
52   In his commentary to *Weiss v Government of Germany* [2000] Crim LR 484, p 485.
53   (1982) 75 Cr App R 276.
54   *Weiss v Government of Germany* [2000] Crim LR 484, explaining *Manjdadria* [1993] Crim LR 73.

## Execution

10-23    The offence in s 20(2) is committed only if D procures the 'execution' of a valuable security. Within the normal meaning of the word, it is suggested, a document is 'executed' when it is signed, or in some other way authenticated. A CHAPS order is primarily an instruction or authority by the customer to the bank to make the money transfer and is, accordingly, signed by the customer. Assuming that the customer is the one practising the deception, then he certainly does not deceive himself and, thus, he does not, by deception, procure his own signature. It was held, in *King*,[55] that he can be guilty of the offence when he, by deception, procures, following his own signature, the signature on it of a bank official, which signature will act as evidence that the bank has carried out its instruction. The signature of the bank official was an execution of the document. The provision, in s 20(2), whereby a valuable security is executed if there is an 'acceptance' of it, does not greatly extend the meaning of 'execution'. Merely receiving possession or accepting delivery of the document is not an 'acceptance' of it. Rather, 'acceptance', in s 20(2), has a narrow technical meaning, referring to the drawee's act of writing on a bill of exchange and signing his assent to the order of the drawer.[56] 'Execution' of the document does not refer to acts implementing the document by carrying out instructions which it may contain (for example, as to making a payment or delivering goods). Rather, it is concerned with, and is confined to, acts done in connection with the document itself.[57]

10-24    Section 20(2) provides that a document is executed when it is 'cancelled' or 'destroyed'. The ultimate fate of a valuable security, the value of which has been paid out, is often that it, the document, is cancelled or destroyed. That is what happens to a cheque when a bank pays out on it. Thus, it was argued in *Kassim* that someone who successfully presents a stolen cheque for payment, is, thereby, guilty of procuring by deception the execution of a valuable security. The argument was rejected as confusing consequences with intention. The Delphic words of Lord Ackner in that case seem to suggest that the crime, in 20(2), requires (i) that the defendant dishonestly procures by deception the execution of a valuable security, and (ii) that he does so with a view to a gain *as a result of that execution* or with intent to cause a loss *as a result of that execution*: 'What the appellant set out to achieve was a gain for himself. The dishonest means by which he intended to achieve this was not by the cancellation or destruction of the cheque. He achieved the profit he sought prior to the cheque's destruction or cancellation.'[58]

---

55  [1992] 1 QB 20.
56  *Kassim* [1992] 1 AC 9 (HL), approving *Nanayakkara* [1987] 1 WLR 265.
57  *Kassim* [1992] 1 AC 9 (HL), disapproving *Beck* [1985] 1 WLR 22.
58  [1992] 1 AC 9, p 19, *per* Lord Ackner, with whom all their Lordships agreed.

## Procure by deception

10-25 'Deception' in s 20(2) has the same meaning as in s 15.[59] The procuring of the execution of the valuable security must be 'by' the deception. This denotes the same requirement of a causal connection between the deception and the obtaining, as in s 15.[60] This requirement is a feature of all the deception offences of obtaining or procuring.

In *Beck*,[61] the Court of Appeal held that 'procure' was a word in common usage meaning to 'cause' or to 'bring about' – a ruling accepted as correct in *Aston and N'Wadiche*, in which it was also held that the defendant must have *mens rea* in relation to procuring the execution of a valuable security.[62] That *mens rea* requirement is that D must have either intended to procure the execution of a valuable security by his deception, or else have been reckless as to that happening. It has already been pointed out that there has to be a causal link between the deception and the procuring of the execution of the valuable security. A further link, however, is also required – this one between the execution of the security and the gain or loss which D anticipates or intends. This link is a matter of *mens rea*, since there is no requirement for D actually to make a gain or cause a loss, merely that he acts with a view to gain or an intent to cause a loss. As stated above,[63] the House of Lords in *Kassim* made it clear that it is not enough that the execution of the valuable security happens to result from the defendant's deception. The defendant must have anticipated making a gain (or intended to cause a loss) *by the execution of the valuable security* and not merely as an incidental result of his activities that bring about the execution of the valuable security.

### *Mens rea*

10-26 For a conviction under either s 20(1) or s 20(2), the prosecution must prove that the defendant acted dishonestly and acted with a view to gain for himself or another or with intent to cause loss to another. Dishonesty has the same meaning as it does in other offences of deception.[64] The expression 'with a view to gain ... or with intent to cause loss' is the same as occurs in the offences of

---

59  See para 8-04, above.

60  See para 8-20, above.

61  [1985] 1 WLR 22, overruled on other grounds in *Kassim* [1992] 1 AC 9.

62  [1998] Crim LR 498. It has been held that the word 'procure' in the Accessories and Abettors Act 1861 means 'produce by endeavour': *AG's Ref (No 1 of 1975)* [1975] QB 773. Putting together the ruling in *Beck* [1985] 1 WLR 22 as to the *actus reus* element of the word and the ruling in *Aston and N'Wadiche* as to the related *mens rea*, the meaning of the word in s 20(2) is not much different.

63  Paragraph 10-24.

64  See *Ghosh* [1982] QB 1053, para 8-34, above.

blackmail and false accounting. Its meaning is set out in s 34(2)(a) and is explained in the discussion of those two offences.[65]

Section 20(2) requires that D had each of the following three elements of *mens rea*:

(1) dishonesty.

(2) either

    (a) an intention by his deception to bring about the execution of a valuable security; or

    (b) recklessness – an awareness that his deception might bring about the execution of a valuable security.

(3) a view to making a gain by procuring the execution of the valuable security or an intent to cause a loss by procuring its execution.

That these are the required elements is clear from the wording of the offence and the decisions in *Aston and N'Wadiche* and *Kassim*, which were explained above. Now consider an example.

## Example

10-27 D dishonestly practises a deception by completing, with false information, an application form which he submits to an organisation which he hopes to deceive into giving him financial assistance. It might be an application for housing benefit, for a loan, for a scholarship, for help from a charity. In the example, D knows that his application is deceptive, but he has no idea if the falsehoods he has told on the form are actually necessary. In other words, he has no idea whether the application might be successful without those falsehoods. Also, he has no idea how, if his application is successful, the funds will be transmitted to him – whether by cheque, by automated transfer into his bank account, or by delivery of cash into his hand. He is aware that it could be by any of these methods. In fact, it turns out that: (i) his application is successful; (ii) that success is because of the falsehoods he put on the application form; and (iii) the result is that the financial help is sent to him by means of a cheque.

## Analysis

10-28 In this example, D has committed the *actus reus* of the crime in s 20(2), because he has procured by deception the execution of a valuable security, a cheque. He was dishonest; the example tells us so. It cannot be said, for sure, that he intended by his deception to bring about the execution of a valuable security. This is because he could not be sure that, even if his intentions were all fulfilled, a valuable security would be executed. Presumably, he knew that it might be –

---

65 See paras 10-09, above, and 11-25, below. In relation to s 20(2), see, also, *Kassim* [1992] 1 AC 9, above.

that he might be paid by cheque. Thus, he can be said to have both the necessary recklessness under 2(b) in the above list of *mens rea* elements and, also, the mental element, at 3 in that list. He has the latter because, realising that, if his deception worked, he might be paid by cheque, he had a view to (an anticipation of) making a gain by procuring the execution of the valuable security (the cheque). If, however, he *assumed* that any funds paid to him following a successful application would definitely be paid to him by cash – it never occurred to him that they might be paid by any other method – then he lacks both the second and third of the required elements of *mens rea* listed above. He lacks the second because he neither intended to procure the execution of a valuable security, nor realised that that might occur. He lacks the third because he did not practise his deception with a view to making a gain by procuring the execution of a valuable security; he practised it with a view to making a gain by other means.

# CHAPTER 11

# BLACKMAIL

11-01    **Section 21 of the Theft Act (TA) 1968 – Blackmail**

(1) A person is guilty of blackmail if, with a view to gain for himself or another or with intent to cause loss to another, he makes any unwarranted demand with menaces; and for this purpose a demand with menaces is unwarranted unless the person making it does so in the belief –

(a) that he has reasonable grounds for making the demand; and

(b) that the use of the menaces is a proper means of reinforcing the demand.

(2) The nature of the act or omission demanded is immaterial, and it is also immaterial whether the menaces relate to action to be taken by the person making the demand.

(3) A person guilty of blackmail shall on conviction on indictment be liable to imprisonment for a term not exceeding 14 years.

## Introduction

11-02    Section 21 represents a substantial reform of the range of offences contained in ss 29–31 of the Larceny Act (LA) 1916. These offences were complex and overlapping and have been described in unflattering terms as, 'an ill assorted collection of legislative bric-a-brac which the draftsman of the 1916 Act put together with scissors and paste'.[1] Moreover, the offences contained in the 1916 Act bore little relation to the common understanding of the term 'blackmail'. In fact, the term itself was not used in the Act. The Criminal Law Revision Committee (CLRC), in its *Eighth Report*[2] recommended both a new terminology and a new configuration of the offence. Accordingly, the present offence, contained in s 21, can properly be characterised as conforming to the ordinary understanding of what 'blackmail' involves. Nonetheless, some of the earlier cases remain useful. This is especially so with regards to the interpretation of the terms 'demand' and 'menaces' which were used in the 1916 Act. A remaining criticism is whether this offence properly belongs in a statute dealing with the law of theft and it may be argued that, like kidnapping, for instance, its proper place lies with offences against the person. The justification appears to be that, as the object of blackmail is to cause either a property gain or loss, it is properly included.

---

1    Hogan, B, 'Blackmail: another view' [1966] Crim LR 474.
2    CLRC, *Eighth Report*, Cmnd 2977, 1966, paras 108–25.

11-03    The offence of blackmail is indictable only (s 17(1) and Sched 1 of the Magistrates' Courts Act 1980) and is a class 3 offence. The offence seems always to have attracted a severe sentence based on deterrence. The case of *R v Hadjou* (1989) 11 Cr App R(S) 29 is illustrative. The appellant demanded money under the threat to disclose sexually explicit videotape of himself and the victim. The tape had been made during a previous liaison between the parties. Lord Lane CJ, in upholding a sentence of four years' imprisonment, adopted the words of the trial judge to the effect that, 'in the calendar of criminal offences blackmail is one of the ugliest ... because it involves what really amounts, so often, to attempted murder of the soul'. Lord Lane went on to hold that 'it is perhaps due to the fact that the courts always impose severe sentences that one so seldom, if ever, finds a person convicted for the second time of blackmail'.[3]

11-04    The victims of blackmailers may often be reluctant to complain to the police because the attendant publicity is precisely the very thing that the blackmailer utilises in his threats. Accordingly, the CLRC considered the possibility of including a provision that would empower the courts to order that the identity of the victim should not be published. The Committee eventually came to the conclusion that this was unnecessary and might even be counterproductive.[4] Any such restriction would run counter to the open justice principle. Nonetheless, in appropriate circumstances, there is an inherent power in the court to impose reporting restrictions supported by s 11 of the Contempt of Court Act 1981.

## Jurisdiction

11-05    Problems may arise where, for instance, the defendant writes a letter of blackmail from London to a victim in the USA or vice versa. This may be illustrated by the case of *Treacy v DPP* [1971] AC 537. The defendant posted, from the Isle of Wight, a letter written by him to his victim in West Germany, demanding money with menaces. At his trial, it was contended that the court had no jurisdiction as the offence had been committed outside the jurisdiction, that is, that no demand had been made by him until the letter had been received in Germany. This was rejected and subsequent appeals to the Court of Appeal and House of Lords were dismissed.

This position was confirmed by the Criminal Justice Act (CJA) 1993. The offence of blackmail is deemed to be a class A offence and, under s 2 of the CJA 1993, a defendant is guilty if any 'relevant event' occurs in England and Wales. Since any 'relevant event' would cover any element of the offence, it follows that making a demand from within the jurisdiction directed to a victim outside the jurisdiction, or vice versa, would be sufficient to constitute the offence. The

3    (1989) Cr App R(S) 29, p 30.
4    *Op cit*, CLRC, fn 2, para 125.

offence would, in these circumstances, be triable by the courts in England and Wales.

## Elements of the offence

11-06    The prosecution is required to prove:

(a) that there was a demand;

(b) made with menaces;

(c) that it was unwarranted; and

(d) that, at the time of making the demand, the defendant made it with a view to gain for himself or another or with intent to cause loss to another.

### *The demand*

11-07    The demand must require the victim to do some act or omission. The demand may be made either orally, or in writing. A further possibility is that the conduct of the defendant may, also, in the circumstances, be sufficient to indicate that a demand is being made. In *R v Collister and Warhurst* (1955) 39 Cr App R 100, police officers threatened to bring a false charge against the victim, but indicated that this could be avoided by making a payment. It was held that the demand need not be explicit: 'Although, there was no express demand ... the demeanour of the accused and the circumstances of the case were such that an ordinary reasonable man would understand that a demand ... was being made of him ...'[5] In the case of *Studer* (1915) 11 Cr App R 307, the appellant led his employer to believe that he (the employer) was under investigation by the police on suspicion of trading with the enemy. Telegrams were fabricated by the appellant, purporting to come from a detective, advising that proceedings would be dropped on the receipt of payment of a sum of money. The final telegram advised that 'matters were serious' and immediate clearance was required as the detective's superiors were 'sure to act at any moment'. Lord Reading CJ held that: 'It is not necessary that the language should be explicit, it may be in language only a request.'[6] Neither is it necessary that the demand has to be communicated to the intended victim. In *Treacy v DPP* (above), the demand was deemed to be effective, even before it actually came to the attention of the intended victim.

11-08     In the cases above, the demand was for money to be made over to the defendant, but it is clear that the offence is not limited to demands for the transfer of money or property. An example of this might be where the defendant makes a threat, in order to cause his victim to abandon a legitimate claim. This is

---

5    (1955) 39 Cr App R 100, p 102.

6    (1915) 11 Cr App R 307, p 311.

made explicit by s 21(2), which provides that 'the nature of the act or omission demanded is immaterial'. If, however, the demand is for something other than money or property it will be vital for the prosecution to show that the demand was with a view to a 'gain' to the defendant, or a 'loss' to the victim

11-09    Lord Diplock in *Treacy* (see above) was clearly of the view that the jury ought to be directed to take a common sense view as to what constitutes a 'demand' and of the way in which it may be made:

> In the course of the argument many other and ingenious ways in which a blackmailer might choose to send his demand to his victim have been canvassed, and many possible, even though unlikely, events which might intervene between the sending of the demand by the blackmailer and its receipt and comprehension by the victim have been discussed. These cases which so far are only imaginary may fall to be decided if they ever should occur in real life. But unless the purpose of the new style of drafting used in the TA 1968 is to be defeated they, too, should be decided by answering the question: Are the circumstances of this case such as would prompt a man in ordinary conversation to say: 'I have made a demand?'[7]

## Menaces

11-10   The courts, when dealing with the provisions of the LA 1916, gave the term 'menaces' a wide interpretation and the CLRC chose to recommend the use of this term rather than the proposed alternative of 'threats'. Two cases are illustrative. In *Thorne v Motor Trade Association*,[8] Lord Wright was of the opinion that: '... the word "menace" is to be liberally construed and not as limited to threats of violence but as including threats of any action detrimental to or unpleasant to the person addressed. It may also include a warning that in certain events such action is intended.'[9]

In *Clear*,[10] a lorry of which the defendant was the driver, and its load, were stolen. The defendant reported to the company that employed him that he had left the loaded lorry for a short time, set the alarm system and taken with him the ignition key and the key of the alarm system. A claim was made against the company's insurers. An action was subsequently brought by the owners of the goods against the company and the defendant was requested to testify as a witness. He visited the managing director of the company on a number of occasions and threatened to withhold or change his evidence unless he was paid £300. In the Court of Appeal, Sellers LJ, dealing with the question as to whether the demand for £300 had been made with menaces, held that:

> Words or conduct which would not intimidate or influence anyone to respond to the demand would not be menaces ... but threats and conduct of such a nature

7    Page 566.
8    [1937] AC 797.
9    *Ibid*, p 817.
10   [1968] 1 QB 670.

and extent that the mind of an ordinary person of normal stability and courage might be influenced or made apprehensive so as to accede unwillingly to the demand would be sufficient for a jury's consideration.[11]

11-11   The emphasis in *Clear* was placed firmly on a comparison with an ordinary person of normal stability and courage. Does this mean that a defendant might. with impunity, take advantage of an unduly susceptible victim? This was dealt with in *Garwood*,[12] where the two possible situations where a jury might need to be guided were laid down:

(a) where the threats might affect the mind of an ordinary person of normal stability, but did not affect the mind of the person actually addressed; or

(b) where the threats, in fact, affected the victim's mind, although they would not have affected the mind of a person of ordinary stability, provided that the defendant was aware of the likely effect on his victim.

11-12   Moreover, the test is not purely an objective one, but must be answered by looking at the actual facts of the case and the extent to which the defendant is, or is not, aware of any special facts. In *Clear*, Sellers LJ went on to hold that, where the defendant is unaware of any special circumstances that would lead the intended victim to disregard the threat, this would have no bearing on the defendant's state of mind. In *Clear* itself, the victim, the managing director, had no direct interest in the outcome of the litigation and, therefore, was not likely to be influenced by the threats. The defendant was unaware of this and this factor was held to be irrelevant. However, the requirement of menace might be lacking where the defendant knew that his threats would have no effect on the victim.

11-13   The judicial approach is best summed up by Cairns LJ in *Lawrence and Pomroy*: 'The word "menaces" is an ordinary English word which any jury can be expected to understand.' Judicial over-elaboration is only likely to confuse the jury in straightforward cases. Nonetheless, exceptional cases may arise where guidance is necessary. Cairns LJ continued: 'In exceptional cases where because of special knowledge in special circumstances what would be a menace to an ordinary person is not a menace to the person to whom it is addressed, or where the converse may be true, it is no doubt necessary to spell out the meaning of the word.'[13]

11-14   This common sense approach ought to be applied to threats which are trivial. This was quite clearly the view of the CLRC, which regarded `menaces' as something stronger in force than 'threats'.[14] This point is illustrated by *Harry*.[15] Here, the student treasurer of a college 'rag' committee sent letters to 115 local shopkeepers offering to sell them indemnity posters for amounts

---

11   [1968] 1 QB 670, pp 679–80.

12   (1987) 85 Cr App R 85.

13   Page 72.

14   *Op cit*, CLRC, fn 2, paras 110–11.

15   [1974] Crim LR 32.

between £1 and £5, the money to go to charity. This was intended to protect shopkeepers 'from any rag activity which could in any way cause you inconvenience'. Fewer than six traders complained and none that complained had paid. The defendant was indicted on two counts of blackmail, but the trial judge directed the jury to return a verdict of not guilty. Common sense clearly indicated that the letter was not to be taken so seriously that it constituted 'a demand with menaces'. This was further supported by the reactions of the recipients.

11-15        By virtue of s 21(1), it is clear that the defendant must make or be a party to the making of a demand with menaces. However, s 21(2) indicates that it is immaterial whether the menaces relate to any action to be taken by the defendant himself, or by someone else. As *Studer*[16] illustrates, this may even cover action to be taken by a purely fictitious person.

11-16        The primary difficulty is in drawing a distinction between mere demands and the kind of demands that constitute 'menaces'. The CLRC considered a number of such examples.[17] Most people, for instance, would agree that a threat to denounce someone as homosexual unless he paid a debt would amount to a demand with menaces. Similarly, a threat to cause physical injury or damage to property would always be sufficient. What, however, would be the position where the defendant demanded money that was legally due to him (perhaps by way of a debt), by threatening to injure the debtor's credit rating by making his non-payment generally known? The answer lies in asking whether the demand was 'warranted' in the circumstances.

### *Unwarranted*

11-17   By virtue of s 21(1), blackmail requires the making of an 'unwarranted' demand. Such a demand will be unwarranted unless the defendant acts in the belief (a) that he has 'reasonable grounds' for making the demand and (b) that his use of menaces in making the demand is 'proper'. The unwarranted nature of the demand is an element in the definition of the offence. In terms of the burden of proof, therefore, this is an element that the prosecution must establish. To put it simply, the prosecution has the burden of proving that the defendant had no such belief. In practice, this will only become a 'live' issue, that is, an issue for the jury's consideration, if the defendant raises some evidence that he was acting under a belief that his demands were warranted.

11-18        In *Lawrence and Pomroy*, it was held that where there are no reasonable grounds for the demand (in this case for the payment of a debt) and the defence does not raise the issue, there is no need for the jury to be directed as to s 21(1)(a). Similarly, where the means adopted by the defendant were, on the

---

16   (1915) 11 Cr App R 307.
17   *Op cit*, CLRC, fn 2, para 119.

face of it, not proper and where the defendant does not set up the case that he believed it to be proper, there will be no need for a direction to the jury on s 21(1)(b).

11-19     The wording of the sub-section makes it clear that the beliefs of the defendant need not be reasonable. This imports an entirely subjective test of what the defendant considers to be 'reasonable grounds' and 'proper' use of menaces, although, of course, it is for the jury to decide whether he held the belief in question. In *Harvey and Others*,[18] the appellants had entered into a transaction with X, by which X would procure a large quantity of cannabis for a sum in excess of £20,000. He did not do so and the appellants kidnapped X, his wife and their small child and subjected them to threats of violence to obtain the return of the money that had been paid over to him. The appellants were convicted on a number of charges, including blackmail. On appeal, one issue related to the directions of the trial judge to the jury in which he ruled that a threat to perform a serious criminal act could never, as a matter of law, be believed to be warranted. Bingham J, in the Court of Appeal, ruled that a trial judge was free to comment on the unlikelihood of a defendant believing threats, such as were made in this case. It would be absurd, for instance, if a trial judge were to be prevented from making an 'appropriate comment on the unlikelihood of the defendants believing murder and rape or threats to commit those acts to be lawful or other than criminal'.[19] Nonetheless, he should have left the question to the jury:

> It matters not what the reasonable man, or any man other than the defendant, would believe, save in so far as that may throw light on what the defendant in fact believed. Thus, the factual question of the defendant's belief should be left to the jury. To that extent the sub-section is subjective in approach, as is generally desirable in a criminal statute.[20]

11-20  Again, it is for the defendant to raise any reasonable grounds he may have. It is the defendant's belief that he has reasonable grounds which is crucial and it appears to be immaterial that he is in error. In *Dymond* (see below), for example, the defendant clearly believed that she had reasonable grounds for believing that she was entitled to make a demand of compensation against the man who, it was alleged, had indecently assaulted her. The question is whether the test of reasonableness is a purely objective one. The pre-1968 Act case of *Thorne v Motor Trade Association* (above), seems to indicate an objective assessment, but there is doubt as to whether this is the case under s 21. The better view would appear to be that, while the jury must consider whether the grounds are reasonable, this must be judged according to the facts as the defendant, not an objective bystander, believed them to be.

---

18   (1981) 72 Cr App R 139.
19   *Ibid*, p 142.
20   *Ibid*, p 141.

11-21 In addition, he must have had a belief (whether reasonable or not) that the use of menaces was a 'proper' means of reinforcing the demand. The term 'proper' is not defined in the Act and Bingham J, in the *Harvey* case (above), described it as, 'an unusual expression to find in a criminal statute'. The learned judge went on to say:

> Thus, no assistance is given to any defendant ... who knows or suspects that his threat, or the act threatened, is criminal, but believes it to be justified by his peculiar circumstances. The test is not what he regards as justified, but what he believes to be proper. And where, as here, the threats were to do acts which any sane man knows to be against the laws of every civilised country no jury would hesitate long before dismissing the contention that the defendant genuinely believed the threats to be a proper means of reinforcing even a legitimate demand.[21]

11-22 The effect of this is that, while a defendant may believe that a threat to cause violence, for instance, may be justified, he cannot contend that it would be 'proper' when he knows that what he threatens would be criminal. However, what would be the position when the defendant contends that he did not know that what he threatens is unlawful? The answer to this might lie in the view taken by the CLRC to the effect that: '"Proper" directs the mind to consideration of what is morally and socially acceptable, which seems right on a matter of this kind.'[22] Accordingly, while the defendant may claim a lack of knowledge that his conduct was unlawful, the jury may, nonetheless, convict by applying a standard of what is morally and socially acceptable. This, in turn, would lead to the reworking of the appropriate test to: Did the defendant believe that what he threatened to do was morally and socially acceptable?

11-23 The problems that this may cause may be illustrated by two cases decided under the previous law. In *Dymond*,[23] a young woman who claimed to be the victim of an indecent assault demanded compensation in the form of a payment from her alleged assailant, threatening to expose him. She was convicted, with the trial judge refusing to allow her to give evidence in support of her complaint. This decision was upheld by the Court of Criminal Appeal. By way of contrast, in *Bernhard*,[24] a woman demanded money that had been promised her as the mistress of the victim. She threatened that, if payment were not made, she would make the relationship known to his wife, as well as to the newspapers. She was convicted and sentenced to nine months imprisonment. The conviction was, however, quashed by the Court of Criminal Appeal on the grounds of her belief that she was entitled to the payment. The requisite *mens rea* was, therefore, lacking. Leaving aside the question as to whether there were reasonable grounds for the making the demands, both the women would, under the present law, be

---

21   (1981) 72 Cr App R 139, p 142.
22   *Op cit*, CLRC, fn 2, para 123.
23   [1920] 2 KB 260.
24   [1938] 2 KB 264.

able to argue that they honestly believed that their threatened action was morally and socially acceptable and, therefore, proper. This was clearly the view taken by the CLRC:

> As to the illegality of making the demand, we are decidedly of the opinion that the test should be subjective, namely whether the person in question honestly believes that he has the right to make the demand ... Since blackmail is in its nature an offence of dishonesty, it seems wrong that a person should be guilty of the offence by making a demand which he honestly believes to be justified.[25]

11-24  *Lambert* may illustrate the problems this approach might cause.[26] The defendant, L, suspected his wife of having an affair with X, her sales manager. In the course of two telephone calls and one meeting, he informed X that, for the sum of £250, X could buy 'rights' to his wife. If X would not pay the money, L threatened to tell X's wife and employer of his suspicions. The trial judge directed the jury as follows:

> The main question in the case was this. Was the demand with menaces unwarranted? Did the defendant honestly believe he had the right or reasonable grounds for making the demand? The prosecution must show that the defendant made the demand not having that belief. The defendant's guilt or innocence depends upon his own opinion as to whether he was acting rightly or wrongly at the time.[27]

In the light of this direction, the jury acquitted. There may be doubts as to whether a present day jury would accept, as in *Dymond* and *Bernhard*, that the actions of L could be said to be morally and socially acceptable. Nonetheless, the approach taken by the trial judge must be correct and it would be open to a jury to come to the conclusion that the defendant must have known that his conduct was unwarranted.

Blackmail may be contrasted with robbery at this point. A defendant who threatens violence in order to recover property borrowed from him by another does not commit the offence of robbery if he honestly believes he is entitled to recover it.[28] However, since he cannot argue that his threats of violence are proper, under the ruling in *Harvey* (above), he would be guilty of blackmail.

*With a view to gain for himself or another or with intent to cause loss to another*

11-25  The demand must be accompanied by either 'a view to gain for himself or another or with intent to cause loss to another'. This terminology is found elsewhere in the Act, for instance, in s 17, in relation to false accounting.[29] This

---

25  *Op cit*, CLRC, fn 2, para 118.
26  [1972] Crim LR 422.
27  *Ibid*, p 423.
28  See *Robinson* [1977] Crim LR 173, para 3-10, above.
29  For a discussion in the context of s 17, see para 10-09, below.

brings into operation s 34(2) of the Act, where the following interpretation appears:

>  (a) 'gain' and 'loss' are to be construed as extending only to gain or loss in money or other property, but as extending to any such gain or loss whether temporary or permanent: and
>
>> (i) 'gain' includes a gain by keeping what one has, as well as a gain by getting what one has not; and
>>
>> (ii) 'loss' includes a loss by not getting what one might get, as well as a loss by parting with what one has.

Although this interpretation is artificial, it nonetheless limits the scope of s 21 to the gain or loss in money or other property. This is in accordance with the remit of the TA 1968, as being only concerned with 'theft and similar or associated offences'.[30]

11-26    Most instances of blackmail are straightforward, in that the blackmailer is seeking to obtain money to which he knows he has no right and, therefore, there is little doubt about his view to gain or his intent to cause loss. If the demand is for property, gain or loss is, similarly, obvious. The intentions of the defendant in demanding that property – even if he was to destroy it – would be immaterial. He still would have a view to gain or an intent to cause loss. Other situations may be more problematic. In *Bevans* [1988] Crim LR 236, the appellant was suffering from osteo-arthritis. He went to a doctor, produced a handgun and demanded an injection of medication to ease his pain, threatening to shoot the doctor unless the doctor complied. The doctor did so, injecting him with pethidine. He was convicted of blackmail and the issue for the Court of Appeal was whether there had been a gain or loss of property. The Court of Appeal took a strictly literal approach. First, the substance injected was 'property'. Secondly, the demand involved a 'gain' to the appellant. It may be true that the appellant's primary motive was relief from pain, but s 21 does not require that the loss or gain should be economic in nature. The view of the CLRC was that 'provided that the element of gain or loss is present, there seems no reason to make any distinction as to the subject matter of the demand'.[31]

11-27    What, then, of the defendant who, at the point of a gun demands sexual intercourse? Would this constitute blackmail? The short answer is that, while this would lead to a conviction for rape (or attempted rape), it would not constitute blackmail, as there is not a gain or loss of either money or property. The problems that might be raised by this approach were explored by Professor Sir John Smith in his 'Commentary' to the *Bevans* case:

> If D demands a massage at the point of a gun he does not commit an offence under s 21. What then if, as D knows, the massage involves the use of some oil or cream on the patient's body? Does D's demand now amount to blackmail? The

---

30   See the long title to the Act.
31   *Op cit*, CLRC, fn 2, para 117.

property involved is only incidental to the service and there is no difference in substance between the demand for the massage with, and the massage without, the oil or cream. If D demands with menaces that P drive him to the station (in P's car), it would seem rather artificial to argue that D has a view to gain or an intent to cause loss in respect of the petrol.[32]

11-28    This analysis would require an examination of the motive that lies behind the defendant's demand. If the gain or loss in either money or property is merely incidental, then the offence of blackmail is not made out. Another potentially useful concept is that of remoteness. If the gain or loss is too remote in the context of the threat, then it may be argued that the offence of blackmail would not be made out.

11-29    A further issue arises in relation to instances where the defendant demands money or property lawfully owed to him by a creditor. Provided that the other ingredients of the offence are satisfied, it may be asked whether the defendant has, in fact, gained anything. In *Lawrence and Pomroy*, it seems to have been assumed that this ingredient of the offence was satisfied, even where the gain related to a debt that was believed to be rightly due to the appellant. In *Parkes*,[33] the defendant was charged with blackmail in relation to a demand for money due under debts legally owing to the defendant. The defence submission was, to the effect that, a demand for what was lawfully owing to the defendant could not be said to be a demand 'with a view to gain' within s 21 of the Act. The trial judge rejected this submission. Such a demand, even for money lawfully due, came within the definition of s 34(2(a), as including 'getting what one has not'. Here, the defendant had a right in action in respect of the debt and he would have gained hard cash. He was, accordingly, getting more than he already had. In the event, the defendant was acquitted and no opportunity to test this ruling on appeal arose. If this ruling is to be regarded as correct, then the existence of a profit might be *prima facie* evidence of the gain, but the absence of a profit would not be conclusive either way. What, then, would be the position if cases such as *D&C Builders v Rees*[34] were to come before the criminal courts? Here, typically, a defendant uses the threat of a refusal to pay to induce a creditor to accept a lesser amount in full satisfaction of a debt. No real problem arises, as it is clear that the defendant has made a gain while the creditor has incurred a loss.

11-30    An essential ingredient of the offences of theft, robbery and obtaining property by deception is that there must be intent permanently to deprive. Regardless of the qualifications to this, in s 6 of the Act, no such requirement pertains to the offence of blackmail. A defendant who, with menaces, obtains the use of another's property, intending to return that property in due course, nevertheless, has done so 'with a view to gain for himself', as s 34(2)(a) extends to both temporary as well as permanent gains and losses. A similar analysis

---

32    [1988] Crim LR 236, p 237.

33    [1973] Crim LR 358.

34    [1966] 2 QB 617.

must be extended to situations where a defendant has an intention to return an economic equivalent to the victim, from whom he has obtained the use of money or property, assuming that full restitution is possible in the circumstances. Here, too, he has obtained a gain and his victim has suffered a loss, albeit a temporary one.

## Attempted blackmail

11-31   The nature of the definition of the offence of blackmail makes it extremely unlikely that a charge of attempted blackmail may be brought. Any conduct that would normally constitute the preparatory acts deemed necessary by s 1(1) of the Criminal Attempts Act 1981 would, in fact, be capable of sustaining a charge for the full offence under s 21.

## Associated offences

11-32   Some of the conduct that would have previously been treated as blackmail under the LA 1916 is now dealt with under a variety of other statutes. In a situation where the defendant coerces the victim into paying money owed under a debt, for instance, he necessarily is acting 'with a view to gain' and may be doing so by 'menaces'. Nevertheless, this situation would be better dealt with under s 40 of the Administration of Justice Act (AJA) 1970, which deals with the specific offence of the harassment of debtors. Two significant distinctions may be noted. First, the defendant's belief in the propriety of his conduct would be crucial on a charge of blackmail, but not on a charge of harassment. Second, the offence under the AJA 1970  is purely a summary one. On the other hand, a threat to induce sexual activity would be unlikely to fall within the range of blackmail, unless the element of gain or loss could be satisfied.

11-33       Other associated offences include the following:

(a) threats to kill or to cause harm – under the Offences Against the Person Act 1861 or under the Public Order Act (POA) 1986;

(b) threats to damage property – s 2 of the  Criminal Damage Act 1971;

(c) threats of violence for the purpose of securing entry to premises – s 6(1) of the Criminal Law Act (CLA) 1977;

(d) bomb hoaxes made with a view to gain – s 51 of the CLA 1977;

(e) threats in connection with the contamination of goods – s 38 of the POA 1986;

(f) demands for payment for unsolicited goods – s 2 of the Unsolicited Goods and Services Act 1972 and the Consumer Protection (Distance Selling) Regulations 2000;

(g) threats contained in letters – Malicious Communications Act 1988; and

(h) harassment generally – the Protection from Harassment Act 1997.[35]

## Reform

11-34 The Law Commission has seen no reason for any reform in the terminology or configuration of the offence of blackmail.[36]

---

35  This listing is not intended to be comprehensive.
36  *A Criminal Code for England and Wales*, 1989, Law Commission No 177, Vol 2, para 16.11.

# CHAPTER 12

# HANDLING STOLEN PROPERTY

## 1 HANDLING

**12-01**   **Section 22 of the Theft Act (TA) 1968 – Handling stolen goods**

(1) A person handles stolen goods if (otherwise than in the course of the stealing) knowing or believing them to be stolen goods he dishonestly receives the goods, or dishonestly undertakes or assists in their retention, removal, disposal or realisation by or for the benefit of another person, or if he arranges to do so.

(2) A person guilty of handling stolen goods shall on conviction on indictment be liable to imprisonment for a term not exceeding 14 years.

**12-02**   **Section 24 of the TA 1968 – Scope of offences relating to stolen goods**

(1) The provisions of this Act relating to goods which have been stolen shall apply whether the stealing occurred in England or Wales or elsewhere, and whether it occurred before or after the commencement of this Act, provided that the stealing (if not an offence under this Act) amounted to an offence where and at the time when the goods were stolen; and references to stolen goods shall be construed accordingly.

(2) For purposes of those provisions references to stolen goods shall include, in addition to the goods originally stolen and parts of them (whether in their original state or not) –

    (a) any other goods which directly or indirectly represent or have at any time represented the stolen goods in the hands of the thief as being the proceeds of any disposal or realisation of the whole or part of the goods stolen or of goods so representing the stolen goods; and

    (b) any other goods which directly or indirectly represent or have at any time represented the stolen goods in the hands of a handler of the stolen goods or any part of them as being the proceeds of any disposal or realisation of the whole or part of the stolen goods handled by him or of goods so representing them.

(3) But no goods shall be regarded as having continued to be stolen goods after they have been restored to the person from whom they were stolen or to other lawful possession or custody, or after that person and any other person claiming through him have otherwise ceased as regards those goods to have any right to restitution in respect of the theft.

(4) For purposes of the provisions of this Act relating to goods which have been stolen (including sub-ss (1)–(3) above) goods obtained in England or Wales or elsewhere either by blackmail or in the circumstances described in s 15(1) of

this Act shall be regarded as stolen; and 'steal', 'theft' and 'thief' shall be construed accordingly.

## Introduction

12-03    Section 22 represents a considerable extension of the pre-1968 offences and has been criticised for the breadth of its provisions, in particular, because some variants of the offence of handling amount to no more than inchoate offences in relation to the main TA offences.[1] For instance, where the goods have, in fact, been stolen 'to order' by A for disposal by B (the 'fence'), B would inevitably come within the terms of s 8 of the Accessories and Abettors Act 1861 as having aided, abetted, counselled or procured the original theft. Nevertheless, it was the view of the Criminal Law Revision Committee (CLRC) that the specific offence was necessary:

> Since thieves may be helped not only by buying the property, but also in other ways, such as facilitating its disposal, it seems right that the offence should extend to these kinds of assistance.[2]

The previous legislation had utilised the term 'receiving', without any definition of this term being provided. In any case, it was the view of the CLRC that the term was inappropriate, as the new offence was intended to be wider in scope than merely 'receiving'. After considering alternatives, which included 'dealing with stolen goods', the Committee decided on 'handling stolen goods'. This term would encompass receivers, as well as:

> ... those who knowingly convey stolen goods to any place after a theft, those who take charge of them and keep them on their premises or hide them on the approach of the police, those who negotiate for the sale of the goods and the like. The definition will also include a person who in the course of his otherwise innocent employment knowingly removes the goods from place to place, for example, a driver employed by dishonest transport owners. If the driver knows that the goods are stolen and that in conveying them he is helping in their disposal, it seems right that he should be guilty of the offence.[3]

## Mode of trial and sentence

12-04    The offence, under s 22, is triable either way by virtue of s 17(1) (read together with Sched 1) of the Magistrates' Courts Act (MCA) 1980. By virtue of the *Practice Note (Mode of Trial: Guidelines)* [1990] 1 WLR 1439 (revised 1995), cases of handling should be tried summarily, unless the court considers that one or more

---

1    Ashworth, p 409.

2    CLRC, *Eighth Report,* Cmnd 2977, 1966, para 127.

3    *Ibid,* para 128.

of the following features is present and that its sentencing powers are insufficient:

(a) dishonest handling of stolen property by a receiver who has commissioned the theft;

(b) the offence has professional hallmarks; or

(c) the property is of high value (at least £10,000).[4]

In terms of sentence, it is worth noting that compensation will not be ordered in situations where the property concerned is recovered undamaged, as in *Tyce*.[5] Here. the stolen property had been recovered and returned to the owner and the Court of Appeal quashed the compensation order that had been made.

12-05    The maximum penalty for handling is higher than that prescribed for theft, reflecting the view that a proportionately more severe sentence may be merited in some cases of handling, than for simple theft. This chimes with the judicial attitude that, if there were fewer receivers of stolen goods, there would be fewer thieves.[6] As the Court of Appeal put it, in *Shelton*:[7] '... handling is the more serious offence, carrying a heavier penalty because those who knowingly have dealings with thieves encourage stealing.' The CLRC, too, was of the opinion that the aim of their revision was 'to combat theft by making it more difficult and less profitable to dispose of stolen property'.[8] A long custodial sentence will, accordingly, be reserved for cases where there is evidence of large scale operations. The judicial view is illustrated by cases such as *Patel*.[9] Here, the offender had received goods valued at £160,000, part of a consignment worth about £1 m which had been stolen from the manufacturer. He, also, had a previous conviction for importing drugs. Lord Lane CJ, in upholding a sentence of four years, held:

> ... proper penalties for cases of handling will vary enormously according to the circumstances. At the top end of the scale come the cases where the handler provides an outlet for the proceeds of very substantial thefts or robberies, where the advantages to the thief of having such an outlet are very great and where accordingly the receiver or handler is indirectly encouraging the thefts to take place, and where also the profits to the handler are likewise very great, as plainly they were going to be here.[10]

12-06    On the other hand, where there are no aggravating circumstances and the court is of the view that the offence was merely one-off and opportunistic, a custodial

---

4    The revised guidelines remain unreported.

5    (1993) 15 Cr App R(S) 415.

6    See *Battams* (1979) 1 Cr App R(S) 15.

7    (1986) 83 Cr App R 379, p 384.

8    *Op cit*, CLRC, fn 2, para 127.

9    (1984) 6 Cr App R(S) 191.

10    *Ibid*, p 192.

sentence is unlikely. An example of this is *Khemlani*,[11] where the offender, a small businessman with no previous criminal record, had bought 350 watches which were part of stolen consignment. He had pleaded guilty and a fine of £1,000 was substituted for a sentence of imprisonment for three months.

12-07    A further point that may be noted at this stage relates to the common position that a defendant may be charged with the handling of the proceeds of several different thefts, burglaries or robberies arising out of several different occasions. If this is the case then, while it is proper for these offences to be dealt with at one and the same time, it is, nevertheless, necessary that there should be separate counts of handling for each occasion.[12]

## Scope

12-08    In the early days of the TA 1968, one issue that posed problems related to the number of offences contained within s 22. In *Griffiths v Freeman*,[13] it was argued that s 22(1) contains a total of 18 separate offences. This was rejected by Lord Parker CJ who held that the section constitutes a single offence of handling stolen goods. Some confusion was generated, however, by the *caveat* that his judgment was confined to proceedings in magistrates' courts only. The issue was resolved in *Sloggett*,[14] when the Court of Appeal expressed its agreement with the judgment in *Griffiths v Freeman*. This was, further, confirmed by the Court of Appeal, in *Nicklin*.[15] The appeal related to the manner in which the indictment had been drawn up.[16] It was held that:

> If the prosecution were to consider and provide for all possible forms of handling ... some 18 counts might be necessary. That would be absurd but the prosecution ought, generally speaking, to nail its colours to the mast of a particular form of handling. If there is any uncertainty about which form of handling, two counts will generally cover every form: one count for the first limb, dishonestly receiving, and a second for the second limb, dishonestly undertaking or assisting in the retention, removal, disposal or realisation, with arrangement to do those things if need be ... If there is any doubt about what form of handling is being charged ... particulars of the charge or charges should figure clearly in the indictment.[17]

12-09    In summary, therefore, s 22(1) contains a single offence containing two possible limbs:

---

11   (1981) 3 Cr App R(S) 208.
12   *Smythe* (1980) 72 Cr App R 8.
13   [1970] 1 WLR 659.
14   (1972) 55 Cr App R 532.
15   (1977) 64 Cr App R 205.
16   For a detailed discussion on the form of the indictment, see *Archbold*, paras 21–271.
17   (1977) 64 Cr App R 205, pp 208–09.

(a) dishonestly receiving stolen goods; or

(b) dishonestly undertaking or assisting in the retention, removal, disposal or realisation of stolen goods.

It was also held that the words 'or if he arranges to do so', at the end of s 22(1), apply to both limbs. One point made clear in all the cases on this issue (as in *Griffiths v Freeman*, above) is that the prosecution should make every attempt to ensure that full particulars are given, so that the defendant may be in the position to mount a proper defence. The fault element required for the offence is that of dishonesty and the offender must know, or believe, that the property is stolen.[18]

## Jurisdiction

12-10    Under s 24(1), the provisions of the Act apply whether or not the stealing occurred in England or Wales 'or elsewhere' provided that the stealing 'amounted to an offence where and at the time when the goods were stolen'. Moreover, by virtue of the Criminal Justice Act (CJA) 1993, the offence under s 22 is designated as a Group A offence. This means that, where any relevant event occurs within the jurisdiction, the English courts have the power to deal with the offence, regardless of the fact that the other relevant events may have occurred outside the jurisdiction. A relevant event would include any event that constitutes any of the elements of the offence. Thus, in a case where A stole goods in France, but the property was disposed of by a defendant in England, the English courts would have jurisdiction.[19] However, it must, first, be proved that the actions of A constituted an offence punishable in France, at the time, and evidence of the relevant French law would have to be strictly proved.

## The elements of the offence

### *Stolen goods*

12-11    It is worth noting from the outset that the concept of 'stolen goods' has an extended meaning provided by s 24 as a consequence of the statutory provisions of the Act. Goods will be considered to be stolen under a number of provisions. In addition to the basic theft offence (s 1), goods obtained through blackmail (s 21), by deception (ss 15, 15A) and through the dishonest retention of a monetary credit (s 24A) are included as 'stolen goods'.

---

18    See paras 12-50 and 12-58, below.

19    See, eg, *Forsyth* [1997] 2 Cr App R 299.

12-12    (a) *Goods*

The term 'goods' is interpreted in s 34(2)(b) as:

> 'goods', except insofar as the context otherwise requires, includes money and every other description of property except land, and includes things severed from the land by stealing.

This definition is narrower than that attached to 'property' in s 4 pertaining to the basic offence of theft. However, the cases seem to indicate that the courts have treated the definition of 'goods' as equivalent to that of 'property' in relation to things that can be the subject of the offence of handling. In relation to land, this does not pose a problem. Although land is exempted, provided it can be brought within the exceptions provided in s 4(2), it can be 'appropriated' and, accordingly, can be considered to be 'goods' which may be the subject of handling. Similarly, if the appropriation of property is made out in relation to wild flora and fauna in s 4(3) and (4), then this, too, may be the subject of handling.

12-13    A problem, however, arises in relation to 'things in action and other intangible property' in s 4(1).[20] A common example of a thing in action would be a debt (in other words, the property belonging to A would be A's right to be paid the sum of money owing to him) while an example of other intangible property would be intellectual property (for instance, copyright). This has not been specifically included in s 34(2)(b) as 'goods'. On one interpretation, this would be dealt with by the fact that s 34(2)(b) contains the phrase 'and every other description of property'. However, the issue is whether in the context of the offence, things in action should be excluded from the range of goods that may be the subject of handling. The pre-Act cases are not of much use due to the fact that under the Larceny Acts (LAs), the *actus reus* was that of 'receiving' and it had been held that it was not possible to receive things in action.

12-14    In *AG's Ref (No 4 of 1979)*,[21] the Court of Appeal confirmed the position that things in action can be handled. The court ruled that a bank account, being a debt due to the account holder, is a thing in action, which falls within the definition of goods and may, therefore, be goods which directly or indirectly represent stolen goods for the purposes of the offence of handling. It has to be said that cases of handling, which involve things in action and other intangible property, are bound to be rare. One example might be represented by cases such as *Forsyth*,[22] where a credit balance in a bank account might be regarded as stolen goods, if it represented the monetary proceeds of a theft. In such a case, if the defendant assists the thief in any of the proscribed ways, then this would amount to handling.

---

20   Things in action are often referred to as 'chose in action'; see, eg, *Preddy* [1996] AC 815.
21   [1981] 1 All ER 1193.
22   [1997] 2 Cr App R 299.

12-15    Moreover, many of these instances might now come within ss 15A and 24A. In particular, under s 24A(8), stolen goods 'include money which is dishonestly withdrawn from an account to which a wrongful credit has been made, but only to the extent that the money derives from the credit.' Consequently, it would be an offence to retain the wrongful credit and it may also, conceivably, amount to handling for another to withdraw the proceeds, or to assist the thief in doing so.[23] Both of these amendments (contained in the Theft (Amendment) Act 1996) were a response to the decision of the House of Lords in *Preddy*.[24] It may also be possible that, in situations of this nature, the 'money laundering' provisions of Pt III of the CJA 1988 may come into play. This may mean, in effect, that those cases which are difficult, if not impossible, to bring within the ambit of handling may be brought, instead, under the 1988 Act. A financial institution, for instance, a bank, accepting money for deposit or investment, where the money represents the proceeds of criminal activity, would run the risk of a conviction for laundering, in a situation where it might well be difficult for the prosecution to sustain a charge of handling. It is also worth noting the possible overlap with s 24(2) in relation to the handling of the proceeds of stolen goods.

12-16    (b) *Stolen*

It is an essential element of the offence under s 22 that the goods in question should be 'stolen goods'. It must be noted, however, that the conviction of the alleged thief is neither essential, nor conclusive, and it is not necessary that the thief be identified in every case. In *Forsyth*,[25] for instance, a conviction for handling was possible, even where the person alleged to be the thief had not been prosecuted, as he was outside the jurisdiction and could not be extradited. Similarly, situations may arise where there is some bar to the alleged thief being prosecuted, for instance, where he enjoys diplomatic immunity.

Nevertheless, it must be proved that the goods have, in fact, been stolen. Where the offender mistakenly believes that the goods he is dealing in are stolen, whereas, in fact, they are not, he could be convicted of an attempt to handle under the Criminal Attempts Act (CAA) 1981. This raises the issue of 'impossible' attempts.[26] In *Haughton v Smith*,[27] the House of Lords had ruled the offender could not be guilty of attempting to handle stolen goods since, at the time, those goods were in the possession of the police.[28] This ruling was nullified by s 1(2) of the CAA 1981:

> A person may be guilty of attempting to commit an offence ... even though the facts are such that the commission of the offence is impossible.[29]

---

23    See para 12-70, below.
24    [1996] AC 815.
25    [1997] 2 Cr App R 299.
26    See para 14-16, below.
27    [1975] AC 476.
28    See para 12-25, below.
29    See para 14-16, below.

12-17   The effect of this provision fell to be worked out in two further cases. In *Anderton v Ryan*,[30] Ryan bought a video recorder under circumstances which showed that she believed it to have been stolen. If it had been stolen, she would, of course, have been guilty of handling. However, there was no evidence to prove that it was, in fact, stolen. The decision of the House of Lords was that, despite s 1(2) of the 1981 Act, she could not be guilty, even of an attempt. However, in *Shivpuri*,[31] their Lordships accepted that their previous decision in *Anderton v Ryan* was wrong. Here the accused had been charged with an attempt to commit an offence under s 3(1) of the Misuse of Drugs Act 1971. He confessed to receiving and distributing what he believed to be an illegal drug, although it later turned out that the substance in question was not a drug at all. In upholding his conviction, the House of Lords held that the crucial element was his state of mind: 'What turns what would otherwise ... be an innocent act into a crime is the intent of the actor to commit an offence.'[32]

12-18       If a conviction for handling can only be sustained where the goods were stolen in the first place, it may be argued that, where the person who 'steals' the goods is a child under the age of 10 years, or someone who is held to be insane, anyone who receives the property from such a person cannot be guilty of handling, despite being fully aware of the facts. In *Walters v Lunt*,[33] the respondents were charged, under s 33(1) of the LA 1916, with receiving from their seven year old son goods which had been stolen. The Divisional Court held that, since the boy could not be found guilty of any criminal offence due to his age, any property taken by him could not be 'stolen', as required by s 33. However, the Divisional Court added that that anyone who received the property could be guilty of other forms of larceny. Under the TA 1968, an offender in the position of the parents, in *Walters v Lunt*, would have appropriated property belonging to another, intending permanently to deprive, it being immaterial under s 3(1) whether the offender has come by that property innocently, or even without stealing it.

Proof that the goods were stolen may take a number of forms:

(a) through the evidence of the thief;[34]

(b) where the thief has already been convicted, the conviction may be proved through s 74 of the Police and Criminal Evidence Act (PACE) 1984;

(c) alternatively, depending on the facts, circumstantial evidence may be admissible.[35]

---

30   [1985] AC 560.
31   [1987] AC 1.
32   p 22, *per* Lord Bridge.
33   [1951] 2 All ER 645.
34   *Reynolds* (1927) 20 Cr App R 125.
35   *Noon v Smith* (1964) 49 Cr App R 55.

12-19   (c) *Proceeds of stolen goods*

By virtue of s 24(2), goods are categorised as stolen goods, if they are the goods originally stolen, or parts of those goods. For instance, it would be sufficient if the defendant handled only the speakers of a stolen stereo system. In addition, anything that represents the proceeds of those stolen goods, in the hands of the thief or the receiver, would also be stigmatised as stolen goods.[36] Consider the following example:

> T steals a bicycle and exchanges this for a pair of roller skates with A, who knows that the bicycle is stolen. A, in turn, sells the bicycle for £60 to B, who is not aware that the bicycle has been stolen and is an innocent purchaser. A deposits the £60 in his bank account while, later, B exchanges the bicycle for a scooter belonging to C.

A may be convicted of handling. While B and C may lack the necessary *mens rea*, the bicycle is, and remains, stolen goods. The roller-skates represent stolen goods in the hands of the thief, within s 24(2)(a), while the £60 represents stolen goods in the hands of the receiver, within s 24(2)(b). On the other hand, the scooter does not become stolen goods, as it is not the proceeds of stolen goods in the hands of either the thief (T), or the handler (A). It must be emphasised that when B, in the example above, acquires the stolen bicycle and then exchanges it for the scooter, whether the scooter is categorised as stolen goods depends primarily on whether B knew that the bicycle was stolen in the first place. The scooter would be stolen goods if he did know; it would not be stolen goods if he did not know. This example illustrates the wide reach of the statutory provisions.

12-20   The difficulty of determining whether property acquired by the thief or handler comes within s 24(2) becomes particularly acute in those cases where stolen goods are converted into monetary form and are then deposited, or mixed with other funds, in a bank account. No difficulty arises where the bank account is a new one or where there is zero balance. The money deposited would amount to intangible property, as being a 'thing in action' and it would be 'stolen goods', under s 24(2), as being the proceeds of the original stolen goods. If, however, the account also contains other funds which have been lawfully obtained, then the question arises as to whether any money drawn out of this mixed account should be tainted as stolen goods. In civil law, this issue would arise in the context of whether the victim of the theft has a right to a claim on the mixed fund. If there is a fiduciary relationship between the parties (as between trustee and beneficiary), then such a claim may well be upheld in equity.[37] The accepted principle being that the victim has an equitable claim to a charge upon the mixed fund.[38]

---

36   In *Forsyth* [1997] 2 Cr App R 299, it was decided that the phrase 'in the hands of' meant 'in the possession or under the control of'.

37   McGhee, J, *Snell's Equity*, 30th edn, 2000, Sweet & Maxwell, para 13-29.

38   See, eg, *Clowes (No 2)* [1994] 2 All ER 316.

12-21     The problem, as it arises under the TA 1968, is illustrated in *AG's Ref (No 4 of 1979)*.[39] Here, the Court of Appeal held that a credit balance in a bank account could be goods which either directly, or indirectly, represent stolen goods under s 24(2). Crucially, it was also the opinion of the Court of Appeal that anyone who accepts a transfer of funds from another's account into his own account (through the receipt of a cheque, for instance), knowing that the funds represent the proceeds of stolen goods, is receiving stolen property, under s 22(1). This opinion was thrown into doubt by the House of Lords' decision in *Preddy*.[40] This was, briefly, to the effect that the money (or credit) that was being transferred represented a new thing in action, not one that has ever belonged to another.[41] Accordingly, the funds which are transferred are not the same funds in the original account. However, this must be viewed in the light of the decision in *Forsyth*.[42] Here, the appellant collected money from a bank in Switzerland, alleged to be the proceeds of a theft in England, and transferred it to another Swiss bank. A proportion was then transferred to an English bank and the balance, in cash, brought into England. The appellant was charged with handling and was convicted. Her appeal, however, came after the decision in Preddy and she sought to rely on it, to the effect that the transaction related to funds which could not be, as Lord Goff had ruled, identified as the property belonging to another. The Court of Appeal, however, ruled that the crucial issue was not whether the funds amounted to 'property belonging to another', but whether the funds 'represented' the property originally stolen. The court ruled that the words 'in the hands of the thief', in s 24(2)(a), meant in his possession or under his control. Despite the fact that the appellant had moved the funds in and out of different bank accounts, the person alleged to be the thief retained control of the funds. Accordingly, it was possible for the appellant to have handled these funds.[43]

12-22    (d) *Stolen under s 2*[44]

The consternation caused by the *Preddy* decision led, via proposals of the Law Commission, to the enactment of ss 15A and 24A.[44] Arguably, if similar facts were to re-occur, the proper charge would be under s 24A, for dishonestly retaining a stolen credit.[45]

---

39   (1981) 71 Cr App R 341.

40   [1996] AC 815.

41   For a full discussion of *Preddy* [1996] AC 815, see para 8-29, below.

42   [1997] 2 Cr App R 299.

43   See the 'Commentary' on this case in [1997] Crim LR 589.

44   Law Commission, *Report on Offences of Dishonesty: Money Transfers*, 1996, Law Commission, No 243.

45   See para 12-70, below, for s 24A and para 8-36 above for s 15A.

12-23    (e) *When goods cease to be stolen*

As far as the requirement that the goods must be 'stolen', it is worth noting the specific provisions in s 24(3). Under this provision, goods cease to be regarded as 'stolen' in the following situations:

(a) where the goods in question 'have been restored to the person from whom they were stolen';

(b) when the goods have been 'restored' to 'other lawful possession or custody'; or

(c) when the person from whom the goods were stolen, as well as any other person claiming through him, ceases 'to have any right to restitution in respect of the theft'.

12-24    The drafting of this sub-section is clumsy. Goods recovered by the police and now in their custody would cease to be 'stolen', in the second limb above, and it is somewhat inappropriate to speak of goods, now in the hands of the police, as having been 'restored'. Moreover, confusion arises as to what precisely is meant by the phrase 'person from whom they were stolen'. Presumably, this must be read in conjunction with the s 5 definition of 'property belonging to another'. If this is so, then 'the person from whom they were stolen' must mean the person who had possession or control of the goods at the time of the theft. In reality, this will not be problematic due to the second limb, above. Obviously, restoration may be to an agent, provided the agent is acting with proper authority. In the case of the police, the element of public policy would displace the fact that the police may not have received the authority of the owner of the goods, or the person from whom they were stolen. In any case, anything less than a full and deliberate exercise of control over the recovered goods cannot be said to be 'restoration. For instance, a telephone call to the owner of the goods telling him where the goods have been left could hardly be said to be a proper restoration.

12-25    As indicated above, the element of restoration would also be satisfied if the stolen goods have been recovered by the police. The problems that may arise in this connection are illustrated by *AG's Ref (No 1 of 1974)*.[46] A police officer came upon a car containing a quantity of new clothes which he suspected of having been stolen. He immobilised the car by removing its rotor arm and kept it under observation. The defendant returned to the car and attempted to drive it away. He was questioned by the police officer and, as his answers were unconvincing, he was arrested and later charged with handling. The trial judge ruled that the goods had ceased to be stolen as the police officer had taken lawful custody of them and he withdrew the case from the jury. The Court of Appeal came to the conclusion that the trial judge had been wrong to conclude, as a matter of law, that the goods had been taken into possession by the police officer. This was a

---

46   (1974) 59 Cr App R 203.

matter that should have been left to the jury. Instead, he should have directed them that, if they came to the conclusion that the police officer had intended to assume control over the goods, then he had taken lawful possession and the prosecution would fail. However, if their conclusion was that he was merely keeping the goods under observation and that the immobilisation of the car was so that the driver should not be able to get away without being questioned, then the goods were still to be regarded as stolen:

> It depended primarily on the intentions of the police officer. If the police officer seeing these goods in the back of the car had made up his mind that he would take them into custody, that he would reduce them into his possession or control, take charge of them so that they could not be removed and so that he would have the disposal of them, then it would be a perfectly proper conclusion to say that he had taken possession of the goods. On the other hand, if the truth of the matter is that he was of an entirely open mind at that stage as to whether the goods were to be seized or not and was of an entirely open mind as to whether he should take possession of them or not, but merely stood by so that when the driver of the car appeared he could ask certain questions of that driver ... then there is no reason whatever to suggest that he had taken the goods into his possession or control.[47]

12-26   The law, therefore, leaves the matter to be settled by raising a collateral issue, that being the intentions and the conduct of the police. This may not be a satisfactory state of affairs. It is not very likely that a police witness would testify that he had intended to take custody and control of the stolen goods when such an admission would destroy the possibility of a conviction. However, the position is consistent with the principles underlying the discussion of abandoned property[48] and with decisions, such as *Parker v British Airways Board*,[49] where it was held that property would not be regarded as abandoned if it was shown that there was a continued intention to treat the property as being in possession.

12-27   A decision along the same lines is that of *Greater London Metropolitan Police Comr v Streeter*.[50] A thief stole cartons of cigarettes from his employers and loaded them onto a lorry owned by them. A security guard employed by them realised they were stolen. He initialled the cartons, as a way of identifying them, and then called the police. The police followed the lorry and noticed that some of the marked cartons of cigarettes were delivered to a shop owned by the appellant. Upon questioning by the police, the appellant admitted to knowing that the cigarettes had been stolen. The defence argued that a charge of handling could not be made out. This was because the security guard (by initialling the cartons of cigarettes), and the police (by keeping them under observation), had taken lawful possession of them. The goods had, therefore, been 'restored.' This

---

47   (1974) 59 Cr App R 203, p 208.
48   See para 2-95, above.
49   [1982] 1 All ER 834.
50   (1980) 71 Cr App R 113.

submission was accepted by the magistrates who ruled that s 24(3) had come into play. Upon appeal, the Divisional Court concluded that this was wrong. Neither the security guard nor the police had *intended* to exercise either possession or control. They were merely waiting to see what happened next. At the time that the appellant received them, the cigarettes were still stolen goods:

> The security officer never in fact took physical possession of the cartons of cigarettes by writing initials on them. He was not thereby exercising ... any control over the goods. Nor was it then [his] intention ... to restore the stolen goods to his employers from whom they had been stolen. Both he and the police intended the goods to remain in the possession of the thief and under his control ... all the police did was to follow the thief in order to discover what he did with the goods but not in any way to control or supervise the disposal of the goods.[51]

12-28   The result of decisions, such as *AG's Ref (No 1 of 1974)*, *Parker v British Airways Board* and *Streeter*, is that whether restoration has occurred becomes a question of fact in each case.[52]

What would the position be if the thief handed in goods to the police? Would this be a case of goods being reduced into 'lawful possession or custody'? The answer is not immediately obvious. In the pre-Act decision of *King*,[53] police officers investigating the theft of a fur coat, went to a flat where they met X. He initially denied the theft, but when he realised they were about to conduct a search, he admitted the theft and produced the coat wrapped in a parcel. The police were examining the parcel when the appellant telephoned and X was heard to tell him to 'come along as arranged'. When he arrived, the police were in hiding and observed X handing over the fur coat. On appeal, it was argued that the police had, in fact, already taken possession of the stolen goods. The Court of Criminal Appeal held, however, that the police had not taken possession and, so, the goods continued to be 'stolen'. The justification for this appears to be that the police were merely examining the goods, prior to making a decision. Nonetheless, the fact remains that the goods had been handed in to the police by the thief who had, moreover, confessed to the theft. It is difficult to see how the prosecution could claim that the goods remained stolen. On the other hand, unless the decision is followed, it would prejudice many undercover police operations aimed at the entrapment of the receivers of stolen property.[54]

12-29   The third category of cases where goods cease to be stolen is where the person from whom they were originally stolen ceases to have 'any right to restitution in respect of the theft'. The justification for this provision was provided by the CLRC:

---

51   (1980) 71 Cr App R 113, p 118, *per* Ackner LJ.
52   See, also, the older decision of *Villensky* [1892] 2 QB 597, p 599.
53   [1938] 2 All ER 662.
54   See, eg, *Christou* [1992] 4 All ER 559.

This is because, if the person who owned the goods when they were stolen no longer has any title to them, there will be no reason why the goods should continue to have the taint of being stolen goods.[55]

This, inevitably, raises issues of ownership and restitution under the civil law. One instance of this may arise in situations where the alleged handler claims that he was a purchaser in good faith who had no knowledge that the goods were, in fact, stolen. In civil law, as far as legal title is concerned, this claim may be defeated by the rule of *nemo dat quod non habet*, as incorporated into s 21 of the Sale of Goods Act (SOGA) 1979:

... where goods are sold by a person who is not their owner, and who does not sell them under the authority or with the consent of the owner, the buyer acquires no better title to the goods than the seller had, unless the owner of the goods is by his conduct precluded from denying the seller's authority to sell.

12-30   Two points need be noted. First, this provision does *not* mean that the purchaser of goods which are later proved to have been stolen, is automatically to be considered a handler, since he may well lack the necessary *mens rea*. Secondly, even here, there are a number of statutory exceptions.[56] In particular, under s 23 of the 1979 Act, where the seller of the goods has a voidable title, but that title has not been avoided at the time of the sale, the buyer acquires a good title, provided he buys in good faith and without notice of the seller's defect of title.

## Handling

12-31   As pointed out above, the term 'handling' was specifically chosen as being wider in scope than the term 'receiving' that had been employed in the previous legislation. Handling is, in fact, a shorthand way of referring to the various ways in which the *actus reus* of the offence may be committed, under s 22(1). In *Bloxham*,[57] Lord Bridge was of the opinion, albeit *obiter*, that the sub-section created two distinct offences: (a) receiving the goods or arranging to do so; or (b) undertaking or assisting in their retention, removal, disposal or realisation by or for the benefit of another, or arranging to do so. The better view, now, is that s 22(1) contains one offence which might be committed in several different ways.[58] Nonetheless, the *dictum* of Lord Bridge serves as a useful reminder of the principle, laid down in the earlier case of *Nicklin*,[59] that as a rule of best practice, indictments should indicate which of the two main forms of handling is being specified. The *Bloxham* case is also an authority for the proposition that the words 'by or for the benefit of another person' do not apply to receiving or arranging to receive.

---

55   *Op cit*, CLRC, fn 2, para 139.
56   See the SOGA 1979, ss 21(2) and 22.
57   [1983] 1 AC 109.
58   See, *inter alia*, *Griffiths v Freeman* [1970] 1 WLR 659; *Sloggett* (1972) 55 Cr App 532.
59   (1977) 64 Cr App R 205.

12-32    (a) *Receiving*

No definition is provided within the Act for 'receiving'. The case law under the LA 1916 had taken the logical position that receiving involved the taking of possession or control of goods in some way,[60] although it was not essential that there should be a physical handling. It was also possible for the possession or control to be joint and not strictly exclusive.[61] An obvious case of this would be where there was doubt as to whether the thief had totally relinquished control over the stolen goods to the handler. It is submitted that, as the same term was used under the old legislation, so the old cases are still good law. Consequently, situations may arise where the defendant might have handled the goods physically, without being in control of them or, alternatively, the defendant may have been in control of the goods, without physically handling them. Both situations would be covered by the section.

12-33        Further, it was not necessary for the defendant to have personally received the goods himself. The goods may have been left at his premises and, subsequently, found there, or they may have been received by an employee or agent (for instance, by a spouse). Provided the requisite *mens rea* is established, the offence is made out. However, it is not enough that the defendant knew that goods were stolen: possession or control, howsoever defined, must still be proved. In *Hobson v Impett*, Lord Goddard CJ ruled:

> It is not the law that, if a man knows goods are stolen and puts his hands on them, that in itself makes him guilty of receiving, because it does not follow that he is taking them into his control. The control may still be in the thief ... It cannot be the law that merely because a man picks up goods which he knows are stolen he is receiving the goods.[62]

12-34    It is essential, bearing in mind the above permutations, that jury directions are clear and unambiguous. This is especially the case, where the only evidence is that the stolen goods were found on the defendant's premises (where no offence is made out) and where the defendant's receipt was only temporary, or where he obtained no discernible profit (where the offence may be made out).

12-35    (b) *Arranging to receive; arranging to undertake or assist*

The words 'or if he arranges to do so' apply to both limbs of s 22(1). This constitutes a substantive offence and may be regarded as a catch-all provision that deals with those situations where preparatory arrangements have been made, but which are not enough to constitute an attempt to receive. Similarly, this would cover occasions where a conspiracy charge would not be possible, perhaps because the arrangements were made with an innocent party. Conversely, arrangements made to receive goods that have not (yet) been stolen

---

60    *Wiley* (1850) 2 Den 37; *Watson* [1916] 2 KB 385.
61    *Frost* (1964) 48 Cr App R 284.
62    (1957) 41 Cr App R 138.

would not be covered while, if the arrangements were made with someone with the necessary *mens rea*, this would amount to conspiracy to steal as well as to handle.[63]

12-36    The provisions of undertaking and assisting take the law very far, indeed, *arranging* to undertake or assist pushes the reach of the Act even further. A mere arrangement to do any of the specified acts would appear to be sufficient. Nonetheless, it is submitted that, if the necessary *mens rea* could be proved, it would normally be the case that a proper charge would be for conspiracy instead.

12-37    (c) *Undertaking or assisting*

This part of the offence focuses culpability on the activities of those persons upon whom thieves rely. In *Tokeley-Parry*,[64] the Court of Appeal began by pointing out that the type of mischief at which s 22 was aimed was to combat theft, by making it more difficult and less profitable to dispose of stolen property. To achieve this end, the definition of handling had been extended to include, not only the buying of stolen property, but also other ways, such as facilitating its disposal. Griew describes this best as follows:

> Once he has accomplished his theft, the thief faces major problems for which he may need all manner of facilities. The goods may need to be stored. They may have to be carried to a place of safety or to a purchaser. Gold and silver articles may require melting down. Stolen cars require new number plates and registration documents and the execution of skilled work to conceal their identity. Contact must be made with 'fences' and negotiations conducted. Anyone who assists in or undertakes any of these or similar operations for the thief or for another handler is guilty ... The net is flung very wide.[65]

12-38    Two points should be noted. First, a mere failure to reveal to the police the presence of stolen property on the defendant's premises does not amount to assisting, although it may be evidence of it.[66] Secondly, the prosecution must bring the impugned activity within the ambit of the words 'retention, removal, disposal or realisation'. The meaning of the 'retention' was held, in *Pitchley*, to be a matter of law and it is submitted that this should be the case with the remaining activities as well.

12-39    (d) *By or for the benefit of another person*

The words 'by or for the benefit of another person' do not apply to receiving or arranging to receive, but only to undertaking or assisting. The words, therefore, qualify the four specified activities: retention, removal, disposal or realisation. This was made clear in *Bloxham*. Lord Bridge, in the House of Lords, drew a

---

63    *Park* (1987) 87 Cr App R 164.
64    [1999] Crim LR 578.
65    Griew, para 15-21.
66    See para 12-60, below.

clear distinction between those situations where the activities of the defendant have benefited himself and those where the activities have benefited another:

> The offence can be committed in relation to any one of [the four specified activities] in one or other of two ways. First, the offender may himself undertake the activity for the benefit of another person. Secondly, the activity may be undertaken by another person and the offender may assist him ... The category of other persons contemplated by the sub-section is subject to the same limitations in whichever way the offence is committed.[67]

12-40 The second way, referred to above by Lord Bridge, is neatly illustrated by the recent case of *Tokeley-Parry*.[68] The defendant was charged under the second limb of handling. He had approached P and, in effect, commissioned him to smuggle antiquities out of Egypt. These antiquities were disguised as crude replicas and, when they were taken to the defendant's workshop, they were restored to their original splendour. The defendant was found guilty, but appealed on the basis that P could not be said to be 'another person'. The appeal was dismissed. Obviously, the handling was not *'for the benefit* of another person', as in *Bloxham*. Instead, the charge related to assisting in the removal of the stolen property 'by another person'.

12-41 (e) *Retention*

The word 'retention', in *Pitchley*, was accorded its dictionary definition, as being 'keep possession of, not lose, continue to have'.[69] The facts of the case were that the defendant had received a sum of money from his son. He, then, paid this money into his savings account on his son's behalf (and, obviously, for his son's benefit). On his own evidence, some 48 hours later, he realised that the money had been stolen but, nonetheless, made no attempt to withdraw the money from the account or to return it to the owner, before being visited by the police four days later. The Court of Appeal held that his conduct in permitting the money to remain in his account and under his control was sufficient to constitute retention. Moreover, the court went on to hold, since the construction of the word 'retention' was a question of law and where the defendant had admitted keeping possession and under his control, it was not necessary to leave to the jury the question as to whether that amounted to retention. This decision has been criticised.[70] The stolen property was, after all, no longer the money; if anything, this was now a 'thing in action'. This thing in action was the proceeds of the stolen property, that is, the money and, therefore, in law rightfully belonged to its original owner. By keeping it in his account, the defendant was, in effect, appropriating it within the terms of s 3(2). Accordingly, he was the thief and not the handler. It is submitted, however, that these criticisms are based on

---

67  [1983] 1 AC 109, pp 113–14.
68  [1999] Crim LR 578.
69  (1972) 57 Cr App R 30.
70  See Griew, para 15-23 (fn 62); Smith, JC, para 13-32 (fn 3).

a pre-*Preddy* understanding of the law.[71] Since the House of Lords decision in *Preddy*, it is clear that a defendant who wrongfully retains the credit in his account is to be treated as a handler and not as the thief.[72]

12-42    The case law has focussed attention on whether it could be said that those who merely use stolen property or allow it to be kept on the premises, come within the ambit of the section, even if they are aware that the goods are stolen. In *Sanders*,[73] the defendant admitted using goods in his father's garage. The goods were later discovered to be stolen and the father was charged with dishonestly handling them by receiving and the defendant with assisting in their retention. The jury had been directed that, if they were satisfied that the defendant had used the goods, knowing or believing them to be stolen, then he would be guilty of the offence, as they had been in his control or possession. He was convicted and appealed. The Court of Appeal, elaborated on the *Pitchley* decision in quashing the conviction:

> The mere use of the goods knowing them to be stolen is not enough. It must be proved that in some way the accused was assisting in the retention of the goods by concealing them, or making them more difficult to identify, or by holding them pending their ultimate disposal, or by some other act that was part of the chain of the dishonest handling.

12-43    The case of *Kanwar* serves as an illustration of the kinds of activity that extend beyond mere use.[74] The police searched the defendant's house during her absence and discovered property, later proved to be the proceeds of a number of burglaries. When the house was searched a second time, the defendant was present and said that there was no stolen property there. She was then questioned about specific items, but she lied and said that they belonged to her. She appealed against her conviction on the grounds that her verbal representations could not amount to assisting in retention. The Court of Appeal dismissed the appeal. Assistance in retention need not be restricted to physical acts, nor need the assistance be successful. The defendant had lied in order to protect her husband; she had done so dishonestly and for his benefit. She was, therefore, assisting in the retention of the stolen property.

12-44    Nonetheless, there has to be clear evidence. In *Coleman*,[75] it was held that assisting meant helping or encouraging, amongst other things. There had to be affirmative evidence of this. If the evidence was circumstantial, the jury should be properly directed as to whether the necessary inferences could be drawn.

12-45    (f) *Removal, disposal or realisation*

The approach of the courts in the cases above of using the dictionary meaning of 'retention' ought to be applied, also, to 'removal, disposal or realisation'

---

71  *Preddy* [1996] AC 815.
72  See para 2-93 for further discussion.
73  (1982) 75 Cr App R 84.
74  (1982) 75 Cr App R 87.
75  [1986] Crim LR 56.

Accordingly, removal would involve carrying or transporting stolen goods. It would almost certainly be the case, however, that a defendant who transported stolen goods would also be assisting in their retention. In *Tokeley-Parry* (above), the defendant had commissioned another to smuggle antiquities out of Egypt and had, therefore, assisted another in the removal of the stolen goods.

12-46    In *Bloxham* (above), the defendant had innocently purchased a car which he later came to suspect must have been stolen. He then sold it on to an unidentified person at a bargain price. While it was agreed that this amounted to a 'realisation' of the stolen property, it was a realisation for the benefit of the defendant himself. Implicit in the opinion of the House of Lords is the clear overlap between the words 'disposal' and 'realisation'. However, it is submitted that, while realisation carries the suggestion that something of value has been obtained in return for the goods, no such connotation need apply to 'disposal'. So, for instance, a defendant, who has assisted the thief by destroying part of the goods to avoid detection, could be said to have disposed of them.

12-47    (g) *Handling by omission*

The general principle under the common law, that an omission is not culpable, applies here. Consequently, while it may be conceivable for a defendant to assist the thief by mere inactivity, no offence is committed, unless the defendant is under some duty to act. Moreover, the words 'receiving', 'assisting', 'undertaking' and 'arranging', all suggest positive actions. Nevertheless, the issue was raised in the case of *Brown*.[76] The defendant was charged with three counts of (a) burglary, (b) handling stolen goods, in that he received them, and (c) handling stolen goods, in that he assisted in their retention. The facts were that a cafe had been broken into and a number of items, including cigarettes, had been stolen. The defendant, when questioned by the police, denied any knowledge of the theft and told the police to, 'Get lost'. Some of these cigarettes were later found at the defendant's flat. Evidence was given that the defendant knew of the presence of the stolen cigarettes. The jury were directed in such a way that seemed to indicate that his knowledge of the presence of the cigarettes was sufficient for him to be guilty of assisting by retention. He was acquitted of the first two counts, but convicted on the third. The Court of Appeal began by pointing out that a mere failure to tell the police was incapable of amounting to the offence of assisting in retention, even if coupled with the words 'Get lost'. It was true that his failure to reveal to the police the presence of the stolen cigarettes in his flat assisted the actual thief. But, there was no duty in English law to give information to the police. Did this mean that the conviction ought to be quashed? The Court of Appeal held that it did not. Lord Parker CJ held that, on the contrary, his conduct amounted to permitting the stolen goods to remain in his flat, in the sense that he provided 'accommodation' for the stolen goods, in

---

76    [1970] 1 QB 105.

order to assist the thief to retain them. As has been pointed out, such a decision comes very close to ruling that a mere omission to remove goods, or to reveal their presence, is sufficient to constitute the offence.[77]

## The relationship between handling and theft

12-48   It must be noted that the handling must be 'otherwise than in the course of the stealing'. At first impression, this rules out the possibility of the defendant being simultaneously the thief, as well as the handler. However, as pointed out by Lord Scarman, in *Dolan*, a thief may be convicted of theft, as well as handling, if the evidence warrants such a conclusion:

> If the defendant's handling of the goods occurs only in the course of the stealing, he cannot be found guilty of handling by receiving; ... But, if he handles them later, that is, after the stealing, he commits an offence under the sub-section. It is, therefore, perfectly possible for a man to be guilty of stealing and receiving the same goods.[78]

If, on the evidence, the handling has occurred only in the course of the theft, then a charge for handling would be misconceived. On the other hand, if the handling occurs at some later point, the defendant may be convicted of both offences.

12-49       Despite this guidance, the problem still remains of determining when the theft ends and the handling commences; this is difficult, in the context of continuing transactions. Further guidance has been provided in the case of *Atakpu and Abrahams*,[79] where it was held that appropriation, for the purposes of theft, continued as long as the thief was 'on the job'. The impact of these decisions is to the effect that the matter becomes one of evidence and proof.[80] A further consideration is that the handler is, by definition, also a thief. This is because receiving property stolen during an earlier theft invariably constitutes a further appropriation of it.[81] Therefore, another factor to be considered is the discretion as to which charge to prefer, or whether to consider them as alternatives. It is submitted that *Shelton* correctly sets out the position to be adopted:

> First, that the long established practice of charging theft and handling as alternatives should continue whenever there is a real possibility, not a fanciful

---

77   Smith, JC, para 13-31.

78   (1976) 62 Cr App R 36, p 39.

79   [1994] QB 69.

80   There are at least two other reasons why the issue of when the theft ends is relevant: first, in relation to the question of the jurisdiction of the courts, and secondly, in cases of robbery, whether the accompanying violence occurs at the time of stealing. See para 3-19 above (in relation to robbery) and para 2-57 (in relation to the issue of appropriation as a continuing act).

81   *Stapylton v O'Callaghan* [1973] 2 All ER 782.

one, that at trial the evidence might support one rather than the other. Secondly, that there is a danger that juries may be confused by reference to second or later appropriations since the issue in every case is whether the defendant has, in fact, appropriated property belonging to another. If he has done so, it is irrelevant how he came to make the appropriation provided it was in the course of theft. Thirdly, that a jury should be told that a handler can be a thief, but he cannot be convicted of being both a thief and a handler. Fourthly, that handling is the more serious offence, carrying a heavier penalty because those who knowingly have dealings with thieves encourage stealing. Fifthly, in the unlikely event of the jury not agreeing amongst themselves whether theft or handling has been proved, they should be discharged. Finally, and perhaps most importantly, both judges and counsel when directing and addressing juries should avoid intellectual subtleties which some jurors may have difficulty in grasping; the golden rule should be, 'Keep it short and simple'.[82]

## Knowledge or belief that the goods are stolen

12-50    It must be proved that the defendant knew or believed that the goods were stolen. Further, this state of mind must coincide with the *actus reus*. When that will be is, of course, dependent upon the particulars of the charge. For instance, if the allegation is 'receiving', then the material time will be the time when he received the goods.[83] In other situations, it may be sufficient if the required state of mind can only be proved to exist at a later point in time. For instance, to continue in assisting or undertaking, or making arrangements for one of the specified activities, *after* discovering that the goods were stolen, would be sufficient. There is no need for the prosecution to be compelled to prove that the *mens rea* existed at the start of these activities.[84] This is particularly important when assessing the impact of s 3(2) of the Act. This declares that a *bona fide* purchaser of goods, who acts in good faith, cannot be considered a thief, if a defect in title becomes apparent later. This protection, however, applies only to theft and cannot be called upon for assistance by a handler who, at the material time, knows or believes that the goods are stolen. In situations where the *bona fide* purchaser, who *now* knows that the goods are stolen, deals with those goods, it is clear that he cannot be proceeded against for theft. Would it be possible for him to be proceeded against as a handler for the actual thief? It is submitted that this would be absurd. The policy that lies behind s 3(2) ought to be applied equally to handling.

12-51    Further, in accordance with general principles, the defendant's knowledge or belief that the goods were stolen need not extend to the identity of the thief or the victim, or even to the nature of the stolen goods. As far as the identity of the

---

82   (1986) 83 Cr App R 379.
83   *Brook* (1993) 60 C App R 14.
84   *Ibid.*

victim is concerned, however, in *Gregory*,[85] the Court of Appeal's view was that, if the property involved was of a common or indistinct type, it would be advisable to name the owner in the particulars of the charge. The rationale of this being that, unless ownership was disclosed, the defendant might have difficulty in understanding fully the nature of the case he had to meet. As far as the nature of the goods is concerned, the defendant's mistaken belief of the true nature of the goods (stolen books instead of stolen diamonds, for instance) would not avail him, if the prosecution could succeed in proving that he knew or believed that the goods were stolen, whatever he thought they were.[86] On the other hand, if he mistakenly thought that the goods were stolen diamonds when, in fact, they were books legitimately acquired, he may be proceeded against for an attempt to handle the stolen diamonds.[87]

12-52      The test for knowledge is clearly a subjective one: the prosecution must prove that the defendant knew the goods to be stolen. Actual knowledge, rather than constructive knowledge, is required. The LA 1916 had used the word 'knowing' by itself and the question which has arisen relates to the possible advantage of the present inclusion of belief and whether this element, in fact, imports an objective element. The CLRC intended, by these words, to extend the *mens rea* to deal with those cases of wilful blindness, which are often, erroneously, thought to allow a defendant to escape liability. In fact, the case law in a number of different contexts indicates that, in the majority of such instances, the courts have been more than capable of interpreting 'knowledge' to encompass a defendant who is wilfully blind.[88] Nevertheless, in the opinion of the CLRC:

> It is a serious defect of the present law that actual knowledge that the property was stolen must be proved. Often the prosecution cannot prove this ... The man who buys goods at a ridiculously low price from an unknown seller whom he meets in a public house may not know that the goods were stolen, and he may take the precaution of asking no questions. Yet it may be clear on the evidence that he believes the goods were stolen. In such cases, the prosecution may fail (rightly, as the law now stands) for want of proof of guilty knowledge.[89]

12-53   The irony is that the case law, under s 22, has been consistently of the view that wilful blindness is not sufficient. In *Griffiths*, the defendant had been charged with handling a pair of candlesticks stolen from a church. The Court of Appeal ruled (*per* James LJ) that:

> To direct the jury that the offence is committed if the defendant, suspecting that the goods were stolen, deliberately shut his eyes to the circumstances as an alternative to knowing or believing the goods were stolen, is a misdirection.[90]

---

85   (1972) 56 Cr App R 441.
86   *McCullum* (1973) 57 Cr App R 645.
87   See para 14-16, below, on attempting the impossible.
88   See, eg, *Westminster CC v Croyalgrange Ltd* (1986) 83 Cr App R 155.
89   *Op cit*, CLRC, fn 2, para 130.
90   (1974) 60 Cr App R 14.

12-54   Consequently, a direction is defective if the jury forms the impression that a set of suspicious circumstances imposed a duty on the defendant to inquire before acting and that his failure to inquire or investigate was sufficient, of itself, to be treated as knowledge or belief. The question posed earlier as to the precise function served by 'belief' has posed problems in the context of directions to the jury. An attempt was made to distinguish 'knowledge' and 'belief' in *Hall*:

12-55       We think that a jury should be directed along these lines. A man may be said to know that goods are stolen when he is told by someone with first hand knowledge (someone such as the thief or the burglar) that such is the case. Belief, of course, is something short of knowledge. It may be said to be the state of mind of a person who says to himself: 'I cannot say I know for certain that these goods are stolen, but there can be no other reasonable conclusion in the light of all the circumstances, in the light of all that I have heard and seen.' Either of those two states of mind is enough to satisfy the words of the statute. The second is enough (that is, belief) even if the defendant says to himself: 'Despite all that I have seen and all that I have heard, I refuse to believe what my brain tells me is obvious.' What is not enough, of course, is mere suspicion: 'I suspect that these goods may be stolen, but it may be, on the other hand, that they are not.' That state of mind, of course, does not fall within the words 'knowing or believing'.[91]

12-56   The words, intended as a guideline to the clarity of jury directions, are, on the contrary, replete with potential confusion. Whoever these suggested guidelines were aimed at, it is certain that they were not aimed at the average jury, or for that matter, the average trial judge and it is not surprising that the case has been criticised. In *Forsyth*,[92] the Court of Appeal doubted whether it was helpful to attempt an exposition of 'belief' for the jury's benefit. Instead, the court suggested a return to an earlier ruling by Lord Lane CJ in *Moys*:

       It must be proved that the defendant was aware of the theft or that he believed the goods to be stolen. Suspicion that they were stolen, even coupled with the fact that he shut his eyes to the circumstances, is not enough, although these matters may be taken into account ... in deciding whether or not the necessary knowledge or belief existed.[93]

12-57   This would certainly be in accordance with the general impact of s 8 of the CJA 1967:

       A court or jury, in determining whether a person has committed an offence ...

       (b) shall decide whether he did intend or foresee that result by reference to all the evidence, drawing such inferences from the evidence as appear proper in the circumstances.

       It also draws attention to the fact that the defendant's suspicion is not, of itself, sufficient to prove his belief, even though it may be a factor to be taken into account when deciding the issue.

---

91  (1985) 81 Cr App R 260, p 264.

92  [1997] 2 Cr App R 299.

93  (1984) 79 Cr App R 72.

Since it is the prosecution that bears the burden of proof and the requisite standard of proof is beyond reasonable doubt, this means that a defendant can be said to believe that goods are stolen, only if there are no serious or substantial doubts as to that fact. On a more pragmatic level, it appears that the advice given in *Reader*[94] is particularly apposite, that is, that the words 'knowledge or belief' are ordinary words to be left to the jury without any attempt to explain them.[95]

## Dishonesty

12-58   It would appear that, although the definition of 'dishonestly' in s 2 is aimed at the basic theft offence, the same test applies, equally, to s 22, there being no special test applicable.[96] However, in *Sloggett*,[97] it was held that a 'dishonest' handling must be established. Consequently, the test being subjective, the possibility may arise of a defendant who comes into possession innocently and then handles it; no offence would be committed. This possibility was explored in *Roberts*:

> A person may come into possession of stolen property innocently and the test for that would be normally as to what he did with it. If, for example, he had taken it straight to the police and said, 'I have found this in my motor car,' then the question would plainly arise because nobody would say that a person acting in that fashion was acting dishonestly if it was true.[98]

12-59   In *Roberts* itself, two valuable paintings were stolen in the course of a burglary and the insurance company concerned had offered a reward for their return. Some months later the defendant contacted the company and told them that they had the paintings. He was arrested when he handed the paintings over. The Court of Appeal, in upholding his conviction for handling, was of the view that, on the facts, it was impossible for the defendant to claim that he had not been acting dishonestly and that, therefore, it had not been necessary for the trial judge to provide the recommended direction laid down in *Ghosh*:

> We start with the proposition that, for the subjective test to arise, somewhere along the line the defendant has to say, 'I did not know that anybody would regard what I was doing as dishonest.' We have come to the conclusion that no one can properly say that, if what he is doing is receiving stolen property knowing it to be stolen and then trying to sell it ... At no stage in the present case did this appellant say on the facts, 'I received the stolen goods and was trying to

---

94   (1978) 66 Cr App R 33.

95   See, also, *Harris* (1987) 84 Cr App R 75; '"knowledge or belief" are words of ordinary usage and in many cases no elaboration was needed', *per* Lawton LJ.

96   See *Ghosh* [1982] QB 1053; para 2-18 above.

97   [1972] 1 QB 430.

98   (1987) 84 Cr App R 117.

sell them for my own profit, but I did not know that anybody would think that dishonest.' He had never raised the problem and unless the problem is properly raised it does not seem to us that it is necessary for the trial judge to embark on the full *Ghosh* direction.[99]

This ruling is significant as, it is submitted, the question of dishonesty is a question of fact for the jury under s 22, just as it is under s 1 of the Act.

## Proof of guilty knowledge or belief

12-60    As indicated above, mere suspicion by the handler that goods are stolen would not be enough. The prosecution has the burden of proving the required elements of guilty knowledge or belief, in the same way as with any other offence. With regard to handling, however, a number of specific evidentiary devices are available to the prosecution. Some of these are in statutory form, within the Act itself, and are derived from similar provisions in the LA 1916. Others are derived from what are sometimes termed rebuttable presumptions of law, or from general common law rules relating to admissibility of evidence. These are summarised below, but it must be noted that such evidence is not automatically admissible. It will be dependent on the discretion of trial judges whether the evidence has sufficient relevance (in the context of probative value) that it ought to be admitted. This is crucial because such evidence may be thought to unfairly prejudice the defendant.[100] If admitted, it is vital that the jury is properly directed on the inferences that may be drawn from the evidence.

12-61    (a) *Evidence admissible under s 27*

(3) Where a person is being proceeded against for handling stolen goods (but not for any other offence than handling stolen goods), then at any stage of the proceedings, if evidence has been given of his having or arranging to have in his possession the goods the subject of the charge, or of his undertaking or assisting in, or arranging to undertake or assist in, their retention, removal, disposal or realisation, the following evidence shall be admissible for the purpose of proving that he knew or believed the goods to be stolen goods –

(a) evidence that he has had in his possession, or has undertaken or assisted in the retention, removal, disposal or realisation of, stolen goods from any theft taking place not earlier than 12 months before the offence charged; and

(b) (provided that seven days' notice in writing has been given to him of the intention to prove the conviction) evidence that he has within the five years proceedings the date of the offence charged been convicted of theft or of handling stolen goods.

---

99  See, also, the pre-Act case of *Matthews* [1950] 1 All ER 137.

100 Under the PACE 1984, s 78, evidence may be excluded if: '... having regard to all the circumstances ... the admission of the evidence would have such an adverse effect on the fairness of the proceedings that the court ought not to admit it.'

(5) This section is to be construed in accordance with s 24 of this Act; and in sub-s 3(b) above the reference to handling stolen goods shall include any corresponding offence committed before the commencement of this Act.

12-62 The above provisions apply to all forms of handling, but, as it makes clear, *only* to handling. Under s 27(3)(a), the evidence which may be admitted relates to previous misconduct, while under s 27(3)(b), previous convictions become admissible. The statutory provisions must, therefore, be seen in the context of an exception to the general rule of admissibility that prohibits evidence of previous unconnected wrongdoing.[101] As a consequence, the case law makes it clear that the provisions are to be strictly construed to avoid unfair prejudice to the defendant. Further, the provisions only come into play when dealing with the proof of guilty knowledge or belief. They may not be relied on when dealing with the question of dishonesty. Similarly, the provisions require that the prosecution must have first proved the essential *actus reus*, primarily the fact of possession. The effect of this is that, in situations where possession is in issue, s 27(3) has no part to play. This will cause problems in those cases where the defendant is faced with a number of counts, in some of which the issue is possession and, in some, where the issue is guilty knowledge. This was dealt with in *Wilkins*:

> Very great care should be exercised by the judge first of all before he allows evidence of the previous convictions to be given at all or, if he does allow that evidence to be admitted, very great care should be exercised in order to ensure that the jury realise the issues to which those previous convictions are relevant.[102]

*Wilkins* was concerned with admissibility under para (b) but, it is submitted, that the same care is required under para (a), also. There are a number of significant differences between paras (a) and (b) of s 27(3) which are explored below.

12-63 (b) *Evidence of other stolen property in the defendant's possession*

Under s 27(3)(a), evidence may be given that other stolen property had been found in the possession of the defendant, or that he had, previously, handled such *other* stolen property. It should be noted that the evidence must relate to stolen property, other than that which is the subject of the present charge. It is, therefore, vital that the prosecution proves that this other property was stolen property and that it was in the defendant's possession. There is also a strict time frame: that the other property must have been stolen not earlier than 12 months preceding the date of the present charge. The conditions must be strictly complied with and it would not be permissible to introduce evidence of the previous transactions, where stolen property had come to be within the

---

101 In the context of the law of evidence, what is permitted by virtue of s 27(3) would ordinarily be barred by the general rules relating to similar fact evidence, evidence of previous bad character, as well as previous convictions.

102 (1975) 60 Cr App R 300.

defendant's possession or control or whether, as a consequence of those previous transactions, the defendant had been, or was being, charged as the thief or the handler. The difficulty with this is that the jury may well infer that, because the evidence has been adduced, the defendant is guilty. This point was made clear by Mustill LJ, in *Wood* (approving earlier authority):

> If s 27(3)(a) ... is to be given a literal interpretation, the consequence will be that the jury is to be told simply that the defendant was on a previous occasion found to be in possession of stolen goods, without being furnished with any facts upon which they could base a conclusion as to whether on that occasion the possession was guilty or innocent; and they may well be tempted to assume that since they had been told about the incident, this must be because some guilty knowledge attending it could properly be inferred. The task of conveying to the jury that the only relevance of the fact is that the previous occasion would have served as a warning to be more careful in future ... will not be easily performed. On the other hand, to let in evidence of circumstances from which the existence of guilty knowledge on the prior occasion could be inferred would be such a striking inroad into the general rule which excludes evidence of prior unconnected offences that one would need clear words in the statute to justify it, and s 27(3) is quite silent.[103]

It remains the case, however, that, in most instances, the real reason for allowing the evidence of possession of other stolen goods is to demonstrate the similarity of the handling involved. If this is the case, then it would be possible for the prosecution to achieve this end by using the common law rules relating to the admissibility of similar fact evidence.[104]

12-64    (c) *Evidence of previous convictions*

Under s 27(3)(b), any previous conviction of the defendant for either theft or handling becomes admissible for the purpose of proving guilty knowledge or belief. This is subject to two conditions: first, that the previous convictions have occurred within the five years preceding the date of the offence presently charged; and, secondly that the prosecution has given at least seven days' notice in writing of their intention to give evidence of such conviction. This runs counter to the general rule that previous convictions are inadmissible and, consequently, this provision has been strictly construed in the sense that only the fact of the previous conviction (together with details of time and place) were admissible.[105] However, the provisions of s 73 of the PACE 1984 also come into play. Under s 73, on all occasions where it is permissible to give evidence of a previous conviction, this has to be done by way of producing a certificate of conviction. By virtue of s 73(2), the certificate of conviction shall give 'the

---

103 (1987) 85 Cr App R 200, p 292.
104 See Tapper, C, *Cross and Tapper on Evidence*, 9th edn, 1999, London: Butterworths, pp 348–53.
105 *Fowler* (1988) 86 Cr App R 219.

substance and effect ... of the indictment and of the conviction' (with a similar provision for summary trials). The consequence of this is that the court (in particular, the jury) becomes aware of matters beyond the bare facts and may, consequently, draw unwarranted inferences.

12-65 These were issues that were considered by the House of Lords in *Hacker*.[106] The defendant had been charged with handling stolen goods in the form of the body shell of a motor car. The prosecution sought to give, in evidence, a certificate of previous conviction, under s 72 of the 1984 Act. This certificate contained various particulars of the offence. The defence objected on the grounds that, under s 27(3)(a), only the bare facts of the previous conviction were allowed. Further, the defence argued, the prejudicial effect of this evidence outweighed its probative value and was another reason for its exclusion.

12-66 The House of Lords was of the opinion that s 27(3)(b) could not be read in isolation: it had to be read together with s 73(2) of the PACE 1984. The certificate of conviction was the way by which the previous conviction could be proved and the identity of the goods was an essential part of the conviction. Lord Slynn agreed with the defence argument that the prejudicial effect of the evidence could outweigh its probative value and, therefore, could have been excluded under s 78 of the PACE 1984. However, this was a matter for judicial discretion. On the facts of the case, Lord Slynn saw no reason to interfere with the exercise of discretion. This was especially as the trial judge had directed the jury properly, pointing out to them the danger of concluding that the defendant was guilty merely because he had a previous conviction.

12-67 (d) *Unexplained possession of stolen goods*

There is, of course, no duty imposed on the defendant to produce an explanation of why it is that stolen goods have been found in his possession (on his premises, for instance). This is part of the general rule on the right to silence and the prohibition against self-incrimination. However, by virtue of the Criminal Justice and Public Order Act (CJPOA) 1994, the defendant's failure to provide an explanation may be used in evidence against him as the court or jury would then be entitled (although not automatically bound) to draw an adverse inference against him. This may take place in the context of a refusal to answer police questions when questioned or charged (under s 34); of a refusal to testify (under s 35), or a refusal to account (under s 36), at the time of arrest, for the presence of any object or substance (a) on his person, (b) in or on his clothing or footwear, (c) or otherwise in his possession, or (d) in any place in which he is at the time of his arrest.

12-68 (e) *Recent possession*

Common sense indicates that, if stolen property was found in the defendant's possession, this raises an inference that he could be either the thief or the

---

106 [1995] 1 Cr App R 332.

handler of the stolen property. Since an explanation from the defendant, to the effect that his possession was innocent, would rebut the inference, there is a considerable overlap with the provisions of the CJPOA 1994. Nevertheless, there is some merit in keeping the distinction separate. Apart from other matters, the adverse inferences under the CJPOA 1994 arise only where the defendant refuses to answer questions put to him. No such limitation arises here. The device being relied on here by the prosecution has sometimes been referred to as the 'doctrine of recent possession'. It is submitted that there is no such 'doctrine'; at its highest, it may amount to a rebuttable presumption of law, that is, in the absence of an explanation, the possession of the stolen property merits (but not compels) a finding that the defendant is a handler. The Court of Appeal has made this clear in *Ravira*j, where Stocker LJ held that this was:

> Only a particular aspect of the general proposition that where suspicious circumstances appear to demand an explanation and no explanation or an entirely incredible explanation is given, the lack of explanation may warrant an inference of guilty knowledge in the defendant. This again is only part of a wider proposition that guilt may be inferred from unreasonable behaviour of a defendant when confronted with facts which seem to accuse.[107]

The Court of Appeal, in *Raviraj*, also disposed of the argument raised in previous cases, that this inference of guilt could not apply there was direct evidence of how the stolen property had come to be in the defendant's possession.

12-69 (f) *Evidence from the thief*

For the sake of completeness, it is worth noting that evidence from the thief to the effect that he had sold or handed the stolen property to the defendant could, of course, be admissible as evidence of handling against the defendant.

## Reform

The Law Commission in its draft Criminal Code did not consider any major reforms necessary, apart from a minor redrafting:

> Our restatement of this offence proposes one piece of clarification. As the offence is currently drafted, a person may commit handling 'if he ... dishonestly undertakes or assists in [the] retention, removal, disposal or realisation [of stolen goods] by or for the benefit of another' or 'if he arranges to do so' (where 'do so' also refers to receiving them). This clumsy expression has caused much unnecessary trouble. It seems clear that what is meant is that one may either (i) *undertake* a relevant act *for the benefit of* another or (ii) *assist* in the doing of a relevant act *by another*. Clause 172 is drafted accordingly.[108]

---

107 (1986) 85 Cr App R 93.

108 Law Commission, *A Criminal Code for England and Wales*, 1989, Law Com No 177, Vol 2, para 16.15.

## 2 RETAINING A WRONGFUL CREDIT

12-70 **Section 24A of the TA 1968 – Dishonestly retaining a wrongful credit**

(1) A person is guilty of an offence if –

    (a) a wrongful credit has been made to an account kept by him or in respect of which he has any right or interest;

    (b) he knows or believes that the credit is wrongful; and

    (c) he dishonestly fails to take such steps as are reasonable in the circumstances to secure that the credit is cancelled.

(2) References to a credit are to a credit of an amount of money.

(3) A credit to an account is wrongful if it is the credit side of a money transfer obtained contrary to s 15A of this Act.

(4) A credit to an account is also wrongful to the extent that it derives from –

    (a) theft;

    (b) an offence under s 15A of this Act;

    (c) blackmail; or

    (d) stolen goods.

(5) In determining whether a credit to an account is wrongful, it is immaterial (in particular) whether the account is overdrawn before or after the credit is made.

(6) A person guilty of an offence under this section shall be liable on conviction on indictment to imprisonment for a term not exceeding 10 years.

(7) Subsection (8) below applies for purposes of provisions of this Act relating to stolen goods (including sub-s (4) above).

(8) References to stolen goods include money which is dishonestly withdrawn from an account to which a wrongful credit has been made, but only to the extent that the money derives from the credit.

(9) In this section 'account' and 'money' shall be construed in accordance with s 15B of this Act.

## Introduction, mode of trial and sentence

12-71 This section was introduced as of December 18 1996 by s 2(1) of the Theft (Amendment) Act 1996. The offence is triable either way under s 17(1) and Sched 1, para 28 of the MCA 1980. When tried on indictment, it is a class 4 offence. The maximum penalty on indictment is 10 years. On summary conviction, it is a six month sentence and/or a fine. There have not, to date, been any sentencing guidelines for this particular offence.

Two preliminary points may be made in relation to the offence under s 24A. These refer to its fundamental difference from other theft offences. The first is that the general exception provided to the bona fide purchaser, such as that provided in s 3 of the Act, does not apply here. Accordingly, if a defendant subsequently discovers that money paid into his account had been derived from theft, he is under an obligation to take reasonable steps to secure that the credit to his account is cancelled. The fact that he had no such knowledge at the time the money was paid into his account is irrelevant.[109] Secondly, the rule that a person cannot be guilty of handling stolen goods, in the course of stealing them, does not apply to the offence of dishonestly retaining a wrongful credit. The offence, under s 24A, can be committed at the same time as the offences of theft, obtaining a money transfer by deception or blackmail.

## Wrongful credits and stolen goods

12-72    One arguable side effect of the decision in *Preddy*[110] is that where a defendant dishonestly obtained a money transfer from an innocent party, the sum now credited to his account could no longer be treated as stolen goods. Furthermore, even where the defendant directly pays stolen bank notes into his account, the subsequent payment from that account to an account held by a co-defendant cannot be classed as stolen goods, on the basis that the new credit balance is an entirely different chose in action. It is true that, in one sense, the credit balance in the co-defendant's account represents the proceeds of the first defendant's theft, but it has never done so in the hands of the original thief. In *AG's Ref (No 4 of 1979)*,[111] it was held that the co-defendant may be guilty of handling in such circumstances. However, this cannot stand in the light of *Preddy*.

Section 24A deals with the problem in a number of ways. First, under s 24A(1), a defendant who has committed an offence under s 15A, now also commits a second offence, if he does not take reasonable steps to cancel the credit. Secondly, under s 24A(4), the same applies to any wrongful credit derived from theft, a s 15A offence, blackmail, or the proceeds of stolen goods. Thirdly, under s 24A(8), any money dishonestly withdrawn from an account to which a wrongful credit has been made, may be categorised as 'stolen goods'.

## Dishonesty

12-73    One effect of s 24A is that it creates an offence of dishonest omission, in that the failure of the defendant to cancel the wrongful credit is culpable. This arises when the defendant 'knows or believes' that the credit is wrongful. However, knowing or believing may not necessarily amount to dishonesty. This would be especially the case, where the defendant was, originally, a *bona fide* purchaser

---

109 See *Pitchley* (1972) 57 Cr App R 30, para 12-41, above.
110 [1996] AC 815.
111 [1981] 1 WLR 667.

who subsequently discovers the true facts, perhaps a considerable time after the transaction in question. It may well prove difficult to persuade a jury that such a defendant is dishonest within the terms of the test set out in *Ghosh*.[112] However under s 93B of the CJA 1988 (one of the so called 'money laundering provisions) dishonesty need not be proved and, in appropriate circumstances, may provide an alternative to a charge under s 24A.

# 3 ADVERTISEMENTS OFFERING REWARDS

12-74 **Section 23 of the TA 1968 – Advertising rewards for return of goods stolen or lost**

Where any public advertisement of a reward for the return of any goods which have been stolen or lost uses any words to the effect that no questions will be asked, or that the person producing the goods will be safe from apprehension or inquiry, or that any money paid for the purchase of the goods or advanced by way of loan on them will be repaid, the person advertising the reward and any person who prints or publishes the advertisement shall on summary conviction be liable to a fine not exceeding level three on the standard scale.

## Mode of trial and sentence

12-75 This is a summary offence, punishable with a fine not exceeding level three on the standard scale.[113]

## Advertisements offering rewards

12-76 As a consequence of s 23, an offence is committed by any person who advertises the offer of a reward *together* with a promise that (a) no questions will be asked or (b) that the person who produces the goods will be safe from apprehension or inquiry, that is, that immunity from prosecution will be granted, or (c) that any money that had been paid for the goods will be repaid. It should be noted that merely offering a reward for the return of stolen goods is not penalised. It is only when the offer of a reward is combined with one of the other three elements above that the section takes effect.

The provision is based on a pre-existing offence and its rationale is clear enough. Certain types of goods may be stolen to order and, if advertisements of this nature were to be allowed, it would be tantamount to encouraging theft. As

---

112 [1982] QB 1053; see para 2-18, above.
113 Under the CJA 1982, s 37(2) (as substituted by the CJA 1991, s 17(2)), this currently stands at a maximum of £1,000.

the CLRC put it, 'advertisements of this kind may encourage dishonesty'.[114] Fully to achieve this purpose, the offence is a strict liability offence that is applicable to anyone responsible for the advertisement. This includes not only the advertiser himself, but also the printer or publisher of the advertisement.[115]

---

114 *Op cit*, CLRC, fn 2, para 144.
115 See *Denham v Scott* (1984) 77 Cr App R 210.

# CHAPTER 13

# GOING EQUIPPED FOR BURGLARY, THEFT OR CHEAT

**13-01**     **Section 25 of the Theft Act (TA) 1968 – Going equipped for stealing, etc**

(1) A person shall be guilty of an offence if, when not at his place of abode, he has with him any article for use in the course of or in connection with any burglary, theft or cheat.

(2) A person guilty of an offence under this section shall on indictment be liable to imprisonment for a term not exceeding three years.

(3) Where a person is charged with an offence under this section, proof that he had with him any article made or adapted for use in committing a burglary, theft or cheat shall be evidence that he had it with him for such use.

(4) Any person may arrest without warrant anyone who is, or with whom he, with reasonable cause, suspects to be, committing an offence under this section.

(5) For purposes of this section an offence under s 12(1) of this Act of taking a conveyance shall be treated as theft, and 'cheat' means an offence under s 15 of this Act.

## Introduction

**13-02**   The phrase 'going equipped for stealing', used as a shorthand description for the offence under s 25, comes from the side note to the section and seems to be sanctioned by long usage. It has the advantage of succinctly describing the crux of the offence as opposed to the alternative term, 'possession of housebreaking implements', which is used as a general title to this part of the Act and is preferred by some writers on the subject. The offence is potentially very wide. In addition to the range of possible articles (not limited to housebreaking implements) and the range of circumstances under which the offence may be committed, the Act also couples s 25 with ss 9, 12(1) and 15. Nonetheless, reasonable limits on the breadth of the section have been recognised and the reported case law is not numerous.

**13-03**     A number of other curious features may be noted. First, despite the fact that the maximum penalty is only three years (as compared to a maximum of seven years for the basic theft offence), the offence is an arrestable one under s 24(2)(d) of the Police and Criminal Evidence Act (PACE) 1984. This makes it one of the only two offences under the TA 1968 (the other being s 12(1) – the taking of conveyances without authority)[1] to be specifically so included. The other theft

---

1   See Chapter 6, above.

offences are simply dealt with by the general provision, in s 24(1)(b) of the 1984 Act, to the effect that any offence, where the sentence that may be handed down to a previously unconvicted offender is five years or more, shall be deemed to be arrestable. Secondly, there is no other theft offence where there is a specific mention of the right to make a citizen's arrest. In practice, this provision is superseded by s 24(5) of the PACE 1984, which states:

(5) Where an arrestable offence has been committed, a person may arrest without warrant –

(a) anyone who is guilty of the offence;

(b) anyone whom he has reasonable grounds for suspecting to be about to commit an arrestable offence.

## Mode of trial and sentence

13-04    The offence is triable either way, by virtue of s 17(1) (read together with Sched 1) of the Magistrates' Courts Act 1980. When tried on indictment. it is a class 4 offence and the maximum penalty is three years. When tried summarily, it is six months or a fine, or both. In circumstances where the offence has been combined with theft or taking of motor vehicles, Sched 2 of the Road Traffic Act 1988, provides for the possibility of disqualification. The judicial view taken, with regard to sentencing for this offence, may be illustrated by the case of *Ferry*.[2] Here, the defendants had gone equipped in relation to thefts from telephone boxes. They had been found to be in possession of a cordless drill, screwdrivers, surgical gloves and a map. A sentence of 12 months' imprisonment was deemed to be suitable.

## Elements of the offence

### *Not at place of abode*

13-05    The offence is not aimed at penalising the mere possession of the proscribed articles. Instead, it is made clear that the offence only arises where the defendant has these articles in his possession when outside his place of abode. The court or jury is then asked to draw the necessary inference that he was intending to use these articles in the facilitation of the specified criminal activity.[3] Section 25 is, therefore, not very different from s 28 of the Larceny Act 1916, which it replaced. Under the 1916 Act, also, it had been the case that mere possession was not sufficient. Indeed, the Criminal Law Revision Committee (CLRC) considered this issue:

---

2    [1997] 2 Cr App R(S) 42.
3    See the CJA 1967, s 8(b).

There is no express provision in s 28 [of the Larceny Act] excluding possession at a person's home, but the section is understood in this way. It appears to be concerned with persons who have started out to commit crime. We considered whether to make the new offence extend to possession at the offender's home. This would have the advantage of catching criminals at an earlier stage. On the other hand, it would change the character of the offence. The present offence is a preparatory one in contemplation of a particular crime; the change would make it one of mere possession for use at some time for the purpose of any of the specified crimes generally. It is only exceptionally that the criminal law extends to possession of articles in a person's own home.[4]

13-06 The Act does not contain a definition of 'place of abode' and the question that arose in *Bundy*[5] was whether a motor car could ever constitute a 'place of abode'. The defendant claimed to have been 'living rough' in the car. Consequently, it was argued, when the offending articles were discovered in the car, they were *at* his place of abode and possession of these articles lay outside s 25(1). The Court of Appeal was willing to accept that there were circumstances in which it might be the case that a car might constitute a place of abode, but went on to rule that the expression 'place of abode' must be construed as referring to a *site* at which the occupier *intends* to abide:

> So, there are two elements in the phrase 'place of abode', the element of site and the element of intention. When the defendant took the motor car to a site with the intention of abiding there, then his motor car could be said to be his 'place of abode', but when he took it from that site to move it to another site where he intended to abide, the motor car could not be said to be his 'place of abode' during transit. When the police arrested him he was not intending to abide on the site where he was arrested. It follows that he was not then at his 'place of abode'.[6]

13-07 Would the ruling in this case apply to a caravan? If so, the 'place of abode' for someone who dwells in a caravan would be the caravan site and not the caravan itself. Consequently, when the caravan is in transit between one site and another, the possession of articles which might be construed as coming within the purview of s 25(1) could, conceivably, render the caravan dweller guilty. This would have potentially grave consequences for gypsies and travellers, who may already be regarded with (unfounded) suspicion, as well as for those who chose to spend their leisure time in this manner.[7]

13-08 A more literal approach to this issue is illustrated by a case which arose by way of a challenge to extradition proceedings, *Re McAngus*.[8] The applicant had been committed for extradition to the USA, on the basis of the evidence of undercover agents that he had agreed to sell them clothing, which he

---

4    CLRC, *Eighth Report*, Cmnd 2977, 1966, London: HMSO, para 126.
5    (1977) 65 Cr App R 239.
6    *Ibid*, p 242.
7    See the discussion of a similar issue in relation to burglary, para 4-28, above.
8    [1994] Crim LR 602.

dishonestly represented as being a brand name manufactured in the USA. The applicant had taken the agents to a warehouse where the clothing was stored. The Metropolitan Stipendiary magistrate decided that this amounted to the offence, under s 25(1) of the TA 1968, in that he had with him articles for use in the course of a 'cheat'. If it had been the case that the applicant had gone from door to door with the counterfeit clothing, it would certainly have been the case that he came within the requirement of having with him such articles when not at his place of abode. However, did this apply to a situation where the articles were stored in a warehouse? The Divisional Court had no hesitation in ruling that the warehouse was not his place of abode and, since he had the offending articles with him, the offence was made out.

## Has with him

13-09    The phrase 'has with him' occurs, also, in s 10(1) and similar problems of construction have arisen.[9] In cases where the article is in the defendant's immediate possession or control, the position is straightforward. In other situations, the difficulty that has to be overcome is whether it can properly be said that he has the article with him for the purpose of committing one of the specified offences.

13-10    The *McAngus* case, above, throws into relief the proper label to be attached to the offence under s 25. The label 'going equipped' comes from the marginal note to the section. It is, of course, true that a marginal note is not part of the section itself. Accordingly, it was entirely right for the court in that case to have dismissed the defence submission that he had not 'gone equipped' with the counterfeit clothing. Nonetheless, the decision has been criticised for departing from the original purpose of the offence:

> Like the offence under s 28 of the Larceny Act … the section is aimed primarily at the person who sets out on an expedition equipped with jemmy, skeleton keys, or such like. If the applicant had been hawking his counterfeit shirts from door to door, there could have been no possible answer to the charge. In that case he would have been 'going equipped'. As it was, he was equipped all right, but did he 'go'? …The side note may well be thought equally to show that 'going' is the essence of the offence under s 25.[10]

13-11    It would appear, therefore, that there are two categories of cases where s 25 would apply. First, where the defendant has, in fact, 'gone equipped' with the requisite offending articles (in the sense that he was carrying them with him), it would be a straightforward matter for the prosecution to raise the inference that

---

9    See para 4-38, above.

10    From the 'Commentary' to *McAngus* [1994] Crim LR 602, p 603. Moreover, there are cases such as *DPP v Schildkamp* [1971] AC 1, where it was the opinion of the House of Lords that regard may be had to a marginal note as an indication of the mischief the Act was dealing with, although it remains the case that such a marginal note could not be utilised to interpret the Act itself.

he did so for a dishonest purpose. Secondly, if he 'possessed' such articles, the inference would equally arise, provided, as in *McAngus*, this took place outside his place of abode and provided, also, that this was not mere possession but showed a close physical link and a degree of control over the articles. Support for this view could be gained from the fact that the expression 'has with him' occurs, also, in s 10 of the TA 1968 in relation to aggravated burglary, as well as in a variety of other statutes, such as the Firearms Act (FA) 1968. In cases under these provisions, the judicial view has been that the mere fact of possession, although crucial, is not enough of itself. One instance of this is *Kelt*.[11] When the police searched the defendant's home, they found a holdall containing, among other things, a sawn-off shotgun. The defendant made a statement in which he said that he was looking after the holdall for a friend. He was charged with 'having with him' a firearm, contrary to s 18(1) of the FA 1968. He was convicted and appealed on the ground that the trial judge had failed to given an adequate direction to the jury on the distinction between 'possession' and 'having'. The Court of Appeal agreed that 'having with him' was not to be equated with 'possession' and that this point should have been made clear to the jury:

> Of course, the classic case of having a gun with you is if you are carrying it. But, even if you are not carrying it, you may yet have it with you, if it is immediately available to you. But if all that can be shown is possession in the sense that it is in your house or in a shed or somewhere where you have ultimate control, that is not enough.[12]

13-12 The Court of Appeal has subsequently decided, in *Pawlicki and Swindell*,[13] that no criteria of 'immediate availability' can be read into the legislation. So, for instance, if the articles were in a bag, or in a car, close to the scene of the intended burglary, the section would be satisfied. Nevertheless, it remains the case that some degree of control is necessary in the sense that the defendant has access to the offending articles. This is to be decided on the facts of each case and in a common sense manner. Applying a similar interpretation to the offence, under s 25, would be consistent with the range of other such offences and would deal with the mischief that the section was intended to deal with. Such an interpretation would also be in keeping with the *McAngus* case.

13-13 An issue which arises concerns the question whether the defendant must have had prior possession, in that he had the article with him and had made a decision to carry the article, for the purpose of committing one of the specified offences. In *Dayle*,[14] the defendant was charged with 'having with him' an offensive weapon under s 1(4) of the Prevention of Crime Act 1953. In the course of a fight, he had picked up a car jack and thrown it at the victim. It was held that 'having with him' indicated a situation where the defendant had the

---

11  (1977) 65 Cr App R 74; see the discussion of this case at para 4-41, above.
12  *Ibid*, p 77, *per* Scarman LJ.
13  (1992) 95 Cr App R 246.
14  (1973) 58 Cr App R 100.

offending article with him for the purpose of committing the offence. In this case, the defendant had the car jack with him for a lawful and reasonable purpose and, therefore, the offence was not made out.[15] The difficulty with such an approach may be illustrated by the example of a defendant on his way to commit burglary and who found a convenient screwdriver lying outside the house he intended to burgle. If he is arrested, he will be found to have the screwdriver in his possession, but has he 'gone equipped'? The reasoning, in Dayle, would be unduly restrictive and it would involve speculation as to the point in time at which the defendant begins to 'have' the screwdriver 'with him'.

13-14     This point was addressed in *Minor v DPP*,[16] where the defendant and an accomplice were arrested while preparing to siphon petrol from the tanks of two cars. They had with them two petrol cans and a siphoning tube. There was no evidence that they had taken these articles with them to the cars. Nonetheless, the conviction of the defendant under s 25 was upheld. In deciding that the defendant came within the ambit of s 25, the court was clearly of the view that, even a momentary possession at the time of the offence, or while engaged in preparatory acts, will suffice. This approach runs the danger of being inconsistent with the cases decided under the similar provision in s 10(1). It may also lead to a straining of language that has been criticised:

> On this view the burglar who picks up a nearby stone to break a window would commit the offence of going equipped, but it is respectfully submitted that 'has with him' requires more than that the acquisition of the article should precede the theft.[17]

Moreover, it may have been far simpler to have charged the defendant with an attempted theft of the petrol, provided, of course that they had gone beyond the 'more than merely preparatory' stage, as required by s 1(1) of the Criminal Attempts Act 1981. On the other hand, the approach taken by the court is certainly pragmatic and is in keeping with the mischief the section was designed to deal with. To put it another way, s 25 would permit the prosecution of a defendant, even *before* he had gone beyond the preparatory stages required by the law on attempts.[18]

## *Any article*

13-15   The difficulty that arises here is obvious: is there any limitation to the sorts of articles the possession of which renders the defendant culpable? Any article 'made or adapted for use in committing a burglary, theft or cheat' is automatically covered by sub-s (3); the fact of possession 'shall be evidence'

---

15   See, also, *Ohlson v Hylton* [1975] 1 WLR 724.
16   (1987) Cr App R 378.
17   Smith and Hogan, *Criminal Law*, 9th edn, 1999, London: Butterworths, p 627.
18   See para 14-08, below.

against him. In relation to other articles under sub-s (1), an alternative might lie in drawing a distinction between those articles which a person would legitimately have had with him and those articles the possession of which would immediately arouse suspicion in the minds of a reasonable person. For instance, possession of an 8 inch screwdriver whilst ostensibly on the way to a pub would raise such a suspicion, whilst an electrician's possession of the same screwdriver would not. The problem with such an approach is the obvious one, that even apparently 'innocent' articles which may be legitimately possessed may be used in furtherance of the specified offences.

The only solution, it is submitted, lies in not considering the *actus reus* in isolation from the *mens rea*. Once the prosecution proves the possession of 'any article', the offence is made out, if they then succeed in proving that the purpose of the possession was for any contemplated burglary, theft or cheat. Take, for instance, a situation where the defendant, when arrested, was found to have in his possession skintight black clothing. If it can be proved that he intended to use the clothing in the course of, or in connection with, one of the specified offences, then the offence under s 25 is made out. Consequently, it becomes a matter of inference for the court or jury to draw from (a) the nature of the article, coupled with (b) the circumstances under which the defendant was in possession.

13-16    Such an approach raises the concept of remoteness: is possession of the article too remote from the contemplated offence? Or, in simple terms, is it too far fetched to expect a jury to believe that the articles were to be used for the specified offences? This point may be illustrated by the case of *Mansfield*.[19] The defendant was charged with possessing documents (including someone else's driving licence), intending to obtain employment as a driver. The alleged purpose of this would be to provide him with an opportunity to steal. His conviction under s 25 was quashed, on the basis that his possession of the articles (the documents) was too remote from the contemplated offence.

### *Use in the course of or in connection with*

13-17    A number of points may be noted. First, it is not necessary for the prosecution to prove that the defendant had the article with him in connection with any specific burglary, theft or cheat.[20] The failure to specify this would not render a charge defective. Secondly, it is not necessary to prove that he had the article with him for his own use; it is enough that the article was to be used, even by another person. In the latter case, however, it might be the case that a charge for aiding and abetting, under s 8 of the Accessories and Abettors Act 1861, would also be made out. Thirdly, as an arrest may be effected before one of the specified

19   [1975] Crim LR 101.
20   *Ellames* (1974) 60 Cr App R 7.

offences has, in fact, been committed, it follows that possession of an article for future use would come within s 25. This would be consistent with the fact that the object of s 25 is to deal with preparatory acts by the defendant. This would, of course, be subject to the limitation of remoteness, as discussed above. Finally, cases, such as *Minor*,[21] indicate that possession during the commission of the offence would be sufficient. What about possession after commission? It is submitted that, if the possession was to enable the defendant to make his escape after the commission of the offence, then the offence is made out. This is because the possession would be 'in connection with' the offence Similarly, the offence is made out if the article is in the defendant's possession, so that he may use it in the disposal of stolen property. An example of this would be where a screwdriver was in the defendant's possession in order to enable him to dismantle and dispose of stolen property. If the defendant is assisting another in the disposal of such articles, then it is conceivable that he may be brought within the terms of the offence of 'handling', under s 22 of the TA 1968.[22]

## Burglary, theft or cheat

13-18 There are situations where the prosecution may be unable to prove that the defendant is either a burglar or a thief. For instance, this may occur where the defendant has been apprehended in the early stages of preparation for these offences. In such cases, s 25 provides an alternative to these charges, as well as an alternative to a charge for attempt.

13-19 The law on burglary and theft does not require further explanation here. What about 'cheat'? In *Rashid*,[23] Bridge LJ was clearly of the view that what was at issue with regard to 'cheat' was, in fact, 'deception', as laid down in s 25(5). The defendant was a railway steward who had with him his own sandwiches, which he intended to sell to passengers, instead of selling those belonging to his employers. The Court of Appeal held that the prosecution was required to prove that the defendant intended to practise an effective and operative *deception* on the passengers. In the court's view, the prosecution failed as it would have been a matter of complete indifference to a passenger whether the sandwiches belonged to British Rail, or to a steward. Moreover, the court held, it had to be a cheat on the passengers, not the defendant's employers.

13-20 The same point arose in the later case of *Doukas*.[24] The defendant, a waiter in a hotel, had with him a number of bottles of wine in order dishonestly to sell them to the hotel's customers. The Court of Appeal upheld his conviction. Lane LJ held that, as far as going equipped for cheat was concerned, it was necessary that s 25 should be read together with s 15. Consequently, the offence is made

---

21  Paragraph 13-14, above.
22  See Chapter 12. A charge under s 4 of the Criminal Law Act 1967 may also be a possibility.
23  (1977) 64 Cr App R 201.
24  (1978) 66 Cr App R 228.

out if the defendant has with him an article for use in the course of, or in connection with, any deception. Some disagreement was expressed with the views of Bridge LJ in *Rashid*, that as it would not have mattered to the customers involved, no operative deception had occurred. This is criticism is justified. The customers in both cases might not have bought the goods in question if they had known that those items belonged to the defendants. This might be especially true in relation to the wine (especially as the wine being sold by the waiter was of a type not stocked by the hotel), as opposed to sandwiches, but this is a difference merely of degree. The decision in *Doukas* has been approved in *Corboz*.[25] Further approval was provided by the House of Lords in *Cooke*.[26] This case was not directly concerned with s 25, but Lord Mackay LC approved the ruling given in *Doukas*: whether deception is proved is a question of fact, dependent upon the evidence of dishonesty in relation to the deception of customers or passengers. In *Doukas*, the prosecution had sought to argue, as an alternative, that there had also been deception of the defendant's employers. Lord Mackay rejected this alternative. This rejection is consistent with Lord Bridge's characterisation of a similar argument, in *Rashid*, as a red herring: the fact that an employee is defrauding his employer is quite separate as to whether he is practising a deception on his employer's customers.

## Mens rea

13-21    Section 25, itself, does not prescribe any particular form of *mens rea*. Nonetheless, on the basis of the case law, it would appear that the prosecution must prove either: (a) that the defendant, knowingly, possessed the article; or (b) that he intended that the article be used in furtherance of the specified offences. In both cases, the state of mind is a matter of inference to be drawn from the facts of the case, in particular the nature of the article and the circumstances of the possession. This would bring into play the general provision of s 8 of the Criminal Justice Act (CJA) 1967. As this is a matter of fact, it must be left to the jury to draw their own conclusions. The general rules relating to proof of intention and knowledge apply. Consequently, the burden of proof rests on the prosecution and the fact of possession does not raise a *prima facie* case against the defendant. Where the defendant puts forward an innocent explanation for his possession, however, it would be accurate to say that this imposes an evidential burden upon him. Similarly, a failure to explain his possession could give rise to an adverse inference that the possession was for a guilty purpose, in the same way as it would for offences of handling, under s 22 of the TA 1968,[27] and

---

25    [1984] Crim LR 629.

26    [1986] AC 909. See, also, paras 8-22–24, below, where the decisions in *Rashid* (1977) 64 Cr App R 201, *Doukas* (1978) 66 Cr App R 228 and *Cooke* [1986] AC 909 are further discussed in relation to the requirements to prove a causal connection between the deception and the 'obtaining'.

27    See para 12-60, above.

within the context of ss 34 and 35 of the Criminal Justice and Public Order Act 1994.[28]

13-22    To this end, s 25(3) offers some assistance, albeit minimal assistance, to the prosecution. Under this provision, it is evidence against the defendant that he has in his possession any article 'made or adapted for use' in committing one of the specified offences. This must, in reality, be considered a rule of evidence and proof, rather than a rule of *mens rea*. The jury may take the fact of possession into account, but it cannot be conclusive evidence of guilt. In particular, the weight to be attached to the possession, together with any forthcoming explanation, is for the jury to decide.

13-23    As 'cheat' encompasses deception, the further question that arises is whether it is necessary for the prosecution to prove that the victim has, in fact, been deceived. Since the essence of s 25 is that it is a preparatory one, this would not be necessary. It is the intention of the defendant that is in issue. Accordingly, it is irrelevant that no customer was, in fact, deceived. However, it is essential that the prosecution must establish that what the defendant was going equipped to commit was the s 15 offence and not something that would fall short of that offence. If this is true, then the decision in *Rashid* is plainly wrong. Here, the conviction was quashed on the basis that the jury had not been directed that they could only convict if the defendant believed that the railway passengers would decline to purchase his sandwiches if they knew the truth. This is irrelevant: it is sufficient that the defendant had the sandwiches with him in order to pass them off as sandwiches belonging to his employer.

13-24    This also raises the question as to whether it would be sufficient to prove recklessness. Under s 15(4), deception may be 'any deception (whether deliberate or reckless) by words or conduct'. If s 25 is to be read together with s 15, as suggested by the Court of Appeal, in *Doukas*, and the House of Lords, in *Cooke*, then there is no reason why recklessness should not also be sufficient under s 25.

## Related offences

13-25    It is not an offence under s 25 to keep or possess articles at one's home, even if those articles may be used for burglary or theft or have even been made or adapted for such a purpose. However, other charges might be brought, instead. Under s 3 of the Criminal Damage Act 1971, an offence is committed by any person who has in his custody or control anything which he intends to use to destroy or damage property. Since the intention may be to destroy or damage property in furtherance of burglary, for instance, this may be a useful charge for the prosecution to bear in mind. Similarly, firearms in the possession of the

---

28    Under these provisions, a failure to provide an explanation at the proper time may result in adverse inference being drawn against the defendant.

defendant for the purposes of one of the specified offences would obviously fall within s 25, although charges would more properly be brought under the various provisions of the Firearms Act 1968.

# CHAPTER 14

# ATTEMPTS

14-01      **Section 1 of the Criminal Attempts Act (CAA) 1981**

1(1) If with intent to commit an offence to which this section applies, a person does an act which is more than merely preparatory to the commission of the offence, he is guilty of attempting to commit the offence.

(1A) Subject to s 8 of the Computer Misuse Act (CMA) 1990 (relevance of external law) if this sub-s applies to an act, what the person doing it had in view shall be treated as an offence to which this section applies.

(1B) Sub-section (1A) above applies to an act if –

(a) it is done in England and Wales, and

(b) it would fall within sub-s (1) above as more than merely preparatory to the commission of an offence under s 3 of the CMA 1990 but for the fact the offence, if completed, would not be an offence triable in England and Wales.

(2) A person may be guilty of attempting to commit an offence to which this section applies even though the facts are such that the commission of the offence is impossible.

(3) In any case where –

(a) apart from this sub-section a person's intention would not be regarded as having amounted to an intent to commit an offence; but

(b) if the facts of the case had been as he believed them to be, his intention would be so regarded,

then for the purposes of sub-s (1) above, he shall be regarded as having an intention to commit that offence.

(4) This section applies to any offence which, if it were completed, would be triable in England and Wales as an indictable offence, other than –

(a) conspiracy (at common law or under s 1 of the Criminal Law Act (CLA) 1977 or any other enactment);

(b) aiding, abetting, counselling, procuring or suborning the commission of an offence;

(c) offences under s 4(1) (assisting offenders) or 5(1) (accepting or agreeing to accept consideration for not disclosing information about an arrestable offence) of the CLA 1967.

## Introduction

14-02   The common law crime of attempt was abolished by s 6(1) of the CAA 1981 and replaced by the offence in s 1(1), set out above. The effect is that, it is a crime to attempt to commit an offence which is triable on indictment. The scope of the crime of attempt is, thus, much wider than attempting to commit one of the offences in the Theft Acts (TAs). However, many of the leading cases have happened to involve situations where the crime alleged to have been attempted was one of those in the TA 1968. When it falls to be considered whether someone has committed a criminal attempt, the following questions are relevant:

(a) was the crime attempted one to which s 1 applies?;

(b) do the English courts have jurisdiction?;

(c) did the defendant do an act which was more than merely preparatory?;

(d) did the defendant have the necessary intention/*mens rea* to be guilty of the attempt?;

(e) was it a case of attempting the impossible and, if so, does that make any difference?

## Mode of trial and sentence

14-03    In the case of attempted crime, these matters are dealt with by s 4 of the CAA 1981, as follows. If the crime attempted is triable either way, then the attempt is triable either way. The maximum penalty on indictment is the same as that for the crime attempted. Following summary trial, the magistrates can sentence up to the maximum for which they could sentence following a summary conviction of the crime attempted.

## Crimes capable of being attempted

14-04    Section 1(4) of the CAA 1981 sets out those crimes which are capable of being attempted. Subject to the exceptions listed in that sub-section, those crimes are all crimes triable on indictment, which means all crimes which are indictable and all crimes which are triable either way. Thus, all three of the offences in the TA 1978 (ss 1–3) are capable of being attempted, as, also, are the vast majority of those in the TA 1968.

From time to time, Parliament changes the law so as to make crimes triable only summarily, which were previously triable either way. Thus, the Criminal Justice Act (CJA) 1988 made the following crimes triable only summarily: assault (including battery) and the offence in s 12 of the TA 1968 (taking a conveyance without authority).[1] The result is that it is no longer a crime to attempt to commit one of these offences.[2] It is, theoretically, possible to be guilty of

---

1    Discussed in Chapter 6 above. For mode of trial, see para 6-02.

2    This hardly amounts to a gap in the law since the CAA 1981, s 9, creates a substantive offence of interference with a motor vehicle or trailer (or with anything carried in or on it) with the intention of committing theft of it or of committing the offence in the TA 1968, s 12(1) – see para 6-03, above.

attempting to commit the offence of aggravated vehicle taking (in s 12A of the TA 1968), though it would, presumably, be necessary to prove that D intended to produce (or was reckless as to whether he would produce) one of the aggravating circumstances listed in s 12A(2).

Currently, the only offences in the TA 1968 which are triable only summarily and which are, therefore, not capable of being attempted are: s 12 (taking a conveyance) and s 23 (advertising rewards for stolen goods). Thus, it is even a crime to attempt to go equipped, contrary to s 25. That does, however, seem an unlikely charge, in practice. After all, the crime of going equipped is itself a kind of preparatory crime, to enable someone to be caught who has not yet done an act sufficiently proximate to the main offence (theft, obtaining property by deception or blackmail) that he can be shown to have attempted it.

14-05     One may wonder what would be the effect upon the law of attempt if, at some date in the future, Parliament were to make certain types of theft triable only summarily. If this were done, it would be likely to be done simply in terms of value. For example, theft of property not exceeding £X would become triable only summarily. Such a change would be likely to make no change to the current position, whereby one can be guilty of attempted theft of property of any value, however low. That would reflect the position in relation to the crime of criminal damage. That offence is triable only summarily, unless the damage exceeds £5,000. It, nevertheless, remains an 'indictable' offence. It, thus, remains an offence to attempt to commit the crime of criminal damage, however low in value the damage attempted.[3] In the case of theft, it is perhaps unlikely that Parliament would decide to make 'low value' thefts triable only summarily, if only because of the difficulties presented by situations, such as that where the defendant succeeds in stealing property of a low value when he actually meant, and tried, to steal more property or property of a greater value. In that situation, the prosecution could charge – as it can at present – (a) theft of property worth £X and (b) attempted theft of property worth £Y (where Y is greater than X).[4] A more likely change would be for the offence to remain triable either way, but for the accused to lose his right to insist upon a trial by jury when the magistrates were otherwise minded to decide upon a summary trial.[5] Such a change would clearly leave unchanged the current position where it is a crime to attempt to steal property, however low in value it might be.

---

3   *R v Bristol Magistrates' Court ex p E* [1999] 1 WLR 390 DC; *R v Fennel* [2000] 1 WLR 2011 (CA).

4   It would be odd, indeed, if (a) were triable only summarily but (b) were triable on indictment.

5   In 1993, the *Report of the Royal Commission on Criminal Justice*, Cm 2263, recommended that, in the case of all crimes triable either way, the right of the defendant to insist on a jury trial be abolished. In other words, if the magistrates decided upon summary trial, the requirement for the defendant's consent to that mode of trial would be removed. In 2000, the Government sought to have that recommendation enacted when it introduced the Criminal Justice (Mode of Trial) (No 2) Bill. Faced with opposition in the House of Lords to this erosion of the right to trial by jury, the Government withdrew the Bill.

## Jurisdiction

14-06    Part I of the CJA 1993 (ss 1–6) was brought into force with effect from 1 June 1999. In the case of a large number of offences in the TAs 1968 and 1978, it has considerably widened the rules on jurisdiction. It creates, what it terms, Group A offences and Group B offences. The offences in the following sections of the TA 1968 are all Group A offences: s 1 (theft); s 15 (obtaining property by deception); s 15A (obtaining a money transfer by deception); s 16 (obtaining a pecuniary advantage by deception); s 17 (false accounting); s 19 (false statements by company directors, etc); s 20(2) (procuring execution of valuable security by deception); s 21 (blackmail); s 22 (handling stolen goods); s 24A (retaining credits from dishonest sources, etc). Group A offences also include the offences in the following sections of the TA 1978: s 1 (obtaining services by deception); s 2 (avoiding liability by deception).[6] Group B offences are: conspiring, inciting or attempting to commit a Group A offence and conspiring to defraud.

In the case of a Group A offence, if a 'relevant event' occurs in England or Wales, then the courts of England and Wales have jurisdiction, s 2(3). A relevant event is any act, omission or other event (for example, a result), proof of which is required for a conviction, s 2(1). Thus, there is jurisdiction to try a Group A offence where any constituent of the offence occurs in England or Wales. An attempt to commit a Group A offence is a Group B offence and, as such, is triable in England and Wales provided that the attempt, if completed, would involve one of the constituent elements of the full offence being committed in England and Wales. A person can be guilty of a Group A or Group B offence, even if he was not in England and Wales at the material time, s 3(1). The reverse situation is where the defendant does acts within the jurisdiction which amount to an attempt to commit a Group A offence outside the jurisdiction. In this situation, s 1A of the CAA 1981[7] is relevant. It applies where the defendant has done an act within the jurisdiction which is more than merely preparatory to the commission outside the jurisdiction of what would, if it were completed within the jurisdiction, be a Group A offence. In that case, the courts of England and Wales have jurisdiction, provided that what the defendant had in view would be a crime under the law in force where the whole or part of it was intended to take place (s 1A(4)).

14-07    Crimes which are not, and attempts to commit crimes which are not, Group A offences remain subject to the common law rules on jurisdiction, which are narrower than the provisions of Pt I of the CJA 1993. The common law rules, developed mainly in conspiracy cases, are that a conspiracy or attempt abroad to commit a crime within England and Wales, is indictable in England and Wales. At one time, it was thought that, for the English courts to take jurisdiction, there

---

6    Group A offences also include a number of offences under the Forgery and Counterfeiting Act 1981.

7    Inserted by the CJA 1993, s 5(2).

had to be some overt act in pursuance of the conspiracy (or attempt) carried out within the jurisdiction.[8] It has, subsequently, been held that it is sufficient that the defendant has entered the jurisdiction, irrespective of whether he has carried out any such overt act within it.[9] In *Stonehouse*,[10] the House of Lords held that, for the offence of obtaining by deception, the basis of the jurisdiction was, not that the defendant had done some physical act in England, but that his acts, wherever they were done, had caused the obtaining of the property in England from the person to whom it belonged; the same principle also covered the inchoate offence of attempting to obtain the property.[11] The converse situation is where an attempt is committed within the jurisdiction to commit a crime outside it. In that situation, however, the common law declines to take jurisdiction.[12]

Robbery and burglary are examples of offences which are not Group A offences and which, therefore, are subject to the common law rules on jurisdiction. Robbery is unusual, however, since it is really only an aggravated form of theft (which is a Group A offence). Proof of all the ingredients of theft is essential for a conviction for robbery. Thus, if the prosecution finds that the common law rules deny jurisdiction to the English courts, in the case of a particular robbery or attempted robbery, it could, instead, simply charge theft or attempted theft, thereby enabling itself to rely upon the wider jurisdictional rules now provided by Pt I of the CJA 1993. The same may be possible in the case of certain types of burglary. Given, however, the nature of these offences (robbery requiring violence or threat of it, and burglary requiring the entering of a building as a trespasser), they are not likely to present jurisdictional problems, other than, perhaps, in the form of conspiracy (or incitement) to commit them.

## An act more than merely preparatory

14-08 Section 1(1) of the CAA 1981 requires 'an act which is more than merely preparatory to', to the commission of the full offence. Prior to the Act, there were many reported cases, some of which were not always easy to reconcile with each other. There were two broad lines of authority.[13] The first was sometimes known as the 'last act' test and was exemplified in *Eagleton*.[14] In applying this test, one looked to see if the defendant had committed the last act which he needed to commit, in order to bring about the full offence. As Lord Diplock, in *Stonehouse*, said:[15] 'In other words, the offender must have crossed the Rubicon

---

8   See *Doot* [1973] AC 870 (HL).

9   *Liangsiriprasert v USA* [1991] AC 225 (PC).

10  [1978] AC 55 (HL).

11  This offence would now, of course, be within the wider rules in the CJA 1993, Pt I.

12  *Board of Trade v Owen* [1957] AC 602.

13  Collated in *Ilyas* (1983) 78 Cr App R 17.

14  (1855) Dears CC 515; [1843–60] All ER Rep 363.

15  [1978] AC 55, p 68.

and burnt his boats.' The other line of authority was based on a statement in *Stephen's Digest of the Criminal Law*,[16] referring to: 'An attempt to commit a crime is an act done with intent to commit that crime, and forming part of a series of acts which would constitute its actual commission if it were not interrupted.' According to Lord Lane CJ, in *Gullefer*,[17] the wording of s 1(1) steers a midway course between those two tests. It does not require the defendant to have 'reached a point from which it is impossible for him to retreat', before the *actus reus* of an attempt is proved. The attempt 'begins when the merely preparatory acts come to an end and the defendant embarks on the crime proper'. This approach requires the defendant to be 'in the process of committing' the full offence or, as it was put in one of the pre-Act cases, 'on the job'.

In *Gullefer*, the defendant had placed a bet on the outcome of a race at a greyhound stadium. Having seen that the dog on which he had placed the bet was losing the race, he jumped on to the track and waved his arms about in an attempt to distract the dogs. As he later admitted, he did this in the hope that the stewards would declare 'no race', thereby, enabling him to recover the stake of his misjudged bet. He was convicted of attempted theft of the £18 stake, which he had wagered with the bookmaker. Quashing the conviction, the Court of Appeal held that his actions had not gone beyond mere preparation. It could not be said that he was 'in the process of committing theft'. It is clear that a defendant cannot be convicted, unless the jury are satisfied that he committed an act more than merely preparatory. Where, as was the case in *Gullefer*, there is no evidence which would entitle the jury to say that he had embarked on the crime alleged to have been attempted, the judge should withdraw the issue from the jury and direct an acquittal.[18]

14-09    In *Jones*,[19] the Court of Appeal approved the approach adopted in *Gullefer*, in particular, that: 'The first task of the court is to apply the words of the 1981 Act to the facts.'[20] To construe the statutory words by reference to previous conflicting law, was held to be misconceived. The matter is accurately summed up by the concluding words of Taylor LJ, in *Jones*:

> Looking at the plain natural meaning of s 1(1) in the way indicated by Lord Lane CJ, the question for the judge in the present case was whether there was evidence from which a reasonable jury, properly directed, could conclude that the appellant had done acts which were more than merely preparatory. Clearly, his actions in obtaining the gun, in shortening it, in loading it, in putting on his disguise and in going to the school could only be regarded as preparatory acts. But, in our judgment, once he had got into the car, taken out the loaded gun and pointed it at the victim with the intention of killing him, there was sufficient evidence for the consideration of the jury on the charge of attempted murder. It

---

16   6th edn, 1904, Macmillan and Co, Art 50.
17   [1990] 1 WLR 1063, p 1066.
18   See, also, *Campbell* [1991] Crim LR 268.
19   [1990] 1 WLR 1057.
20   In *Gullefer* [1990] 1 WLR 1063, p 1065, *per* Lord Lane CJ.

was a matter for them to decide whether they were sure that those acts were more than merely preparatory.

The decisions in *Gullefer* and *Jones* leave an intriguing question. This arises from a consideration of the case of *Robinson*.[21] Robinson was a jeweller who hid a quantity of his jewellery and then contrived to be found in his shop bound and gagged and with the safe door swinging open. He lied to the police that he had been robbed. He later admitted that his intention had been to make a fraudulent claim upon his insurance policy. He had not submitted that claim. He was charged with attempting to obtain property (money under his insurance policy) by false pretences.[22] In a decision under the common law offence of attempt, it was held that he had not committed any act which went beyond mere preparation. He had not got as far as making the attempt to obtain the insurance money. If those facts arose again today, how should the judge direct the jury? Should he leave it to them to decide the proximity issue – to decide whether the defendant had gone beyond mere preparation – or should he withdraw the issue and direct an acquittal? It is a fair guess that, if the proximity issue were left to the jury, they would convict. After all, the jury did convict in *Robinson* and, on somewhat analogous facts, the jury convicted the accused in *Ilyas*.[23] In each of these cases, both of them decided on the law before the CAA 1981, the convictions were quashed on appeal, it being held that the judge should have withdrawn the issue from the jury. It seems that the result in these cases would be the same today. The judge still has the duty to withdraw the proximity issue from the jury, if there is no evidence upon which the jury, properly directed, could reasonably come to the conclusion that the defendant had moved beyond the realm of mere preparation. Cases, such as *Robinson* and *Ilyas*, where an accused has merely set the scene in which to perpetrate his intended offence, are not ones where a jury, properly directed, can reasonably conclude that he has gone beyond mere preparation. That this is so, seems clear from the fact that the decision in *Ilyas* has been cited (apparently with approval) in a number of cases, since the CAA 1981.[24] Setting the scene is not the same as being embarked on the full offence.

14-10 Setting the scene, getting equipped, getting into position, lying in wait, reconnoitring the target, none of these will usually amount to an attempt. In *Geddes*,[25] the defendant, who had no right to be there, entered school premises and went into the boys' lavatory, carrying a bag containing a large knife, a length of rope and a roll of masking tape. Before being arrested, he never had any contact or communication with any pupil. His conviction for attempted false

21 [1915] 2 KB 342.
22 This would now be attempting to obtain property by deception, contrary to the TA 1968, s 15(1).
23 (1983) 78 Cr App R 17.
24 Including *Widdowson* (1986) 82 Cr App R 314, *Gullefer* [1990] 1 WLR 1063 and *Jones* [1990] 1 WLR 1057.
25 [1996] Crim LR 894 (CA).

imprisonment was quashed, since there was no evidence that he had gone beyond preparation. Similarly, if the defendant has not even reached the place where he would be in a position to carry out the offence, it is unlikely that he can be said to have got so far as to have attempted it. In *Campbell*,[26] the defendant arrived in the vicinity of a sub-post office. He was arrested in front of the sub-post office and found to be carrying an imitation gun and a threatening note. He admitted that he had intended to use the note to threaten the counter assistant in the sub-post office, but claimed to have changed his mind. It was held that he was not guilty of attempted robbery because his actions had not gone beyond preparation.

Whether a defendant has gone beyond mere preparation may well depend upon the crime which he is charged with attempting. Suppose a man intends to force his way into someone else's house, without consent, and to rape a woman inside. Suppose that, in pursuance of that intention, he arrives outside the house of the proposed victim, masturbates himself, gets out a condom and knocks on her front door. He is not, at that stage, guilty of attempted rape, since he has not got beyond preparing to commit rape; he is equipped for, but he has not yet embarked upon, the rape. He has, however, got very proximate to committing burglary – entering premises as a trespasser with intent to commit rape inside – and, thus, there is evidence entitling a jury to conclude that he was guilty of attempted burglary: *Toothill*.[27] In his planned sequence of events, burglary will be committed before rape. Burglary is committed by entering premises as a trespasser (with the necessary intent). Knocking on the door could well be seen as more than preparation and as part of an attempt to enter the premises.

## *Mens rea* of an attempt

14-11    Section 1(1) of the CAA 1981 requires, as the previous common law offence of attempt required, the defendant to have an intention to commit the full offence. This means that where, as in the crimes of theft and obtaining property by deception, the full offence requires proof of an intention to deprive the owner permanently, the same intention must be proved on a charge of attempt. Similarly, where, as is the case with most of the offences in the TAs, the full offence requires proof of dishonesty, that requirement applies equally on a charge of attempt. Again, where an element of knowledge must be proved on the full offence, that knowledge must be proved also on an attempt charge. So, where an accused is charged with attempted handling, it must be proved that he knew or believed the goods had been stolen.

---

26    [1991] Crim LR 269.
27    [1998] Crim LR 876 (CA).

14-12    It is quite common for an offence to require *mens rea* as to a circumstance. Sometimes – though this is not generally the case with offences in the TAs – the *mens rea* required as to a circumstance is either knowledge or recklessness, as to whether the given circumstance exists. It has been held that, where for the full offence, the *mens rea* as to a circumstance is satisfied by proof of something less than knowledge (for example, recklessness), then that is sufficient *mens rea* as to that circumstance on a charge of attempt.[28] Thus, on a charge of attempted rape, the *mens* required to be proved is: (a) the defendant intended to have sexual intercourse with another person; and (b) the defendant either knew that person was not consenting, or was reckless as to that fact.[29] Suppose, to adapt an example given earlier, a man intends to enter, by force if necessary, a woman's house with intent to have sexual intercourse with her. Suppose that, in pursuance of that intention, he arrives outside the house of the proposed victim, masturbates himself, gets out a condom and knocks on her front door. Assuming that when knocking on the door he commits an act more than merely preparatory, is he guilty of attempted burglary – of attempting to enter premises as a trespasser with intent to commit rape? It is submitted that the following *mens rea* is required – namely that, when he knocks on the door: (1) he intends to enter the premises; (2) he knows he will lack consent to enter *or is reckless* as to whether he will have consent to enter; (3) he intends to have sexual intercourse with his proposed victim; (4) he knows the victim will not consent *or, not caring less whether she will consent, intends to press on regardless*.

## 'Conditional' appropriation

14-13    The full offence of theft requires an intention to deprive the owner permanently. Since the crime of attempt requires an intention to bring about the full offence, the same intention must be proved on a charge of attempted theft. It also so happens that the same intention must be proved in certain versions of the crime of burglary – in particular the crime of entering as a trespasser, with intent to steal (commit theft). The decision of the Court of Appeal in *Easom*,[30] where the accused was charged with theft, has caused difficulties in cases of attempted theft and, also, in cases of burglary. The facts were that, in a cinema, the defendant had taken a handbag of a woman who was sitting there, looked through it (presumably, to see if there was anything worth taking) and had then (presumably, without having found anything worth taking) left it with all of its contents intact. He was charged with theft of 'one handbag, one purse, one notebook, a quantity of tissues, a quantity of cosmetics and one pen'. The Court of Appeal quashed his conviction on this charge, Edmund Davies saying:[31]

---

28   *Khan* [1990] 1 WLR 813 (CA); *AG's Refs (No 3 of 1992)* [1994] 1 WLR 409 (CA).

29   *Khan* [1990] 1 WLR 813 (CA).

30   [1971] 2 QB 315.

31   *Ibid*, p 319.

In the respectful view of this court, the jury were misdirected. In every case of theft, the appropriation must be accompanied by the intention of permanently depriving the owner of his property. What may be loosely described as a 'conditional' appropriation will not do. If the appropriator has it in mind merely to deprive the owner of such of his property as, on examination, proves worth taking and then, finding that the booty is valueless to the appropriator, leaves it ready to hand to be repossessed by the owner, the appropriator has not stolen. If a dishonest postal sorter picks up a pile of letters, intending to steal any which are registered but, on finding that none of them are, replaces them, he has stolen nothing, and this is so notwithstanding the provisions of s 6(1) of the TA 1968. In the present case the jury were never invited to consider the possibility that such was the appellant's state of mind or the legal consequences flowing therefrom. Yet the facts are strongly indicative that this was exactly how his mind was working, for he left the handbag and its contents entirely intact and to hand, once he had carried out his exploration. For this reason we hold that conviction of the full offence of theft cannot stand.

14-14 The simple reason for this decision was that the defendant had no intention to deprive the owner permanently of any of the items he was charged with stealing. When someone is charged with theft, it is only right and normal that the indictment should identify specific items, the property which he is said to have stolen. It is necessary for the prosecution to prove that the defendant intended to deprive the owner permanently of those specific items. There is, it seems, no room for the doctrine of transferred malice to be applied in these circumstances.[32] It is, thus, not enough for the prosecution to prove that the defendant intended to deprive the owner permanently of some other, perhaps unidentified, property. Easom was, therefore, not guilty as charged. The fact was that he had stolen nothing. Was he guilty of attempted theft? He had not been charged with attempted theft. However, the Court of Appeal, when quashing a conviction, has power[33] to substitute a verdict of guilty of attempting to commit *the offence charged*. Thus, the only attempt verdict open to Court of Appeal was for attempting to steal one or more of the specific items (the handbag, etc) listed in the indictment for theft. The Court observed[34] that 'it is implicit in the concept of an attempt that the person acting intends to do the act attempted, so that the *mens rea* of an attempt is essentially that of the complete crime'. Thus, there could be no substituted verdict of attempted theft, unless it were established that the defendant had the intention permanently to deprive the owner of the specific items listed in the indictment. Easom had not committed attempted theft of a handbag, purse or notebook, etc. Although he had no intention to deprive the owner of the items listed in the indictment, he plainly did intend to deprive the owner permanently of some or all of the contents of the handbag, if and when he

---

32 'If you indict a man for stealing your watch, you cannot convict him of attempting to steal your umbrella.' *R v M'Pherson* (1857) Dears & B 197, p 200, *per* Cockburn CJ, cited in *Easom* [1971] 2 QB 315, p 321.

33 Criminal Appeal Act 1968, s 3 and CLA 1967, s 6(3) and (4).

34 [1971] 2 QB 315, p 321.

got them into his possession – and that is sufficient intention for a conviction, provided that the charge is appropriately worded. If Easom had been charged with an attempt to steal 'some or all of the contents of the handbag', he could properly have been convicted.[35]

14-15     After *Easom*, matters became confused by an unfortunate statement of Lord Scarman, when giving judgment in the Court of Appeal, in *Husseyn*, where he said:[36] 'It cannot be said that one who has it in mind to steal only if what he finds is worth stealing has a present intention to steal.' As it stands, this statement is incorrect. It is correct, only where the defendant is charged with theft (or attempted theft) of specific items. As explained by Roskill LJ, in *AG's Refs (Nos 1 and 2 of 1979)*,[37] the sentence would present no problem if lengthened as follows: 'It cannot be said that one who has it in mind to steal only if what he finds is worth stealing has a present intention to steal *the specific item charged*.' Thus, in cases where the defendant has looked in a handbag or has rifled through the contents of a car, but has taken nothing, it is perfectly possible for him to be charged with attempted theft of 'some or all of the contents of a handbag' or 'some or all of the contents of a car' or, possibly, with 'attempting to steal from a handbag'.[38] Certainly, 'An intention to steal can exist even though, unknown to the accused there is nothing to steal'[39] and attempting the impossible can be a crime.

So, in cases where, as in *Easom*, the prosecution is unable to prove an intention permanently to deprive the owner of any specific item, a conviction for an attempt can properly be sought on a charge which alleges an intention to steal, but which does not identify any specific item. The prosecution needs only to prove a general intention to steal and does not have to prove an intention to steal a particular item or items. The matter was reviewed in *AG's Refs (Nos 1 and 2 of 1979)*,[40] where it was held that this approach is appropriate, not only for attempted theft, but also on a charge of burglary (or attempted burglary) contrary to s 9(1)(a) of the TA 1968 – where the charge is that the defendant entered (or attempted to enter) as a trespasser with intent to steal. The Court applied the decision in *Walkington*,[41] where the defendant had entered the area of the store, normally occupied by staff, where a cash till was situated. There was, as it turned out, no cash in the till. The defendant was held to have been properly convicted of burglary on an indictment which charged him with having 'entered as a trespasser part of a building known as Debenhams Store with intent to steal therein'.

---

35   See *AG's Refs (Nos 1 and 2 of 1979)* [1980] QB 180, p 189.

36   (1977) 67 Cr App R 131, p 132.

37   [1980] QB 180.

38   See *Smith* [1986] Crim LR 166 and Professor Smith's 'Commentary', p 167.

39   *DPP v Nock* [1978] AC 979, p 1000, *per* Lord Scarman.

40   [1980] QB 180.

41   [1979] 1 WLR 1169 (CA).

## Attempting the impossible

14-16 At common law, prior to the CAA 1981, it was not an offence to attempt to commit a crime which was, at least in some senses, impossible. Steps on the way towards something which, if achieved, would not amount to an offence, could not amount to a criminal attempt – even if the defendant mistakenly believed in circumstances which, if true, would make it an offence. Thus, handling goods which were not 'stolen', in the belief that they were stolen, did not amount to attempted handling: *Haughton v Smith*.[42] Initially, the House of Lords held, in *Anderton v Ryan*,[43] that this rule had not been reversed by s 1(2) and (3) of the CAA 1981, holding that a woman was not guilty of attempting to handle stolen goods when she purchased a video recorder, believing it to be stolen when in fact it was not. This decision was, however, soon itself reversed by the House of Lords' decision in *Shivpuri*.[44] The result is that it is now possible for someone to be convicted of attempting to commit an offence which is, in fact, impossible to achieve. This is true, irrespective of whether the impossibility is absolute (as in the case of trying to kill a corpse), or is merely the result of the defendant having inadequate resources to achieve success. For this purpose, the law looks at the facts as the defendant believed them to be (irrespective of whether the facts were, in reality, as he believed them to be): s 1(3). Thus, the following are all criminal attempts:

(a) attempting to steal from an empty pocket or handbag;

(b) attempting to steal a specific diamond under the mistaken impression that the diamond is in the particular location where the attempt is carried out, when, in fact, it has been removed to the other side of the world;

(c) attempting with a hammer to break into, and steal the contents of, a safe which is impregnable to any force short of a nuclear explosion;

(d) attempting to handle goods in the belief that they are stolen, when, in fact, they are not.

---

42 [1975] AC 476 (HL).
43 [1985] AC 560.
44 [1987] AC 1 (HL).